15.00

Date Due

DISCARDED

Comparative
Social Policy
and Social Security

Comparative
Social Policy
and Social Security

A TEN-COUNTRY STUDY

P. R. Kaim-Caudle

DUNELLEN
New York

First published in 1973 by Martin Robertson and Company Ltd.
17 Quick Street, London, N1 8HL

This edition published by The Dunellen Company Inc.,
386 Park Avenue South, New York, N.Y. 10016

International Standard Book Number 0-8424-0072-9
Library of Congress Catalog Card Number 73-82262

Printed in Great Britain at The Pitman Press, Bath

Contents

Preface

THE object of this study is threefold : to heighten the reader's understanding of the nature and implications of the social security provisions of his own society, to enable him to learn from the experiences of the different provisions of other societies and to make him familiar with an important facet of the social organisation of other countries.

The first three chapters are mainly analytical. In each of the subsequent five, a major social security scheme and its organisation in all ten countries are discussed. In two of these chapters – 'Employment Injury' and 'Temporary Disability' – each country's provisions are examined in relation to a number of questions. In the other three the provisions of each country or pair of countries are discussed separately and a comparison is incorporated into the review, in which the main findings of each chapter are summarised. This diversity of treatment aims at maintaining the reader's interest in a subject-matter where there is an inherent danger that he will not see the wood for the trees.

In order to keep the study at a reasonable length, survivors' benefit schemes (the sixth major social security system) have not been discussed. For the same reason no reference has been made to the social security provisions for migrant workers, which is a topic of great and increasing importance but too complex to be included in a basic study covering as many as ten countries. The organisation of medical care, which is an integral part of social security, is outlined in Appendix I. An adequate treatment of this subject would require another book.

This study is written in the past tense, looking back to 1969. All comments and statistics, unless otherwise stated, refer to that year. The concept of the standard wage-earner is discussed in Appendix II. A currency conversion table is given in Appendix III.

I wish to express my gratitude for the unstinting assistance I have received from Jane Dunkelman, B.A. (Psychology) Dunelm. She typed several versions of the manuscript and made innumerable and most helpful suggestions for changes in the form and style of the draft chapters.

P.R.K.-C.

CHAPTER I

Introduction

SOCIAL POLICY

Factors in Policy Decisions. Policy is the adoption of one among several courses of action. It presumes the possibility of choice, is normally based on assumptions and/or facts and aims to achieve one or several particular objectives. However, the persons deciding on a policy may be unaware of all the courses of action which could be adopted; they may act on implicit or explicit assumptions which are erroneous; for a variety of reasons not all the relevant facts may be known to them at the time a decision is taken; they may fail to distinguish between relevant and irrelevant facts or may err in the evaluation of the relevant facts; they may misjudge the consequences of pursuing a policy by failing to envisage its incidental effect; finally, a policy objective may be inconsistent with another which was adopted previously or which is adopted simultaneously. For all these reasons a policy may be bad in the sense that it would not necessarily have been adopted if the persons taking the decision had had greater knowledge or greater understanding.

In the field of social policy many decisions are bad in this meaning of the term. The multiplicity of choice is often so great that not all possibilities are properly considered. The validity of assumptions about human behaviour in such fundamental matters as incentive to work, desire to have children, propensity to malinger or willingness to accept degrees of economic, social or racial inequality is much disputed. The one matter beyond dispute is that such behaviour is influenced by a variety of factors, including traditions, recent experiences, future expectations, standards of education and access to services and work opportunities, which themselves vary over time and between places. The proven validity of an assumption in one place at one time does not necessarily hold in another place or at another time. This is of course one of the marked differences between the social and the natural sciences and a legitimate reason for doubting

1

some of the scientific deductions of economics, psychology and sociology.

In all the developed countries data about social phenomena have increased quite considerably in the post-war period, but even today statistics available to the decision-makers are often incomplete, out-dated, unreliable or the by-product of administrative procedures which were not designed for the purpose for which they are used. Data of age and sex distribution or of infant mortality rates are more readily available for administrative areas than for socio-economic groups or for levels of education attained. Data relating to income and wealth distribution based on tax returns cannot easily be adjusted for tax evasion or avoidance and it is notoriously difficult to distin-guish, at least for the top 10 per cent, between income and capital gains. Even the allocation of certain types of income to income groups presents great difficulties.

Side-Effects.   The side-effects of social policies are often as unex-pected and unpredictable as they are in medicine. The effect of an incomes policy on emigration of skilled professional workers is inherently difficult to assess. A policy aimed at reducing poverty among families having four or more children may result in an increase in large families. Higher old-age pensions may increase rather than diminish the number of old people living in poverty because some of them may opt to maintain or establish independence of their families in preference to maintaining or attaining a higher material standard of living. A policy encouraging self-reliance – standing on your own two feet – is inconsistent with one encouraging people to apply for all means-tested welfare benefits to which they are entitled. High levels of old age pensions, subject to a means test, are inconsistent with a policy encouraging high levels of personal savings. Charging of fees to patients to prevent them from cluttering up the doctor's waiting-room is inconsistent with discouraging them from practising self-medication.

Many social policies are not merely bad because they are based on lack of knowledge of other possibilities, wrong assumptions, in-sufficient data, incorrect assessment of the facts, failure to realise the nature of side-effects and objectives which are inconsistent with other policies, but their very shortcomings are frequently not properly realised, evaluated and quantified. The natural bias of people who administer a service is to stress its benefits, not to underline its failures.

Legitimate Concern of Many Interests. The choice of the policy objectives reflects the values and ideology of the decision-makers. This is the case both in deciding between different courses of action and even more in deciding whether to act or refrain from acting. Almost all policies favour some people and affect others detrimentally. The primary beneficiaries are usually easy to identify, while the consequential benefits to other persons are often diffuse, and difficult to ascertain and assess. The position of those detrimentally affected is similar. Examples to illustrate beneficiaries come easily to mind. In countries where health care is a free-enterprise service, higher old-age pensions not only benefit the old but also dentists who supply dentures and opticians who supply spectacles. They also enable the children of old people to give less support to their parents either in cash or in kind. Free medicines or spectacles on doctors' prescriptions benefit the patient as well as the pharmacist and the dispensing optician.

Social policy decisions affect large numbers of people directly or indirectly, favourably or detrimentally, currently or subsequently, in all circumstances or only in certain contingencies. However, in addition they play an important role in shaping social relationships and the environment in which a society functions. For all these reasons social policy is not merely a subject of academic study but is the very core of party politics and the legitimate concern not only of many different economic interests – insurance companies, trade unions, medical associations, employers' federations – but also of the churches and various voluntary organisations.

A Non-controversial Policy Objective: An Example. Public discussion of social policy in all countries is generally ill-informed, tendentious and based on misconceptions. The complexity of the issues and the importance of judgement are too often underrated and the dilemmas facing decision-makers, or which would face them if they understood all the implications of their decisions, are usually not appreciated. This can be illustrated by briefly examining some of the issues involved in formulating a policy which has a quite non-controversial objective : to reduce the number of people suffering from handicaps due to physical disability. The prevalence of handicap can be reduced in at least four different ways. First, to prevent the occurrence which causes the disability. This will include the prevention of accidents at the place of work, on the roads and in the home; vaccination against such disabling diseases as poliomyelitis and tuberculosis, as well as health education to encourage moderation in smoking and drinking and thereby reduce the propensity to bronchitis, lung cancer and heart conditions. Second, to restore the facilities which have been impaired. This can be achieved by surgery (for hernia, stomach ulcer and varicose veins) or by medicine (for tuberculosis and some kidney diseases). Third, several diseases cannot be cured but can be controlled so as to eliminate or at least reduce the handicap. This applies to some forms of diabetes, asthma and epilepsy. Fourth, a prosthesis – spectacles, hearing aids, dentures and increasingly ingenious devices to replace limbs – can compensate for some disabilities. Restoration and control are mainly the concern of biochemists, pharmacologists, medical practitioners and the professions allied to medicine, but prevention and compensation are also the concern of factory inspectors, police officers, and civil and traffic engineers. Most of these measures require expenditure by public bodies, firms or private citizens. Others, however, require no expenditure but the acceptance of restrictions not generally acceptable in Western countries. The prohibition of motor-cycles, the raising of the minimum age for a driving licence to 21 years and the strict enforcement of laws prohibiting driving while under the influence of alcohol would without doubt reduce the number of road accidents and thereby the occurrence of people suffering from disabilities, but at a price, though non-monetary, which is not acceptable.

Higher standards of safety in factories and mines and on building sites and roads will increase cost and the prices charged to consumers. This in turn may reduce exports and affect the balance of payments. It will also, by raising prices, reduce the standard of living of all people, but to different degrees. Higher prices for motor-cars will hurt the poorer motorists, some of whom will be driven off the road, more than those who are comfortably off. The higher price of coal may result in the closing of pits and redundancy of miners. Raising the minimum age for a driving licence to 21 and prohibiting motor-cycles would be considered as discrimination by the establishment against youth. The enforcement of laws against drinking while driving would lead to an outcry among brewers and publicans and in a parliamentary democracy would lead to political agitation which quite likely would affect policy.

Difficulties of Implementing Policies.   However desirable and noncontroversial a policy objective may be, the formulation of a policy implementing it is far from simple. How should the limited public funds be distributed between prevention and cure? How much of the sum allocated to prevention should be spent on health education and how much on stricter enforcement of safety in factories? Finally, there is yet another issue : should the objective of reducing the number of people suffering from handicap due to physical disability be considered in isolation from the equally desirable and non-controversial objective of minimising the degree of handicap of people who have suffered a loss of faculty which was not prevented and which cannot be restored, controlled or compensated? If these two objectives are considered simultaneously, the issues become even more perplexing. How should scarce resources be allocated between prevention and vocational rehabilitation or between cure and subsidising handicapped workers or their employers?

The Importance of Judgement. To all these questions there are no answers which can be derived from a set of assumptions, an assessment of known data and a political ideology. At the point of decision the *sine qua non* is judgement. Some of the implicit or explicit assumptions on which social policy decisions are taken are technical, others are political. Traffic experts may suggest that it would be reasonable to assume that the raising of the minimum age for driving licences or the prohibition of motor-cycles on certain roads would result in reducing serious road casualties by a certain number. This is a technical assumption which has to be supplemented by judgement of what would be the political consequences of such a course of action. Judgement is also essential in determining priorities. Ideology is a guide in deciding whether a policy objective is desirable, but judgement is required in determining the relative importance and urgency of different desirable objectives. Judgement is also required in deciding when and to what extent concessions should be made to groups whose interests are affected by a particular policy.

The central place of judgement in decision-making explains why intelligent and reasonable people, on the same technical assumptions, relying on the same data and sharing a similar outlook on life, will adopt quite different policies in attempting to achieve the same objective. In an international comparative study one should therefore expect countries to adopt different policies even if they share the same ideology and face problems which appear similar.

Different Meanings of the Term.   The meaning attached to the term *social security* varies greatly from country to country, and even within a country it often means different things to different people. In the U.S.A. the term is popularly used to refer to the old-age, survivors', disability and health insurance programme of the Federal government. In this, health insurance is restricted to partial reimbursement of certain health-care expenditure to persons aged 65 and over. In 1969 the cash benefits paid under this programme accounted for approximately half the aggregate payments under public income-maintenance programmes. A much wider meaning is attached to the term in *Social Security Programs in the United States,* an official publication of the U.S. Department of Health, Education and Welfare. This contains a description of all public programmes providing protection against loss of income, retirement provisions for government employees, veterans' compensation and pensions as well as privately organised pensions and other employee-benefit plans. In official statistics the phrase *social security* is not used at all. *Social welfare expenditure* is the term employed to cover six services : social insurance, public aid, health and medical programmes, veterans' programmes, education and other social welfare. Public expenditure on social welfare is compared and aggregated with private expenditure for welfare purposes which includes all expenditure on education and health services which is not financed out of public funds as well as all private cash transfer payments provided under organised income-maintenance programmes.

In the U.K. *social security benefits* in published statistics cover social insurance (national insurance and industrial injuries), social assistance (supplementary benefits), children's allowances (family allowances) and veterans' pensions (war pensions). It includes all cash transfers to individuals for social purposes except educational grants. *Social services* in British official terminology includes social security benefits, health services, education and local welfare services, but excludes housing. The local authority Social Service Departments set up in 1970 are, however, in spite of their name, concerned only with welfare services – social case work, residential institutions and community services.

The New Zealand Social Security Act, 1938, set up a comprehensive system of cash benefits and a universal health service. The term *social security* is nowadays used to refer to the functions of the department of this name. These include responsibility for social work and welfare services as well as income-maintenance provisions including war pensions but excluding workmen's compensation. The term *social services* in Australia covers virtually all income-maintenance provisions except workmen's compensation. *Welfare* is the collective term used in reference to social and health services. In Canada, as in Australia, there is no reference to social security in official statistics.

Cash benefits and health services in Germany and Austria are closely integrated in the various social insurance schemes. *Social security* is not a term employed in official statistics, but in academic and official publications it is used in reference not only to social insurance but also to veterans' pensions, public health services and housing subsidies.

Borderline areas. In all countries there are problems in determining the borderline between public social welfare services (in the U.S. terminology) or social services (in the U.K. terminology) and other public and private services. In the U.K., cash transfers to the unemployed in the form of unemployment benefit or supplementary benefit are classed as social services, but if they take the form of retraining allowances or statutory redundancy payments they are considered not as social but as labour services. Financial assistance to the unemployed in the form of public works programmes or special allocation of funds to finance public capital expenditure in areas of high unemployment are difficult to distinguish from economic services, and are usually classified as such. Services in kind, for example the cost of operating employment exchanges and enforcement of occupational safety regulations, are classed as labour services in the U.K. but included in social security in Denmark.

The distinction between private and public provisions is also not easy to make. In the U.K., employees who, as members of an approved occupational pension scheme, have been contracted out of part of the graduated retirement pension scheme, pay graduated contributions at a lower rate than those who are not contracted out. The premiums to the approved private schemes are not classed as a social service in spite of the fact that they are a condition for paying reduced contributions to the public-service graduated scheme. In Australia and New Zealand workmen's compensation is a statutory obligation of employers who normally insure against this liability with commercial

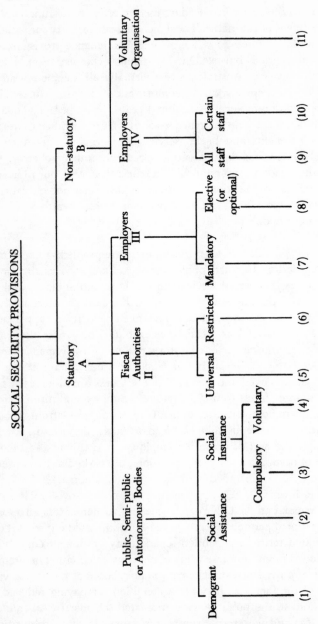

FIG. 1:1   *Classification of Social Security Provision*

insurance companies. This privately organised provision is not classed as a social service, though the payments are made under statute.

The ILO Criterion. In this study the scope of social security and the use of the term are the same as that adopted by the International Labour Organisation :[1] it refers to rights of individuals to provisions which have the object of (*a*) granting curative or preventive medical care; (*b*) maintaining income in case of involuntary loss of earnings or of an important part of earnings, or (*c*) granting supplementary incomes to persons having family responsibilities.

The Social Divisions of Welfare. Social security services provided by public authorities have effects which are very similar to those of certain tax allowances and of certain payments and services rendered by employers to their staff. The variety of provisions in the social security field can best be shown diagramatically, as in Fig. 1.1.

Notes to Fig. 1.1

In the notes below, (*a*) refers to examples of income maintenance; (*b*) refers to examples of health services. The examples are taken from different countries and are illustrative rather than comprehensive.

A. STATUTORY PROVISIONS

    I. *Expenditure borne by a public, semi-public or autonomous body*

        (1) Provided universally without means and/or income test and without contribution conditions (demogrant):

            (*a*) Children's allowances in most countries, superannuation pensions in New Zealand.

            (*b*) Health services in the U.K., pharmaceutical benefit in Australia.

        (2) Provided subject to a means and/or income test (social assistance):

            (*a*) Non-contributory old-age and widows' pensions in Ireland, unemployment benefit in New Zealand and Australia.

            (*b*) Health services for the full-eligibility group in Ireland, Medicaid in the U.S.A.

        (3) Provided subject to compulsory insurance contributions (social insurance):

(*a*) Old-age and invalidity pensions in Austria and Germany, sickness benefit in the Netherlands and the U.K.

(*b*) Medicare in the U.S.A., health insurance benefits in Austria and Germany.

(4) Provided subject to voluntary insurance contributions (voluntary social insurance):

(*a*) Sickness and unemployment benefit for married women in the U.K., incapacity benefits for persons who had been compulsorily insured in the Netherlands.

(*b*) Medical benefits for persons with low incomes who are not compulsorily insured in the Netherlands, medical benefits (as for limited-eligibility group) for persons who had been compulsorily insured in Ireland.

II. *Tax allowances or concessions*

(5) Universal:

(*a*) Dependent relative allowance and tax concessions to old persons in the U.K. (similar to old-age pension), dependent children's allowance in the U.S.A. and Canada (similar to child endowment).

(*b*) Medical expenses (less amount recouped from hospital and medical funds) in Australia and Ireland.

(6) Restricted to persons participating in approved schemes:

(*a*) Contributions to superannuation funds in Denmark (similar to old-age pension), premiums for life insurance in Austria (similar to widows' pension).

(*b*) Premiums to hospital and medical funds in Ireland and Australia.

III. *Obligations on employers*

(7) Mandatory on all:

(*a*) Payment of wages during sickness in Germany (similar to sickness benefit), workmen's compensation pensions in Denmark (similar to invalidity pension), redundancy payments in the U.K. (similar to unemployment benefit).

(*b*) Health care under workmen's compensation acts in the U.S.A. and Australia, occupational health services in Germany.

(8) Elective or optional:

    (*a*) Workmen's compensation in several states of the U.S.A.; occupational pensions giving entitlement to contract out of the graduated pension scheme in the U.K.

B. NON-STATUTORY PROVISIONS (voluntary or contractual)

IV. *By employers for their staff*

    (9) To all staff:

        (*a*) Full or half pay during sickness (similar to sickness benefit), superannuation pensions (similar to old-age pensions).

        (*b*) Payments of employees' contributions to hospital and medical funds, occupational health services.

    (10) To certain grades of staff (e.g. directors or administrative):

        (*a*) Top-hat pension schemes, superannuation.

        (*b*) Payment of hospital or nursing-home fees.

V. *By voluntary organisations*

    (11) (*a*) Payments to which persons are entitled on satisfying prescribed conditions (excluding discretionary charity), e.g. trade union pension and sick-benefit programmes.

        (*b*) Health care similar to (*a*), e.g. trade union medical benefit schemes.

These 'social divisions of welfare', a phrase coined by R. M. Titmus, are not only characteristic of social security – income-maintenance and health services – but also, with some modifications of housing, education and personal welfare services.

The classification of social security provisions by eleven systems dispensed by four types of agency is logically satisfactory. However, the classification of specific provisions to these systems presents some perplexing problems. Civil servants and local government officers' pensions which are provided by statute ought strictly to be allocated to (7), but they are economically and socially very similar to private employers' superannuation payments in (9). The gross cost of some provisions should be divided between two headings: tax savings by employers and employees which are the result of contributions to superannuation schemes should be classed as (6), while the remainder should be classed as (8), (9) or (10).

Voluntary Social Insurance and Employee-Benefit Plans.   Payments by public, semi-public or autonomous bodies to persons who are compulsorily insured are social security provisions irrespective of how they are financed. Compulsory social insurance contributions by employees are a tax which is allocated to a specific purpose. Benefits paid to voluntary social insurance contributors present some problems in classification. To the extent that they are subsidised out of public funds and to the extent that they offer in other ways greater benefits than could be obtained by premiums to commercial insurance companies, they are clearly social security provisions. Otherwise, they are similar in character to sums paid out by commercial insurance companies to their policy-holders. This similarity, however, is more apparent than real. In practice, benefits paid to voluntary contributors cannot, in most countries, be distinguished from benefits paid to other contributors. They are also usually of a different character from payments made by insurance companies; for example, health service benefits in Ireland and sickness benefits for married women in the U.K. are unlimited in duration. Furthermore, persons may in most countries become voluntary contributors in conditions which would be unacceptable to insurance companies, for example without a medical examination and without regard to their medical condition. For these reasons it is proper and in accordance with the facts to class all social insurance benefits, irrespective of the status of the contributor, as social security provisions.

Privately organised pensions and other employment benefits should also be considered as social security provisions irrespective of how they are financed. Employee contributions to occupational pension schemes are generally quite as compulsory as social insurance contributions and the schemes themselves give employees as little discretion and freedom of choice as they have under public social insurance provisions.

Personal Security.   The purchase by individuals of insurance policies, however, is different in character. The policies will provide them with security in stated contingencies, but this security is personal rather than social in the sense that it is based on a personal decision which moreover is taken in conditions which allow considerably more freedom of choice than is provided by social security provisions.

Varieties of Purpose and Motivation.   While the economic and social effects of provisions by different types of agency are in many but not all respects similar, the four agencies tend to favour different sections of the community. Employers' non-statutory provisions are by definition restricted to employees and are in general more generous for white-collar than for manual workers and usually more favourable for higher than for lower-paid staff. Tax allowances are biased in the same direction; they do not benefit at all people who are so poor that they are not liable to pay tax. As taxes on income in all ten countries are progressive, allowances received by the well off result in greater tax savings than those received by the less well off. Social assistance payments successfully aim to benefit the less well off. Social insurance benefits, in practice though not necessarily in intention, often have a similar effect. The less well off tend to be more frequently unemployed, sick and the victims of employment injuries than the better off.

The four types of agency also have different purposes and motivation for the provisions they make. Tax allowances (system 5) do not aim at assisting people in need but at achieving equity in tax burdens between persons who have the same income but differ in ability to pay. The £2,000-a-year man who has three dependent children or who supports his parents-in-law has less ability to pay tax than the bachelor with the same income. The purpose of children's and dependent relatives' allowances is to adjust taxable income so as to increase equity. Other tax allowances (system 6) are means of encouraging certain actions, e.g. allowances for life-insurance premiums are meant to promote this type of saving. Non-statutory provisions by employers generally aim to maintain and improve morale and thereby increase productivity. Their superannuation schemes are often designed to tie an employee to the firm for which he works. In conditions of labour scarcity a variety of fringe benefits of a social security type may be set up to assist recruitment.

The purpose of public social services has changed over the years. The Poor Law in the nineteenth century gave minimum support to destitute people in dire need. Present-day health services in all European countries, except Ireland, serve the vast majority of the population irrespective of need. This is also increasingly the case in invalidity and old-age pensions. However, whether this trend should be encouraged or reversed is, in the field of social policy, one of the great ideological divides.

THE TEN COUNTRIES

Ten countries have been selected for this comparative study :

> Austria
> Germany (Federal Republic)
>
> Ireland
> United Kingdom (U.K.)
>
> Denmark
> Netherlands
>
> Canada
> United States of America (U.S.A.)
>
> New Zealand
> Australia

Compared with the 131 member states of the United Nations, these countries have many common characteristics. They enjoy a relatively high average standard of living, their governments require the support of the electorate at regular intervals, most of their people are of European stock, and they speak one of the Germanic languages.

Developed Economies. All ten have a per capita income of more than U.S. $1,000 per year. This is high if compared with an average income of U.S. $120 in Africa in the mid-1960s, of U.S. $200 in East and South-East Asia and U.S. $400 in Latin America. The level of social security provisions depends at least partly on the degree of economic development, as in a society where average incomes are barely above the subsistence level it is inherently difficult to provide social services. The taxable capacity to finance these services does not exist. In the countries selected for study the high average income makes it possible to divert large sums, both in relative and absolute terms, to provide social security as well as other social services.

Common Political Characteristics. The ten countries also have important constitutional characteristics in common. All are democracies in which the survival of the government depends on gaining the support of, or at least not being opposed by, a relative majority of the adult population at elections, which are held every three, four or five years. Governments are changed as the result of elections in which adult suffrage, secret ballot, freedom of the press and the right of the opposition to criticise the government on television and radio are part of the accepted way of life. In Africa north and south of the Sahara, and in most countries in Asia and Latin America changes of government are rarely the result of elections.

The need to consult the electorate at fairly short intervals makes it necessary for governments to strive for popularity at all times and especially so in the second half of their term of office. This makes for preference being given to measures which yield, or appear to yield, short-term benefits over those where benefits are delayed for some time.

In all the countries, governments are fairly stable. In the twenty-five years up to 1972 there were four heads of government in Austria, Germany, Ireland and New Zealand, five in the U.S.A., and six in the U.K., Canada and Australia.

A second common political characteristic is the prevalence of the rule of law in the administration of social security provisions and of tax allowances which are of a social security character. This enables the citizen to enforce his statutory right, by resort to administrative tribunals or courts of law. Benefits are received by those entitled to them and corruption and bribery are a rare and exceptional occurrence. (Political patronage and discrimination in other social services, for example the allocation of subsidised houses or the granting of discretionary public assistance, are not unknown in at least some of the ten countries.) The enforcement of statutory rights by employees against employers presents some difficulties in all societies. Workers who are not organised and who are in a weak bargaining position may find it difficult to obtain the benefits which they may legally claim.

Six of the countries are English-speaking, though Irish in Ireland and French in Canada are also recognised as official languages. Five of the countries were at some time ruled by Britain. Canada, Australia and New Zealand gradually evolved into independence, while the U.S.A. and Ireland gained their independence through revolutions. These two countries experienced bitter civil wars which, even after time-lags of over a hundred and over fifty years respectively, are still influencing people's minds. After gaining their independence none of the English-speaking countries experienced a non-constitutional change of government.

Other Similarities and Differences between the Ten.   Two of the four Continental countries are German-speaking and the other two also speak Germanic languages. In both world wars Germany and Austria were fighting the U.S.A., the U.K., Canada, Australia and New Zealand as well as Russia and France. In the First World War Denmark and the Netherlands were neutral, while in the second both were occupied by Germany for five years. These two countries have been parliamentary democracies for more than a hundred years. Germany and Austria prior to 1945 had only a short spell of parliamentary government, between 1918 and the early 1930s. Germany and the Netherlands are founder members of the European Economic Community and the U.K., Ireland and Denmark joined the community in 1973. Prior to that date the U.K. and Denmark had belonged to the European Free Trade Area.

The Reasons for the Choice of the Ten.   In selecting countries for a comparative study of social policies, several different schemes can be adopted. One possibility is to compare some developed (rich) countries and some developing (poor) countries. Another is to compare some countries with market economies (free enterprise) and some with planned economies (communist). Both these schemes were rejected as it was thought that a comparative study of one facet of social organisation in countries which are reasonably homogeneous would be more enlightening than a study comparing countries which differ fundamentally in many other respects. A comparison of provisions for the unemployed in two countries, in one of which large-scale unemployment is endemic, the G.N.P. per capita is $80 and corruption among minor functionaries is part of the way of life, while in the other there are normally more jobs than men to fill them, the G.N.P. per capita is $2,500 and the rule of law prevails, may well be considered an interesting but futile exercise.

Four Pairs of Countries.   The countries selected for this study include four groups of two countries which are closely linked with each other. They speak the same language, are neighbours, one is markedly more populous and richer than the other and both had at some time a direct or indirect political association. Austria was annexed to Germany between 1938 and 1945; the Republic of Ireland was part of the United Kingdom of Great Britain and Ireland between 1801 and 1922 (or, as the Irish see it, was occupied by Great Britain). Canada and the United States in the eighteenth century and New Zealand and Australia in the nineteenth century were British colonies.

An indication of the closeness of the economic ties between the pairs of countries is that in 1968, 41 per cent. of Austria's, 51 per cent. of Ireland's and 73 per cent. of Canada's imports came from their larger neighbours. New Zealand's closest trading partner was the U.K., only 18 per cent. of its total imports coming from Australia.

Denmark and the Netherlands are included in this study because their social security provisions and their demographic data contain many interesting features.

CHAPTER II

Factors Influencing the Level and Nature of Social Security

DEMOGRAPHIC and economic factors as well as policy considerations are the three major factors influencing the level and nature of social security provisions. In all these three respects the differences between the ten countries are small compared with those between them and the majority of other countries. All the same, the differences between the ten are sufficiently great to be relevant in the shaping of policy.

DEMOGRAPHIC FACTORS

The Size of the Ten. The ten countries differ greatly in size (see Table 2 : 1). The population of the U.S.A. exceeds 200 million and is greater than the combined total of the other nine countries. The two smallest are Ireland and New Zealand with less than 3 million, next are Austria, Denmark, the Netherlands and Australia with between 4 and 13 million, Canada has a population of more than 20 million and those of Germany and the U.K. exceed 55 million.

Population Growth. The annual rate of population growth in the period 1963–9 varied between 0.4 per cent. in Ireland and 2.0 per cent. in Australia. All countries except Ireland experienced during these years immigration from less prosperous areas. Ireland and New Zealand in 1969 had a fertility rate – number of births per 1,000 women aged 10–49 years – in excess of 80, while in the other eight the rate varied only between 60 and 68. In most countries this rate fluctuated fairly widely in the post-war years and this brought about quite remarkable changes in the annual number of births. In Germany and the U.K. births increased by more than a quarter between 1955

	I	II	III	IV		V			VI	VII			VIII		IX		X
	Popu-lation	Annual Rate of popu-lation Growth (1963-9) Rate(a)	Fertility Rate(a)	Index of Births (1955=100)		Legitimate Birth Rate by age of mother			Infant Mor-tality Rate	Proportion of population surviving up to 65 years			Average life expectation at 65 (1966-8)		Proportion of population under 15 and over 65 (1965-9)		Depen-dancy Ratio (b)
	Millions	‰	‰	1965	1969	20-24	25-29	30-34	‰	Year	M	F	M	F	U.15	O.65	
						%	%	%	‰		%	%	(yrs.)	(yrs.)	%	%	%
Austria …	7.4	5	65	119	111	29	17	11	25	1959-61	65	79	11.6	14.9	24.1	13.9	61
Germany …	58.7	10	64	127	110	29	18	11	23	1964-5	68	81	12.1	15.0	23.4	12.1	55
Ireland …	2.9	4	83	103	102	49	37	28	21	1960-1	70	78	12.6c	14.4c	31.2	11.3	74
U.K. … …	55.5	6	65	126	117	26	18	9	19	1963-5	69	82	12.0	15.9	23.6	12.8	58
Denmark …	4.9	8	67	112	92	30	18	10	15	1963-4	73	83	13.6	16.1	23.7	11.4	54
Netherlands …	12.9	12	67	107	108	29	23	13	13	1961-5	74	85	13.7	16.4	27.6	10.0	60
Canada …	21.1	18	60	95	84	26	17	9	21	1960-1	69	81	13.6	16.7	31.7	7.7	65
U.S.A. …	203.2	12	62	92	87	35c	22c	12c	21	1965	64	79	12.8	16.3	29.2	9.6	63
New Zealand ..	2.8	16	82	108	112	42c	30c	17c	19	1960-2	70	80	12.8c	15.5c	32.4	8.5	69
Australia …	12.3	20	68	108	120	27	20	11	18	1960-2	68	81	12.5c	15.7c	29.2	8.4	60

a Number of births per 1,000 women aged 10—49.
b Number of persons aged under 15 and 65 or over per 100 aged 15—64.
c 1960—2.

Sources:

Column I   *United Nations Demographic Yearbook, 1969* (United Nations, New York, 1970), Table 2.
     II   Ibid.
    III   Ibid., Table 3.
    IV   Ibid., Table 11, and *United Nations Demographic Yearbook, 1970* (United Nations, New York, 1971), Table 13.
    V   *United Nations Demographic Yearbook, 1969*, Table 26.
    VI   *United Nations Statistical Yearbook, 1970* (United Nations, New York, 1971), Table 21.
    VII   *United Nations Demographic Yearbook, 1966* (United Nations, New York, 1967), Table 23.
  VIII   *United Nations Demographic Yearbook, 1970*, Table 20.
    IX   *United Nations Demographic Yearbook, 1969*, Table 6.
    X   Ibid.

and 1965 but declined by 15 and 8 per cent. respectively in the next four years. In Austria the trends were in the same direction but not quite so pronounced, while in Denmark the number of births declined drastically in the four-year period. In Canada and the U.S.A., however, births declined by 5 and 8 per cent. respectively in the first ten-year period and by a further 10 and 5 per cent. in the next four years. The reasons for these changes are recognised to be complex, and attempts to project births have generally been subject to wide margins of error. Only in Ireland has the annual number of births shown little variation over the last fifteen years.

The Fertility Rate.   The fertility rate is influenced by changes in the age at which women marry, by the proportion who never marry, by the number of illegitimate births, by the age composition of women of child-bearing age and by the age-specific fertility of married women. In all the countries the median and average age at which women marry has been declining over the last two decades. Other things being equal, this increases the number of births in years when the age is declining but will result in a reduction in the number of births when the decline ceases. In the U.S.A. as many as 36 per cent. of all women in 1969 married under the age of 20 years, in seven countries 23 to 30 per cent. of women married below that age, while in the Netherlands and especially in Ireland marriages of teenage girls were still comparatively rare. In New Zealand and Australia only one in five of all women married when aged over 25, while in Ireland the corresponding proportion was two in five.

Among women aged 30 to 34 only 5 per cent. in the U.S.A. but 25 per cent in Ireland were not married. Spinsters of that age were also relatively common in Austria but in the other seven countries accounted for only between 7 and 10 per cent. of that age group. The proportion of women who do not marry not only affects the fertility rate but also impinges on social security provisions in several other respects. They tend to require more health and welfare services than married women and in old age generally receive higher pensions than married women are paid as adult dependants.

In all countries except Austria and Germany the proportion of children born out of wedlock has increased between 1958 and 1968. In New Zealand it went up from 5 to 13 per cent. and in the U.S.A. from 5 to 10 per cent. Why this has happened, during a period when in general the availability and efficacy of contraceptives have increased and when in most countries the proportion of spinsters has declined, is not easy to understand. Social security provisions for children born out of wedlock are more costly than for children who have married parents. Unmarried mothers are more likely to slide into poverty and their off-spring often have to be taken into public care.

Women aged between 20 and 25 years are more prone to child-bearing than those aged between 40 and 45. The age composition of women of child-bearing age is therefore an important factor influencing fertility. This composition is determined by the number of female births between 15 and 49 years ago, by the mortality experience of females under 49 in the past 49 years and by the number and ages of female immigrants and emigrants. In countries where immigration is relatively important, the age composition tends to be lower than it would have been but for the immigrants.

The age-specific fertility of married women depends on the use and efficacy of contraceptives, on the ages at which women marry, on the number of children desired and on the spacing of children. Economic factors, such as changes in the level of unemployment and earnings, influence the spacing of children and possibly to a lesser degree the number of children in a family. To what extent the assistance in cash and kind which public authorities render to parents in the rearing of their children influences fertility or the age-specific fertility rates is a much disputed question. In the countries which are the subject of this study, free education and to a lesser extent free or subsidised health services (except in the U.S.A.) are so much an accepted way of life that it is virtually impossible to assess their influence on fertility.

In all but three countries in 1969 the number of births per 100 married women aged 20 to 24 years was between 26 and 30, while in the U.S.A. it was 35, in New Zealand 42 and in Ireland 49. This can be expressed differently by saying that in Ireland half, in the U.S.A. more than a third and in the U.K. and Canada a quarter of all married women in that age group had a child that year. Married women aged 30 to 34 having children were about three times as common in Ireland as in the U.K. and Canada.

Impact of Variations in the Number of Births. Changes in the annual number of births make an impact on social security provisions in several respects. They affect expenditure on maternity (birth) grants, on maternity allowances to working women and on family (children's) allowances. They may also result in excessive strain on or under-utilisation of maternity hospitals, public education, school health, domiciliary and dental services; on the long-term age composition of the population their impact is even greater.

Mortality Rates.   Birth rates move up as well as down and fairly large movements over short periods of time are quite common. Death rates are more stable, especially for the older age groups, and tend to decline but not to rise. Their effect on age composition is more marked than that of birth rates and they are more easily influenced by measures in the social policy field.

The infant mortality rate – the number of children dying in the first year of life per 1,000 children born – was at one time considered the best single indicator of standards of living. It has declined in all countries since the Second World War, but between the ten still varied greatly in 1969 – 13 in the Netherlands, 15 in Denmark and 25 in Austria. Germany, Canada and the U.S.A. had a somewhat higher rate than the U.K., New Zealand and Australia. In spite of the disparity in their standards of living, Ireland and the U.S.A. both had a rate of 21. This is all the more remarkable as two factors which make for a higher rate, large families and a relatively high age of the mother at birth, are more prevalent in Ireland than in the U.S.A. If, in the late 1960s, the infant mortality rate in the U.S.A. had been the same as it was in the Netherlands, the number of very young children dying would have been less by some 30,000 a year.

The proportion of men and women surviving up to the age of 65 years does not differ as widely as the infant mortality rate, but the differences are all the same quite remarkable. In the Netherlands 74 per cent. and in Denmark 73 per cent. of all males survived to that age. At the other end of the scale the proportion was only 64 per cent. in the U.S.A. and 65 in Austria. In the other six countries the rate varied between 68 and 70 per cent. The proportion of females surviving to the age of 65 is in all countries markedly higher than that of males. The differences between countries are somewhat less but the pattern is much the same, the proportion being highest in the Netherlands and Denmark and lowest in Austria, Ireland and the U.S.A.

In all countries the average expectation of life at the age of 65 was longer for women than for men. The difference was as much as 3.9 years in the U.K. but only 1.8 years in Ireland. For men the expectation of life was greatest in the Netherlands (13.7 years), Denmark and Canada and least in Austria (11.6 years). If men in Austria after reaching the age of 65 were to live as long as men lived in the Netherlands, the cost of old-age pensions, *ceteris paribus,* would have been greater by more than one-sixth. In the other six countries, the expectation of life was very similar overall. For women the expectation of life at 65 was highest in Canada (16.7 years), second highest in the Netherlands (16.4 years) and least in Ireland (14.4 years).

Impact of Reduction in Death Rates. Any reduction in death rates has a direct and important effect on the cost of social security provisions. The larger the proportion of people who survive up to 65 years and the longer their expectation of life after reaching this age, the higher will be the cost of old-age pensions. Reductions in the death rates at lower ages will tend to have the offsetting advantage of increasing the number of people in the labour force. An increase in longevity requires higher taxes and/or social insurance contributions to finance the additional cost of old-age pensions and health services.

The Burden of Dependancy. A large proportion of expenditure on education and on social security provisions benefits two population groups : those who who have not yet started to work and those who have retired from work. The financing of the services which benefit these two groups is borne directly or indirectly by those engaged in the economic process. There is no definite age in any country at which young people start work. This depends on *inter alia* three factors : the statutory minimum school-leaving age, the proportion of young people who stay at school or college beyond that age and the length of time for which they continue their education. The position in respect to retirement is very similar. The age at which people retire also depends on *inter alia* three factors : the minimum age at which old-age pensions may be claimed, the proportion of people who stay at work beyond that age and the length of time for which they continue working. All these six factors in turn are influenced by a variety of circumstances which include the employment opportunities for the young and the old, the state of health of the old, the level of various types of old-age pension and possibly the cost of education. There is thus no definite working age, any more than there is a specific age for starting work or for retiring. The proportion of the population which is engaged in the economic process also depends, in addition to the factors already mentioned, on the level of involuntary unemployment, on the ability and willingness of married women to work outside their homes and on the number of people who are mentally or physically so impaired that they cannot work.

Age distribution is therefore only one among several factors which influence the division of the population into three groups : not yet working, of working age, and no longer working. It is, however, the most important and lends itself most readily to international comparison. The proportion of the population under 15 years in Ireland, Canada and New Zealand exceeded 30 per cent., while in Austria, Germany, the U.K. and Denmark it was less than 25 per cent. The proportion of the population over 65 years ranged from 8 per cent. in Canada, New Zealand and Australia to 13 per cent. in the U.K. and 14 per cent. in Austria. With the exception of Ireland the proportion of under-15s was inversely related to the proportion of over-65s. The four countries outside Europe have relatively many children and few old people, while in the European countries, except Ireland, the position is reversed.

The relative burden of dependancy can best be measured by computing a dependancy ratio showing the number under 15 and over 65 per 100 persons aged 15 to 65. This ratio indicates the relative burden of providing services which especially benefit the young (education and children's allowances) and the old (pensions and health services). It is highest in Ireland (74) and lowest in Denmark (54). Germany and the U.K. have comparatively low ratios, while those for New Zealand and Canada are relatively high. To provide any specific standard of service to the young or the old requires on average the levying of 37 per cent. more taxes in Ireland than are required in Denmark to provide the same services. Even then the services would not be the same in absolute terms but only the same relative to the G.N.P. per head.

The importance of demographic factors in the level and nature of social security provisions requires little emphasis. Any projection or discussion of future demographic trends is well beyond the scope of this study. The changes which might possibly occur over the next ten or twenty years would have repercussions in the social policy field which are at present very difficult to visualise. The combined effect of improvement in contraceptive techniques, greater availability of abortion and fear of over-population may result in quite drastic reductions in the number of births. Advances in medical knowledge might well lead to equally drastic changes in the prolongation of life, resulting in a substantial increase in the proportion of the population past what at present is the conventional retirement age.

Measuring Economic Growth. It is more difficult to compare the economic wealth (income) of different countries than their demographic characteristics. In relatively affluent and sophisticated societies people consume individually and collectively thousands of commodities and services which can only be aggregated by measuring them in money units. Money, however, is itself a variable, which differs in purchasing power in at least three dimensions – over time, between countries and between regions of the same country. The post-war years were for all ten countries a period of economic growth, but the rate of growth varied between countries. International comparisons of real growth per head have much greater validity than those of income per head expressed in a common monetary unit. (The term *real* is applied to changes in volume – value deflated by an index measuring average price increases.) Comparisons per head of population rather than of totals are more meaningful as they allow for changes in the size of the population.

Income Aggregates and Social Expenditure. There are a number of income aggregates which can be used to measure growth. The Gross National Product (G.N.P.) at market prices is the most appropriate in a discussion of social policy. Expenditure on health services and social security cash benefits is invariably expressed (and spent) at market prices and therefore ought to be related to totals valued at these prices. For international comparisons this aggregate has the disadvantage of incorporating taxes and subsidies on goods and services and thus it distorts the relative size of the G.N.P. of different countries. This distortion can be avoided by valuing G.N.P. at factor cost (market prices less taxes on consumption net of subsidies), but this concept has little meaning in the social security context.

Growth will Cease. Between 1960 and 1968 the rate of real growth per head exceeded $3\frac{1}{2}$ per cent. in Austria, Denmark, the Netherlands, Canada and the U.S.A., was more than 3 per cent. in Ireland, Germany and Australia and was about $2\frac{1}{4}$ per cent. in the U.K. and New Zealand (see Table 2 :2). If this rate of growth were maintained in future years, real income per head in the first group of countries would double in twenty years, in the second in about twenty-three years and in the third in about thirty years. Projecting this rate of growth to the year 2072 gives for the first group a 31-fold, the second a 19-fold and the third a nine-fold increase. Put in a different way, the grandchildren of 1972 university students in Germany, Ireland and Australia, if still alive in 2072, would be living at a time when average incomes would be nineteen times what they are today.

TABLE 2:2   *Economic Indicators.*

	I	II
	Average annual rate of growth at market prices of real Gross Domestic Product per capita (1960-8) %	*Consumer Prices General Index,* 1969 (1963 = 100)
Austria	3.6	123
Germany	3.2	116
Ireland	3.3	134
U.K.	2.3	127
Denmark	3.7	137
Netherlands	3.8	135
Canada	3.7	122
U.S.A.	3.7	120
New Zealand	2.2	128
Australia	3.2	120

Sources:
Column I *United Nations Yearbook of National Accounts Statistics,* 1969 (United Nations, New York, 1970), vol. II, Table 4A.
Column II *United Nations Monthly Bulletin of Statistics* (July 1971), Table 60.

It is not merely difficult but wellnigh impossible to imagine what life would be like if this were to happen. In any case, for a number of reasons it is quite impossible that it will happen. The purpose of the projection is to show that the rate of growth in the 1960s, which was much like that of the 1950s, was quite exceptional and is most unlikely to be maintained for any length of time. In considering the future development of social security this is a most important fact to keep in mind.

G.N.P. per Head in U.S. Dollars. The apparently most straight-forward method of comparing the levels of economic wealth (income) in different countries is to express their G.N.P. per head in U.S. dollars. This is based on the implicit but invalid([1]) assumption that the purchasing power of the dollar is the same in all countries. In reality the value of the dollar in different countries varies widely. In 1963 the G.N.P. per head expressed in U.S. dollars (rounded off to the nearest $100) was 3,200 in the U.S.A., between 1,600 and 2,100 in Germany, the U.K., Denmark, Canada, New Zealand and Australia; only Austria, Ireland and the Netherlands had G.N.P.s below 1,200. In the subsequent five years the price indices of the G.N.P. increased at widely different rates, ranging from 36 per cent. in Denmark and 30 per cent. in the Netherlands to 13 per cent. in Germany and 14 per cent. in the U.S.A. During the same period the official exchange rate between the national currency and the dollar remained unaltered in Austria, Germany, the Netherlands, Canada and Australia but was devalued by 20 per cent. in New Zealand, by 14 per cent. in Ireland and the U.K. and by just under 8 per cent. in Denmark. The com-bined effect of changes in the internal purchasing power and in the official exchange rates was that even if the dollar had had the same purchasing power in all countries (a purely hypothetical proposition) in 1963, it certainly did not have it five years later in 1968.

The same distortion is shown when comparing the G.N.P. per head in U.S. dollars of 1963 and 1968 : that of Denmark increased by 50 per cent., that of the Netherlands by 63 per cent., but that of the U.K. by only 17 per cent. and that of New Zealand by a mere 1 per cent. The changes are completely out of line with the changes of per capita product at constant prices : Denmark 22 per cent., the Netherlands 25 per cent., the U.K. 15 per cent. and New Zealand 9 per cent.[2] It is therefore proper to view the G.N.P. per head statistics with great care and possibly with some little suspicion. It just does not make any sense to assert that the G.N.P. per head in Australia in 1963 was 3 per cent. and in 1968 was 39 per cent. higher than in New Zealand. Nor can it easily be accepted that the G.N.P. per head was 5 per cent. higher in Denmark than in the U.K. in 1963 and that five years later this difference had increased to 39 per cent. The apparently simple device of expressing G.N.P. per head in U.S. dollars is only of very restricted use in international comparisons of income and frequently is positively misleading.

There are also other reasons for doubting that the G.N.P. per head

TABLE 2:3　Indicators of Standard of Living, 1969.

	I	II	III	IV	V	VI	Year	Housing Statistics			
	G.D.P. at market prices per capita (U.S. $)	Private Cars per 1,000 population	Telephones per 1,000 population	Television Sets per 1,000 population	Net Food Meat grams per day per capita	Consumption Milk and Milk Products Grams per day per capita		VII Rooms per Dwelling	VIII Persons per Room	IX Dwell'gs with W.C. %	X Dwell'gs with fixed Bath or Shower %
Austria ...	1,734	152	180	173	188	544	1969	3.1	1.0	68	52
Germany ...	2,519	208	211	262	200	532	1960	4.1	0.9	83c	64c
Ireland ...	1,166	125	99	153	207	740	1966	4.5	0.9	54d	33d
U.K. ...	1,950a	210	254	284	205	595	1966	5.5b	0.6b	98b	85b
Denmark ...	2,861a	208	328	250	166	722	1965	3.5	0.8	91	63
Netherlands ...	2,149a	177	243	223	159	671	1956	5.1	0.8	68	27
Canada ...	3,473a	305	440	294	251	632	1967	5.4	0.7	93	90
U.S.A. ...	4,574a	427	566	399	299	671	1960	4.9	0.7	90	88
New Zealand ...	1,949	308	430	222	302	762	1966	4.9	0.7	94	98
Australia ...	2,708a	298	292	215	290	631	1966	5.2	0.7	—	—

aData in terms of present system of National Accounts while the other figures in column I are calculated in terms of the former system of National Accounts.
bEngland and Wales only.
c1965.　　　　　　　　　　　　　　　　　　　d1961.

Sources:
Column I　　United Nations Yearbook of National Accounts Statistics, 1970 (United Nations, New York, 1972), Table IC.
Column II　　United Nations Statistical Yearbook, 1970, Table 148.
Column III　Ibid., Table 159.
Column IV　Ibid., Table 212.
Column V　　Ibid., Table 161.
Column VI　Ibid.
Column VII　Ibid., Table 201.
Column VIII　Ibid.
Column IX　Ibid.
Column X　　Ibid.

is a proper measure of real income. It does not allow for such items as congestion, noise and air pollution which are not priced but are a type of negative real income. Furthermore, the implicit assumption that all heads are homogeneous is dubious. It is quite as arbitrary to count a child irrespective of age as one head as it would be to count children under the age of 15 as only half a head. If this latter method were used, it would increase the G.N.P. per head in Ireland and New Zealand relative to that of other countries. Another problem is that the prices of goods and services relative to each other differ between countries; this is an additional problem quite different from that of the variation in general purchasing power of the dollar.

Other Indicators of Standards of Living. The purpose of comparing average G.N.P.s per head in U.S. dollars is to find an approximate measure of variations in average standards of living. As this measure suffers from all the disadvantages to which reference has been made in the previous paragraphs, it may be of interest to show other indicators of standards of living. This is done in Table 2:3, which gives the number of private cars, telephones and television sets per 1,000 people and the net food consumption per head in grams per day for meat and milk, as well as a number of statistics related to domestic dwellings.

It is interesting to note that while the G.N.P. per head in U.S. dollars in Australia is a third higher than in New Zealand, New Zealand shows the same or more favourable data for all the other indicators except for the housing data, which are somewhat less favourable, but these differences are fairly marginal. The Accounts data show G.N.P. per head to be almost half as great again in Denmark as in the U.K., but the number of cars per 1,000 people is the same, there are more television sets in the U.K. and a greater amount of meat per person is eaten in the U.K., while in Denmark the number of telephones per 1,000 people is about a third greater than in the U.K. and the consumption of milk and milk products is considerably higher. In the housing statistics the figures for the U.K. appear in most respects more favourable and in the rest not less favourable than those of Denmark.

Each one of these indicators, however, may be influenced by many factors which invalidate international comparisons if these are made on the basis of any one indicator alone. For instance, the number of private cars per 1,000 population may be much influenced by a country's taxation policy as this affects the prices of cars, petrol and licences. Another influence on the number of cars will be the need for cars, which varies both with the standards of public transport and the distances which have to be traversed. Likewise, the proportion of telephones is at least partly a function of the installation charges, annual rents and call charges. If the rent is high fewer telephones are installed, whereas if the rent is low but the call charge high many telephones will be installed but not used so often.

The net food consumption figures published by the F.A.O. are presumably as comparable as any that can be obtained, but it is somewhat astonishing that in a relatively poor country such as Ireland meat consumption is markedly higher than in Denmark or the Netherlands. This may possibly be explained by differences in the relation of meat prices to earnings.

The housing statistics give a partial picture of housing standards, but by their nature do not distinguish between rooms on the seventeenth floor of a tower block, in a city-centre condemned dwelling or in a pleasant suburban house. Nor do they distinguish the Irish owner-occupier of a dwellinghouse on a subsistence farm from the owner-occupier of a house in a Copenhagen suburb.

In spite of all these drawbacks in the comparability of such indicators of the standard of living, it must be emphasised that, if the indicators are taken in aggregate, a truer picture is given than is provided by the G.N.P. per head; the shortcomings of these other indicators are most pronounced when they are taken singly, but in aggregate they are a relatively good basis for international comparisons.

Regional Dispersal of Income.   In discussing social policy, differences in average income between countries are important but so is the distribution of income between regions and between persons. Variations in the dispersal of income are quite as relevant as variations in averages.

J. G. Williamson[3] has computed a weighted coefficient of variation which measures the dispersal of regional income per head relative to the national average (weighting each regional variation by the share in the national population). Unfortunately, with the data available the coefficients had to be based on regions of varying sizes, on different numbers of regions for each country and on heterogeneous definitions of income.[4]

They estimate rather than measure regional inequalities. Williamson comes to the conclusion that regional inequalities are quite minor among mature economies, although for any country they may be politically significant. There appears also to be a trend for regional inequalities to diminish with increasing economic wealth (income). As will be argued in later chapters, social security provisions tend to contribute to this diminution.

These conclusions, however, can easily be misunderstood. In any population, variations between individuals are greater than those between averages of small groups, and those in turn are greater than variations between averages of large groups. A low coefficient of variation shows that differences in the average income of regions having relatively large populations are small. It does not exclude the possibility that there may be pockets or areas with relatively small populations, where incomes are high or low in relation to the national average. Small low-income areas may be a manifestation of Galbraith's structural poverty and as such of interest in formulating a social policy.

Problems of Measuring Income Distribution.   The study of income distribution is beset with methodological difficulties, absence of appropriate data and unreliability of existing data. The term *income* itself is notoriously awkward to define. The borderline between income and expenses, between income and capital gains and between money income and a variety of incomes in kind is inherently vague and it is often to the advantage of many people to keep it so.

Income data may refer to households (how much of the income of earners other than husband and wife is to be included?) or to individuals, to men or to women or to both combined, to adults or to all age groups; they may refer to all incomes earned or unearned, to earnings of employees or to all earnings including those of the self-employed, to salaries or to wages or to both combined, possibly including or excluding pensions, to earnings from any activity or to manufacturing or non-farm incomes only; they may refer to people in full-time employment only or include also those in part-time work, to full-period workers only or also to those working for only a part of the year; they may refer to earnings of an hour, a week, a month or a year, and may include or exclude overtime, piecework, holidays or Christmas bonuses. In any case income data may for a variety of reasons be overstated, for instance to gain prestige for the individual or to adhere to minimum wage regulations, or more likely be understated to evade tax liability. Income data in particular tend to exclude the income derived from 'second jobs', the value of services rendered within the family and the notional income derived from the ownership of certain capital goods, for example, houses.

Lydall's Findings. Harold Lydall[5] has attempted to measure the dispersal of income in twenty-five countries including those of this study except Ireland. He stresses that his estimates are partly based on personal judgements on account of the scarcity and diversity of the published data. Allowing for these limitations he concludes that at various dates between 1956 and 1961 the dispersal of income among the nine countries of this study was somewhat less in Australia and New Zealand and somewhat greater in the Netherlands than it was in the other six countries, which had rather similar levels of dispersal. It seems reasonable to assume that the dispersal of income is greater in Ireland than in any other of the ten countries. (This is partly due to low levels of income in the relatively large agricultural sector and relatively high incomes of white-collar and professional workers.) Not unexpectedly, Lydall's findings confirm the generally accepted view that with some remarkable exceptions, the degree of dispersal of income is inversely related to the general level of economic development – prosperity makes for equality.

Restricted Validity of Dispersal Measures. The dispersal of income is one facet of differences in standards of living within a country. The degree of dispersal may, however, partly reflect items which themselves are relevant in assessing standards of living. In a community where all married women stay at home, the dispersal of household income is likely to be less, *ceteris paribus,* than in one where some women go out to work. It does not necessarily follow, however, that the differences in degree of dispersal reflect real differences in standards of living : an income of £50 per week earned jointly by a married couple is in some significant way which is not easy to quantify less than the same income earned by the husband. Similarly, any degree of dispersal where all men work 40 hours per week has a different meaning from the same dispersal where some men work 70 and others 30 hours per week. A degree of dispersal of money income may also exaggerate dispersal of real income whenever there are significant regional differences in retail prices.

Several statistical studies in different countries have found that the distribution of income has not significantly changed during the last four decades. By this is meant that the proportion of all personal incomes received by the top fifth and the bottom fifth of all income received is substantially unaltered. If these findings are accepted as valid, it still does not mean that the level of material inequality is the same today as it was before the war. The general increase in material prosperity as well as post-war technological changes have brought about greater similarity in standards of living quite independent of the distribution of income.

Alternative Indicators of Inequality. In pre-war Europe the difference between the way of life of the worker who rode a pedal cycle and the bank manager who had a small car was much greater than it is today between the worker who has a secondhand car and the bank manager who has a large new one. The fact that before the war the ratio of the price of a pedal cycle to that of a car may have been the same as that today of a small second-hand car to a big new one is quite irrelevant. Before the war the worker's wife would do the weekly wash in the tub in her kitchen while the manager's wife would either have a woman come in to do the washing or send it to a laundry; today the worker's wife will have a small washing-machine and the manager's wife a super de-luxe one. There can be no doubt that here too there has been a move towards equality. Today in Europe most workers' homes have hot water and a bathroom while before the war this was comparatively rare; the manager's house always had one bathroom even before the war and today often has two. Here again the difference between no bathroom and one is much greater than that between one and two bathrooms. The same move towards equality can be observed in holidays, personal clothing and house furnishings. The number of bathrooms can of course be easily recorded, but the greater similarity in the way of life between the one- and the two-bathroom family than between the family that has a bath and the family with none cannot be quantified, but is real all the same.

Increase in Relative Deprivation. Greater prosperity has, however, not merely led to greater equality between the majority of the working class and the professional managerial class but has also tended to widen the gap between the 5, 10 or 15 per cent. of families who are poorest and the majority of the population. In all the countries of this study these families have today a higher standard of living than they had before the war, but they are all the same relatively more deprived. Today not to have a car, a washing-machine, a bathroom or an annual holiday is an indication of deprivation, while before the war it was part of the normal way of life of the majority of the population in every Western European country.

Redistribution of Income.   Social policy is much concerned with income redistribution of three different kinds : redistribution by contingency groups – from the employed to the unemployed, from the childless to those with children; redistribution over the life-span – from those at work to children and the retired, and also to those who are ill at present from those who were ill yesterday and may again be ill tomorrow; redistribution by income group – from those with high income to those with low income, or possibly vice versa. The redistribution effect of social policies will be discussed in later chapters.

Social policy, however, also affects the distribution of income in other ways which are no less important. Social security provisions are likely to influence the demographic characteristics of a population, and the taxes levied to pay for services may in their turn possibly also affect the demographic pattern. It is probable that those beneficiaries who receive more in benefits than they pay in taxes spend their net receipts on different goods and services from those who contribute more than they receive. The net recipients may also save less of the income transferred to them than the net contributors. The taxes required to provide public services may encourage the substitution of tax-free leisure for taxable earnings. It is thus quite probable that social security provisions will alter the distribution of factor income – return on capital goods and labour. In practice it is impossible to measure these different types of redistribution. Any calculations would have to be based on assumptions about the behaviour of people in many hypothetical circumstances and would be of most dubious validity.

Economic Growth and Social Expenditure.   The rate of economic growth expressed in G.D.P. per head may well be influenced by the nature and level of social security provisions. Higher taxes may lead to the substitution of leisure for work, benefits may reduce participation in the labour force, reduced personal savings may stimulate inflationary pressures, the number of consumers who do not produce, for example the old, may increase and births may be stimulated. However, the extent to which these factors are influenced by social security provisions is impossible to determine. There are other phenomena exerting similar influences while still others have a counter-balancing effect.

Two facts, however, appear to be beyond dispute. The developed, rich, industrial countries experienced during the last seventy years a period of unprecedented growth in both the economic and social spheres. While it is not possible to express an opinion on whether the rate of economic growth would have been even greater if the rate of social progress had been slower, it can be confidently asserted that high rates of growth of the two are not incompatible. Second, the economic history of the post-war period provides no evidence to confirm the hypothesis that high social security expenditure in developed countries inhibits economic growth or that low expenditure promotes it. The verdict must be 'not proven'.

RISING EXPENDITURE[6]

Varieties of Rising Expenditure. Three different types of rising expenditure on social security can be distinguished. In an economic environment where annual increases in the retail prices of goods and services are a normal occurrence, rising expenditure in terms of the monetary unit requires little comment. Rising expenditure in real terms (money cost adjusted for price changes) is also to be expected in countries which enjoy economic growth. This enables social security beneficiaries to participate in the improved general standard of living, which is the result of higher productivity. The third type of rising expenditure – an increased proportion of G.N.P. spent on social security – requires some elucidation. There are three broad categories of factors involved in this : those operating automatically, relative price rises and improved services. These groupings are of analytical interest but the boundaries between them are imprecise.

Automatic Factors. Automatic factors are those which necessitate higher expenditure to maintain the present level and quality of service. They may be of economic, demographic or social origin. For example, in Britain in the period from 1964 to 1969 the population aged between 15 and the minimum retirement age remained constant while the number of persons above the minimum retirement age increased by 9 per cent. A similar increase was experienced in Germany. These changes in the age composition of the population caused a higher proportion of G.N.P. to be spent on social security. Some automatic expenditure increases are the consequence of people availing themselves of services to which they had been entitled but had previously not taken up, for example a reduction in the proportion of men and women who delay retirement beyond the minimum pensionable age, thus increasing expenditure on pensions. Other automatic factors are a higher incidence of the contingencies that lead to interruptions of earnings, for example an increase in unemployment and sickness benefit claims due to an influenza epidemic.

Relative Price Rises.   Relative price rises can best be described by an example; an increase in the cost of health services by the same proportion as the rise in prices of other goods and services does not require higher expenditure relative to G.N.P., but if doctors' or nurses' remunerations rise faster than the prices of other services, a higher proportion of G.N.P. is required to meet them. In this case the costs rise but the quality and the quantity of the services remain the same.

Improved Services.   Improved services can take three different forms : an extension in the number of persons entitled to a service, an increase in the quality of services or the formation of new services. Examples from the U.S.A. can illustrate each of these. First, the extension of monthly benefits in 1967 to disabled widows aged 50 to 59; second, the increase in 1968 of the maximum earnings base that is creditable for benefit from $6,600 to $7,800 under the O.A.S.D.H.I. programme; and third, the establishment of a comprehensive health insurance programme for persons aged 65 and over, in 1965. Some changes may take more than one form : the extension of the earnings limit for pensioners to $1,680 per annum in 1968, both increased the number of beneficiaries and improved the quality of the service for some of them – their standard of living went up. Any rise in pensions which exceeds increases in average earnings is an improvement in social security services in the form of higher quality.

Multiplicity of Causes. Changes in expenditure on social security of all three types to which reference has been made are caused by a multiplicity of demographic, economic and social developments. Many of these are inherently complex and interrelated. A reduction in the proportion of old people deferring retirement beyond the minimum pensionable age may be caused by an increased level of unemployment, higher social security pensions, more frequent or higher company superannuation pensions, changes in the nature of work which are detrimental to older people or possibly more ill-health amongst people in their 60s. However, demographic, economic and social factors cannot fully explain the differences in the nature and development of social security provisions in the ten countries. These are also largely the result of tradition, economic pressure groups and underlying ideologies.

POLICY CONSIDERATIONS

Civil Service Standards for All? Field-marshals in Britain and university professors in Germany retire on their full emoluments. Civil servants, teachers, local government officers and other public servants retire in all ten countries on pensions which amount normally to about two-thirds or more of their final salaries. They also enjoy security of tenure and usually receive full pay for some months if they are absent from work on account of illness. These conditions of service are enjoyed by all grades of staff without any income ceiling in assessing pensions or sick pay.

Social security provisions are invariably less favourable than those for public servants. The state in all the ten countries accepts to a greater or lesser degree some responsibility for the economic well-being of its citizens, but even today the extent of this commitment is quite limited. In fact one possible yardstick of the success of social security provisions might be the extent to which the state provides for all its citizens the economic security enjoyed by its public servants.

The Beveridge Approach. In his report *Social Insurance and Allied Services,* Beveridge in 1942 recommended a social insurance scheme which was universal (in that it covered the whole population irrespective of employment status, occupation or income), comprehensive (in that it covered all contingencies resulting in interruptions or cessations of earnings) and adequate (in that it provided benefit levels sufficient 'without further resources to provide the minimum income needed for subsistence in all normal cases'[7]). The scheme recommended flat-rate contributions and flat-rate benefits which could be claimed as a right, irrespective of income. The Beveridge recommendations were implemented in the National Insurance Act, 1946, and were the basis of what later was often referred to as 'the welfare state'. However, the flat-rate benefits were right from the start and have remained ever since below subsistence level, that is, below the national assistance (now supplementary benefit) which could be claimed subject to a means test.

The Beveridge plan envisaged a greater commitment to social security than had ever been attempted previously. The New Zealand Social Security Act, 1938, had provided benefits in all contingencies but limited them to those who had incomes below prescribed limits. Beveridge in recommending an extensive state commitment had made it one of his guiding principles that

> Social security must be achieved by co-operation between the state and the individual . . . The state in organising security should not stifle initiative, opportunity, responsibility; in establishing a national minimum, it should leave room and encouragement for voluntary action by each individual to provide more than that minimum for himself and his family.[8]

This was quite explicit; the state should provide a minimum standard, neither more nor less. A higher standard was quite as undesirable as a lower one. Everybody who wanted to maintain in sickness, unemployment or old age a standard of living above mere subsistence was to rely on 'voluntary action'.

Five Official Viewpoints. The Beveridge view was reiterated in the 1958 British White Paper *Provision for Old Age* :

> The Government believe that it would not be right to force everyone to contribute more through a state scheme than would be needed for a reasonable provision for old age. For the state to go further would be to arrogate to itself the individual's right to dispose of his income in what he thinks the right way, and would seriously undermine the individual's sense of responsibility for his own affairs.[9]

The minimum standard had become a reasonable provision but otherwise the attitude was much the same. It was still unaltered in the 1971 British White Paper *Strategy for Pensions* :

The central issue for the future is how to shape the relationship between the state scheme and occupational schemes . . . this issue can only be satisfactorily resolved by a partnership in which the state scheme provides basic pensions and occupational schemes provide pensions related to earnings.[10]

Reasonable provision had now become a basic pension but there was still the firm adherence to the policy that the state should not provide more than a reasonable basic minimum.

The same spirit was reflected in an official U.S. publication in 1968 :

The benefits under the government social insurance programs are payable as a matter of right and as an addition to, and not a substitution for, other financial resources. The individual is thus encouraged to supplement these benefits and build up additional protection through his own initiative, thrift and personal effort.[11]

The New Zealand Royal Commission of Inquiry into Social Security recommended in 1972 that every citizen should have a level of income which enables him

'To belong and participate' – no-one is to be so poor that he cannot eat the sort of food that [citizens] usually eat, wear the same sort of clothes, take a moderate part in those activities which the ordinary [citizen] takes part in as a matter of course. The goal is to enable any citizen to meet and mix with other [citizens] as one of them, as a full member of the community – in brief, *to belong.*[12]

They assessed the *belonging* standard as 80 per cent of the lower quartile level of adult male earnings for a married couple[13] and the same proportion of median earnings for a couple with three children.[14] The Commission also recommended, and this was accepted by the government, that New Zealand should adhere to its long-established practice of selective benefits (except in the case of superannuation and family benefits) subject to an income test. The belonging principle is a distinct advance on the subsistence standard – sufficient to maintain life and health.

A similar attitude towards a desirable minimum standard is expressed in the 1970 White Paper *Income Security for Canadians* in discussing the meaning of poverty :

It [poverty] involves the lack of income, opportunities and self-respect that is regarded as normal in a community . . .

But poverty must be recognised as not simply a lack of income. It means also a lack of opportunities – for good health, for education, for meaningful employment and for recreation. It means a depressing environment, a sense of failure and a feeling of alienation from society.[15]

A Spurious Argument. The New Zealand Royal Commission[16] and the Canadian White Paper[17] adhere after an interval of thirty years to the Beveridge view that voluntary action in the field of income maintenance is desirable and should be encouraged. In discussing the cost of social security pensions neither made any reference to the cost of subsidising private pension schemes by tax exemptions. The New Zealand Royal Commission also queries

. . . whether the community has a right to compel individuals to provide in this particular way [earnings-related social insurance contributions] for their old age, or for sickness and other eventualities. Some may not wish to make such provisions. They may prefer to spend their money on a higher standard of living now, on educating their children, or on buying a house.[16]

They well may, but these arguments, like the stress on individual responsibility in the British White Papers quoted, are spurious. In the U.K. and New Zealand judges and senior civil servants, headmasters and town clerks are deprived of a choice between higher salaries and retirement pensions. Superannuation is part of their terms of employment and is not individually negotiable. In all the ten countries public servants suffer, in the phraseology of the British White Paper, from a serious undermining of responsibility for their own affairs. All the same, public servants accept the pension arrangements made by the state and refrain from pressing through their professional associations for higher salaries in lieu of pensions. In this they are prudent, as most people attach more importance to the apparently pressing needs of today than to the needs of tomorrow. Even amongst the best-educated section of the population, free choice in the provisions for old age is considered undesirable : the risk of some making no provisions or only inadequate ones is realised.

The Central Position of Occupational Pensions. In the countries which adhere to the 'belonging' principle in determining social security benefits, the only realistic way to receive a pension more related to pre-retirement earnings is through membership of an occupational pension scheme. For the great majority of male clerical, administrative and technical staff and to a lesser extent male manual workers in these countries, membership of the employer's pension scheme is a condition of employment. These schemes do no more to encourage individual responsibility and offer no greater choice of pension terms to the employee than social insurance schemes, nor are they any less of a compulsory imposition.

The proper place for occupational pensions and private annuities is quite possibly the most controversial issue in social policy. The preference of policy-makers for these provisions is one of the major restraints on the expansion of social security. The relevant issues are complex and some of the data required to make a rational decision cannot be obtained as they depend on what is going to happen in the future.

Robert J. Myers, the Chief Actuary of the Social Security Administration in the U.S.A., writing in 1970, presents the case for private provisions :

> If the foregoing goals of the expansionists on Social Security benefits [the doubling of the maximum earnings base that is creditable for benefit, the increase of benefits by at least 50 per cent and the enlargement of eligibility for disability benefit] were achieved, the consequences must be clear to anyone. There would not only be the direct effect of eliminating most private sector efforts in economic security; there would also occur a most significant effect on our national economy. Private savings of all types, including pension plans and deferred profit-sharing plans (which had assets of $104 billions at the end of 1967), would be appreciably diminished. This in turn would result in a shortage of investment funds for private industry to maintain and expand its economic productivity. Accordingly private industry would have to turn more and more to the government for such funds and this could well mean increasing governmental regulation, control and even ownership of production.[18]

Myers forcefully expresses views which are usually not put quite so frankly. He emphasises that in social security policy it is not a few welfare cents but billions of dollars which are at stake, and that this is not a subject on the periphery of economic organisation and power, but at its very centre.

Supporters of public provisions stress that occupational pensions are normally non-transferable and thus hinder labour mobility and involve those who change their employment in losses. They also express much doubt as to whether, in a world where industrial structure and technology are undergoing rapid changes and where inflation is ubiquitous, any system of annuities or occupational pensions can offer people in retirement incomes which not only increase with prices but which also enable the old to participate in rising standards of living. They claim that earnings-related social insurance benefits are an efficient means of achieving their objective of replacing income which has ceased, and that they do so in a way greatly superior to the commercial alternative.

Scope for Occupational Pensions. The major objective of social security, in the I.L.O. phraseology, 'to maintain income in case of involuntary loss of earnings or of an important part of earnings',[19] can in a social insurance system be restricted in four ways : by excluding some groups of the population according to occupation or employment status, by excluding those who earn more than a specified amount, by limiting the earnings base that is creditable for benefit and by replacing only a small proportion of the income lost. All four of these devices encourage the private provision of economic security. In the eight countries which have social insurance schemes, that is, all of the ten except for New Zealand and Australia, there has been since the Second World War a marked trend, which will be described in later chapters, towards expansion by modifying or removing some of these restrictions.

The Case for Earnings-Related Benefits. The arguments for relating benefits to earnings are developed in a paper by Detlev Zöllner, a principal officer of the Federal German Ministry of Labour and Social Affairs. He writes :

> . . . wages cover not only minimum needs but specific needs as well; they are not only the means of meeting needs but are also felt by the individual to be the mark of his social status. It is therefore understandable that what workers want is a wage guarantee. If social benefits are to provide security, they must replace the wages lost and must therefore at least be related to them . . .

> In general it would not be considered just if, on the one hand, in the distribution of wages one proceeded on the basis of the inequality of individuals, and on the other hand, if social income distribution were based on equality . . .

> Furthermore, one can say that in the light of the inequalities discussed above, both the human need for security and the

criterion of justice call in principle for full wage compensation. A partial wage replacement would oblige the recipient of social benefits, particularly of long-term benefits, to adjust his standard of living. To prevent, or at least modify as much as possible, such an adjustment is the very aim of wage-related benefits.[20]

Zöllner's views represent an important influence in the shaping of German social legislation, just as Myers' views represent an important influence in discouraging American social legislation. Their explicit and implicit objectives differ so widely that they virtually argue on two different planes.

The Case Against Earnings-Related Benefits. The New Zealand Royal Commission in their discussion of earnings-related benefit doubt the equity of these benefits :

> The "equity" principle ("the greater the loss the greater the need") must itself be approached with some reserve. There can be "equity" in preserving income differentials only if there was equity in the differentials themselves. But differentials in market earnings are based on ability to take advantage of the market rather than considerations of equity.[21]

They also emphasise that earnings-related schemes would only benefit 'those whose earnings are, or have been, above the level with which the flat-rate is proportionally aligned'. On the basis of the Commission's recommendations that would be, for three-children families, those whose earnings exceeded 80 per cent. of the median wage for adult men. Both these comments refer to points of substance.

The Case for Private Provisions and Selectivity. In recent years in Britain and the U.S.A. the increased cost of social services and the realisation that poverty and low-standard social services are still quite common have led to the growth of political forces pressing for limitations rather than expansions in the commitment of the state to the economic well-being of all its citizens. They favour, wherever possible, the provision of services to be made by the private sector rather than by the state, and advocate the principle of selectivity in the sphere of public social services. In other words, they mean that individuals or families should receive free or subsidised services and benefits only on the basis of proven need. Moreover, they believe that universal benefits tend to be too low – spreading the butter too thinly

– to help adequately those in greatest need. They argue that the high levels of taxation which are required to pay benefits to people who do not need them tend to discourage enterprise and the will to work. The same people generally fear that universal benefits undermine the individual's sense of responsibility and cause the growth of state bureaucracies.

These views are reflected in the Canadian White Paper *Income Security for Canadians*,[22] the British White Paper *Strategy for Pensions*,[23] as well as in the British Housing (Financial Provisions) Act, 1972, and the Family Income Supplements Act, 1971. It is difficult to envisage how the social policy of the British government elected in 1970 can be reconciled with those of the other member states of the European Economic Community. The trend in Britain is in the opposite direction to that of the rest of Western Europe and goes against the spirit of Article 118 of the Treaty of Rome:

> . . . it shall be the aim of the Commission to promote close collaboration between Member States in the social field, particularly in matters relating . . . to social security . . . [and] to protection against occupational accidents and diseases.

Therefore British social policy may require considerable adjustment.

Reverse Income Tax. In Britain and the U.S.A. the introduction of a system of reverse income tax (R.I.T.) has been proposed as a means of simplifying and co-ordinating income-maintenance and taxation policy. The basic idea is that people whose income, allowing for variations in family circumstances, exceeds a specified level would be liable to pay tax and those whose income is less than this level would receive payment equal to a proportion of the difference between their actual income and the specified amount. It is claimed that because both taxpayers and R.I.T. recipients would have to fill in the same forms, the stigma involved in applying in person for benefits, and the consequent failure to do so in many cases, would be eliminated. Some advocates of R.I.T. envisage it replacing not only means-tested benefits but also family allowances, pensions, and sickness, unemployment and other social insurance benefits. But there are numerous objections to R.I.T. on ideological as well as practical grounds.[24] In theory it would be possible to specify an amount sufficiently high to guarantee everybody a subsistence minimum. However, assuming the proportion of the deficiency which is to be made up is 50 per cent., a figure which is often quoted,[25] the specified amount would have to be twice the subsistence level and much of the reverse tax would be paid to people with incomes well above subsistence, a consequence which the proponents of this scheme would abhor. If, however, the specified amount were to be about equal to subsistence, those who earn less would receive an allowance insufficient to bring them up to the subsistence level and those who have no income would receive an allowance sufficient to meet only half their minimum need. This dilemma could be avoided by replacing the whole and not merely a proportion of the difference between the specified amount and the actual income, but this would remove from persons with low incomes any incentive to earn an income[26] – to stand on their own two feet – another prospect which the proponents of this scheme would abhor.

For these reasons any R.I.T. scheme is almost certain to guarantee less than a subsistence level. It is an anti-welfare device which as yet has not been implemented by any country, although it has been widely discussed.

The Influence of Opposition Parties. Party-political ideology in the democratic countries with which this study is concerned is not as important in shaping social legislation as it may appear. Governments tend to disappoint their more enthusiastic supporters because they are concerned with gaining and keeping the support of the uncommitted voters. Opposition parties, however, have more influence on legislation than is generally thought. They may lose the elections and votes in parliament, but their programmes and attitudes can and do sway the many whose political alignments are uncertain and changeable, and in this way influence the government.[27] Economic interests are much more difficult to sway. The influence of the American Medical Association in the U.S.A., which is well documented,[28] and that of the Association of Life Insurance Officers in the U.K., which is not so well documented, has certainly been profound.

Policy considerations specific to employment injury, sickness, old age, unemployment and child endowment will be discussed in the chapters which are concerned with these subjects.

Social Control. When social insurance was first introduced in the 1890s in Germany, the avowed object was to protect the state against political upheavals, to integrate the proletariat into society and to shield them from being seduced by revolutionary influences. Similar considerations were in the minds of policy-makers in many countries in the 1930s. If social security developments over the last eighty years are judged by these criteria, they must be pronounced a success. It is of course not possible to isolate the effect of any social or economic measure on the state of society, but except in Germany and Austria in the 1930s, none of the countries experienced political upheaval. The revolutionary influences which did prevail in Germany and Austria were certainly not of the kind which Bismarck wanted to guard against. Nor was Ireland's revolution of 1916-22 the result of an uprising of the working class.

Conflict between Economic and Social Objectives.   The distinction between economic and social policy is often blurred, but their objectives are not always identical. If the major aim of economic policy is to increase G.N.P. per head, one of the fastest ways of achieving this is not 'officiously to keep alive' the over-65s. Not many of that age group normally assist in producing the G.N.P. and the fewer of them that survive, the larger is the share which will go to all below that age. This very extreme example illustrates well the difference between economic objectives and the more sophisticated and humanitarian objectives of social policy. It may also serve as a warning to the worshippers of the paramountcy of economic goals. It must, however, be stressed that without the economic advances that have been achieved since the 1890s, the progress of social development would have been less. In particular, the maintenance of a full and stable level of employment must be a major objective of social as well as of economic policy. The high post-war level of employment as compared with the widespread unemployment of the inter-war period has been an important contributory factor in social development.

Freedom of Choice.   Some argue that the power of the state has increased, is increasing and ought to diminish. They believe that the diffusion of power in society is the basis of individual liberty and that the dependence of the individual on the state in many important facets of life diminishes that liberty. They suggest that services solely supplied by the state, whether in health, education, housing or pensions, deprive the individual of the freedom of choice which is an inherent characteristic of liberty. They believe that the patients, parents, tenants and policy-holders have a right to change their custom from one supplier to any of several competing ones. This not only gives the individual more liberty and power to have his wishes respected, but also produces, through the competitive forces of the market, services which are more efficient, in greater variety and better adapted to changing needs than services rendered by government agencies. These views deserve respect and are a valid criticism of many public social services. It is undoubtedly eminently desirable to give the consumer of social services the greatest possible freedom of choice and the most ample opportunity to appeal against the refusal of services or the award of benefits. This, however, has to be limited so as not to override other goals of social welfare. On the criteria of freedom of choice and opportunity to appeal, the present state of social security provisions is usually at best indifferent – the 'take it or leave it' attitude is all too common.

Absence of Clearly Defined Objectives. If the success of social security provisions for all citizens is measured against the terms of service, in respect of security of tenure, sick pay and pensions, enjoyed by public servants, it becomes obvious that the scope for social development in all the countries of this study is still very great and, as will be seen in later chapters, much greater in some than in others.

Anyone surveying social policies pursued in the ten countries will share the views of the New Zealand Royal Commission reporting on their overseas study tour in 1971 :

> It soon became apparent, however, that social welfare policies were in a state of flux all over the world. Everywhere old ideas and techniques . . . were being questioned and re-examined. Nowhere did there seem satisfaction with the *status quo* . . .
>
> Nowhere did we find the aims of social security policy or of community responsibility clearly defined. Social security administrators are everywhere prisoners of history, tradition and political will. Nevertheless if any trend can be discerned, it was towards more selectivity, better income redistribution techniques and better identification of need.[29]

CHAPTER III

Levels and Trends
of Social Security

DIFFICULTIES AND LIMITATIONS OF INTERNATIONAL COMPARISONS

Sources of Data. A number of international organisations collect
information on social security expenditure. Unfortunately, much of
this is quite out of date by the time of publication. The International
Labour Office (ILO) issues at three yearly intervals a comprehensive
report, *The Cost of Social Security.* The Seventh report[1] in this series,
which covers 68 countries, was published in 1972 and refers to the
period 1964–66. For many countries, including six of the ten under
review, the most recent data are for the financial year ending in 1966.
This was normally March 1966, almost exactly six years prior to the
publication of the report.

Two regional inquiries give more recent data. First, *Social Security
in the Nordic Countries* (covering Denmark, Finland, Iceland,
Norway and Sweden) was most recently published in 1971[2]. It refers
to 1968 (1968–69) and contains a very brief summary of data for the
following year. Second, the European Economic Community (EEC)
publishes *Social Accounts of the Member States of the EEC* at irregular intervals. The volume issued in 1970[3] gives data for 1967 and
covers Belgium, France, Federal Germany, Italy, Luxemburg and the
Netherlands. Both these reports and the ILO report are edited by
highly competent staff who endeavour to make the data relating to
each country as much as possible comparable with those of the other
countries covered.

The Social Security Administration of the U.S. Department of
Health, Education and Welfare publishes every other year a report,
Social Security Programs Throughout the World. This contains a
summary of the principal provisions of social security programmes.
The volume published in November 1970[4] relates in the case of most
of the 128 countries to the status of their social security systems in

mid-1969. The material is presented in the form of a separate chart for each country.

Definition of 'Social Security'. The use of the term *social security* varies somewhat in all three reports. The I.L.O. in its comprehensive 68-nation inquiry did not attempt an *a priori* definition of social security but found it more expedient to formulate certain criteria which had to be satisfied before a scheme or a service was considered as part of the 'national social security system'. These criteria in 1966, as in previous inquiries, were :

(1) the objective of the system must be to grant curative or preventive medical care, or to maintain income in case of involuntary loss of earnings or of an important part of earnings, or to grant supplementary incomes to persons having family responsibilities;

(2) the system must have been set up by legislation which attributes specified individual rights to, or imposes specified obligations on, a public, semi-public or autonomous body;

(3) the system should be administered by a public, semi-public or autonomous body.

However, any scheme of employment-injury compensation should be included in the inquiry, even if it does not meet the criteria in (3) above, because the compensation of employment injuries is imposed directly on the employer.[5]

The I.L.O. data thus include all compulsory and certain voluntary social insurance schemes, family allowances, public employees' pensions, public health services, public assistance and benefits granted to war victims. They cover all provisions shown in (1) to (3) and some provisions in (4) and (7) of Fig. 1.1, but exclude most statutory obligations imposed on employers, all non-statutory provisions and all fiscal reliefs of a social character.

The E.E.C. social accounts follow closely the I.L.O. criteria but exclude public health services, public assistance (except unemployment assistance) and benefits to war victims. In the data for the Nordic countries, pensions of public employees are excluded but safety and accident-prevention services, employment and placement services, public works for the unemployed and estimates of tax rebates for children are included.

It is important to realise that while some criteria may be more expedient than others in determining whether a particular programme is part of a national social security system, all decisions of what constitutes social security provisions or policies are necessarily arbitrary. This can be illustrated by an example. A government may prevent loss of income on account of unemployment and maintain income in case of unemployment in a number of different ways. It can :

(1) ensure by its economic policy a high and stable level of employment;
(2) organise public works to provide temporary employment;
(3) make grants to individuals, enterprises or public bodies to promote employment;
(4) allow tax reliefs of various kinds to provide work in areas with high unemployment;
(5) impose on employers the obligation to give extensive notice before making a man redundant;
(6) compensate men who are made redundant irrespective of whether they are becoming or remain unemployed;
(7) pay unemployment benefit.

All these seven measures have some social policy component; they benefit the unemployed or those who would have been unemployed but for these measures. However, only the seventh is part of the social security system according to the I.L.O. criteria.

Methods and Pitfalls of Comparing Levels of Expenditure. Even figures as expertly compiled and edited as those of the I.L.O. report do not cover expenditure on identical items in all countries. This is not due to any shortcomings in the data but to differences in legislation, organisation, policies and attitudes which, even for countries as homogeneous as the ten under review, are so great as to make standardised accounting not merely difficult, but possibly even misleading. It is a truism that international comparisons are hazardous, and that they compare items which are not identical cannot be doubted. In all countries the majority of social security expenditure is on a few major services which are comparatively easy to identify, but relatively minor provisions vary between countries to an extent which is not negligible. However, in spite of all dangers, difficulties and limitations, international comparisons are useful and suggestive, especially if they are regarded with some scepticism. They should not be viewed as a league table and even less as revelations of truth.

The most straightforward international comparison of levels of social security provisions can be made by computing the cost per head and expressing it in U.S. dollars at the official rate of exchange. This method is based on two implicit assumptions : that the purchasing power of the U.S. dollar does not differ between countries, and that the items classified as social security are the same in all countries; but both these assumptions have already been shown to be of limited validity. In any case the differences in cost per head also reflect variations in G.N.P. per head.

A second method is to express expenditure on social security as a proportion of G.N.P. This overcomes the difficulty of purchasing-power variations and is independent of the G.N.P. per head, but still hides differences between the items considered as social security.

A third method is to ascertain the per capita benefit expenditure at constant prices for a number of years and to compute an index of the real purchasing power of these benefits. This allows a comparison of the changes in the public social security provisions of different countries but not a comparison of the relative levels in these countries.

The interpretation of statistics relating to cost, even if they are based on uniform definitions, standardised accounting and are free from distortion by differences in the purchasing power of money, is still exceedingly difficult. This too can best be illustrated by an example.

If the cost of cleaning in hospitals per 100 beds is half as great in country A as in country B, there could be at least seven reasons for this :

(1) factor cost – wages, prices of consumables and equipment are higher in country B;
(2) level of mechanisation – more or better-designed floor-polishing machines in country A;
(3) nature of buildings – hospitals in country A are more modern and have a superior layout requiring less cleaning;
(4) standard of training – higher in country A resulting in higher productivity;
(5) industry of workers – cleaners in country A work harder;
(6) level of cleanliness – lower in country B owing to habits of patients or nurses or to air pollution;
(7) required cleanliness – lower in country A and excessive in country B.

Differences in the cost of hospital cleaning may be due to any of these seven factors or combinations of them. The supposition that low cost necessarily implies low standards is certainly unjustified.

In the same way high levels of expenditure, whether per head of population or relative to G.N.P., are not necessarily an indication of high standards of services. Thus high expenditure on unemployment compensation may be due to many people being unemployed, to high rates of unemployment benefit or to a large proportion of all unemployed being entitled to benefit. High public expenditure on drugs may be due to, among many other factors, a high incidence of illness, the high price of drugs or doctors prescribing too many or unnecessarily expensive drugs. High expenditure on pensions may reflect a relatively large proportion of old people or a higher pension rate given to fewer people. Thus in order to indicate standards of social services, expenditure must be related to needs and possibly also to prices and levels of efficiency. The more familiar one is with the nature and intricacies of a particular service, the more one becomes aware of the multiplicity of factors which may be the cause of differences in national expenditure and the more one realises that these differences may in part reflect the unit of measurement chosen and the base period selected.

In the following section a comparison is made of the levels and trends of public social security provisions in the ten countries. The figures quoted will exclude the revenue loss due to tax remissions and the cost imposed on employers in meeting their statutory obligations (except in the case of employment injury compensation). They will also not take into account the non-statutory provisions which have a social security character. In examining and interpreting these figures it is therefore essential to remember not only all the difficulties and limitations to which reference has been made in this section, but also that they represent merely a fraction of the aggregate of social security expenditure and that the fraction of the aggregate which they represent varies both between countries at any given time and within each country over time.

THE COST OF SOCIAL SECURITY

Expenditure Proportions, 1952–66. The aggregate expenditure on public social security schemes (according to the I.L.O. criteria) expressed as a percentage of the G.N.P. at current market prices (as defined in the United Nations' *System of National Accounts*) is given in Table 3.1. In 1966, the most recent year for which the I.L.O. data

TABLE 3:1   *Total Expenditure on Public Social Security as a proportion of G.N.P. at Current Prices.*

	PROPORTION			INCREASE	INDEX			RANK ORDER		
	1952 %	1961 %	1966 %	1952-66 %	1961 (1952=100)	1966 (1961=100)	1966 (1952=100)	1952	1961	1966
Austria ...	15.9	16.5	18.5	2.6	104	112	116	1	1	1
Germany ...	14.6	15.9	17.4	2.8	109	109	119	2	2	2
Ireland[a] ...	8.0	9.3	10.2	2.2	116	110	128	7	8	7
U.K.[b] ...	10.0	11.2	12.6	2.6	112	113	126	4	4	5
Denmark[a] ...	9.5	10.8	13.2	3.7	114	122	139	5	6	4
Netherlands ...	8.3	11.1	16.7	8.4	134	150	201	6	5	3
Canada[a] ...	6.1	9.6	9.6	3.5	157	100	157	8	7	8
U.S.A.[a] ...	4.3	7.0	7.2	2.9	163	103	167	10	10	10
New Zealand[a] ...	10.9	13.1	11.8	0.9	120	90	108	3	3	6
Australia[a] ...	6.1	8.5	8.2	2.1	139	96	134	8	9	9

[a] Figures refer to 1951-2, 1960-1 and 1965-6 respectively.
[b] Figures refer to 1952-3, 1961-2 and 1966-7 respectively.

Source: The Cost of Social Security (International Labour Office, Geneva, 1972) Table 2.

are available, the expenditure proportion in Austria, Germany and the Netherlands was more than one-sixth, while in Canada, the U.S.A. and Australia it was less than one-tenth. In New Zealand and the other three European states expenditure varied between these proportions. In all the countries expenditure on social security had increased since 1952. The increase was a mere 0.9 per cent. of G.N.P. in New Zealand but a massive 8.4 per cent. in the Netherlands, and varied between 2.1 per cent. and 3.7 per cent. in the other countries. The increase in this proportion relative to what it had been in 1952 was also greatest in the Netherlands, where it more than doubled, and least in New Zealand, where it increased by less than one-tenth. Otherwise the increase was least in Austria and Germany, where expenditure had already been high in 1952, and greatest in the U.S.A. and Canada, where expenditure had been low in 1952. Denmark was the only country which had both a comparatively high increase and a fairly high proportion in 1952. In three of the pairs of countries – the two German-speaking, the two English-speaking European and the two North American – the relative increase (index) was much the same for both countries.

The rank order of the proportion shows that the countries in all the pairs except New Zealand and Australia were fairly close to each other in this respect also. In the fourteen-year period the rank order of the proportion of social security expenditure to G.N.P. showed little change, with two exceptions : the Netherlands moved up from sixth to third place and New Zealand came down from third to sixth place. At the beginning as well as at the end of the period Austria and Germany had the highest and the U.S.A. and Australia the lowest proportions (see Fig. 3.1).

Changes in the proportions over time are indicative of shifts in resources within one country, but identical changes in different countries are not necessarily of the same importance. In both Austria and the U.K. social security expenditure as a proportion of G.N.P. increased by 2.6 per cent. between 1952 and 1966, but as in Austria the average annual rate of growth of real product was some 5.4 per cent. and in the U.K. some 2.9 per cent., the relative increase in expenditure was almost twice as great in Austria as in the U.K.

Expenditure on social security as a proportion of G.N.P. was in 1966 inversely related to G.N.P. per head in U.S. dollars. Among the four countries with the highest G.N.P. per head were the three – Canada, the U.S.A. and Australia – with the lowest expenditure

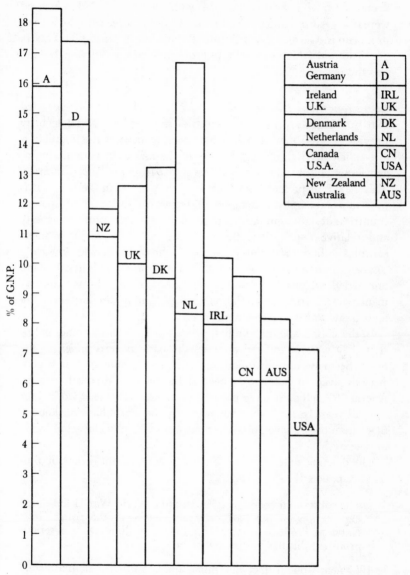

FIG. 3:1 *Expenditure on Public Social Security Schemes as percentage of G.N.P. at Current Prices, 1952 and 1966.*

NOTE: The bar below the initials shows expenditure in 1952; that above, expenditure in 1966.

proportions, while among the three with the lowest G.N.P. per head were two – Austria and the Netherlands – of the three with the highest proportions. Germany and Denmark both had a fairly high G.N.P. per head and a high expenditure proportion; the position in Ireland was the reverse.

Low Proportions Due to Absence of Need?   It has been suggested that in relatively prosperous countries the need for social security provisions is less than it is in poorer ones, as most of the population are sufficiently well off to take care of themselves in various contingencies without having to rely on assistance from public programmes. This view is at present less widely held than it was in the 1950s. It is now more generally recognised that even in the most prosperous countries substantial minorities of the population are prone to poverty and relative deprivation; these include not only people without earnings – the retired, the unemployed, the mentally and physically disabled and women who have the care of young children but are unmarried, widowed or deserted – but also men in full-time employment whose earnings in relation to their family circumstances are inadequate to keep them out of poverty.

In the U.S.A. about 26 million persons in 1967 had incomes so low that they were considered poor by the basic poverty index of the Social Security Administration. An estimated $7\frac{1}{2}$ million of these poor persons lived in households headed by aged or disabled persons. Another $8\frac{1}{4}$ million lived in households in which the head worked for the full year. In the most affluent society the world has ever known, more than one in seven of all persons were officially classed as living in poverty.[6]

The opening statement of a Canadian government review of anti-poverty policies in 1970 read :

> The substantial economic growth after World War II led to the expectation on the part of many that with the rising Gross National Product poverty would steadily diminish as a serious problem; this has not proved to be so.[7]

In 1967 nearly one-fifth of all families and two-fifths of all unattached individuals in Canada had low levels of income on the basis of a Dominion Bureau of Statistics study on income distribution and poverty in Canada.[8] This study took $4,060 for a family of four as the low-income cut-off. This was approximately 69 per cent. of the average weekly wages of male workers in manufacturing industries.

The first survey in Australia measuring the extent of poverty was conducted by the Melbourne University Institute of Applied Economic and Social Research under the direction of R. F. Henderson in 1966. The survey was confined to the metropolitan area of Melbourne but was thought to give a good indication of poverty in urban Australia. The findings showed that some 7 per cent. of income units lived in poverty. This was defined for a married couple and two children as an income equivalent to less than the minimum statutory wage of an unskilled labourer plus child endowment. The low prevalence of poverty in comparison with the U.S.A., Canada and the U.K. was attributed by R. I. Downing[9] to the virtual absence of unemployment, the high level of average earnings, minimum wages not 'uncomfortably' below the average and universal welfare provisions. He observed :

> An expenditure on cash social benefits which is not high by international standards but which, on the other hand, is concentrated by the means test on those demonstrably in need, ensures at least a minimum subsistence for those not in the work force – though it is among this group, naturally, that most of our poverty and need is found.[9]

This last point refers to the finding that 15 per cent. of the old and 31 per cent. of fatherless families lived in poverty. Henderson and his associates believed that the extent of the poverty was higher among that sixth of the population of Australia living in rural areas and especially among the aboriginal population (a mere 0.6 per cent. of the total) than it was among those living in the urban parts of the country. They also presumed that the prevalence of poverty increased between 1966 and 1970 on account of social security cash benefits' rising more slowly than average earnings.

Low Proportions Due to Generous Non-statutory Benefits? A second possible explanation of the relatively low expenditure on public social security in the most prosperous countries might be sought in the prevalence of non-statutory social security schemes provided by employers, for example superannuation, redundancy compensation and pay during sickness. Ubiquitous and liberal schemes might replace, at least to some extent, the need for public provisions. The available evidence does not confirm this hypothesis. In the U.S.A. in 1967 a mere 6 per cent. of the incomes of married couples with one or both members aged 65 or over came from private pension funds. For the unmarried the corresponding proportion was 3 per cent. Only 19 per cent. of the couples and 7 per cent. of the unmarried persons received any benefit from private group pensions.[10] In future, owing to the expansion of group pension schemes in the last thirty years, the number of beneficiaries will be greater and so will the benefits they receive. This, however, does not explain the stringency of public provision in 1967. There is no reason to presume that private pensions in number or liberality were more generous in Canada and Australia than they were in the U.S.A.

The relatively low expenditure on public social security provisions in the three countries with the highest G.N.P. per capita can thus neither be explained by the absence of poverty, especially among the groups prone to poverty, nor by the extent and liberality of non-statutory schemes.

Per Capita Expenditure, 1952–66.   Increases in per capita expenditure on public social security between 1952 and 1966 at constant prices are shown in Table 3 : 2. In all countries except the U.K., New Zealand and Australia per capita expenditure more than doubled.

TABLE 3:2   *Indices of per capita expenditure on Social Security Benefits at Constant Prices.*[a]

	(1964 = 100)			(1952 = 100)	
	1952	1961	1966	1966	Rank Order
Austria	45	83	112	249	3
Germany	41	87	113	276	2
Ireland[b]	54	84	112	207	7
U.K.[c]	63	90	113	179	9
Denmark[b]	50	77	118	236	5
Netherlands	34	67	126	371	1
Canada[b]	46	90	108	235	6
U.S.A.[b]	46	87	112	243	4
New Zealand[b]	84	98	103	123	10
Australia[b]	56	86	105	188	8

[a] Values adjusted according to cost-of-living indices.
[b] Figures refer to 1951-2, 1960-1 and 1965-6 respectively.
[c] Figures refer to 1952-3, 1961-2 and 1966-7 respectively.

Source: I.L.O., *The Cost of Social Security*, Table 6.

The three countries which had the largest increase in per capita expenditure – Austria, Germany and the Netherlands – were also those countries which in 1966 spent the largest proportion of G.N.P. on social security. Other countries with comparatively large increases were Denmark, Canada and the U.S.A. By far the lowest increase, a mere 23 per cent., was experienced in New Zealand. In Ireland, the U.K. and Australia increases were relatively low but not insubstantial. Only one country was among the three lowest on both counts – Australia.

There was a tenuous relation between increases in per capita expenditure on public social security benefits (Table 3 :2) and annual growth per capita of real Gross Domestic Product (G.D.P.) (Table 2 :2). Germany and Austria scored high and the U.K. and Ireland low in both respects. Canada and Denmark experienced the same rate of growth of G.D.P. and also had the same proportionate increase in expenditure. The Netherlands had the most substantial increase in per capita expenditure combined with a rate of growth slightly above average, while the U.S.A. had an above average increase in expenditure with a rate of growth well below average. New Zealand and Australia had low increases in expenditure but average rates of growth.

Per Capita Expenditure Changes Affected by Needs? Changes in per capita expenditure on public social services might possibly have been related to increased need for such expenditure. Since in all the countries a large proportion of the cost of social security cash benefits is accounted for by pensions for the old, a meaningful but by no means comprehensive measure of the required change in expenditure per head is an old-age index (see Table 3 :3). This index was relatively high in Austria, Germany and the Netherlands, all of which had substantial increases in per capita expenditure, and also in Denmark where the increase in expenditure was about average. The index was low in Ireland, New Zealand and Australia, all of which had low increases in expenditure, and also in Canada where the increase in expenditure was about average. The correspondence between the expenditure index and the old-age index is also tenuous but is somewhat greater than that between the expenditure index and the rate of growth of G.D.P.

Changes in Expenditure Proportions, 1960–70. The most recent

TABLE 3:3   *Changes in population and number of old[a] people, 1952-66*

	Population (1952 = 100) 1966	Number of old[a] people (1952 = 100) 1966	Old-age index[b]
Austria	105	131	124
Germany	119	141	118
Ireland	97	102	106
U.K.[c]	109	120	109
Denmark	111	138	124
Netherlands ...	120	144	120
Canada	138	137	100
U.S.A.	131	142	108
New Zealand ...	133	123	92
Australia	134	140	104

[a] 65 and over.

[b] Index of people aged 65 and over in 1966 with 1952 as the base, multiplied by 100 and divided by the index of total population in 1966 with 1952 as the base (calculated by author).

[c] England and Wales only.

Source: United Nations Demographic Year Book 1970, Table 6.

comparative statistics of social security expenditure, which relate to 1966 (1965–6), are somewhat out of date although they were only published in 1972. It is, however, possible to gain a quite reliable indication of the trend of public social security in any given country by relating its expenditure on social security (according to its national definition) to its G.D.P. The proportion calculated by this method cannot be compared with that of other countries, as the items included and their definitions are not always the same for each country. The figures shown in Table 3 :4 are all based on official statistics covering income-maintenance provisions including family endowment and (except for Canada) expenditure on health services; they all exclude public employees' programmes and some exclude employment injury compensation. The indications are that in Germany, Canada, New Zealand and Australia the proportion of G.D.P. spent on social security provisions has declined, and whereas this decline was only marginal in Canada and Australia, it was somewhat greater in Germany and New Zealand. There were quite marked increases in Ireland, the U.K.[11] and the U.S.A. and a steep increase, similar to that in the Netherlands in the previous period, in Denmark. The changes in these proportions will have been caused by the factors discussed in the section on 'Rising Expenditure' in the previous chapter.

TABLE 3:4 *Indications of the trend of Social Security expenditure as a proportion of G.D.P., 1966–70.*

								1966 %	1970 %
Germany[a]	...	...	...	...	...	...	...	17·4	17·0
Ireland[b]	...	...	...	...	...	...	...	9·8	11·4
U.K.[c]	...	...	...	...	...	...	...	11·2	12·9
Denmark[d]	...	...	...	...	...	...	...	13·3	18·3
Canada[e]	...	...	...	...	...	...	...	5·0	4·9[f]
U.S.A.[g]	...	...	...	...	...	...	...	7·3	9·6
New Zealand[h]	...	...	...	...	...	...	...	9·9	9·1
Australia[i]	...	...	...	...	...	...	...	4·2	4·1

Note: The proportion indicates *only* the trend over time; it has no validity for inter-country comparisons (see text).

Sources: The expenditure data are taken from the sources shown below and are expressed as proportions of the G.D.P. statistics published in the *U.N. Monthly Bulletin of Statistics* (May 1972) Table 61.

a Sozialbudget in *Ubersicht über die Soziale Sicherung* (Bundesminister für Arbeit und Sozialordnung, 1970) p.26. The proportions quoted in this publication are: 1966, 17·8 per cent.; 1970, 17·9 per cent.

b *National Income and Expenditure* 1970 (Stationery Office, Dublin, 1972). Table A23.

c *National Income and Expenditure* 1971 (Central Statistical Office, H.M.S.O., 1971). Table 50, pp. 63-4.

d *Social Security in the Nordic Countries,* no. 22 (1971). Tables 1A and 1C.

e *Income Security for Canadians* (Department of National Health and Welfare, Ottawa, 1970) p. 58; excludes health expenditure.

f Refers to 1969.

g *Statistical Abstract of the United States* 1971 (U.S. Department of Commerce, Washington, 1971). Table 430, p. 271.

h *Social Security in New Zealand : Report of the Royal Commission of Inquiry* (Wellington, 1972). Appendix 15, p. 558.

i *Official Yearbook of the Commonwealth of Australia* (Commonwealth Bureau of Census and Statistics, Canberra, 1971) p. 385.

NUMBER OF BENEFICIARIES

Absence of Compilation of the Number of Beneficiaries.   Another
measure of the level of social security provision in a country is the
number of persons receiving cash benefits (excluding children's
allowances) 'to maintain income in case of involuntary loss of earnings or of an important part of earnings'. None of the countries, to
the author's knowledge, publishes annual statistics of this type. This
is so for quite good reasons. The number of recipients of specific
benefits is usually known, but even this is not invariably the case,
for example for workmen's compensation in the U.S.A., Australia
and Canada. The real difficulty, however, is that in all the countries
there are some people who receive two or more quite unrelated
benefits and in some countries insurance benefits are supplemented
by means-tested assistance schemes.

In Germany in 1969 the number of pensions and similar payments
made each month was 18 million, but a micro-census in 1968 ascertained that 6·6 million people received one pension only while 11·4
million pensions were paid to 2·4 million people[12]. It is, for example,
quite common in Germany for a woman to receive a widow's pension
on her husband's insurance as well as an old-age pension in respect
of her own earnings. The position in Austria is rather similar.

Estimates of the Number of Beneficiaries in Five Countries.   In
Ireland, where the duplication of benefits is minimal, the total
number of persons and their dependants in receipt of weekly social
welfare benefits was 717,000 – approximately one-quarter (24 per
cent.) of the population. The 403,000 people receiving benefit (about
half subject to a needs test) had 99,000 adult dependants and 215,000
child dependants in their households. These figures were compiled
by the Research Services of the Irish Congress of Trade Unions on
the basis of information furnished by the Departments of Social
Welfare, Health and Central Statistics. The figures for recipients
are referred to as 'firm' while those for dependants are partly
estimated 'but can be taken to be of the correct order of magnitude'[13].

In the U.K. the duplication of benefits is more common than in
Ireland. Thus in 1969 about 23 per cent. of recipients of unemployment benefit and 28 per cent. of retirement pensioners also received
supplementary benefits. It is, however, on the basis of published

information, possible to estimate that in 1969 the number of social security beneficiaries and their dependants was about 12·6 million – approximately 23 per cent. of the population[14]. Among the nearly 10 million beneficiaries some 93 per cent. received insurance benefit without a needs test, but a substantial proportion of these beneficiaries (22 per cent.) also received supplementary assistance subject to an income test.

The proportion of beneficiaries and their dependants in New Zealand was much lower. Excluding supplementary benefits (which are always paid in addition to other benefits) and workmen's compensation recipients, the number of beneficiaries in 1970 was about 280,000 (about half of whom were subject to an income test) plus 23,000 dependants, equivalent to some 11 per cent. of the population[15]. The corresponding proportion for Australia was about 9 per cent. In Australia in June 1970 just over 1 million benefits were paid[16], all of which were subject to an income test. These were supplemented by an estimated 100,000-150,000 allowances for dependants.

In the U.S.A. in December 1969 some 20½ million people received social insurance benefits (excluding workmen's compensation) and a further 4 million received public assistance (excluding those who also received social insurance). The latter group was subject to a variety of means tests, different in each state. These payments were supplemented in respect of approximately 13 million dependants[17]. The proportion of the population covered by social security payments was thus about 19 per cent.

Heterogeneity of Award Conditions. The proportions of the populations in these five countries receiving social insurance or assistance benefits ranged from 9 per cent. in Australia to 24 per cent. in Ireland. However, great care is needed in evaluating the meaning of this. The conditions for awarding social assistance differ widely. Public assistance in the U.S.A. in general and in the southern states in particular involves elements of discretion and even arbitrariness which are quite alien to the income test for old-age pensions in New Zealand. It seems indeed doubtful whether a programme such as A.F.D.C. (Aid to Families with Dependent Children) in the U.S.A. qualifies as a social security provision according to the I.L.O. definition – a 'system . . . which attributes specified individual rights to, or which imposes specified obligations on, a public . . . body'.

Even if it does qualify according to the letter of the law, which is different for each of the 50 states, it may well be disqualified in at least some of them by the way the law is administered.

In Australia all benefits are awarded on the basis of an income test, in New Zealand and Ireland half of all beneficiaries are tested in respect of their income, while in the U.K. the corresponding proportion is about 28 per cent. and in the U.S.A. about 21 per cent. Both insurance benefits and assistance payments, however, differ widely between countries in their magnitude relative to wages, and even within a country there are often great divergences between benefits awarded under different schemes. In Germany, the U.K. and New Zealand virtually all beneficiaries are entitled in law as well as in practice to have their benefits brought up to what is officially considered as the subsistence standard, while this is not the case in Australia and the U.S.A., where most pensions are well below that standard. The average monthly payment of $48 in January 1970 for a family of four under A.F.D.C. in Mississippi is very different indeed from the payment which such a family would have received in the U.K. or New Zealand. Similarly, the 5 million single retired women in the U.S.A. who in December 1969 received an average pension of $86 per month – 58 per cent. of the official poverty level – were in a much worse position than their counterparts in the U.K. whose national insurance retirement pension was £5 per week – about 71 per cent. of the average subsistence level of a single householder.

Mere Numbers Poor Indicator.   The number of beneficiaries and their dependants may possibly be considered as an indication of the spread of social security. It is, however, a poor indicator of the degree to which social security provisions satisfy needs. This depends on demographic, economic and social characteristics. Sources of income other than social security available to citizens who are un-employed, disabled, widowed or retired are particularly relevant.

CHAPTER IV

Employment Injury

Introduction. In most countries protection against employment injury has four characteristics : it is the oldest branch of social security, it provides the most generous benefits, it is a pace-setter for other social security provisions and it is administered as a separate entity. The first social security law anywhere, introduced in Germany in 1883, was compulsory sickness insurance for certain employees in industry. A year later Germany was also the first country to set up an accident insurance scheme to protect workers against employment injuries. Austria followed suit with a similar scheme in 1887. Ten years later the U.K. (which then included the whole of Ireland) imposed on employers in some industries a legal liability to compensate their employees for part of their loss of earnings due to accidents arising out of and in the course of their employment irrespective of fault. Denmark introduced similar legislation in 1898 and the Netherlands in 1901 adopted an accident insurance scheme. By the outbreak of the First World War, New Zealand and most, but not all, parts of the U.S.A., Canada and Australia had introduced Workmen's Compensation Acts (W.C.A.s) following broadly the original British Act of 1897.

In all ten countries, with the possible exception of the Netherlands, in spite of long legislative histories, the principles on which employment injury protection is based have remained curiously unsatisfactory. The basic questions – who is to be compensated? by whom? in what circumstances? for what? by how much? – have not been answered in a generally acceptable and consistent way[1].

WHO IS TO BE COMPENSATED?

The I.L.O. Standards. The General Conference of the International Labour Organisation adopted certain proposals with regard to benefits in the case of industrial accidents and occupational diseases

65

which are incorporated in the Employment Injury Benefits Convention, 1964. This provides in Article 4(1):

> National legislation concerning employment injury benefits shall protect all employees, including apprentices, in the public and private sectors, including co-operatives, and, in respect of the death of the breadwinner, prescribed categories of beneficiaries[2].

This general principle is modified in Article 4(2):

> Any Member may make such exceptions as it deems necessary in respect of – (a) persons whose employment is of a casual nature and who are employed otherwise than for the purpose of the employer's trade or business; (b) outworkers; (c) members of the employer's family living in his house, in respect of their work for him; (d) other categories of employees, which shall not exceed in number 10 per cent. of all employees other than those excluded under clauses (a) to (c)[3].

U.K. and Ireland. The U.K. industrial injuries scheme which commenced in 1948 covered all employees including married women and persons over pension age. Also included were unpaid apprentices, children under school-leaving age in part-time employment and persons excluded from other social insurance schemes because their employment was subsidiary or inconsiderable. The Irish occupational injuries scheme which commenced in 1966 provided broadly the same cover against employment injuries as there was in the U.K., except that non-manual workers earning more than £1,200 per annum (£1,600 since 1971) were excluded.

Germany and Austria. The coverage of the German accident insurance scheme based on the law of 1963 was more extensive. It protected not only all employees and most self-employed and their spouses but also several other groups. These included persons injured in rescue work or in assisting the police, the unemployed when following the duties imposed upon them by law, blood donors and persons undertaking civic duties. Even students and pupils were protected. The circle of persons protected in Austria was similar to that in Germany but was not quite as extensive.

Denmark and the Netherlands. In Denmark industrial injuries insurance included all employees as well as persons carrying out civic duties and shore fishermen. Self-employed persons were able to take out voluntary insurance provided their annual income did not exceed specified limits. The Netherlands was the only country among the ten and indeed the only country anywhere which made no special provisions for persons suffering accidents connected with their employment. Since 1967 all persons who were unfit for work owing to physical or mental illness or whose incapacity was due to an accident or an industrial disease received the same benefits irrespective of the cause of the illness or accident. The legislation providing such benefits covered all employees as well as commercial travellers, outworkers and similar categories.

U.S.A. In the U.S.A.[4] each of the 50 states had its own workmen's compensation programme, independent of any Federal legislative or administrative responsibility. In all states, coverage against employment injury was more restricted than in the six European countries. All the states covered employees only. Moreover, in 23 states coverage was elective, that is, the private employer had the option of accepting or rejecting the state legislation; however, if he rejected it he lost the customary common law defences against suits by employees. In 24 states employers with fewer than a specified number of employees – in most states 3 but in one 15 – were exempted from any liability. Other common exclusions were: agricultural employees (three-fifths of all states), domestic servants (five-sixths of all states), casual employees (three-fifths of all states) and employees in non-hazardous occupations (a quarter of all states)[5].

These and similar exclusions had the net result that in 1968 the 15 states with the least extensive protection covered less than 70 per cent. of the workers who potentially could have been protected. The proportion of all employees covered in these states was even lower. Nationally, protection against employment injury was afforded to about 84 per cent. of the 68 million civilian wage and salary workers who potentially could have been eligible for such protection.

Canada. Each of the ten Canadian provinces had its own workmen's compensation scheme. Coverage was similar to that of the U.S.A. Employees in industry and commerce were included, while agricultural workers (except in Ontario) and domestic and casual employees and those of small firms were excluded. However, in contrast to some of the state programmes in the U.S.A., all the provincial programmes were compulsory.

New Zealand and Australia.   In New Zealand in 1970 protection
against employment injury covered all persons (defined as workers)
who were employed under a contract of service or apprenticeship
and also certain designated groups such as share farmers. In Australia employment injury protection for all but Commonwealth
employees was the responsibility of the states. Most employees were
covered with the exception of casual workers, outworkers and shore
fishermen. In Victoria cover was restricted to employees earning less
than $6,000 per annum, while in none of the other states was there
an income limit.

Common Exclusions and their Effects.   The largest group of pro-
ducers excluded from protection against employment injury were
employers and the self-employed. The latter were covered, if only
to a limited extent, in Germany, Austria and Denmark. Many self-
employed worked in agriculture, where the risk of industrial accidents
was comparatively great. In Great Britain claims to industrial injury
benefit were higher for agricultural workers (40 per 1,000 at risk)
than for men in engineering and electrical goods (35 per 1,000) or
in the vehicle industry (31 per 1,000)[6]. Australian statistics bear
this out. In Victoria the claim rate for employees in primary industries (excluding mining) was 58 per 1,000 at risk, compared with 40
per 1,000 in manufacturing industries[7].

In the six European countries and New Zealand all employees
were covered against employment injury, with the exception of non-
manual employees in Ireland earning more than £1,600 per annum.
The exclusion of agricultural workers in most of the states of the
U.S.A. and in all but one of the Canadian provinces left unprotected
a group of workers whose earnings were often comparatively low
and among whom trade union organisation was weak. Their chances
of obtaining damages in a common law suit even when their employers
were negligent were therefore much less than those of higher-paid
industrial workers who were backed by a strong trade union. This
applied equally to domestic servants, most of whom were excluded
in the U.S.A., and to casual workers who frequently were not covered
in the U.S.A., Canada and Australia.

The relative importance of excluding employers and the self-
employed from protection against employment injury depends on
two factors : their proportion in the labour force and the alternative
social security services available to them. In Ireland employers and

the self-employed accounted for 31 per cent. of all males in the labour force; the corresponding proportion was 16 per cent. in Australia and a mere 7 per cent. in the U.K. In Ireland the self-employed were entitled to free health services only if their income and/or the rateable value of their farm was below a specified amount; they were not entitled to any income maintenance in the case of disability, unless they were completely destitute. In the U.S.A. in the case of employment injury the self-employed had no entitlement to either free medical services or, for at least 26 weeks, any social security income maintenance. In the U.K. the self-employed were entitled to free health and rehabilitation services irrespective of income and also to sickness benefit for an unlimited duration, supplemented by dependants' allowances.

WHO BEARS THE LOSS?

Damages for Negligence. Prior to the passing of accident insurance and W.C.A.s the only remedy available in any country to the worker suffering a work-connected injury was to prove his employer's negligence and to claim damages from him. Negligence has always been a difficult legal concept. It is related to an objective standard of reasonableness. The conduct which is alleged to be negligent has to be compared with that to be expected of a reasonable man of ordinary prudence in the same circumstances. The law in the six English-speaking countries allowed the defendant in an action for negligence three defences : *volenti non fit injura* – the principle that a workman accepts responsibility for the normal risk of his employment; *common employment* – the judge-made rule that an employer is not responsible to an employee if the accident was the result of another employee's negligence; and *contributory negligence* – proof that the employee was himself negligent and that notwithstanding his (the employer's) negligence, the injury was proximately caused by the negligence of the employee.

The combined effect of these three defences, coupled with the difficulty of collecting evidence and the high cost of legal advice and representation, was succinctly commented on by the Irish Commission on Workmen's Compensation, 1962 : 'In the harsh social climate which prevailed in the latter part of the nineteenth century it was, therefore, very difficult for a workman to succeed in a common law action for damages.'[8] The 'harsh social climate' referred to Great

Britain and Ireland, but could equally well have referred to any of the other eight countries.

If the injury was caused by a purely fortuitous work-connected accident, the legal rule applied was 'the loss lies where it falls'. The Royal Commission on Compensation for Personal Injuries in New Zealand, 1967, commented on this :

> To common lawyers . . . [the] thought that a person who is the innocent cause of an injury might reasonably be asked to share with his equally innocent victim the loss he has caused . . . approaches heresy . . .[9]

There can be little doubt, although it would be very difficult to substantiate this with concrete evidence, that in all the countries most of the economic loss caused by work-connected injuries was borne by the worker. Full indemnity must have been rare, but some limited and partial compensation of a semi-charitable character was presumably somewhat more common.

U.K.   In the U.K. the W.C.A. of 1897 imposed on employers in certain industries the statutory duty to compensate a worker injured in an accident arising out of and in the course of his employment for part of his loss of earnings. The intention was to share the losses resulting from the accident between the employer and the worker. Prior to the passing of the Act, virtually the whole loss was borne by the worker who possibly shared it with the Poor Law guardians.

The National Insurance (Industrial Injuries) Acts which came into operation in the U.K. in 1948 substituted a state insurance system awarding flat-rate benefits and making provision against loss of faculty, for the liability previously borne by employers under the W.C.A.s. The system was financed by equal contributions from employers and employees, which were supplemented in Great Britain by state grants equal to one-fifth of all contributions paid. The contributions were flat-rate, that is, unrelated to either the level of earnings or the degree of risk in different occupations and industries. All contributions were credited to an Industrial Injuries Fund out of which all benefits were paid.

The expenditure of this fund did not, however, show the value of all benefits received by the beneficiaries. The consequences of an industrial accident frequently led to payment of sickness benefit (for example in supplementation of disablement benefit after exhaustion of injury benefit), which was paid out of the National Insurance Fund. The earnings-related supplement to injury benefit paid to persons having an underlying title to sickness benefit was also paid out of the National Insurance Fund. All costs of medical care and rehabilitation were borne by the National Health Service and to a lesser extent by the Department of Employment.

The costs resulting from an industrial accident in the U.K. were thus widely diffused, although the injured worker himself still bore a major share in any loss of earnings not replaced by social insurance benefits. This loss varied directly with pre-accident earnings – the higher the wage, the smaller the proportion replaced by insurance benefits.

The industrial injury scheme was financed in such a way that all risks were pooled. This meant that industries and occupations which had a low risk of accidents did effectively subsidise those which had a high risk; for example, the coal-mining industry in 1967–8 paid about $2\frac{1}{2}$ per cent. of the contributions received by the Industrial Injuries Fund and drew about one-quarter of all benefits paid out.

Lord Beveridge might have approved of these provisions although he did not recommend them. However, he did pinpoint some of the drawbacks involved :

> This argument for pooling of social risks is in accord with the general stream of public opinion and has force. It must be realised, however, that pooling of a risk between industries makes it difficult or impossible to maintain that the cost should be borne by employers only. In so far as industries depend on one another, both employers and employees in each industry depend upon all other industries. There is no reason why the employer of a bank clerk or domestic servant, rather than the clerk or domestic servant himself, should contribute for the cost of accidents in mines or ships.[10]

Another possibly undesirable consequence of all industries sharing equally risks which affect them unequally is that of price distortion : the cost of providing for industrial accidents is not fully incorporated in the price of those commodities whose production involves exceptionally heavy costs in industrial injuries compensation. Thus in Britain in 1969 the price of coal might have been some 15p per ton higher had not much of the cost of injury caused by coal mining been borne by insurance contributors rather than coal consumers.

Ireland.   Ireland introduced an occupational injuries scheme in 1966 on broadly the same lines as had been operating in the U.K. since 1948. The major difference was that the Irish scheme was financed entirely by weekly flat-rate contributions – 11p for men and 8p for women – paid by employers. No payments were made by either employees or the state. The contributions paid by employers covered in addition to cash benefits the cost of medical care incurred by a workman as a result of an occupational injury (to the extent to which such cost was not met under the Health Acts), and the disability (sickness) benefit to which an injured worker might have been entitled in supplementation of occupational injury disablement benefit.

Germany.   In Germany the cost of accident insurance was normally borne by employers. Contributions were based on expenditure incurred in the previous year. For employers in industry and trade they were expressed as a percentage of employees' earnings (excluding those in excess of DM36,000 per annum). The contributions were graded by industry according to risk. For individual firms there was an additional merit rating similar to the no-claims bonus in motor insurance. The justification of merit rating was the belief that accidents are not entirely fortuitous but are frequently the result of inadequate accident prevention. This is undisputed, but whether the expectation of lower insurance contributions effectively encouraged preventive measures and thereby reduced the incidence of accidents is doubtful. The average contribution paid by employers, excluding the mining industry, was about 1·5 per cent. of wages. In mining the contribution equalled about 9·6 per cent, of wages. Contributions for the self-employed in agriculture were related to either the productive capacity of the farm or the standard labour units required to work it.

The German accident insurance was administered by occupational associations which were statutory bodies but which assessed contributions on very much the same basis as commercial insurance companies. The rates were, of course, much lower than commercial rates as they neither contained any element of profit nor had to cover the cost of selling the insurance.

A notable feature of the German scheme was that employees injured in work-connected accidents, like those incapacitated for any other reason, were entitled to receive full wages from their employers for the first six weeks of temporary disability. Compensation for this period was thus an employer's liability not covered by any insurance and was virtually complete indemnity for the pecuniary loss the worker would otherwise have suffered. Persons who were not employees received from the accident insurance funds injury benefit at the normal sickness benefit rates from the first day of incapacity. Employees were paid sickness benefit by their sickness funds from the seventh to the thirteenth week for which they were incapable of working. These funds also provided health services without reimbursement for the first 18 days for their members who suffered work-connected accidents. Only after this period did the accident insurance funds normally assume financial responsibility for health services. The burden of compensation in Germany as in Britain was thus widely diffused and correspondingly difficult to quantify.

Austria. Accident insurance, except for the self-employed, was financed in Austria by contributions from employers. These were statutory percentages for salary-earners (0·5 per cent.) and wage-earners (2 per cent.) for incomes up to Sch100,800 per year. There was no risk rating of industry and no merit rating of firms – all risks were pooled. For the first 26 weeks of temporary disability employees were paid benefits at the same rate irrespective of cause by the sickness funds. They also provided health services for the first 45 days without reimbursement. For the non-agricultural self-employed the accident insurance contribution was a uniform flate rate; for farmers it was related to the rateable value of their farms.

Denmark and the Netherlands. Under the Danish system of workmen's compensation employers had to insure against employment injury liability and pay premiums either to an approved private insurance company or to an employer's mutual association. The premiums were risk-rated. In certain circumstances, however, employers were not required to insure for payment of cash benefit during the first 13 weeks following the accident. Employers' liability for medical expenses was limited to appliances and some specialist services. Health services were provided under the sickness funds for all disabilities irrespective of cause. The government bore two-fifths of the cost of accident insurance of the low-income self-employed, whose benefits were subject to a 13 weeks' waiting period. Thus the self-employed bore a considerable share of the loss caused by their employment injuries.

In the Netherlands the cost of compensating injured workers was borne by employers and employees in the same proportions as they contributed to sickness and invalidity benefits.

U.S.A.   In the U.S.A. workmen's compensation benefits with some minor exceptions were entirely employer-financed. The exceptions were minimal : employee contributions – primarily towards the cost of medical care – in a few states and very limited supplemental pensions financed out of general taxation.

Employers in most jurisdictions had either to insure against employment injuries with a commercial insurance company or produce proof of their ability to carry their own risks. In 6 states they had to insure with a statutory insurance fund and in 12 there was a statutory fund that competed with commercial companies. The premiums charged were related to the employer's industrial risk classification and were sometimes adjusted by experience (merit) rating. In some industries which employed mainly clerical staff premium rates could be as low as 0·1 per cent. of the payroll, while in industries involving hazardous occupations the rate could exceed 20 per cent. The premium rates paid by employers in the same industry also differed according to the level of benefits provided in the state in which the employer operated. In 1969 the average cost of workmen's compensation was 1·1 per cent. of payroll.

All the benefits received by injured workers for temporary incapacity were provided under workmen's compensation laws. The diffusion of the cost of supporting the victim of a work-connected accident through various agencies, which was common in Europe, did not exist in the U.S.A., as general health services for persons under the age of 65 years were not financed by public authorities and there was no scheme for temporary disability or sickness benefit of which the injured worker could avail himself. Even the four states which provided such benefits restricted them to non-occupational disabilities.

Canada.   The Canadian system of workmen's compensation was financed by compulsory insurance contributions levied by statutory bodies on employers. The contributions in different industries varied with the risk involved and were expressed as percentages of earnings but were not subject to experience rating. As in the U.S.A., the whole cost of workmen's compensation was borne by employers. The victims were not assisted by general social security provisions as these did not include temporary disability benefit nor, until 1970, disability pensions.

New Zealand. The position was quite different in New Zealand. There the government-financed national health system provided health services, including rehabilitation and appliances, for all irrespective of the cause of the incapacity. Workmen's compensation insurance was financed by premiums varying with risk, paid to commercial insurance companies or mutual associations. The maximum premium rates for all classes of employment were fixed by law. For all employments they were about 1 per cent. of the payroll. Large employers were permitted to carry their own risk. For temporary disability the injured worker had to rely on workmen's compensation, but for permanent disability he was frequently also entitled to social security benefit. As workmen's compensation benefits were limited to a maximum period of six years and were in any case usually converted into a lump sum, such entitlement was by no means uncommon.

Australia. Australian workmen's compensation was financed by premiums paid by employers to licensed commercial insurance carriers and it provided all the benefits to which an injured worker was entitled. As in the U.S.A., there was no possibility of benefit from other social security provisions. The premiums charged varied with risk. In New South Wales the premiums averaged about $2\frac{1}{4}$ per cent. of payroll in 1968.

WHAT CIRCUMSTANCES GIVE RISE TO A CLAIM FOR COMPENSATION?

The I.L.O. Standards. The Employment Injury Benefits Convention, 1964, was rather imprecise in defining what circumstances should give rise to a claim for compensation :

> Each member shall prescribe a definition of 'industrial accident', including the conditions under which a commuting accident is considered to be an industrial accident . . .
> Where commuting accidents are covered by social security schemes other than employment injury schemes, and these schemes provide in respect of commuting accidents benefits which, when taken together, are at least equivalent to those required under this Convention, it shall not be necessary to make provision for commuting accidents in the definition of 'industrial accident'.[11]

U.K. and Ireland.   The British W.C.A. of 1897 had set out to define precisely the circumstances which should give rise to a claim : a personal injury by an accident 'arising out of and in the course of employment.' With this definition it succeeded in coining the words which are reputed to have engendered more litigation than any others. The Act, however, established clearly that a claim to compensation was to be quite independent of any question of negligence on the part of the employer or any person employed by him, nor was negligence on the part of the worker to be a bar to compensation except when it amounted to serious and wilful misconduct. The W.C.A. of 1906 removed this last stipulation (as an employer's defence against a claim) where the accident had resulted in death or serious and permanent disability.

Revision of statutes, judicial interpretations and, since 1948, the decision of the National Insurance Commissioner had led to many changes in the circumstances which gave rise to a claim for compensation (benefit after 1948) in the U.K. By 1969 the term 'accident' had been given a wide interpretation so as to cover any unexpected occurrence resulting in a personal injury irrespective of whether the effects of the accident were immediate or delayed. The phrase 'arising out of employment' was taken to mean that the injured person was engaged in doing something he was employed to do or that he was exposed to a special risk by his employment. An accident was deemed to have arisen in the course of employment unless there was evidence to the contrary. The course of employment was normally taken as the time from the arrival at to the departure from the employer's premises. It also included the journey to and from work if it was made in transport provided by the employer, but not otherwise.

The interpretation of the phrase 'arising out of and in the course of employment' had also been liberalised by three other statutory provisions. Accidents sustained in meeting an actual or supposed emergency at any premises used for the employer's business were included. So were accidents happening in the course of employment which were caused by another person's misconduct but which were no fault of the injured person. Accidents which happened while a person was acting in breach of regulations or orders, so long as the act was done for the purposes of the employer's business and was within the scope of his employment, also gave entitlement to benefit.

Up to 1966 the circumstances which gave entitlement to compensation in Ireland were very similar to those in force in Britain prior to

1948. The Irish Social Welfare (Occupational Injuries) Act, 1966, made the circumstances giving rise to occupational injury benefit very similar to those giving rise to industrial injury benefit in the U.K.

Germany and Austria. The position in Germany was much like that in Austria. In both countries benefit was paid irrespective of fault and 'industrial accident' had a wide definition. Cover, however, was more extensive than it was in the U.K. and Ireland as it included accidents while travelling to and from the place of employment. Road accidents in Germany in 1969 accounted for more than one-tenth of all industrial accidents. Another difference was that Germany and Austria provided employment injury benefit to people involved in accidents while rendering various types of public service.

The Other Six Countries. In Denmark and under most programmes in the U.S.A., injuries arising out of accidents due to the employee's intoxication, wilful misconduct or gross negligence did not qualify for the award of compensation. Under the programmes in the U.S.A., Denmark, Canada and New Zealand, accidents while travelling to and from work were not considered industrial accidents. They were, however, considered as such in Australia. In the Netherlands, as all employees were entitled to social insurance sickness and invalidity benefits at the same rates irrespective of the cause of the incapacity, the notion of an industrial accident and the circumstances giving rise to compensation were irrelevant in social insurance.

Absence of Uniformity. The circumstances which led to claims for employment injury benefit differed between the ten countries in many particulars and even in some respects within the several jurisdictions in Canada, the U.S.A. and Australia. Nor was there, of course, complete uniformity in the judicial interpretations of identical words or phrases. The 'wilful misconduct' which disqualified an employee from a claim to compensation was possibly not quite the same in Denmark as it was in Tennessee.

Commuting Accidents. By far the most important and readily ascertainable factor which varied from programme to programme and which was relevant in an appreciable proportion of accidents was the injured employee's eligibility for or exclusion from claims to benefit or compensation when the accident occurred while he was travelling to or from his place of employment. The Employment Injury Benefit Convention required these commuting accidents to be covered unless other social insurance benefits to which an injured employee was entitled were at least 60 per cent. of the pre-accident earnings for the standard beneficiary – a married man with two dependent children. Commuting accidents in general were covered in the employment injury schemes of only Germany, Austria and the Australian states. The U.K., Ireland and New Zealand provided restricted cover for those injured while travelling in transport provided by the employer. In the Netherlands the levels of benefit for all types of incapacity were well above those laid down by the Convention. This was also the case in Denmark for employees suffering a permanent injury who were entitled to an invalidity pension, but the sickness benefit rates for temporary incapacity were below the levels required by the Convention. In Canada and the U.S.A. there were no cash social security benefits at all for the great majority of employees who were injured in an accident while travelling to or from work. There was some entitlement in the U.K., Ireland and New Zealand, but except for very low-paid employees this was below the level required by the Convention.

In any employment injury scheme there must invariably be some arbitrariness in the rules which determine the circumstances giving rise to a claim to benefit. There seems to be at least some legitimate doubt whether commuting accidents should be considered as industrial accidents. They differ from accidents at the place of work in several important respects. The probability of an employee suffering an accident while travelling to work depends at least partly on the distance he travels and on the mode of travel. The shorter the distance, the less the likelihood of an accident; the man who travels in a private car or, even worse, rides a motor-cycle is more exposed than the man who uses public transport or walks. Why should an employee who runs a greater risk, either on his own volition or for reasons which may be compelling but which are unconnected with the nature of his employment, be compensated in circumstances where a man visiting his wife in hospital would not be compensated? The employer will have some scope, depending on circumstances, to make working conditions safe at the place of employment, but he cannot in any way influence the safety of his employees on their journey to work.

It is also frequently difficult to define what travelling should be included under the journey to work. Should a man who is injured on his way to work while unnecessarily crossing a road to buy a packet of cigarettes be considered as having been travelling to work at the time of the accident? If a man takes his children to school on his way to work and is involved in a car accident near the school but half a mile from the direct route to work, should he be considered as having been injured while travelling to work? Should it be relevant whether the accident happened on his way to work after dropping the children or on the diversion from the direct route to work on his way to the school? The difficulties which arise in answering these questions possibly explain why, in the majority of countries, commuting accidents are not considered as industrial accidents.

WHAT IS THE NATURE OF THE LOSS COMPENSATED?

Complete Indemnity. There are five different ways by which a person may be compensated for the loss he experiences as a result of an employment injury. At one extreme he may receive full indemnity for all pecuniary and non-pecuniary damage and at the other he may receive no compensation at all. In between he may be entitled to such benefits as are received by persons experiencing a similar injury due to other causes, to partial or complete compensation for loss of earnings or to receipt of benefit for loss of faculty.

In none of the countries did social security provisions provide complete indemnity for employment injuries. This could only be obtained by an injured worker in an action for damages in respect of his employer's negligence. Such actions could be brought in the U.K., Ireland, Denmark, the Netherlands, New Zealand, Australia and the U.S.A. (by employees of firms which had elected not to be covered by the workmen's compensation acts in the 23 states where such election was permitted). This remedy was also available to all those employees in the U.S.A. and Canada who were not covered by W.C.A.s. In Germany, Austria, the U.S.A. (the other 27 states) and Canada persons entitled to accident insurance benefits or workmen's compensation could not bring actions for negligence against their employers. The very nature of claiming damages from the employer precluded the self-employed from ever benefiting from this remedy.

Damages for negligence aim, at least in theory, at putting the injured worker, as far as humanly possible, in the same position as if he had not suffered the accident. They endeavour to secure redress for all its foreseeable consequences. Special damages are awarded for disbursements such as medical and legal charges incurred as a result of the injury and for loss of earnings up to the date of the settlement or trial. General damages cover all foreseeable future consequences and include pecuniary losses – diminution or cessation of future income resulting from impaired capacity to earn – and non-pecuniary losses – compensation for the specific losses suffered by the injured worker who makes his claim. These losses include : reduced expectation of life, diminished capacity to enjoy life (inability to have sexual relations or play golf), impairment of physiological functions (loss of sense of touch, smell or hearing), reduced physical functions (limp arm, arthritic elbow), disfigurement (facial injuries), pain and suffering and mental agony. In the case of fatal injury the deceased's dependants can claim damages for the pecuniary loss they have suffered as a result of the death.

The social importance of the right to bring an action for damages depends mainly on two factors : the difficulty of establishing negligence and the spirit and social climate in which damages are awarded. In all countries it was easier to prove damages in the 1960s than it had been sixty years previously, but all the same such actions remained hazardous and expensive. In some countries the law made it more difficult for some workers to prove negligence than others. In Ontario the W.C.A. provided for the removal of some common law defences in actions for damages brought by employees in industries and occupations not covered by the Act, but specifically excluded farm workers and domestic servants from this provision. In the U.S.A., in the 23 states where employers could elect to accept or reject the W.C.A., employers who rejected it lost the customary common law defences against suits by employees, but this advantage was not enjoyed by those employees (casual or agricultural workers) who were outside the scope of the Act.

A third factor of some importance is the difficulty the injured worker experiences in filing a suit for damages. In countries which permit lawyers to charge contingency fees, as was the case in the U.S.A., lawyers will be more willing to represent a client whose chances of success, while fair, are not overwhelming, than in countries where such fees are considered as unprofessional conduct. Under the contingency-fee system the price the injured worker has to pay to have his suit filed and his claim pressed will be a substantial proportion of any damages he may be awarded. The British system of legal aid –

assistance to claimants in defraying legal costs out of public funds
subject to a quite severe means test – was more advantageous to the
victim of an employment injury. To what extent it was more advantageous depended on the stringency of the means test and the
liberality with which legal aid certificates – issued after examining
the prima facie chances of a claim succeeding – were granted. Actions
for damages in all countries could be brought more readily by a
member of a strong trade union than by an unorganised worker.

While an action for damages could result in an injured worker
receiving full indemnity, this was not the case in the vast majority
even of those actions which were successful. The operation of the
doctrine of contributory negligence often reduced damages well below
the level of full indemnity and, even more important, for a variety
of reasons most claimants in all countries compromised their claims
by accepting offers made to settle out of court. Actions for damages
in employment injury cases have been widely criticised in all countries.
The Report of the Royal Commission on Compensation for Personal
Injury in New Zealand summarised these criticisms :

(1) The adversary system hinders the rehabilitation of injured
persons after accidents and can play no effective part before-
hand in preventing them.

(2) The fault principle cannot logically be used to justify the
common law remedy and is erratic and capricious in
operation.

(3) The remedy itself produces a complete indemnity for a
relatively tiny group of injured persons; something less (often
greatly less) for a small group of injured persons; for all the
rest it can do nothing.

(4) As a system it is cumbersome and inefficient; and it is
extravagant in operation to the point of absorbing for administration and other charges as much as $40 for every $60 paid
over to successful claimants.[12]

Statutory Partial Compensation. The workmen's compensation or
accident insurance acts introduced in all ten countries prior to the
First World War provided some compensation for industrial
accidents, irrespective of the cause of the accident. The acts, however,
did not provide full indemnity for the loss suffered by the worker,
but divided this loss between the worker and his employer. Compensation for total, temporary or permanent, incapacity was a proportion
of pre-accident earnings subject to a statutory maximum. The worker

thus bore the whole of all non-pecuniary losses as well as suffering a reduction of income. For partial incapacity compensation was proportionate to loss of earnings. The worker was thought to gain the certainty of receiving compensation for all employment injuries covered by the Act, at the price of accepting compensation which was always inadequate to indemnify him fully.

U.K. In the U.K. the W.C.A. which operated between 1897 and 1948 had placed on the employer the legal liability of compensating his employees who suffered employment injuries. Beveridge in his *Report on Social Insurance and Allied Services*[13] argued that while the system had conferred great benefits on the victims of employment injuries, it also had many disadvantages. Some of these were similar to those which had been advanced against actions for damages in common law; these included : (1) the systems resting upon the threat of litigation and thereby involving the risk of considerable expense; (2) the lack of machinery for assisting the employee in presenting his claim; (3) the uncertainty of payment of compensation, as employers were not compelled to insure against their liability; (4) the frequent failure of the lump-sum payments, which the acts permitted in certain circumstances, to provide a permanent source of income where earning capacity had ceased; (5) the unavoidability of demarcation disputes if compensation were determined by *inter alia* the cause of the incapacity. Beveridge concluded his case against W.C.A.s in clear and unmistakeable language :

> The pioneer system of social security in Britain was based on a wrong principle and has been dominated by a wrong outlook. It allows claims to be settled by bargaining between unequal parties, permits payment of socially wasteful lump sums instead of pensions in cases of serious incapacity . . . and over part of the field, large in the numbers covered, though not in the proportion of the total compensation paid, it relies on expensive private insurance. There should be no hesitation in making provision for the results of industrial accident and disease in the future . . . [a] branch of a unified Plan for Social Security.[14]

The National Insurance (Industrial Injuries) Act of 1948 brought compensation for industrial accidents and diseases within the British system of national insurance. It repealed the W.C.A. and replaced it by a scheme which set out at its inception to compensate for loss of faculty – loss of health, strength and the power to enjoy life compared with a healthy person of the same age and sex – rather than for loss of earnings. It provided the injured worker with compensation for several types of non-pecuniary loss, for example, facial disfigurement, which had not been covered by the W.C.A., but the damages compensated were less comprehensive than those for which the common law indemnified; for example, it did not compensate for 'pain and suffering'. One provision of the industrial injuries scheme, contrary to the original intention, injected into it an element of compensation for loss of earnings. An injured worker could be awarded a special hardship allowance in addition to disablement benefit which was based on medical assessment of loss of faculty. He was entitled to this allowance if, as the result of an accident or disease, he was incapable of following his regular occupation or suitable employment of an equivalent standard. The rate of allowance was, within the limits of several statutory restrictions, the difference between the standard of remuneration in his former occupation and his probable standard of remuneration in any suitable occupation which he was now capable of undertaking.

Ireland. Ireland in 1966 replaced its W.C.A. with a social insurance occupational injuries programme. This introduced the principle of compensation for loss of faculty very much on the same lines as the British industrial injuries scheme, except that the Irish scheme did not provide a special hardship allowance. Although compensation was nominally based solely on loss of faculty, it contained an implicit compensation for loss of earnings. This was for two reasons : first, the benefits under this programme were substantially higher than the corresponding standard social insurance benefits; and second, there was a provision which restricted, subject to certain exceptions, the aggregate of all social insurance benefits which an injured person could receive to his pre-accident earnings. This reduced the benefits, to which they would otherwise have been entitled, of many family men, especially those who were most severely disabled or had a large number of children.

The Other European Countries. In the other four European countries compensation was for loss of earning capacity and was supplemented by comprehensive health and rehabilitation services which were rendered free of charge and were generally of a high standard. These countries provided no compensation for any non-pecuniary damage. Disfigurement and mutilation did not give rise to compensation unless they caused loss of earning capacity.

U.S.A.   In the U.S.A. benefits for temporary or permanent total disability were intended to replace wages in part and were usually expressed as a proportion of weekly earnings at the time of the accident, but were limited to a statutory maximum. In the case of permanent partial disability compensation was not only related to reduced earning capacity but in certain circumstances also took into account loss of faculty. Most state laws distinguished between two types of such disabilities : schedule (loss of an arm, leg or eye) and non-schedule (less clearly measurable disabilities such as injuries to the back). Schedule injuries were compensated at the same rate and subject to the same maximum as total disability. The compensation was restricted to a prescribed number of weeks depending on the severity of the injury, but was awarded without regard to loss of earning capacity. Non-schedule disabilities were assessed on the difference between pre-accident earnings and estimated post-accident earnings. The compensation was normally the same proportion of that difference as total disability was of pre-accident earnings. This compensation was also normally restricted to a fixed period or a maximum amount.

In the U.S.A. compensation was in most cases partial in a twofold sense : it was a proportion of earnings and was limited in duration or amount. Only in 31 states was benefit paid for as long as a total disability lasted; in the remainder it was limited to a prescribed number of weeks or a maximum monetary sum. In 11 states compensation for expenditure on health services was also restricted in duration or aggregate cost. The employer generally had the right to nominate the medical practitioner who provided medical services. The liability of the employer to pay for medical charges was normally limited 'to such charges as generally prevail in the community for treating persons who are of the same general economic status as the employee and who pay for their own treatment'[15]. This could well mean that the poorer the victim of an employment injury, the poorer the standard of health care he was likely to receive. This would be the natural consequence of the not unreasonable assumption that the size of the fee bore some relation to the quality of the care. In 20 states containing more than a quarter of all persons covered by W.C.A.s there were no specific obligations on employers or public authorities to provide rehabilitation services for injured workers.

Canada. Entitlement to comprehensive and free health care was one of the original provisions of the first Canadian W.C.A.s of 1914. In addition, comprehensive and free rehabilitation services were later provided in all the provinces. Cash benefits were a proportion of pre-accident earnings excluding earnings in excess of $5,000-$6,000 (varying with the province). All benefits, for temporary or permanent and total or partial disability, were payable for the duration of the incapacity in all provinces.

New Zealand. In New Zealand the level of compensation was related to the injured worker's pre-accident earnings subject to two limitations : weekly compensation was limited to $25 and the duration for which compensation was payable, irrespective of the duration of the disability, was limited to six years. Permanent partial disability was compensated by statutory percentages (graded according to the severity of the injury) of pre-accident earnings. Compensation was thus based on loss of faculty rather than on loss of earnings. The Royal Commission, while criticising the operation of the schedule of the W.C.A. which contained the statutory percentages for various disabilities, commented : 'We think that the loss of physical capacity by itself and regardless of its effect upon future earnings, is a factor which deserves to be compensated. . . .' [16] In general the Royal Commission considered that the W.C.A. suffered from many serious failings, including the low ceiling of $25 per week, the six-year limit, the common practice of lump-sum payments, the relatively more generous compensation of the more minor injuries, the high expense ratio (30 per cent. of premium for administration) and the legal process inherent in the scheme. They, like Beveridge before them, considered that W.C.A. legislation was 'based on a wrong principle dominated by a wrong outlook.'

Australia. Compensation for employment injury in Australia had many features in common with that in the U.S.A. In only two states – Victoria and South Australia – were health-care expenses compensated in full. In the other four states reimbursable expenditure was limited to amounts varying between $660 and $2,500. These restrictions were contained in legislation passed in 1969. Compensation in the case of total disablement was payable for an unlimited duration only in New South Wales; under the other programmes the employer's total liability was limited to payment of compensation for six years at the maximum statutory amounts. The method of compensating for permanent partial disability was similar to the schedule provisions used in the U.S.A. and New Zealand.

The W.C.A.s have been widely criticised. Already in 1925 the Australian Royal Commission on National Insurance, 1923–7, recommended that workers' compensation be co-ordinated with the national insurance scheme which it proposed. Kewley, writing in 1965, referred to the W.C.A.s as 'an uncharted wilderness' and considered them as 'in urgent need of scrutiny'.[17]

The I.L.O Standards.   The Employment Injury Benefits Convention, 1964, provided in Article 9 that

> . . . each member state shall secure to the persons protected, subject to prescribed conditions, medical care and allied benefits in respect of a morbid condition and cash benefits in respect of specified contingencies. These benefits shall be granted throughout the contingency.[18]

The laws of all six European countries and Canada were in accordance with this clause of the Convention, but in the majority of the states of the U.S.A., New Zealand and all the Australian states benefits were restricted in a way which was irreconcilable with the Convention.

WHAT IS THE LEVEL OF COMPENSATION?

Factors Determining Benefit Levels.   In all the ten countries the level of compensation under social security schemes was well below what would have been required to indemnify the person suffering an employment injury for all the damage suffered. Benefits for temporary or permanent disability were adequate to compensate for the pecuniary loss in only three countries; in none did they allow for all non-pecuniary losses. It was only for permanent partial loss of earning capacity or faculty that compensation in any appreciable number of cases exceeded the pecuniary loss. The compensation ratios for total temporary and permanent disability in different countries can be compared by expressing the levels of compensation received by the standard wage-earner as a proportion of the standard wage. However, the compensation ratios in some countries fluctuated quite widely over short periods of time (depending on the dates of changes in benefit rates), and in most countries the ratios for different levels of wages were not identical. They also depended on a number of other factors, which included age, marital condition, employment status of the wife, number of children and duration of the incapacity.

Benefit for Temporary Total Disability. In three countries – Austria, Germany and the Netherlands – compensation for temporary total disability was a proportion of earnings for all injured persons whose income was up to one and a half (or more) times the standard wage. In most countries – Denmark, Canada, the U.S.A., New Zealand and three of the Australian states (New South Wales, Victoria and South Australia) – compensation was nominally also a proportion of earnings, but restricted to a weekly money maximum which was so low that a large proportion of employment injury victims received compensation at less than the statutory proportions. In the U.S.A. in 1968, for example, the maximums in only five of the 52 W.C.A. programmes were high enough to permit a worker with average earnings to receive a weekly benefit that provided the statutory proportion of wage replacement.[19] Thus while the average weighted statutory compensation ratio for the 52 programmes was 64 per cent., the weekly compensation at the average wage level was only 53 per cent.[19]

In the U.K., Ireland and the other three Australian states compensation was at a weekly flat rate which in the U.K. was augmented by an earnings-related supplement in respect of weekly wages between £9 and £30.

Increases for dependants were awarded at weekly flat rates in Ireland, the U.K., 17 of the U.S. programmes, New Zealand and all the Australian states and at rates proportionate to the earnings in Austria. The same compensation irrespective of family circumstances was paid in Denmark, the Netherlands, all the Canadian provinces and 36 of the U.S. programmes. In Germany workers continued to receive their full wages and thus the issue of increases for dependants did not arise.

Waiting Days for Temporary Total Disability. Compensation in Germany, New Zealand and Australia was payable from the day of the accident, while in Ireland, the U.K. and Denmark it only commenced on the fourth day unless the incapacity lasted for two weeks

TABLE 4:1   *Compensation Ratio for the Standard Wage Earner, 1969, in respect of Three Weeks' Temporary Total Disability and the Data for Basis of Assessment.*

	Single man or woman %	Married man with two children %	Basic benefit	Maximum earnings[a] as proportion of standard wage %	Number of waiting days	Dependants' allowances Spouse	Two children
Austria[b] ...	45	63	50%	156	3	10%[k]	10%[k]
Germany[c]	100	100	100%	238	none	none	none
Ireland ...	30	51	£5·75	–	3[g]	£2·63	£1·50
U.K. ...	36	56	£7·75	113[f]	3[g]	£3·10	£2·20
Denmark ...	53	53	75%	80	3[g]	none	none
Netherlands ...	69	69	80%	184	2	none	none
Canada (Ontario)	73	73	75%	97	1–4[h]	none	none
U.S.A. ...	44	47[d]	64%[e]	n.k.	7[j]	n.k.	n.k.
New Zealand ...	43	53	80%	53	none	$3	$3
Australia (N.S.W)	32	48	75%	23	none	$7	$6
(Victoria) ...	24	38	$20	–	none	$6	$5

[a] Maximum earnings taken into account for benefit purposes.
[b] Manual employees only. It was considered the normal practice for employers to pay salaries to their non-manual staff for several weeks during incapacity.
[c] Since January 1970. As from that date employers have had to pay to their employees full wages for the first six weeks of incapacity, irrespective of cause.
[d] Ratio refers to 1968. Only 16 states paid increases for dependants.
[e] Weighted average for all programmes.
[f] Refers to earnings-related supplement based on range of earnings between £9 and £30 per week, payable after a two-week waiting period.
[g] None if incapacity lasted at least two weeks.
[h] Varied according to province.
[j] In 32 states employing 78 per cent. of all covered employees.
[k] Proportion related to earnings.

or more, when it was due as from the first day. In the Netherlands benefit commenced on the third day and in Austria on the fourth day without any retroactive payments. All the programmes in the U.S.A. required some waiting days; in 32 states having 78 per cent. of all covered workers, benefits were payable only after seven days of incapacity. In almost all states payments were retroactive if the incapacity lasted more than a specified period. This varied widely. As the average period of temporary disability in manufacturing industries in the U.S.A. was about 18 calendar days, the rules as regards waiting days and retroactive payments were of considerable importance.

Compensation Ratio for Temporary Total Disability. Table 4 : 1 shows that the compensation ratios for the single standard wage-earner and the married standard wage-earner with two children at the end of 1969 in respect of three weeks' temporary disability, and also some of the data which determined these ratios.

Compensation ratios relating to any particular period partly reflect the interval since the last statutory change was made. The British ratios, for example, are comparatively favourable as benefit levels were increased in November 1969, while the Irish ratios are relatively unfavourable as benefit levels increased (quite substantially) only in the month after the date to which the table refers. In Denmark too there was a substantial increase in the maximum level of compensation from Kr54 to Kr67 in January 1970. Only the German compensation ratio is shown for January 1970, as this was the date when a new system commenced.

The combined effect of waiting days, retroactive payment for waiting days after a specified period of incapacity and the earnings-related supplement in the U.K. was that the ratios varied with the length of the disability. In the extreme case of the incapacity lasting only one day, compensation would have been due in Germany, New Zealand and Australia but in none of the other countries. However, comparisons of the statutory provisions for very short periods of incapacity are somewhat unrealistic, as in some countries most and in all some employers made voluntary payments for such days. The extent to which this happened is not known. In general, the shorter the period of incapacity, the lower the compensation ratio. In the U.K. for a single worker it was less than 15 per cent. if the incapacity was limited to one week but as much as 51 per cent. in the third week. In the U.S.A. the effect of the long waiting period was particularly great; for example, in California the compensation ratio in the first week was zero but in the third was 62 per cent.

The effect of both low weekly maximums of compensation and flat-rate benefits was that the compensation ratios varied inversely with earnings; those of the lowest-paid worker were highest and those of the best paid were least. As women's earnings were in general lower than those of men and as benefits and maximums were independent of sex in all countries,[20] the compensation ratios for women tended to be higher than those for men.

In only four countries – Germany, Denmark, the Netherlands and Canada (Ontario) – did the compensation ratio for a single worker exceed 50 per cent. In Germany and the Netherlands more than 95 per cent. of all injured workers did receive the compensation proportion shown in Table 4 :1, while in Denmark and Canada (Ontario) the proportion for workers earning more than the standard wage would be very much lower on account of the relatively low maximum earnings limit for benefit assessment. In Ontario, for example, the compensation ratio for the single standard wage-earner was about 73 per cent. but for the man earning one and a half times the standard wage it was only 50 per cent.

For a married man with two children the compensation ratio exceeded 60 per cent., the minimum laid down by the I.L.O. Convention, in only four countries – Austria, Germany, the Netherlands and Canada (Ontario). In the U.S.A. and in most of the Australian states it was less than 50 per cent.

In Austria, Germany and the Netherlands during this three-week period the level of compensation was the same as that paid for incapacity due to any other cause. In Ireland, the U.K., Denmark and the four states in the U.S.A. (California, New Jersey, New York and Rhode Island) which had temporary disability insurance schemes, compensation levels for employment injury were higher than the corresponding sickness benefit rates.

The other four countries – Canada, the U.S.A. (46 states), New Zealand and Australia – had no temporary disability (sickness) insurance schemes and their workmen's compensation schemes thus placed the injured worker in a more favourable position than the man incapacitated for any other reason. In all countries he was entitled not merely to compensation without a means test, but he also received a higher level of compensation (only marginally more in New

Zealand) than he would have received had be been incapacitated for any other reason.

The compensation ratios refer to gross earnings but understate somewhat the economic position of the injured worker, as in all countries, except Denmark, compensation was exempt from taxes and other deductions.

Benefit and Compensation Ratios for Permanent Total Disability. Benefits for permanent total disability for the single as well as for the family man were higher than benefits for temporary disability, except in Germany. In the European countries and Canada periodical benefits were paid for the duration of the incapacity. This was also the case in 31 states in the U.S.A., but in the others benefits were limited in duration, amount or both. Duration in these 19 states was limited to periods ranging from 330 to 550 weeks. In New Zealand benefits were limited to a six-year period. In Australia they were unrestricted in amount and time only in New South Wales and Victoria; in the other four states benefits were limited in amount to the equivalent of about six years' compensation.

In Denmark the annual benefit could, wholly or in part, be commuted into a lump sum, subject to the consent of the beneficiary and provided this would improve the beneficiary's employment opportunities or financial conditions, in the view of the official agency which supervised the approved insurance companies. Benefits which were not commuted were automatically adjusted annually for movements in the retail price index. In the other five European countries permanent total disability benefits could not be commuted. Germany, Austria and the Netherlands adjusted benefits annually in line with changes in average earnings; in the U.K. such adjustments were made broadly at two-year intervals (annually since 1972), while in Ireland there have been annual *ad hoc* adjustments in recent years. Only a few programmes in the U.S.A. provided for the revision of awards. In Connecticut benefits were raised annually according to increases in the average wage of covered workers. Beneficiaries under the programme for Federal employees had their benefits raised whenever retail prices advanced by at least 3 per cent. In another three states there was a predetermined procedure for increasing current awards, and in two or three others there have been *ad hoc* increases. For the vast majority of beneficiaries in the U.S.A., benefits remained unaltered once they had been awarded except for increases in the minimum compensation levels. Their purchasing power declined over time and this has happened quite quickly in recent years. In New Zealand and Australia long-term benefits were normally commuted into lump sums.

In the U.K. the rate of injury benefit plus the earnings-related supplement for the standard wage-earner in the first three weeks of incapacity was less than the disablement pension plus unemployability (or sickness) benefit received by the permanently totally disabled worker. The full disablement pension in Ireland was the same as the injury benefit rate, but for the man who was unable to work it was supplemented, as in the U.K., either by unemployability or sickness benefit.

In the other European countries benefits were statutory proportions of earnings subject to prescribed maximums. In Denmark benefits were supplemented by the invalidity pension. In all these six countries, except the Netherlands, benefits were increased in respect of dependants. The compensation ratios in the case of permanent total incapacity are summarised in Table 4 : 2.

TABLE 4:2   *Compensation Ratio for the Standard Wage-Earner, 1969, in Respect of Permanent Total Disability.*

	Single man or woman	Married man with two children
	%	%
Austria	67	80
Germany	67	80
Ireland	46	68
U.K.	48	68
Denmark[a]	67	94
Netherlands	80	80

Note : The ratios refer to gross earnings; only in Denmark were compensation payments and benefits liable to income-tax.

[a] Refers to 1968 and includes invalidity pension; taken from *Social Security in the Nordic Countries,* no. 22 (1971) p 70.

In Canada compensation for permanent total disability was based on 75 per cent. of pre-accident earnings subject to a weekly dollar maximum which was in some provinces not even up to the standard weekly wage. Once awarded, this benefit had not in the past been adjusted for changes in the value of money, except for increases in the minimum compensation rates. In 1969 Quebec followed British Columbia in tying compensation benefits to the cost of living.[21] For the variety of reasons to which reference has already been made it is not possible to give comparable ratios for the U.S.A., New Zealand and Australia.

The compensation ratios in the six European countries for a married man with two children were all well above the 60 per cent. minimum laid down in the I.L.O. Convention.

THE NEW ZEALAND ACCIDENT COMPENSATION BILL, 1971

Objectives. This Bill implemented recommendations made by the Royal Commission on Compensation for Personal Injuries in New Zealand[22] (Chairman : Mr. Justice Woodhouse) as amended by the Select Committee on Compensation for Personal Injury in New Zealand.[23] Its provisions were to come into force in October 1973.[24] The Bill not only proposed major changes in the employment injury compensation but had several features which may well be taken up by other countries in the future.

The Explanatory Note attached to the Bill stated :

> The purposes of this Bill are to make provision for general safety and the prevention of accidents; for the rehabilitation and compensation of earners who suffer personal injury by accident in respect of which they have cover under the Bill, and of persons who in New Zealand suffer personal injury by a motor vehicle accident in respect of which cover is afforded under the Bill; and for the compensation of certain dependants of those earners and persons where death results from the injury.[25]

The Bill placed heavy emphasis on the prevention of accidents and on the rehabilitation of victims and required two special divisions of the Accident Compensation Commission, which the Bill proposed to establish, to be set up for the promotion of these objectives.

Major Provisions of the Bill. Subject to prescribed residential qualifications, self-employed and employees (earners) were to be insured against personal injury by accident irrespective of the place and time of the accident. Employees were to be paid by their employers for the time lost from work as the result of an accident during the working week comprising the day of the accident and the six days thereafter. Self-employed persons were not to receive any compensation during this period. For any loss of earnings thereafter, self-employed persons and employees were to receive compensation for loss of earning capacity at the rate of 80 per cent. of their pre-accident earnings up to $200 per week. The widow of a person who died as the result of an accident would be paid a pension equal to one-half, increased by one-sixth for each child, of the pension to which he would have been entitled. All compensation was to be paid out of a fund to which employers contributed premiums (which were to be risk-rated by classification of earners, industries or occupations or any of these) in respect of the wages paid to their employees up to a maximum earnings limit of $10,400 per year.

The Bill also proposed to establish a motor-vehicle accident scheme to compensate persons who had become incapacitated as the result of personal injury by a motor-vehicle accident and for certain dependants of persons who had died as the result of a motor-vehicle accident. This scheme was to be financed by a levy on motor vehicles (the rate of which had not been fixed by the date of the Bill's publication) and a levy on drivers of motor vehicles at the rate of $2 per annum. There were provisions to impose penalty rates on drivers whose accident records were significantly worse than the average.

Under both the earners' and the motor-vehicle accident schemes there were also provisions for the payment, in addition to any other compensation, of (1) lump sums not exceeding $5,000 in respect of an injury involving the loss or impairment of any bodily function, and (2) lump sums not exceeding $7,500 in respect of loss of the capacity to enjoy life, including loss from disfigurement and in respect of future pain and suffering.

All earnings-related pensions and levies were to be periodically adjusted, but the details of how this was to be done had not been determined at the time the Bill was published.

All rights to actions for damages in respect of personal injury or death by accident covered under either scheme were abolished.

The earners' compensation scheme thus replaced the W.C.A.s by a social insurance scheme administered by a public statutory body which was to provide generous benefits up to an exceptionally high level of earnings. It extended the contingency from the traditional personal injury 'arising out of and in the course of employment' to all accidents, and the compensation from one which only replaced earnings (and this quite inadequately) to a scheme which also covered non-economic losses and provided a full rehabilitation service. The motor-vehicle accident scheme provided certain compensation for non-earning road-accident victims. As these non-earners would not lose any income as the result of an accident, they were not to be paid income maintenance.

Objections of Interest Groups. The Bill overrode the interests of what are in any developed country two powerful groups : the insurance companies and the lawyers. The insurance companies would lose a considerable volume of business not only in workmen's compensation but also in employers' liability insurance. There was an acrimonious debate on whether the insurance companies should be permitted to administer the two schemes.[26] The recommendations of the Royal Commission on this issue deserve to be quoted in full :

(1) In the absence of personal liability and with the disappearance of any element of voluntary contribution there can be no place for the insurance companies. Their purpose is to seek business from individuals who might wish to cover themselves at their own choice in respect of personal contingencies of their own definition.

(2) It is said that the State should hesitate before interfering with private enterprise in what is claimed to be a legitimate field of operation. There is much confusion of thought about this matter. Private enterprise cannot claim as of right to handle a fund such as the compulsory road injury fund or workers' compensation fund in New Zealand. Those funds have arisen not because owners of vehicles or employers have been persuaded to provide the business, but because Parliament has ordained that they must do so.

(3) Moreover, the insurance system itself can offer no central impetus in the important areas of accident prevention and rehabilitation. It is operating in an area which ordinarily would be handled by the central Government as a social service. It cannot avoid adversary problems. In terms of administration it is very expensive.[27]

These views prevailed in essence, but the Bill empowered the Commission to appoint agents, which could be insurance companies, local authorities, government departments or any other 'body that is operating in New Zealand',[28] to collect the levies due to the Commission, and to terminate the appointments of such agents at any time. This provision could give some limited scope for participation to the insurance companies.

The Bill provided for quite an extensive machinery for appeals against the decisions of the Commission. This, however, would only to a very limited extent compensate the legal profession for the loss of work due to the abolition of the right to bring actions for negligence.

Earnings-Related Benefits.   The Bill's provisions for earnings-related benefits were not in accordance with New Zealand's tradition in social security provision, but the Royal Commission argued :

> The community should accept responsibility for all victims of accident : and if that responsibility is to be fairly discharged every man should be provided with a fair measure of his actual losses.[29]

The Royal Commission, in recommending a high earnings limit for benefit assessment, was influenced by the awareness that at the 1967 level of incomes the cost of the scheme if the limit were $120 per week would be less than 2 per cent. more than if the upper limit were $40 per week.[30] The Select Committee, in supporting the Royal Commission on this point, commented :

> Even if this course were not dictated by the need to provide an acceptable substitute for common law rights, the earnings-related approach seems desirable : it enables all those affected by the economic consequences of a sudden disablement to continue their accustomed way of life and it frees the injured from financial worries which can often impede rehabilitation.[31]

Demarcation between Accident and Sickness.   The Bill's provisions overcame the difficulty experienced in all countries of defining an industrial accident, but introduced a new demarcation problem – the distinction between accident and sickness. The Royal Commission was aware of the lack of logic in treating sickness differently from accident : 'A man overcome by ill-health is no more able to work and no less afflicted than his neighbour hit by a car . . . but logic on this occasion must give way to other considerations.'[32] These considerations were that it would be more expedient to introduce reforms gradually than in 'one massive leap', that action in the injury field was long overdue and that the 'statistical sign posting' demonstrating the feasibility of a similar sickness scheme was lacking.

The New Zealand Bill Compared with the Netherlands Provisions.
In conclusion, it is of interest to compare the proposed New Zealand
earners' compensation scheme with the 1967 Netherlands Incapacity
for Work Law which is often considered as the most advanced and
comprehensive scheme in this field. Both have a relatively high
maximum earnings limit and a compensation ratio of 80 per cent.,
but they differ in many other respects.

The Netherlands scheme covers employees only, grants earnings-
related compensation for loss or reduction of earning capacity irrespective of cause after two waiting days, does not affect the eventual
right of an insured person to compensation under common law,
finances compensation by wage-related contributions from employers
and employees which are the same for all occupations and industries,
is not concerned with accident prevention or medical rehabilitation
and is administered by 26 self-governing associations representing
employers and employees.

The New Zealand scheme will cover all earners (the self-employed
as well as employees), will grant earnings-related compensation for
loss or reduction of earning capacity resulting from any accident (but
excluding sickness except industrial diseases), as well as substantial
lump-sum payments for loss or impairment of bodily functions and
for non-economic losses including future pain and suffering, will
impose on employers the duty to pay wages to their injured employees
for (on average) the first seven days of incapacity, will abolish the
right to compensation under common law, will be financed by wage-
related contributions from employers which will be both risk- and
merit-rated, will charge the Accident Compensation Commission with
undertaking accident prevention and rehabilitation and will be
administered by a commission of three members appointed by the
government.

Each scheme clearly has some strong points : in the Netherlands
the equal compensation for all incapacity irrespective of cause and
the uniform contributions; in New Zealand the cover of all earners,
the lump-sum payments for loss of bodily functions and impaired
capacity to enjoy life, the duty placed on employers to pay wages for
about seven days (thereby reducing much administrative cost) and
the abolition of common law actions. On balance the strength of the
New Zealand scheme seems to point the way in which social policy
in the developed countries will advance. The New Zealand government has shown commendable courage in brushing aside powerful

sectional interests and in so doing disappointing their expectations which to many would appear legitimate.

Administration of Schemes.   Some statutory employment injury compensation has been provided in all ten countries for the last sixty years, but there has been comparatively little movement towards a uniform pattern of administration. The agencies providing the services were as heterogeneous as the services themselves. In Ireland and the U.K. a government department administered the cash benefits which were provided under separate acts but which were an integral part of the general social insurance system. In these two countries accident prevention was part of the employment service which was the responsibility of another government department, while rehabilitation was the responsibility of the National Health Service in the U.K. and of the Rehabilitation Board and the Health Boards in Ireland. The position was quite different in Austria and Germany where accident insurance was administered by public bodies specially set up for this purpose whose executives were representatives of employers and employees. These bodies were not only responsible for the payment of cash benefits, but also had a major role in accident prevention and rehabilitation. The occupational associations in the Netherlands which administered the Incapacity for Work Law had a composition similar to that of their counterparts in Germany, but were in addition responsible for the administration of unemployment and sickness insurance. Their functions in incapacity compensation, however, were more narrowly confined to the awarding of cash benefits and to the provision of a variety of relatively minor non-medical vocational rehabilitation services.

Denmark was the only one among the six European countries in which workmen's compensation was provided either by insurance companies or by mutual associations. These private corporations, however, were fairly closely supervised by the Directorate of Industrial Injuries Insurance, a public agency which also decided on questions of disability and compensation. In the Canadian provinces workmen's compensation was administered as a public service by Workmen's Compensation Boards appointed by the governments. These Boards had wide responsibilities in accident prevention and rehabilitation.

Most compensation in the U.S.A. was provided through private insurance carriers or self-insurance, with the exceptions to which reference was made earlier. Insurance companies or mutual associations under public supervision provided all compensation in New Zealand and the Australian states. A large proportion of benefit expenditure in the U.S.A. and Australia went to meet medical and hospitalisation costs. In the U.S.A. this accounted for about one-third of all benefits.

The effectiveness of the self-government incorporated in the Austrian, German and Dutch schemes has been doubted. The doubts may well have been justified, but it is noteworthy that the overall level of services provided in these three countries was more satisfactory than in the others.

In Canada, the U.S.A. and Australia workmen's compensation schemes were a state or provincial responsibility. The reasons for this are mainly historical and possibly constitutional. It is not easy to find a logical justification of the American and Australian arrangements whereby workmen's compensation was a state and old-age pensions a Federal responsibility; the other way round would have made more economic sense. The diversity of the programmes within these countries, as has been shown in previous sections, was quite extensive. Skolnik and Price suggested that one of the reasons for the recent improvements in workmen's compensation was 'the growing concern among States that failure to bring their laws up to commonly accepted standards will increase the possibilities of Federal participation'.[33]

In Canada the White Paper *Income Security for Canadians* proposed Federal–provincial discussions concerning the integration between the Canada Pension Plan and workmen's compensation.[34] This had become necessary on account of the changes in the plan which would have led to an unco-ordinated overlapping of benefits.

Persons Covered. The circle of persons covered by employment injury compensation schemes has widened continuously in all countries. However, even among employees the cover in Canada, the U.S.A. and Australia was far from complete. This, it is suggested, was for three reasons : (1) W.C.A.s in these countries were within state and provincial jurisdiction and unco-ordinated with other social security provisions; (2) private insurance carriers in the U.S.A. and Australia wished to avoid the relatively high cost of insuring large numbers of very small employers, especially if they lived in sparsely populated areas; and (3) the legislatures were unwilling to burden the small man with much office work.

The self-employed benefited only rarely from protection against work-connected injuries. The only countries which provided schemes for certain of the self-employed were Austria, Germany and Denmark, and even there the conditions and terms were less favourable than those applying to employees. Some of the reasons for the exclusion of the self-employed are similar to those which have been mentioned above. Another is the danger of abuse; in any scheme restricted to industrial accidents it is fairly easy for the self-employed to claim benefit for accidents which are not work-connected. The quantitative importance of this can easily be exaggerated, but the fear of abuse is uppermost in the minds of many policy-makers all over the world. The New Zealand Accident Compensation Bill removes the possibility of abuse by proposing compensation for all accidents.

Diffusion of the Burden of Loss.   In all countries except Germany and Austria (in the case of non-manual workers) a considerable proportion of the pecuniary loss resulting from industrial accidents was borne by the injured employee, who also bore the whole of the non-pecuniary loss in all countries in the case of total disability. The New Zealand Bill proposes to relieve the victim of a work-connected accident of a greater proportion of the total loss resulting from accidents than is as yet provided by any social security scheme anywhere.

In the European countries and New Zealand it was not easy to ascertain the cost to the community of work-connected accidents. This was not only borne by the special employment injury pro- grammes but was shared with other income-maintenance schemes and the health services. In the remaining three countries virtually all compensation was financed through the W.C.A.s.

Employment injury provisions were normally paid for by employers; only in the U.K., at the express wish of the trade unions, and in the Netherlands did employees contribute. Two issues are outstanding in the financing of these schemes : should industries' contributions be risk-rated, that means be roughly proportionate to the risk of industrial accidents in particular industries? Should contributions be merit-rated, that means should the employer be awarded a 'no-claims bonus' or be charged a penalty premium according to the frequency of accidents in his works? The main argument in favour of risk rating is that it makes for the incorporation of the full cost of production, including the cost of accidents, in the price of goods and thereby avoids price distortion. It is, however, against the general spirit of social insurance which is based on the pooling of all social risks. If risk rating is adopted in employment injury insurance, the question arises of whether it should not also be adopted in unemployment or sickness insurance where differences in risk between various industries are also appreciable. Merit rating is based on the frequently asserted but little substantiated belief that employers will pay more attention to safety if they are apprehensive about having to pay higher premiums when their safety record is unsatisfactory.

Commuting Accidents. In deciding on the definition of an industrial accident some arbitrariness is unavoidable. On balance the arguments for excluding accidents while travelling to and from work appear to be the more convincing. In the Netherlands this issue did not arise as the same wage-related benefit was paid for all incapacity whatever its cause, nor will it in future arise in New Zealand as the same wage-related compensation will be paid for all incapacity due to accidents wherever they happen.

Common Law Damages. Common law damages in theory indemnify against all pecuniary and non-pecuniary losses; in practice, in the words of the New Zealand Royal Commission, they are erratic, capricious in operation, cumbersome, inefficient and extravagant in cost. The right to sue for damages ought to be abolished in all countries where it still persists. This makes it desirable, as is proposed in the New Zealand Bill, to provide social security benefits also for the non-pecuniary losses resulting from accidents. Workmen's compensation through private insurance carriers has considerable disadvantages to which reference has already been made. The survival of common law actions and W.C.A.s through private insurance carriers was partly due to the general feeling against public services in such countries as the U.S.A. and Australia, and partly to the advantages derived from these procedures by insurance companies and the legal and medical professions.

Restriction of Compensation. The practice prevailing in New Zealand and in some states of the U.S.A. and Australia of not paying compensation for as long as a disability lasts, but restricting it in time or amount, appears as indefensible as the practice, also prevailing in some states of the U.S.A. and Australia, of limiting compensation expenditure on health services in duration or aggregate cost.

Adequacy of Compensation. The compensation ratio for the standard wage-earner with two children in respect of three weeks' temporary disability was less than 60 per cent. in four countries and in respect of permanent disability was less than 60 per cent. in three countries.

The Case for 'Privileged' Treatment of Employment Injury Victims. Employment injury compensation, however, even in those states of the U.S.A. and Australia and in those other countries where it was least adequate, was still higher than the compensation or benefit, if any, paid to those suffering from sickness or any other incapacity. As long as the provisions for sickness and disability are so meagre, the case for separate provisions for employment injury is overwhelming. They remain as much today as they have been in the past the pace-makers of social security. In this they are greatly helped by the fact that in all countries the number disabled by work accidents (including industrial diseases) or indeed any accidents is much less than that incapacitated by sickness. This makes it less expensive to provide adequate compensation for the relatively small number of persons who suffer industrial injuries than it is to provide for all who are incapacitated.

The logical case for maintaining the 'privileged' position of the victims of industrial accidents may be weak but, as the New Zealand Royal Commission remarked in the same context, 'logic on this occasion must give way to other considerations'.

CHAPTER V

Temporary Disability

GENERAL CONSIDERATIONS

Sickness and the Ability to Work.   Sickness is a more frequent cause of absence from work than industrial injury. In the U.K., for example, at least nine days are lost because of short-term sickness for every one day lost because of industrial injury. Absence from work on account of industrial accidents is inherently undesirable; the undisputed objective of policy in this field is to eliminate all accidents and the consequent absences from work. It is, of course, equally desirable to minimise the incidence and severity of sickness, but in the present state of knowledge such endeavours can only be partially successful. There always have been many people who go to work in spite of suffering some degree of ill-health. If, however, some ill-health is accepted as an integral part of human life, a rise in the sickness rate (as a result of more people being able to take time off work when they are ill) may be regarded as a desirable side-effect of economic progress.

Little is known about the causes of the diseases which prevent people from following their usual occupation, and little more is known about the incidence and prevalence of these diseases and the characteristics of the people who suffer from them. While it is recognised at present that certain illnesses are psychosomatic, it is still not known to what extent, if any, the more common illnesses are either caused or aggravated by psycho-social factors. The views of the German Sozialenquête-Kommission on this subject are of interest :

> It is . . . well established that psychological disorders lead to illnesses which have symptoms very similar to those of physical illnesses; indeed, psychological disorders can induce physical illnesses. It would be erroneous to consider people whose symptoms are of such origin fraudulent or malingering . . . [1]

There is also a distinct possibility that changes in industrial techniques may diminish or increase the incidence of certain diseases.

Sickness is not a state which can be easily defined or measured. Neither its beginning nor its end can be precisely determined. There is a continuum with perfect health at one end and excruciatingly painful and completely disabling sickness at the other. The great majority of the population are at any one time somewhere between these two extremes. Moreover, the physical and mental states which individuals accept as normal vary widely and to some extent influence the type of work they are willing and able to undertake. Most people continue working even if their state of health falls somewhat below what is their norm, and everybody has to give up working at some level of ill-health, but there is an indeterminate area between these two states. The willingness and ability to turn up at work are affected by many complex factors which include *inter alia* the nature of the work, the attitude of the individual to his work, the level of his income and the short-term and long-term effects of his absence.

Absenteeism.   A man whose earnings per hour have increased may rationally wish to adopt one of three basic courses of action : work the same hours and thereby enjoy a higher income, work regularly shorter hours and thereby enjoy more leisure, or work the same basic hours but less regularly and thereby have the option of not turning up at work when he does not feel like it, possibly because he is a little 'off colour'. The freedom of the consumer to spend his income as he chooses and the right to choose between income and leisure are widely established, but absence from work without good cause is almost universally condemned. People disapprove of this mainly because absenteeism, especially short-term, non-anticipated absenteeism, frequently causes an economic loss to a firm which far exceeds the wage of the absent worker. The general work ethics of Western society contribute further to this attitude.

The cost of absenteeism to the firm in terms of excessive manning, idle machinery and the disruption of teamwork is passed on to the consumer in higher prices. This, of course, also happens to the high costs of advertising and retailing, which are inherent features of an economic organisation based on the consumer's freedom of choice. In the years to come it will probably be considered as unreasonable to expect a worker to suffer the discomfort, or worse, of having to work when he is not feeling well, as it is today to expect him or his wife to stand in a long queue when shopping, as would be the case if the cost of retailing were kept down at the expense of the consumer's freedom of choice.

Many people consider that absence on account of ill-health, even minor ill-health, is legitimate, while wilful, unauthorised absence for other reasons is unacceptable. It is, however, easier to distinguish between these types of absence in theory than it is in practice. There are many pathological conditions causing symptoms, especially pain, which are not capable of medical verification. Any scheme of sick leave is therefore always in danger of being abused, although this danger is easily exaggerated. The Sozialenquête-Kommission comments on this subject :

> There is . . . no justification for the suspicion that it [the high sickness rate] is due to fraud, malingering or carelessness at sport. Detailed investigations of the sickness funds of large industrial enterprises indicate that fraud is only responsible for an insignificantly small proportion of all absences due to sickness.[2]

It is commonly found that the sickness rate increases following the introduction of organised sick leave, the setting-up of a social insurance sickness benefit scheme or a rise in the rate of sickness benefit. Some people consider this to be evidence of abuse, but this is not necessarily the case. The purpose of these schemes is twofold : to provide the worker with an income when he is incapable of working and to remove from him the burden of having to work when he is not well, even if his state of health would have made it posible for him to continue working had the alternative been the loss of wages. If these objectives are the proper ones, it must be accepted that in low-wage employments, increased benefits will lead to higher sickness rates because they enable workers to stay away from work when previously they could not have afforded the loss of wages. In high-wage employments the effects will not be so marked, as the workers will have been able to stay away from work even without receiving sick pay or benefit.

Sick Pay.   Non-statutory social security provisions in sickness are for a number of reasons more important than and different from provisions for other interruptions or cessations of work. Sick pay (including employer-financed, sickness insurance cash benefit) was received in all ten countries in any given year by more persons than any other employee benefit. Expenditure on superannuation pensions may have been greater than that on sick pay, but the number of persons affected was much smaller. Sick pay tended to be socially divisive : it was a normal condition of service for administrative, technical and professional staff, but less common for manual workers in all countries. This was accentuated by the fact that some workers, particularly those in the public service, received 100 per cent. income replacement for short, and sometimes even for relatively long, periods of sickness, while others lost all pay as soon as they were off sick. In pensions the contrast was not so marked : 100 per cent. income replacement was exceptional. Expenditure on employer-financed sick pay was also greater in relation to publicly financed sickness benefit than any other employee benefit was in relation to the corresponding public social security provision.

Discouraging Malingerers? Not only is ill-health often more difficult to define than other social contingencies, such as widowhood or old age, but the decision whether to go to work or stay at home is mainly that of the individual. The level of income replacement and the day of the commencement of benefit will therefore have greater influence on the number claiming sickness benefit than on that claiming widows' or old-age pensions. If ill-health were a definite state, capable of independent verification at reasonable expense, the case for full or at least partial income replacement irrespective of duration would be very strong. As this is not so, some consider it inadvisable to award sick pay or temporary disability benefit on conditions which do little to discourage and possibly even encourage the weaknesses inherent in all individuals. A waiting period before the receipt of benefit and partial rather than complete income replacement are two devices designed to overcome such weaknesses.

THE FIRST WEEK

Duration of Sickness and Waiting Days. A large proportion of all absences due to sickness are very brief. The exact proportion is not known for any country, as days of incapacity not resulting in claims to benefit are usually not properly recorded. In Austria in 1967 the duration of the incapacity of 35 per cent. of all beneficiaries was one week or less.[3] In Great Britain 28 per cent. of the men and 30 per cent. of the women whose spell of certified incapacity ended in 1968-9 were absent for one week or less.[4] In Germany in the 1960s about half of all absences of manual workers lasted a fortnight or less ;[5] the corresponding proportion in Great Britain was almost three-fifths. These figures indicate the relative magnitude of brief absences but for a variety of reasons cannot be compared with each other.[6]

The International Labour Office (Minimum Standards) Convention, 1952, appeared to condone waiting days before the commencement of benefit :

> The benefit . . . shall be granted throughout the contingency, except that the benefit may be limited to 26 weeks in each case of sickness, in which event it need not be paid for the first three days of suspension of earnings.[7]

Seventeen years later, in the Medical Care and Sickness Benefit Convention, 1969, reference was again made to three waiting days but with a slightly different emphasis :

> 1. The sickness benefit . . . shall be granted throughout the contingency : provided that the grant of benefit may be limited to not less than 52 weeks in each case of incapacity, as prescribed . . .
> 3. Where the legislation of a Member provides that sickness benefit is not payable for an initial period of suspension of earnings, such period shall not exceed three days.[8]

The position as regards waiting days in the ten countries in 1969 is shown in Table 5 : 1. From this it will be seen that half the countries had more than three waiting days and only one country had dispensed with them altogether.

The German Wage Payment Continuation Act. In Germany the Wage Payment Continuation Act, 1969, required employers to pay an incapacitated worker for a period of up to six weeks the gross remuneration which he would have earned had he remained fit. The employee's right to receive his remuneration did not depend on any qualifying period of employment. (The Act did not change the position of salaried staff, who were already entitled to continue payment of salary for six weeks under previous legislation.) Its main purpose was to give manual workers a claim to continue pay to replace the previous arrangement under which they had received sickness benefit for six weeks from the day following the issue of a medical certificate of incapacity, as well as a supplement from their employers. This supplement had been assessed in such a way that, combined with sickness benefit, it was equal to the previous net wages.

The 1969 Act thus did not in any marked sense improve the

TABLE 5:1 Temporary Disability Benefits, 1969.

	Qualifying Employment	Maximum Duration of Benefit Wks.		Income Replacement	Maximum Assessed Earnings	Flat Rate	Addition for Wife and two Children	Benefit as a percentage of the Standard Wage	
		Wait-ing Days	Benefit Wks.					Single	Couple
Austria ...	Nil	3	78	50% 6 wks.>60%	Sch 4,725 p.m.	N.A.	10%	53f	58f
Germany ...	Nil	None	78	N.W. 6 wks.>75%	DM 228 p.w.	N.A.	10%	59f	65f
Ireland ...	26–48 wks.	3	N.L.	N.A.	N.A.	£3·75	£4·67	19	43
U.K. ...	26–50 wks.	3a	N.L.	F.R. +⅓£9 p.w.	£30 p.w.	£5	£5·30	41g	61g
Denmark ...	40 hrs.	6b	52	N.A.	N.A.	Kr. 54	Kr.13.50	49	61
Netherlands.	Nil	2	52	80%	Fl.89 p.d.	N.A.	None	80	80
Canada 1971	20 wks.	12	15	67%	$150 p.w.	N.A.	None	h	h
U.S.A. ...	4–17 wks.	6	26	50–67%	$97–$130 p.w.c	N.A.	None	40	40
New Zealand	Nil	6	N.L.	N.A.	N.A.	$13.25	$11.50	23	43
Australia ...	Nil	6	N.L.	N.A.	N.A.	$10	$13	12	27

Notes: N.L.—no limit; N.W.—normal wage; N.A.—not applicable; ∧—above; >—thereafter; F.R.—flat rate.

a Retroactive payments if incapacity lasted a fortnight or more.
b Retroactive payments if incapacity lasted longer than three weeks.
c Maximum benefit in New Jersey and New York. In 1970 the maximum weekly benefit under new group disability insurance programmes was $66 (Kolodrubetz, 1972, p. 19).
d Except for low-income families.
e In the second week of incapacity, except for Austria, Germany and the U.K.
f As from the seventh week.
g Between the third and the 28th weeks only. At other times 19 per cent and 39 per cent. respectively.
h No scheme in 1969.
j With two dependent children; excludes family allowances.

N.B.—For sources see text.

economic position of manual workers. It did eliminate what was in law, but not always in practice, one waiting day, and to some limited extent improved a manual worker's entitlement to old-age and invalidity pension. However, the force behind the change in the law was the desire to remove the favoured social position of the salaried employee. As from 1970, when the Act came into operation, salaried employees and wage-earners enjoyed the same rights when sick to continued payment of wage or salary and after six weeks to sickness benefit. In Germany this was considered a significant step towards equality in the employment field.

The Netherlands. In the Netherlands as from 1967 all employees except public servants were covered by sickness insurance. They were entitled when incapacitated by illness or accident to sickness benefit after a statutory period of two days. Large groups of insured persons, however, received benefit from the first day of incapacity as a non-statutory benefit from the occupational associations which administered the sickness insurance schemes.[9]

Austria. Austria had a compulsory sickness insurance scheme for all employees except public servants. Benefit was paid after three waiting days for normally up to 78 weeks. The right to benefit was suspended as long as the incapacitated employee was receiving wages from his employer. If he received half pay he would receive sickness benefit at half the standard rate. Salaried employees were not often entitled to sickness benefit because as a rule their salaries continued to be paid for at least the first six weeks. For this reason they paid only 4·8 per cent. of their salaries in contributions to the sick funds, while wage-earners paid 7·3 per cent. (These percentages were paid on earnings up to a statutory ceiling which was the same for both wage and salary earners.)

The Beveridge Recommendations. Beveridge in 1942 had recommended that benefit should 'not be paid for the first three days of a period of unemployment or disability unless and until it lasts in all for four weeks'.[10] This recommendation adopted for unemployment and disability the principle of retroactive payment and the four-week period, both of which had been applied to workmen's compensation claims since 1923. It was also in accordance with the then prevailing practice of British trade unions in regard to out-of-work benefit.[11]

The Beveridge recommendation of retroactive payment was incorporated in the British National Insurance Act, 1946, but the four weeks were reduced to two. Between 1948 and 1971 benefit for the first three days of sickness was paid whenever an applicant qualified for payment of unemployment, sickness or industrial injury benefit for at least 12 days (excluding isolated days and Sundays) within 13 weeks of the onset of sickness.

Retroactive Payments in the U.K.   In 1971 the National Insurance Act abolished the retroactive payments but left the three day waiting period unaltered, thereby reverting to the pre-1948 position. The government gave four reasons for this change. First, the general standard of living since 1948 had increased to such an extent that the retroactive payment of benefit was no longer needed. Second, these payments did not assist the lowest paid, but were for them merely an offset against supplementary benefit which they claimed when incapacitated. Third, the savings resulting from the discontinuation of these payments were available to meet needs of a higher priority, for example increased allowances for the chronic sick. Fourth, there was a possibility of abuse; the guarded reference to this deserves to be quoted verbatim :

> Often retrospective payment of benefit for waiting days means a tax-free bonus when the person concerned has returned to work. There is even the possibility of a suspicion that the prospect of a retrospective payment for waiting days could sometimes conceivably be a distorting factor tempting some people to prolong a spell of sickness. No-one knows for sure, but it may be a factor.[12]

There was no need for the Secretary of State to be quite so guarded. Retroactive payment of waiting days was only one among several distorting factors tempting people to prolong an illness. In the U.K. benefit was paid on the basis of a six-day week, but most people worked a five-day week. A man who returned to work on a Friday instead of on the following Monday thus gained one day's pay but lost two days' benefit. His pay was subject to income tax at 30 per cent. while the benefit was exempt from tax. Furthermore, in respect of the one day he worked he had to pay one week's insurance contribution (at the end of 1969 for a man 88p a week and for a woman 75p). A single woman who earned £15 a week, well above the average of women's wages at that time, was 65p better off if she delayed her return to work until Monday; a single man earning £20 a week was 8p better off if he did the same. In 1969 both the woman and the man who had already been ill in the previous week also received a retroactive payment for the first three waiting days if they delayed their return until Monday. This increased the advantage of not working on Friday to £3·65 for the woman and £3·08 for the man.[13] The factors which could have tempted people to delay their return to work were quite complex and included the number of days per week for which benefit was paid, the rates of both benefit and dependants' allowances, the tax exemption of benefit, the tax threshold for various family compositions, the tax rate, the mechanism of tax collection and the liability to social insurance contributions, as well as the retroactive payment of waiting days.

The government also claimed that the need for retroactive payment was reduced because more than half of all employees received some sick pay in addition to insurance benefit. They might have added that most salaried employees were not affected by the abolition of the retroactive payment because they received full pay less insurance benefit during periods of sickness. A reduction in benefit would thus be offset in their case by increased sick pay from the employers. The change, therefore, affected neither the comparatively well off nor the poorest, but it did harm the interest of the manual worker whose earnings were above those of the lowest paid.

The change was aptly described by the opposition's chief spokesman as 'robbing the sick to help the poor'.[14] It also had the undesirable feature of diminishing long-established rights under social insurance.

Ireland. Disability (sickness) benefit in Ireland was paid after three waiting days. Prior to 1967 retroactive payments had been made under the W.C.A. and thereafter such payments were incorporated in the occupational injuries scheme, but at no time were they applied to disability benefit.

Denmark. In Denmark all insured employees received cash benefits for incapacity due to sickness after six waiting days (three before 1961), but if the incapacity lasted more than three weeks a retroactive payment was made for the first week. In spite of the fact that the waiting period was longer than it was in the U.K., retroactive payment in Denmark did not give as much encouragement for prolonging a spell of sickness. There were three reasons for this : an interval of three rather than two weeks had to elapse before repayment; sickness benefit was subject to income tax; social security contributions for one or two day's work were markedly lower. Self-employed and non-employed voluntary contributors to sickness insurance received benefit only after a waiting period of two weeks.

A large-scale survey conducted by the Danish National Institute of Social Research in 1966 found that among persons losing income on account of sickness, 30 per cent. did not receive any benefit because their illness lasted less than six days.[15] This proportion is similar to those quoted above for Austria and Great Britain. The Danish survey excluded those who, though incapacitated, did not lose any income; it therefore must have referred mainly to manual workers.

U.S.A.   In the U.S.A. only the railroad industry and four states had compulsory temporary disability schemes for employees. These schemes covered about a quarter of all employees in private industry in the U.S.A. Another third of employees were covered by a variety of optional sickness benefit schemes mainly through group insurance policies sold by commercial insurance companies. The five compulsory schemes and almost all the commercial schemes had a waiting period of one week before payment of benefit.

New Zealand and Australia.   New Zealand and Australia had no social insurance temporary disability programmes, but they both provided sickness benefit subject to an income test as part of their social security provisions. These benefits were paid after a waiting period of one week.

The Report of the New Zealand Royal Commission on Social Security recommended that there be no waiting period for sickness benefit when there is medical evidence of incapacity for three weeks or more.[16] The report did not discuss the justification or merits of the waiting days, nor did it give any reason for the Commission's recommendation. It merely expressed agreement with the Social Security Department, which in its evidence to the Commission had suggested this change. In this evidence the department described in detail how it exercised its statutory discretion to waive the waiting period and concluded :

> The majority of applications for sickness benefit where the waiting period is waived are those where the applicant remains incapacitated for three weeks or more and has a dependent child.

Experience has shown that there are other classes of beneficiary who may have genuine difficulty in meeting their commitments for the first week without benefit. Accordingly it is considered that it would be reasonable to waive the waiting period in all cases where the medical evidence certifies incapacity for a period of three weeks or more.[17]

Apparently the Department, like the Royal Commission, did not consider that changes in the waiting-days rule required the support of research or reasoned argument.

Canada.   Canada had, before 1971, neither sickness benefit insurance nor special assistance programmes for the incapacitated.

Justification for Waiting Periods.   Except for Germany, all countries which had sickness insurance schemes had a statutory waiting period for manual workers. The German official attitude in recent years has been quite clear : 'Waiting periods for social benefits which replace earnings are not in accord with sound social policy.'[18]

Three justifications for waiting periods are usually advanced : it is claimed that they discourage malingering, avoid the high administrative cost of processing small amounts and are unnecessary if the beneficiary has a high income. It is, however, erroneous to argue that waiting days are required on account of the administrative difficulties and expense of paying benefit within a day or so of the commencement of a spell of sickness : as wages and salaries are normally paid in arrears, the claimant will have the previous month's or week's wages to live on when he falls ill; it is therefore quite sufficient in all but exceptional circumstances if the benefit is paid a week after the start of the illness.

CHARACTERISTICS OF SCHEMES

The Persons Covered.   In 1969 only two of the countries – Austria and the Netherlands – had statutory income-maintenance provisions for all employees : those in the public service were entitled to sick pay and all others were compulsorily covered by a contributory sickness insurance scheme. In Germany non-manual employees whose earnings exceeded DM11,800 a year were excluded. This ceiling was raised twice in the following two years and as from 1971 was adjusted annually so as to equal one and a half times the average earnings (in the first three of the last four years) of all persons covered by pension insurance. The law was also changed in 1971 so that whenever the income of non-manual employees rose above the ceiling for compulsory insurance they had the opportunity of becoming voluntary members of the social sickness funds, the official bodies which administered the cash-benefit scheme.

The U.K. had a comprehensive national insurance system which provided sickness benefit not only for all insured employees but also for all the self-employed with only minor exceptions. Insurance was compulsory for all employees except married women (about one-fifth of all employees) and most widows. Both these groups of women could voluntarily pay national insurance contributions and thereby become entitled to all insurance benefits.[19] The Labour government had suggested in 1969 that social insurance should become compulsory for married women and widows,[20] but the change of government following the election of 1970 made this come to naught. They had in fact proposed a major reconstruction of the social insurance system, but decided that the time was not appropriate to make radical changes in the structure of short-term benefits. They did, however, intend to 'explore further the possibility of introducing a statutory scheme which would provide a minimum of sick pay [to be paid by employers] for all employees'.[21]

In Ireland the social insurance scheme provided compulsory cover for all employees except non-manual workers earning more than £1,200 a year. The employees excluded by the income ceiling could at no time became voluntary contributors to gain cover for disability benefit. The author in a research paper published in 1964 recommended the extension of social insurance to all employees irrespective of income and also compulsory supplementation by employers of social insurance disability benefits during the first four weeks of incapacity.[22]

In Denmark public servants received sick leave at full pay for prescribed periods and employers were normally required to continue the payment of wages to salaried employees. For all those not covered by either of these schemes, the sick funds paid daily cash benefits. The same scheme allowed the self-employed and the non-employed, including housewives, to contribute voluntarily to cash-benefit sickness insurance. Only 50,000 persons – some $1\frac{1}{2}$ per cent. of all adults – availed themselves of this provision.

By the beginning of the First World War, compulsory and contributory sickness insurance in Austria, Germany, Ireland and the U.K. covered most manual workers, as well as most non-manual workers of the same income range. In Denmark the state had subsidised the sickness benefit association since 1892, but compulsory insurance came much later and for women employees was made compulsory only in 1961. Sickness benefit insurance in the Netherlands was a live political issue for twenty years before it was finally enacted in 1930.

Temporary disability insurance in the U.S.A. was provided neither under a Federal programme, as were old-age, survivors' and disability[23] insurance, nor under a Federal–state system, as was unemployment insurance. It was a state responsibility like workmen's compensation, but while all states in 1969 had a W.C.A., only four had temporary disability schemes. All of these were of comparatively recent origin – Rhode Island (1942), California (1946), New Jersey (1948) and New York (1949). After an interval of twenty years Puerto Rico (1969) and Hawaii (1970) brought the number of jurisdictions with mandatory temporary disability insurance up to six. In these jurisdictions about four-fifths of employees were covered, including almost all in commerce and industry. The exclusions were similar to those for unemployment insurance (which is discussed in Chapter 7 below). The law of California, like that of Denmark, permitted the self-employed to opt for cover.

In 1939 New Zealand introduced a sickness assistance scheme with benefits subject to an income test, as part of a comprehensive social security plan, and Australia began a scheme on very similar lines some six years later.

Duration of Temporary Disability.   The period for which a disability was considered temporary varied widely (see Table 5 : 1). The I.L.O. Convention had laid down 52 weeks. In all but two countries temporary disability benefit was paid for 52 weeks or more to all those who satisfied prescribed conditions. In Ireland and the U.K. sickness (temporary disability) benefit was continued without a time limit subject to a minimum of 156 weekly contributions having been paid. In New Zealand and Australia benefits were available to those who were temporarily incapacitated for work, but in both countries benefit was continued without time limit until the beneficiary recovered, died or was medically certified to have a permanent disability.

The duration of temporary disability was important because in most countries benefit was awarded on conditions which were markedly different from those for permanent disability (invalidity) pensions. Long-term benefits were lower than short-term ones in Canada (after 1971), the U.S.A. and (although to a lesser extent) in Austria and Germany. The opposite was the case in Denmark and Australia, while in Ireland, the U.K., the Netherlands and New Zealand the rate of benefit was the same but the conditions of award were different.

The income-maintenance provisions in four countries varied even within the period of temporary disability. In Germany and Austria (non-manual workers) the economic position of the incapacitated employee deteriorated at the end of the first six weeks of incapacity when sickness benefit replaced the continued wage payment. In Australia (as from 1970) the rate of sickness benefit was raised after six weeks to the level of the invalidity pension. In Austria (manual workers) the rate of benefit was increased after six weeks from 50 per cent. of previous earnings to 60 per cent. As from 1965 in the U.K. the flat-rate sickness benefit was augmented after the first fortnight for the following 26 weeks by an earnings-related supplement of one-third of the amount by which the average weekly earnings in the last financial year exceeded £9; this supplement was subject to a maximum of £7 a week.

Assessment of Benefit. In Ireland, Denmark, New Zealand and Australia the standard benefit was a flat rate and the compensation ratio was thus inversely related to income. In all four countries the benefit rates tended to be low and for the standard wage-earner with a wife and two children were well below the 60 per cent. compensation ratio of the I.L.O. Convention.[24] The U.K. was the only country with a two-tier system and the U.K. and New Zealand were the only countries where a person, especially a householder, could obtain supplementary benefit in addition to the maximum rate of sickness benefit. In the other five countries – Austria, Germany, the Netherlands, the U.S.A. and Canada (as from 1971) – benefit was proportionate to previous earnings but subject to maximums, either of the amount of benefit, for example $65 a week for temporary disability benefit in New Jersey and New York in 1969, or of the earnings assessed for benefit, for example DM11,800 a year in Germany.

Administration. The sickness funds in Austria, Germany and Denmark, which financed their members' health services, also paid their cash benefits. The occupational associations in the Netherlands, which awarded sickness benefit, administered invalidity and unemployment benefit as well but were not responsible for health services. In both the U.K. and Ireland one government department was responsible for the administration and award of all social security cash benefits.

Canada's Unemployment Insurance Act of 1971 provided unemployment cash benefits for temporary loss of earnings due to illness. The qualifying period of 20 weeks' employment during the preceding 52 weeks was the same as that for unemployment benefit. The rate of benefit was two-thirds of earnings in the qualifying period, with a maximum of $100 a week; this maximum was adjusted annually with changes in the wage index. The sickness benefit provisions were an integral part of unemployment insurance and were administered by the Unemployment Insurance Commission. This was composed of three Commissioners of whom one was appointed after consultation with employers' organisations and another after consultations with employees' organisations.

In the U.S.A. the administration of mandatory temporary disability schemes, like that of workmen's compensation schemes, differed widely between states. In Rhode Island mandatory insurance was operated exclusively through a state fund, while in Hawaii all cover had to be provided by private carriers. In California and New Jersey cover was provided through a state-operated fund, although employers could contract out by making private arrangements, while in New York cover was normally provided by private carriers, but could also be obtained from a state insurance fund. In the railroad industry there was a separate Federal scheme under which the mandatory insurance was operated through public funds.

New Zealand and Australia had governmental social security agencies which administered all cash benefits except workmen's compensation.

Financing. In only two countries – Denmark and the Netherlands – was temporary disability benefit financed independently of other social security measures. In Austria and Germany the contributions to the sick funds paid for both health services and cash benefits, while in Ireland and the U.K. one contribution covered all social security cash benefits. In Canada (as from 1971) one contribution covered unemployment and sickness benefit. The schemes of New Zealand and Australia were non-contributory and financed out of general tax revenue.

In Denmark cash benefits were financed by a contribution of 11 øre from employers plus 5½ øre from employees for each hour worked. The combined contribution amounted to approximately 1 per cent. of the standard wage. It was supplemented by grants from public funds which, up to October 1969, equalled one-fifth of the contributions paid.

Benefits in the Netherlands were financed on a quite different basis. All employees contributed 1 per cent. of their earnings up to Fl89 a day (in 1970) but employers' contributions differed between the various occupational associations; they averaged 5·2 per cent. of wages up to the same amount. The differences in the rates charged reflected partly the differences in the incidence of sickness between various branches of industry and partly the extent to which the associations awarded benefits in excess of the statutory minimum. The Dutch system of contributions thus had two peculiar characteristics : it incorporated riskrating to some extent, and the benefits which employees received for uniform contributions of 1 per cent. of earnings differed according to the industry in which they worked. Contributions were substantially higher in the Netherlands than they were in Denmark on account of a number of factors, which included the absence of state grants; fewer, if any, waiting days; considerably higher benefits, especially for employees with earnings in excess of the standard wage; the provision of benefits for incapacity due to accidents as well as sickness.

Benefit without Medical Certification.   Both Denmark and the Netherlands differed in another important respect from the other eight countries : they were the only ones in which medical certification was not a requirement for a claim to benefit. (A medical certificate was even necessary in Ireland, the U.S.A. and Australia in spite of the fact that general practitioners' services were not free for the majority of the population.) To obtain benefit in Denmark it was sufficient to make a statutory declaration giving particulars of the nature of the illness, earnings, place of employment and family responsibilities. Some of these had to be confirmed by the employer in a written statement. The sick funds could require the applicant to produce a medical certificate from his doctor, but this was not the normal practice for short-term illnesses.

In the Netherlands either the employer or the claimant could report the incapacity to the occupational association. Benefit was paid irrespective of the verification of the incapacity, but if it exceeded a short duration a sick-visitor employed by the occupational association would call at the house of the claimant and make a report on his condition. This was a layman's assessment and not in any sense a medical report. If the illness was prolonged the claimant would be asked to report to a doctor employed by and responsible to the occupational association or, if necessary, would be visited by this doctor. The underlying idea of this arrangement was that the doctor who treated a patient should not be concerned with the conditions which entitled his patient to social security cash benefit. It was thought that if the doctor were relieved of this task the quality of the doctor–patient relationship would be enhanced. The Danish and Dutch attitudes to medical certification were thus not identical, but their common feature of payment of benefit for short periods of incapacity without a medical certificate may well deserve the consideration of other countries.

Level of Benefits. The main features of temporary disability schemes in the ten countries are summarised in Table 5 : 1. Only in Germany, the Netherlands and Denmark was benefit up to the I.L.O. Convention's standard : a compensation ratio of 60 per cent. for a man and a wife and two children for 52 weeks of incapacity. Austria reached the 60 per cent. ratio only after the seventh week.[25] The U.K. attained it for 26 weeks, but benefit was much lower for the first two weeks and again from the 29th to the 52nd week. In the other five countries benefits were nowhere near the Convention's standard.

In evaluating the table, two subsequent changes which brought about a marked improvement and to which reference has already been made should be remembered. The ceiling for the assessment of earnings in Germany was raised substantially in 1971, so that the compensation ratio for the single standard wage-earner was from the seventh week 75 per cent. and for the man with two children 85 per cent. In Australia as from 1970 the benefit paid after seven weeks of incapacity was the same as the invalidity pension, a rate which exceeded sickness benefit by at least 50 per cent.

In Austria the earnings ceiling was raised by about 20 per cent. in 1971 and a proposal to vary it annually, as in Germany, in line with the ceiling for pension insurance was under consideration.[26]

Proposed changes in Danish Legislation.   Major changes in Danish short-term social security benefits were foreshadowed in a document submitted to the United Nations Conference of Ministers Responsible for Social Welfare, 1972. This stated :

> At the present time, a reform of the daily cash benefit schemes (sickness, maternity and accidents at work) is in progress. That reform work is based on the following main principles :
> (1) In principle, any person who suffers loss of income during temporary incapacity for work shall be eligible for daily cash benefit.
> (2) In principle, daily cash benefit shall be paid under uniform rules in all cases of temporary incapacity for work, whether due to sickness, maternity or accident at work.
> (3) The amount of the daily cash benefit should to a larger extent than has been the case so far under Danish legislation, be adjusted to the amount of the individual loss of income of the eligible person as a result of incapacity for work.[27]

Recommendations of the New Zealand Royal Commission.   In New Zealand too, major changes in the sickness benefit provisions must be anticipated in the not too distant future. The Social Security Department in their evidence to the Royal Commission on Social Security referred to the lack of statistics on work absence and to 'the present practice for Government and some firms to provide sick pay'.[28] The Report of the Royal Commission was more emphatic :

> Sick leave provisions are very common in awards and industrial agreements, and are becoming more common. True there is a great variation in the provisions made, and because of the nature of their employment (casual or intermittent) many workers receive little protection.[29]

These statements do not appear to be based on documentation or evidence but on general impressions. The New Zealand Treasury in estimating the cost of an earnings-related sickness benefit scheme apparently assumed that about two-thirds of all employees received some sick pay and that the average absence due to sickness of each worker was about two weeks a year.[30]

In discussing sickness benefit the Royal Commission re-emphasised their view that it was not the community's responsibility to compensate for loss of income and expressed disagreement with the principle that the aim of social security was to cover the loss of income.[31] The Commission expressed their view positively :

We have already emphasised that the social security system is needed to correct defects in, but not to replace, the general market system. This is already dealing to some extent with the problem of sickness, and could do so more completely. . . .

. . . insurance in various forms is already available to cover loss of earnings through sickness. . . . It is obvious . . . that individual employers could insure against any such liability [sick-pay provisions] they accepted.[32]

The Royal Commission's conclusions on earnings-related sickness benefit were :

Providing social security benefit levels are raised to the extent we suggest in this report, the institution of earnings-related sickness payments is not urgent. That could be postponed until the accident compensation scheme is operating and has been tested, and until sufficient time has elapsed to enable better material to be gathered from employers on sickness absences and other relevant matters.[33]

Their recommendations, however, were not primarily based on the arguments they advanced but on the probability that the government would implement the proposals of the Select Committee on Compensation for Personal Injury. On any other basis the Commission's recommendations are difficult to reconcile with the general tenor of their report. They recommended that :

Favourable consideration be given by the Government to the future introduction of earnings-related 'compensation' for limited periods during incapacity caused by illness, to be administered separately from the social security system as an addition to the scheme for accident compensation. . . .[34]

SOME ECONOMIC AND SOCIAL CONSEQUENCES

Income Redistribution. Any scheme of sickness benefit insurance redistributes income within a given year among those insured, giving it to those who claim benefit and taking it from those who do not claim it. In a private insurance scheme based on actuarial principles, where premiums are strictly graded by risk, redistribution takes place among individuals according to the incidence and duration of the sickness they experience. In social insurance, where contributions are in general independent of risk, income is redistributed among groups of insured persons according to their proneness to claim benefit. Certain groups – the old, women, and unskilled and manual workers –

are everywhere more prone to sickness than other groups – the young, men, skilled workers and salaried staff. As the groups most likely to be claimants are on average less well off than those less likely to be claimants, sickness insurance benefits tend to redistribute income vertically, from the better off to the less well off. For this reason the exclusion of non-manual workers whose incomes exceed prescribed limits, as was the case in Germany and Ireland, reduces the vertical income redistribution of sickness insurance, if only to a minor degree.

In addition to these variations in the incidence of sickness by age, sex, skill and status, there is variation by occupation and industry, which follows a fairly regular pattern.

A sickness benefit scheme which charges all employees a fixed proportion of earnings (like the uniform contribution of 1 per cent. of earnings in the Netherlands) and pays benefits in proportion to earnings thus redistributes income among employees in several different ways. Those who are more likely to be sick benefit in that the aggregate contributions they pay are insufficient to finance the total amount they receive, while those less likely to be sick contribute too much in relation to what they receive. The same degree of redistribution also takes place in a scheme where all contributors pay the same flat-rate contribution and receive the same benefit.

The schemes of the European countries, except the Netherlands and Denmark, contain another element of redistribution : benefits are graded according to family responsibilities while contributions are independent of these. This results in a redistribution of income from the single to the married, and from couples without dependent children to those with many children.

In addition to income redistribution within a particular year, sickness insurance schemes involve some redistribution of income over the life-span. Young men contribute too much in the first ten years of their working life in relation to the cost of the benefit they are likely to claim, but too little in the last ten years. Similarly, the bachelor, the young married man who has not yet got any children and the older married man whose children are no longer dependent contribute too much, while the not-so-young married man with dependent children contributes too little.

The German scheme of continued wage payment for the first six weeks of incapacity had characteristics which were similar to risk-rating by industry. The building industry, with a notoriously high incidence of sickness, paid out a larger proportion of wages in sick pay than an industry employing mainly office staff, where the incidence of sickness was low. As the cost of sick pay, like other costs, was passed on to the consumer, the price he paid incorporated to a larger extent than under a scheme of flat-rate contributions the real cost of production processes.

In New Zealand and Australia the non-contributory sickness benefit programmes, which were financed out of general revenue, redistributed income vertically and by contingency. The amount redistributed was, however, relatively small. The number receiving benefit was on average 6 per 1,000 of the labour force in New Zealand and 2 per 1,000 in Australia, while the corresponding ratio in the U.K. was 29 per 1,000.

Vertical redistribution in Denmark, where sickness benefit covered mainly manual workers, was on a smaller scale than it was in the Netherlands, where all employees were covered. The importance of this redistribution of income among insured persons was, however, limited in both countries by the large proportion of the cost of benefit which was borne by employers and the exchequer. In the Netherlands the employers' contributions varied to some extent with the incidence of sickness among employees in different industrial groups, while in Denmark (as well as in the U.K. and Ireland) employers' and employees' contributions were flat rates, related to neither risk nor income.

In Austria and Germany each sickness fund fixed its own contribution rates within limits laid down by statute. Contributions, which were shared equally between employers and employees, covered both the health services and the cash benefits rendered to their members. The contributions varied between funds because of differences between them in both the incidence and the duration of sickness among their members and the award of additional, non-statutory benefits. In these two countries, therefore, in contrast to the Netherlands, contribution rates varied not only between employers but also between employees.

The Cost of Providing Insurance.   The cost of providing income replacement through private insurance is inherently high. In the U.S.A., for example, benefit payments under individual insurance were 57 per cent. of premiums paid in 1970 (50 per cent. in 1958 and 40 per cent. in 1948).[35] The 43 per cent. difference covered such items as contingency reserves, administration, commission for the sale of insurance, acquisitions, claim settlements and profit. The corresponding ratio of benefit to premium for private group insurance was 73 per cent. in 1970. In the states in which temporary disability insurance was mandatory the ratio for group insurance was the same as it was in those in which insurance was voluntary.

In public social insurance the administrative cost of any scheme is the difference between the benefits paid out and the contributions and grants received. It is not easy, however, to calculate the administrative cost of any country's sickness benefit scheme except on an arbitrary basis, because sickness insurance was always an integral part of some other social security scheme. All the same, it is beyond question that sickness insurance programmes are less expensive to administer than assistance programmes, which require an income test, but more expensive than old-age pensions, which require less checking of claims.

The administrative cost ratio of any social security provision is generally inversely related to both the amount paid out and the period over which payments extend. Thus, as the administrative cost of paying sickness benefit equal to 40 per cent. of earnings is the same, or virtually the same, as that of paying benefit equal to 80 per cent. of earnings, the cost ratio of the former scheme will be twice that of the latter. Similarly, the cost ratio of paying benefit for a three-day spell of sickness will be much greater than that of regular weekly payments over three months. In general, 4 to 5 per cent. would appear to be a generous estimate of the administrative cost – benefit ratio of social security sickness benefit schemes.

Continued wage payment by employers involves less administrative cost than any other method of income maintenance, while unnecessarily high costs are involved when the employer supplements social security benefits with sick pay. This frequently happened in the U.K. when employees had their sickness benefit made up to their normal earnings. In these circumstances, because sickness benefit was exempt from tax, they were actually better off in sickness than in health. In the U.S.A. salaried employees often received sick leave at their normal rate of pay for the first few days of incapacity (but limited to a specified number of days per year) and thereafter benefit at a reduced rate of pay under a group insurance plan. This dual system also led to high administrative costs.

The German Wage Payment Continuation Act. Sickness insurance in Germany has had, since it began in the 1880s, three characteristics : it has been compulsory, it has rendered services in kind and it has paid cash benefits as income replacement. At first cash benefits were restricted to 13 weeks and replaced about half a man's wages; they amounted to more than three-fifths of the expenditure of the sick funds which administered the scheme. Contributions to the sick funds were shared between employers and workers (salaried staff were not insured) in the ratio of 1 :2. The original law was in the nature of a compulsory self-help scheme for workers and required employers to assist workers in this. By the early 1970s cash benefits as a proportion of the sick funds' expenditure had declined to one-ninth. This was partly the result of the continuous increase in costs of health services and partly the result of employers becoming responsible for wages and salary payment for the first six weeks of incapacity.

The Wage Payment Continuation Act, 1969, also introduced a system of compulsory insurance for small employers to give partial coverage of the expenditure involved. Insurance was compulsory for employers of fewer than 20 manual or non-manual workers. The premiums paid were a proportion of the wages bill and entitled employers to a reimbursement of 80 per cent. of the wages paid to incapacitated workers under the provisions of the Act. The insurance carriers designated by the Act were the sick funds which were responsible for paying cash benefits from the seventh week. The purpose of this provision was to relieve small-scale enterprises of the financial risk of irregular and exceptional incidence of sickness among their employees. In order to ease the financial burden of these enterprises the government made transitional grants between 1970 and 1973 amounting to DM550 million to the sick funds to enable them to charge lower premiums to the employers.[36]

The provisions of the 1969 Act placed the incapacitated worker in Germany in a financial position unequalled anywhere in the world. The nature of sickness benefit was now completely different from what it had been in the 1880s; the cherished German ideal of self-help for employees had changed to the point where the state compelled employers, or at least small employers, to insure themselves to cover the obligations to their employees which the state had imposed on them. Compulsory insurance of employers to meet statutory obligations was common under W.C.A.s in many countries, for example Denmark, but it had not been the rule for other social security provisions.

Entitlement to Benefit. Insurance benefits as a form of income maintenance in sickness may have the disadvantage of excluding people whose contributions are insufficient to entitle them to benefit. This was especially the case in Ireland, the U.K. and Canada (after 1971), as these countries required quite lengthy periods of contribution for entitlement to benefit. The great majority of insured persons experienced no difficulty in obtaining benefit at the maximum (standard) rate, but small groups, often of especially vulnerable people, had difficulties in satisfying the conditions. In the U.K. deserted wives who took up work, single women who stayed at home to look after their parents, men and women returning home after a spell abroad, immigrants and young people starting work were not entitled to benefit in their first year of work and even after a year received benefit only at a reduced rate.[37]

An employed, incapacitated person in the U.K. could have been in many different positions as regards income replacement. He might have been entitled to no sickness benefit at all or to benefit only at a reduced rate. He might have received sickness benefit at the maximum flat rate or received in addition after two weeks an earnings-related supplement for 26 weeks. Moreover, in any of these four positions he might have been awarded supplementary benefit on the basis of a means test. The amount of supplementary benefit he was awarded took into account any sickness benefit he received as well as the rent he paid and the number of dependants he had. With respect to his wages he would have been in one of three positions : receiving no pay from his employer, a specified proportion of his pay or his ordinary pay less sickness benefit.

The position in Ireland was very similar to that in the U.K. except that self-employed persons and relatives helping farmers were not entitled to disability benefit in the first year of insured employment.

In Austria, Germany and the Netherlands entitlement to benefit depended on working in insured employment, but was independent of any qualifying period of employment. This was also in general the case in Denmark, except that 40 hours of employment in the four weeks preceding a claim were required to qualify for benefit.

In Canada (as from 1971) cash benefits for temporary loss of earnings depended on a qualifying period. The duration of employment also determined the rate of benefit. In the U.S.A. each state which had a mandatory temporary disability scheme had earnings or employment requirements for entitlement to benefit, but the nature and severity of the requirements varied widely. Their purpose was to limit benefits to individuals who had shown substantial attachment to the labour force.

Income Disparity. In all countries there was a greater disparity in incomes among incapacitated persons than there was among those at work. Very little information is available about paid sick leave. Public servants everywhere were in the most favourable position in this respect. Some employees in all countries and all salaried employees, or the great majority of them, in some countries (Austria, Germany and Denmark) received full pay during periods of incapacity. Only in Germany were manual workers in this favourable position, but all employees in the Netherlands received social security benefits which approximated very closely to their previous net earnings. In all countries except Germany substantial groups of manual workers received no pay when incapacitated, but in the European countries they virtually all received some insurance benefit. In the four non-European countries there were large groups of workers who received neither pay nor insurance benefit when they were sick.

In all sickness insurance schemes cover was incomplete : the self-employed, except in the U.K., were excluded; in the U.S.A. only a quarter of employees in private industry and commerce were covered by mandatory schemes; in Ireland and the U.K. the lengthy qualifying periods excluded quite a few of those paying contributions from benefit, while others received benefit at reduced rates.

Prognosis. In the European countries two developments appear probable : more continued wage payment for the first few weeks of incapacity and less medical certification for the award of insurance benefit or for continued wage payment. One of the consequences of continued wage payment would be the abolition of waiting days. This, in addition to the factors discussed above, would result in an increased sickness rate. The cost to employers would be quite considerable, possibly of the magnitude of 3 to 5 per cent. of the total wages bill.

While it is recognised that medical assessment of incapacity for work serves a useful purpose in the case of disabilities which last for more than a short time, it is increasingly thought that the medical certification of all illnesses by the doctor treating the patient discourages malingering only slightly. If medical certificates were required less often, doctors would be freed of an unwelcome task and the quality of health services would improve.

In the four non-European countries developments are more difficult to predict. In New Zealand a compulsory sickness insurance scheme with earnings-related benefit appears probable. Australia may well in future, as in the past, follow policies not unlike those of New Zealand. In Canada benefits for temporary disability are of such recent origin that the scheme set up in 1971 may well remain unaltered in essentials for many years yet. In the U.S.A. the spirit prevailing in the early 1970s appears to be unfavourably disposed to any further dose of 'welfare'. Future developments there are more likely in private group insurance benefits, in spite of the high cost ratio of this type of provision.

NOTE ON INCOME-MAINTENANCE PROVISIONS FOR PERSONS
INCAPACITATED BY SICKNESS IN GREAT BRITAIN

Information about expenditure on sickness benefit and sick pay and the nature of the provisions for persons incapacitated by sickness can be gleaned from a number of official surveys. This makes it possible to ascertain the magnitude of various items with a fair degree of accuracy.

Expenditure on national insurance sickness benefit in 1969 was £375 million.[38] About £225 million (60 per cent.) of this was spent on those whose spell of sickness had lasted for less than six months.[39] In addition, £35 million was paid in industrial injury benefit.

A large-scale survey of labour costs conducted by the Department of Employment ascertained that 0·4 per cent. of wages paid to manual workers in manufacturing industries was for periods of absence due to sickness or injury.[40] The corresponding proportion for non-manual workers (administrative, technical and clerical) was 1·3 per cent.[41] The aggregate ratio for all wage- and salary-earners is estimated at 0·7 per cent. Wages and salaries totalled £24,215 million[42] so that sick pay will have amounted to about £170 million. Employers in manufacturing industries paid an additional 0·4 per cent. of total wages and salaries either into sick funds for the benefit of their employees or directly to sick and injured employees (other than in wages or salaries).[43] If it is assumed that the corresponding proportion for employees in all employments was about 0·2 per cent, the amount paid would have been some £5 million in all.

The Family Expenditure Survey conducted annually by the Department of Employment recorded payments for 'sickness and accident insurance, subscriptions to sick clubs, friendly societies' as 4p a week per household in 1969,[44] equivalent to a national expenditure of some £34 million. At most three-quarters and possibly as little as half of this sum was paid to sick and injured persons; the remainder will have been swallowed up in the conduct of the business. Employers and private households spent a total of about £209 million on income-maintenance provisions for sickness and injury, which amounted to 80 per cent. of national insurance sickness and industrial injury benefit expenditure on spells lasting less than six months. The combined governmental and non-governmental expenditure of this kind was about 2 per cent. of all wages and salaries paid in 1969.

The Department of Employment conducted a large scale sample survey of earnings, covering employees in all employments and referring to one pay period (April 1970). This showed that among manual workers 4·7 per cent. of the men and 4·3 per cent. of the women lost some pay on account of certified sickness during this period. In addition, 1·2 per cent. of the men and 2·8 per cent. of the women lost pay on account of uncertified sickness. Markedly fewer non-manual employees lost salary : 1·2 per cent. of the men and 1·9 per cent. of the women for certified illness and 0·2 per cent. and 0·5 per cent. respectively for non-certified illness. Losses of wages were more frequent among the unskilled than among the skilled for both sexes.[45]

The same survey also recorded that 93 per cent. of all adult men and 90 per cent. of all women in non-manual employment were covered by employers' sick-pay schemes.[46] The corresponding proportions of men and women manual workers were 65 per cent. and 48 per cent. These percentages only referred to the existence of sick-pay schemes; no information is available about the proportion of earnings compensated or the length of time for which sick pay continued.

Of all men incapacitated and claiming benefit on 31 May 1969, about one-third had been absent for less than four weeks, one-third for between four weeks and one year and another third for more than a year. Thus two-thirds of all incapacity was temporary (or the first 52 weeks of long-term incapacity) and the other third was permanent (invalidity). Both temporary and permanent disability increased greatly with age, as is shown in Table 5 :2—the rate of incapacity lasting for 4 to 26 weeks trebled between the late 20s and the early 50s and doubled between the early 50s and the early 60s. The incapacity rate for up to four weeks was, however, much the same for all age groups.

TABLE 5:2   *Male Claimants for Sickness Benefit analysed by duration of spell, expressed as a proportion of those at risk in the relevant age group.*

GREAT BRITAIN				
	Age at 31st May, 1969			
Duration of incapacity at 31st May, 1969, *in weeks*	25—29 0/00	50—54 0/00	62 0/00	All ages 0/00
Up to 4	15	16	17	16
4—25	6	17	34	13
26—57	1	5	16	4
52 and more	2	20	88	17
All durations	24	58	154	50

N.B.—Male claimants refers to all employees and self-employed persons except non-industrial civil servants for the first six months of incapacity.

Source: adapted from Table 32 in *Digest of Statistics Analysing Certificates of Incapacity, June* 1968—*May* 1969 (Department of Health and Social Security, HMSO, 1972).

The similarity in the incidence of absence from work due to incapacity in the U.S.A. and Great Britain is remarkable, especially in view of their great economic and social differences. It has been estimated that in the U.S.A. an average of 7 out of a possible 255 working days were lost in 1970 owing to short-term non-work-connected disability and the first six months of long-term disability.[47] Expressed differently, 27 out of every 1,000 men and women employees were absent every day. This figure is almost exactly the same as the corresponding proportion for 1969 in Britain.[48]

CHAPTER VI

Old Age and Invalidity

The Number of Old People. The number of beneficiaries of old-age pensions was in all ten countries greater than the number of beneficiaries of any of the other six cash-benefit services.[1] In most it was greater than the combined number of all the beneficiaries of the other services. Consequently, expenditure on social security provisions for the old was the largest item in most social security budgets.

The number of old people (however defined) has increased during the last twenty years in all countries, and in all but Canada and New Zealand there has been an increase in the proportion of old people in the population (see Table 3 :3). This increase is the result of many complex factors, the most important of which was the decline of mortality in childhood, adolescence and middle age, which has enabled many more people to survive into old age. Increased longevity has been comparatively less important. (In the U.K. the average expectation of life at the age of 65 increased between 1871 and 1969 from 10·5 to 12·0 years for men and from 11·2 to 15·9 years for women.) The proportion of old people in the population of Canada, New Zealand and Australia was low compared with that in the population of the European countries because of the large-scale immigration experienced by the former countries in recent decades.

The Position of Insurance Companies. Social security provisions for the old tend to be a controversial subject for a number of reasons. They operate in a field where commercial insurance companies have much experience and claim to provide a flexible and efficient service. The position is rather different for the other cash-benefit services. For a variety of reasons commercial insurance companies have no or very little interest in providing unemployment and maternity insurance; this also applies, except in the U.S.A., to temporary disability benefit and, to a lesser extent, to invalidity insurance. Ireland and New Zealand have recently changed to social insurance systems for employment injuries and commercial companies now operate in this field only in Denmark, the U.S.A. and Australia. Old-age and survivors' pensions are therefore the only field of social security where the insurance companies have an interest in impeding the expansion of a public service. For public social insurance the companies favour low income-replacement ratios, low contribution ceilings (to which benefits are related), the exclusion of persons whose income exceeds prescribed limits and the restriction of cover to employees. These are the conditions which encourage the sale of occupational pension schemes to employers and life endowment and annuity policies to individuals.

Occupational Pensions and Savings.   The insurance companies claim that private provisions for old age have many advantages over public provisions. Some of these are spurious but one appears valid and important. The growth of the funds of the insurance companies and the self-administered trust schemes in the field of occupational pensions has in the past been an important source of private savings. Such savings are desirable as they restrict consumption and thereby make it possible to increase investment without generating inflationary pressures. The reasons why these funds have increased have been elaborated in a British White Paper :

> [The] growth [in occupational pension funds] derives from four factors : growth in membership; expansion in the scale of provision, resulting in higher contributions (as a proportion of earnings) towards more generous future benefits; the extent to which new schemes are still at the stage when funds are being built up while there is little expenditure yet on benefits; and the fact that when incomes are rising current contributions relate to higher earnings rather than current pensions, which are based on former earnings.[2]

The desirability of savings in a dynamic economy is beyond dispute and so is the fact that occupational pension schemes of the traditional type generate large savings for the reasons outlined in the above quotation. It is, however, by no means certain that this particular type of saving is socially desirable. Contributions to occupational pension schemes are, from the employee's point of view, no different from social insurance contributions. It may be argued that taxation ought to be the prerogative of the government rather than the employer.

The emphasis on the savings element in occupational pension schemes tends to distract attention from another factor. If people of working age today provide for their retirement through contributions to occupational schemes, they cannot be expected to contribute simultaneously to the pensions of their parents or grandparents through social insurance. Thus persons who retire before occupational schemes start or during the first two decades of their operation will have to be wholly or partly supported by pensions financed out of general revenue. The cost of such pensions represents an expenditure which, at least in part, offsets the savings of the occupational pension schemes. Not to pay any pensions to old people who have not accumulated rights under occupational pension schemes is clearly as socially undesirable as it is politically inexpedient.

The most essential characteristic of social insurance pensions based on the pay-as-you-go principle is that they compel the present generation of working age to provide pensions for the generation of their parents and grandparents, on the implied promise that the generation of their children and grandchildren will be compelled to provide pensions for them when they have retired. Such a scheme does not necessarily generate any savings. Any desired level of savings, however, can be produced through the operation of social insurance schemes, as is done with the retirement pension scheme in Canada, which has some of the consequences of occupational schemes.

The essence of occupational pension schemes, irrespective of whether they are contributory or non-contributory, is that the member is compelled to purchase a life endowment policy without having any discretion as to the type or terms of the policy, which is converted on his retirement into an annuity. The premiums paid under the life endowment policy normally accumulate until the member either dies or retires.

The savings generated by occupational schemes in all the ten countries are gross rather than net. The contributions of employers to approved schemes are allowable expenses for tax purposes and so are the contributions of members. If, for the purpose of illustration, it is assumed that companies pay tax at 40 per cent. on their profits and employees at 30 per cent. on their marginal earnings, and if contributions are shared equally between employers and employees, it follows that private pension funds receive a government subsidy of 35 per cent. of the contributions paid. The net private savings of the occupational plans are therefore the gross savings minus the government subsidy (the tax concession on contributions).

GERMANY AND AUSTRIA

History of German Pensions.   Germany was the first country to make public provisions for the maintenance of workers in old age and invalidity. An Act passed in 1889 set up a compulsory social insurance scheme for all manual workers who earned less than 40 marks a week. Old-age pensions were paid at the age of 70 as from 1891. The pension rate was assessed according to very complicated rules and was supplemented by a grant of 50 marks a year paid to all pensioners by the state. The scheme was financed by premiums which were a proportion of wages, averaging 1·7 per cent., and which were shared equally between employers and employees.

The pension scheme was conducted right from the start by autonomous bodies composed of equal numbers of 'masters and men'. (The co-operation of masters and men in these bodies was considered to have a good effect on the relations of the classes.) Under the close supervision of public authorities they administered complex procedures which were designed to meet the varying needs of individuals. The Germans have never had the preoccupation with simplicity which has often characterised social security provisions in the Anglo-Saxon countries.

In 1916 the pension age was lowered to 65 years and the premium raised to 2·6 per cent. of earnings. Five years earlier a separate pension scheme had been set up for non-manual employees. In the course of time the scope and organisation of pension provisions and especially the level of pension have changed greatly, but four characteristics have remained unaltered : the compulsory nature of insurance, the payment of pensions without an income or a means test, the variation of premiums and pensions with the level of the insured person's wages and the administration of the scheme by representatives of both employers and employees.

Since 1968 all employees have had to contribute to pension insurance; they themselves have been entitled to invalidity and old-age pensions and their surviving spouses and children have been entitled to widows' and orphans' pensions. Before that year non-manual employees earning more than a prescribed amount were exempt from pension insurance.

Pensions in the 1960s were administered under three different systems : one for manual workers, one for non-manual workers and one for miners. The administration of manual workers' pensions was the responsibility of 18 self-governing, autonomous bodies, each covering a geographical area (which often coincided with a Federal state) and two industry-wide bodies, one for the merchant navy and one for the railways.

The schemes for non-manual workers and miners were each administered by an autonomous body which covered the whole country. As from 1942 the schemes for manual workers and non-manual workers levied contributions at the same rate, subject to the same ceiling, and assessed pensions with the same formula. Thus in essentials the two systems operated as if they were one, although they remained separate entities, differing in the award of discretionary, non-monetary benefits, for example places in convalescent homes.

The Pension Formula. The pension rate was determined by a sophisticated formula which consisted of four components. The first of these was the personal element – the earnings of the claimant while in insured employment, expressed as a proportion of the average earnings of all manual and non-manual workers covered by compulsory insurance during the same years. Thus, if the average earnings of a claimant during his working life exceeded by 20 per cent. the average earnings of all insured persons over the same period, the personal element was 120 per cent.; if they were 20 per cent. below the average earnings, the personal element was 80 per cent. (The maximum personal element taken into account in assessing pensions was 200 per cent.)

The second component was the general earnings base – the average earnings of all employees covered by pension insurance in the first three of the four years before the pension claim was made. The earnings base for pensions which were claimed in 1970 was DM10,300, the average earnings of 1968 (DM10,800), 1967 (DM10,200) and 1966 (DM9,900).

The third component was the number of years for which the claimant had been in insured employment. In the case of claimants of old-age pensions in the 1960s this averaged about 35 years for men and 25 years for women. The minimum length of time in insured employment which gave entitlement to a pension was 180 months for an old-age pension and 60 months for an invalidity pension.

Persons under the age of 55 who claimed an invalidity pension were allowed to add to the years they had been in insured employment the years between the onset of the invalidity and the date of their 55th birthday. Thus a man who commenced work at the age of 18 and had an accident when he was 25 was deemed to have been insured for 37 years.

The fourth component was the statutory contingency percentage. This varied with the contingency – old age, type of invalidity (see below, p. 137), widowhood – and was meant to give a person who had been in insured employment throughout his working life a pension appropriate to the standard of living he had had while at work. The statutory percentage for an old-age or total invalidity pension was 1·5 and for a vocational invalidity pension 1·0.

The pension paid was the multiple of the four components. Thus the pension of a man who had worked for 35 years in insured employment (J), whose lifetime earnings averaged 125 per cent. of the average earnings of all insured persons (P), who claimed an old-age pension (S) in 1970 when the general earnings base was DM10,300 (B), was

$$J \times P \times B \times S = \frac{35 \times 125 \times 10,300 \times 3}{100 \times 200} = DM6,759$$

For the insured person whose earnings during his working life were the same as the average earnings of all insured persons, the pension was DM5,407. As the average gross earnings had risen to DM13,300 in 1970, an insured person with average earnings and average length of service who retired in that year received a pension equal to only 41 per cent. of current average gross earnings.

In theory the pension formula could provide insured persons with the 75 per cent. retirement pension which was normally received by public servants. This happened only when wages were stable (so that the earnings base was the same as the current gross earnings) and when the insured person had worked for 50 years, from the age of 15 to 65. Actually the earnings base in 1970 was only 78 per cent. of current gross earnings and the average duration of insurance only 35 years.

The pension formula provided a pension which was inflation-proof to the extent that the pension was not related to lifetime earnings but to the general level of wages in the four- to five-year period prior to retirement. However, as money wages increased by more than a third between 1966 and 1970, owing to a combination of rising prices and rising real wages, pensions were assessed on a base which lagged far behind current earnings. The formula was meant to relate the standard of living during working life to that in retirement. This did happen, but as salaried staff had pre-retirement earnings higher than average (revalued) earnings, their pensions were a lower proportion of pre-retirement pay than of (revalued) lifetime earnings. For manual workers the opposite was frequently the case. The pension was increased by one-tenth of the general earnings base (DM1,030 in 1970) for each dependent child under the age of 18 or under the age of 25 if still at school or college. There was no increase in respect of a dependent wife, but many wives received pensions in their own right.

Pension Adjustments. As from 1959 pensions in payment were annually adjusted by the same proportion as that by which the earnings base had increased in the previous year. Thus in 1969 pensions were adjusted by the increase in the general earnings base between 1967 and 1968, that is, between the increase in average earnings for the three years 1963–5 and the three years 1964–6. Pensions were not automatically adjusted, but each year a law proposing an adjustment was presented to parliament by the government after it had received a report from a statutory committee on the effect that such an adjustment would have on both the pension funds and the economy in general.

Early Pensions. A person who had been insured for at least 15 years was entitled to an old-age pension at 65; if he had been continuously unemployed for one whole year and still was unemployed he could claim an old-age pension at any time after 60. Women could claim a pension at any age after 60 if they had been in insured employment for most of the 20 years preceding the claim and had now retired. Pensions received at the normal retirement age of 65 were not subject to a retirement condition. Persons who had been working for a specified minimum period in mining could retire at an earlier age; they also received a higher pension.

Invalidity Pensions. There were two types of invalidity pension in Germany. One could be claimed on account of a reduction in earning capacity, due to sickness or accident, to less than half the amount which could be earned by a person of the same qualifications, knowledge and ability who was in good physical and mental health. This was designated the vocational invalidity pension. The other, the total invalidity pension, could be claimed by an insured person who was unable or virtually unable to earn a livelihood on account of a physical or mental disability and who was expected to remain in this position for the foreseeable future.

Financing of Pensions.   The cost of pensions relative to wage levels has increased very steeply over the last eighty years. In 1892 the combined contributions of employers and employees averaged 1·7 per cent. of earnings up to 40 marks a week. The subsidy of pensions out of general revenue at that time equalled about a third of pension expenditure. By 1950 the combined contribution, still shared equally between employers and employees, had increased to 10 per cent.; by 1969 it was 16 per cent. and in 1970 it was 17 per cent. The contribution paid out of general revenue to pension funds in the mid-1950s had amounted to about a third of expenditure on pensions, but this proportion declined to 16 per cent. in 1969 and to 15 per cent. in 1970. Between 1957 and 1969 the subsidy to pension funds declined from 12 per cent. to 8 per cent. of the Federal budget.

The development of the pension programme between 1955 and 1969 can be seen by considering the following data : while average earnings of manual and non-manual workers combined had increased by 160 per cent. and the subsidy to pension funds out of general revenue had increased by 180 per cent., the expenditure on pensions had increased by 530 per cent. This massive increase in pension expenditure was due partly to the fact that the number of pensions increased by half and partly to the steep increase in pension rates : old-age and invalidity pensions for manual workers increased by 220 per cent. and those for non-manual workers by 260 per cent. The old and the disabled thus had a faster increase in their standard of living during this period than those who were still working, in spite of the fact that the number of pensioners had increased simultaneously.

Income Redistribution.   The German pension insurance scheme involved virtually no element of vertical redistribution of income between income groups. There was a substantial redistribution of income over the life-span and between contingency groups, but redistribution was intentionally restricted to take place within rather than between income groups.

Rehabilitation. The German pension institutions were not only concerned with the award and payment of pensions but also had statutory duties in the field of rehabilitation. They were concerned with measures to maintain, improve and restore the earning capacity of insured persons and they even provided vocational training and retraining. The justification for these measures was that expenditure on health care and training which prevented the need for regular pension payments was in the interest of society as well as in that of the individual. The extent of the health-care activities of the pension institutions can be judged by the fact that in 1969 they provided 30,000 beds in a variety of convalescent homes and health institutions. Expenditure on health-care rehabilitation in that year was about 4 per cent. of the aggregate expenditure of the pension funds. A further 8 per cent. (an average of DM39 a month per pensioner) was paid to the sick funds for the provision of health services to pensioners.

Public Servants. In addition to the general pension scheme for employees there were four other statutory schemes, covering public servants, self-employed craftsmen, farmers and self-employed professional persons.

As in all other countries, the pension terms for public servants were the most generous. The minimum retirement pension was 35 per cent. of the final salary after ten years' service and this increased by 2 per cent. for each of the following 15 years and by 1 per cent. for each year thereafter, up to a maximum of 75 per cent. A public servant retiring after 35 years' service at the minimum retiring age of 62 would normally be entitled to the maximum pension. Public service pensions were adjusted whenever the pay scales of civil servants were altered.

Craftsmen. A pension scheme for self-employed craftsmen was first introduced in 1938. The craftsmen were given the option of joining the non-manual workers' pension scheme or buying a life endowment policy from a private insurance company. If they opted for the latter the premiums paid under the policy had to be at least equal to the contributions they would have paid under the public scheme. In 1962 this scheme was drastically remodelled. The option of buying private insurance was abolished and instead insurance under the manual workers' scheme became compulsory for all self-employed craftsmen, irrespective of their income. This gave entitlement to old-age, widows' and orphans' pensions on the same terms as applied to other insured persons, and to invalidity pensions on somewhat different terms, appropriate to the self-employed status of the craftsmen. This scheme differed, however, from the employee's scheme in two important respects. First, contribution to compulsory insurance was limited to 18 years, and second, contributions were not related to earnings but were at a flat rate, equal to the average contributions in the general pension scheme (DM153 a month in 1970), although lower ones could be paid in certain circumstances. The craftsmen's scheme thus restricted the old-age pension to 27 per cent. of what had been the average earnings of all insured men and women some three years earlier. The scheme was not meant to provide adequate minimum pensions but merely a base for the other arrangements self-employed craftsmen were expected to make for their retirement and survivors.

Farmers.   The farmers' pension scheme was amended several times in the twelve years following its introduction in 1927. All full-time farmers were covered by compulsory insurance. The status of a full-time farmer did not depend on the hours he worked on the farm but on whether his farm was of sufficient size to provide a man with full-time employment. Entitlement to an old-age pension was subject to three conditions : first, attainment of the age of 65; second, 15 qualifying years in the scheme; and third, retirement from the management of the farm. The last condition was usually fulfilled by the farm being either handed over to younger members of the family or sold. There were provisions for the payment of a pension at an earlier age in the case of invalidity, as long as a qualifying period of five years' insurance had been paid and the farm had been sold or handed over.

The pension was paid at uniform rates irrespective of the duration of insurance, the past income of the farmer and any means he had. The three rates current in 1969 were DM175 for a married man, DM115 for an unmarried man or woman and DM57·50 for a member of the family who had assisted on the farm. The married and unmarried rates had increased by almost 200 per cent. since the scheme was introduced in 1957, but even so the rate for a couple was barely half of the average pension paid to manual workers in 1969. The pension was originally meant to give the retired farmer spending money, as it was assumed that he received board and lodging from his family, who had taken over the farm.

The transitional rules giving entitlement to benefit were drawn up liberally so that large numbers of farmers qualified for pensions straight away. This fact, and the unfavourable age structure in farming, resulted in more than half a million pensions being paid while the number of contributors was only three-quarters of a million, The 2 :3 ratio of pensioners to contributors caused a financial imbalance. The modest contributions of DM27 a month from farmers and DM13·50 from members of families helping on the farm financed only a quarter of the expenditure on pensions; the remainder was met by the Federal government out of general tax revenue.

The farmers' pension scheme was administered by 18 self-governing, autonomous bodies each covering a particular area of the country. These bodies were authorised in 1965 to provide health care in order to maintain, improve and restore the working capacity of insured persons and in certain circumstances also that of their spouses or widows. The nature of the health care was similar to that provided by the manual workers' pension institutes, but a farmer could also claim a payment to enable him to employ a deputy while he was receiving the care.

The farmer's pension scheme had a dual purpose : to improve the standard of living of farmers in old age and invalidity and to encourage older occupiers to hand over their farms to younger people. In 1969 the Federal government introduced another scheme which provided pensions for occupiers of small, uneconomic units when they gave up farming. The 'farm vacators' pensions could be claimed at the age of 60 by occupiers who had been engaged full-time in farming for the previous five years and who had during that time contributed to the farmers' pension scheme. They could even be claimed at the age of 55 if the occupier had little or no prospect of finding employment in industry. They were paid at maximum rates of DM275 a month for couples and DM180 for unmarried persons. If the claimant was also entitled to an old-age pension it was deducted from the vacators' pension. These pensions were meant as an additional incentive to small occupiers to give up farming. The scheme was not permanent and claims were only accepted if made before 1973. The whole cost of the scheme, which was as much an economic measure aimed at agricultural reconstruction as a social security measure, was borne by the Federal government.

Professional Persons. Most of the 250,000 self-employed professional people were covered by one of three types of public pension provisions : compulsory insurance under the scheme for non-manual workers, continuation as voluntary contributors under the non-manual workers' scheme or compulsory membership of professional associations' pension funds under the laws and supervision of the state governments. (There were separate laws in each of the 11 states in the Federal Republic, but not necessarily for every profession in each state.)

Certain groups of self-employed professional people were included compulsorily in the non-manual workers' scheme because they were considered to require social security protection as much as employees. These groups included all private teachers, instructors, nurses, midwives, artistes, musicians and people in similar occupations. They paid the same contributions and received the same benefits as employees.

The groups of self-employed persons which were not subject to compulsory insurance included architects, consulting engineers, accountants, solicitors (in some states), actors and authors. Members of these professions who had been employees for at least five years in any ten-year period could become voluntary contributors to the non-manual workers' pension scheme. They had to pay in contributions 16 per cent. of their earnings up to the statutory ceiling and were entitled to the same benefits, pensions and health-care rehabilitation as employees.

The third group of self-employed professional people, which included medical and dental practitioners, veterinary surgeons, pharmacists, solicitors (in some states) and architects (in some states), had to belong to pension schemes which were set up by their professional associations under a state law. All members of these professions could apply to be exempted from contribution to the general employees' scheme and instead could voluntarily join the scheme of their professional association. The nature of these schemes varied widely. Contributions were assessed in some on net income, in some on gross income and in others were graded by age. The earnings ceilings for contributions and the contributions also varied, but not infrequently were of the same magnitude as those for non-manual workers. The benefits were equally diverse. The retirement age was often higher than the 65 of the employees' schemes. Some pensions were dynamic like those of the employees' schemes, while others remained unaltered after they had been awarded.

The complexity and variety of these schemes was remarkable. They were the result of long-established institutions which had been gradually built up over the years, set up by professional people who combined strong individualism with corporate loyalty and solidarity. Many of these institutions were not well adapted to the needs of the 1970s; to one outside observer there seems a strong case for rationalising the pension schemes for the self-employed.

Common Characteristics of German and Austrian Pensions. In Austria pension insurance for non-manual employees commenced at about the same time as in Germany, but a scheme for manual workers was only set up in 1939 during the German occupation. Since the end of the Second World War the Austrian general pension insurance scheme has developed along somewhat different lines from the German scheme, but they both still have many common characteristics. These include :

(1) the compulsory insurance of all employees except public servants;

(2) three separate pension systems – for manual workers, non-manual workers and miners;

(3) pensions for invalidity, old age, widows and orphans as part of the same scheme;

(4) benefits (with one relatively minor exception) and contributions assessed by the same formula and levied at much the same rate for manual and non-manual workers;

(5) contributions proportionate to wages up to a statutory ceiling and shared equally between employers and employees;

(6) the automatic adjustment of the statutory ceiling for changes in average earnings;

(7) the dynamic but not automatic adjustment of pensions in line with average earnings;

(8) the maintenance, restoration and improvement of earning capacity as the responsibility of the pension institutes;

(9) self-government – the management of the pension institutes by representatives of employers and employees.

Entitlement to Pensions in Austria. Old-age pensions were paid to men of 65 and to women of 60 who had retired and who had been in insured employment for at least 15 years, including at least 12 months in the previous 36 months. Pensions could be paid five years earlier to claimants who had received either unemployment or sickness benefit for 52 weeks during the preceding 13 months, or who had been in insured employment for a minimum of 35 years.

Disability pensions were paid to persons who had been in insured employment for not less than five years. A pension could be claimed by non-manual workers and skilled manual workers if their earning capacity had declined, owing to mental or physical impairment, to below half of what could be earned by a man of the same qualifications, experience and ability who was in good physical and mental health. (A plumber or a bank clerk would be entitled to disability pension if he could not earn at least half of what a plumber or a bank clerk normally earned). Unskilled workers could claim a pension if their earning capacity had declined, owing to mental or physical impairment, to less than half of what could be earned by an unskilled manual worker in good physical and mental health in regular employment. (An unskilled building worker who had earned a high wage would receive disability pension only if he could no longer earn at least half of what a low-paid unskilled worker would earn in any regular employment.) The criteria for the award of a disability pension were thus mainly economic rather than medical, and the degree of disability which entitled non-manual and skilled manual workers to a pension was less than that required by an unskilled manual worker.

The Pension Formula. The pension rate depended on the 'basis of assessment' and the reckonable years of insurance. The basis of assessment was normally the wage or salary received during the last 60 months, divided by 70. Any earnings in excess of the amount on which contributions were levied were not taken into account and earnings of past years were revalued. Insured persons could opt to have the earnings in the first 60 months after their 45th birthday as the basis of assessment.

In calculating the reckonable years of insurance, not only years spent in insured employment were taken into account but also years spent on national service and years worked as an employee before the manual workers' pension scheme was set up in 1939.

The monthly pension, which was paid fourteen times a year, was made up of three components. The first of these was the 'basic amount', which was 30 per cent. of the basis of assessment. The second was annual increments, which were 0·6 per cent. of the basis of assessment for each of the first ten reckonable years, 0·9 per cent. for each of the second ten years, 1·2 per cent. for each of the third ten years and 1·5 per cent. for each of the following 15 years. Thus a man who could count 30 insurance years received a pension of 57 per cent. of the basis of assessment, and one who could count 45 years (the maximum) received a pension of 79·5 per cent. The third component was a supplement which was given if the basic amount plus the annual increments came to less than 50 per cent. of the basis of assessment. The supplement was either 10 per cent. of the basis of assessment or the proportion of that sum which was required to bring the three components of the pension up to half that sum, whichever was the smaller. Thus for a man who could count 20 years' insurance the basic amount plus increments came to 45 per cent. and the supplement to 5 per cent. – a total pension of 50 per cent.; for a man who was invalided after ten years in insured employment the basic amount plus increments came to 36 per cent. and the supplement to 10 per cent. – a total pension of 46 per cent.

Pensions were increased in respect of three factors. First, for each dependent child there was an increase of 5 per cent. of the basis of assessment or Sch76 (in 1969) a month, whichever was the greater. Second, a degree of disability which required constant attendance by another person gave entitlement to an allowance equal to half of the pension but not less than Sch575 or more than Sch1,150 a month. Third, pensioners whose total income, including the pension but excluding family and rent allowances, was below prescribed limits received an equalisation allowance to bring their income up to these limits, which in 1969 were Sch1,217 a month plus Sch473 for a wife and Sch132 for each child. For a single pensioner the limit was about 23 per cent. of the standard wage.

The ceiling for pension contributions was automatically adjusted each year. It varied with the proportionate change in earnings between the second and the third year before the year in which the adjustment took place. Thus in 1969 the ceiling was increased by the proportionate increase in earnings between 1966 and 1967. The pensions in payment, the equalisation allowances and the minimum increase for dependent children were also adjusted annually, by a method very similar to that used in Germany.

Financing of Pensions. The pension scheme was financed by contributions of 17 per cent. of earnings up to Sch7,200 a month (16·5

per cent. for non-manual workers); if special bonuses had been paid
the average total earnings taken into account could reach Sch8,400
a month. The Federal government subsidised the pension institutes
normally by about 28 per cent. of their expenditure excluding
equalisation payments, but in 1969 the subsidy was restricted to the
difference between the income and the expenditure of the institutes.
It also reimbursed them in full for the equalisation allowances which
they had awarded. Sickness insurance contributions for pensioners
were paid by the pension institutes and in 1969 amounted to 9·2
per cent. of the aggregate expenditure on pensions.

Public Servants.   In addition to the general pension scheme there
were three special schemes covering public servants, the self-
employed and farmers. All three provided old-age, invalidity, widows'
and orphans' pensions. The scheme for public servants was by far
the most generous. They received a maximum pension of 80 per cent.
of their final salary on retiring at the age of 60 after 35 years' service;
after only ten years' service their pension was 40 per cent. of their
final salary.

Self-Employed Persons.   Most groups of self-employed persons were
covered by a compulsory pension insurance scheme as from 1958
which was in most respects very similar to that for employees. The
common features were : the assessment of pensions according to the
three components, the equalisation and constant attendance allowances, the increases in respect of dependent children, the revaluation
of past earnings and the adjustment of contribution ceilings and of
pensions after they had been awarded. There were also some differences – in the qualifying period for entitlement to pensions, in the
method for determining the basis of assessment and in the definition
of invalidity. The contribution of insured self-employed persons in
1969 was 8·5 per cent. of their earnings of three years previously
(that is, of earnings in 1966) up to the statutory ceiling. The Federal
government reimbursed the pension institutes for the expenditure
on equalisation allowances and granted them a subsidy of the
difference between their income and expenditure. Part of this subsidy
was derived from an appropriation out of the proceeds of the trade
tax (which was levied on the self-employed). One peculiarity of the
pension scheme for the self-employed was that it provided for higher
pensions if retirement was postponed beyond 65. Those who retired

at 75 received a pension which was 40 per cent. higher than the one they would have received had they retired at 65.

Farmers. A compulsory pension scheme for farmers started in 1958. It was normal practice for a self-employed farmer to have a contract with his successor which ensured that the former owner would have his board and lodging provided for him on the farm when he retired, or in the event of his becoming an invalid. The pension was therefore meant to provide spending money rather than a means of subsistence. The maximum pension in 1969 was only Sch220 a month (twice that if he was a married man) after 35 years of reckonable insurance. The contributions levied on farmers were not proportionate to their income but an annual flat rate, which was Sch550 in 1969.

The general pension scheme and the schemes for the self-employed and farmers made provision for increasing the pension by voluntary contributions. The level of these monthly contributions could be determined by the insured person, but was not to be less than Sch30 or more than Sch600. The increase in invalidity and old-age pensions was 1 per cent. a month of the total sum paid in contributions. These higher pensions were adjusted for changes in earnings in the same way as all other pensions, and the contributions paid were revalued in the same way as were earnings for the basis of assessment.

DENMARK AND THE NETHERLANDS

History of Danish Pensions. Denmark was the first country, in 1892, to pay non-contributory pensions, following Germany which a few years earlier had introduced a contributory old-age pension scheme. The pensions were paid at the remarkably early age of 60 to men and women of good character who had lived in Denmark for the five years immediately before applying for the pension without receiving poor-law relief. There was no fixed pension rate; payment in cash or kind (food or fuel) was meant to be sufficient for maintenance and was determined according to the means and circumstances of each applicant, at the discretion of the pension authority.

The original Danish pension scheme was more in the nature of public assistance than what would now be called a pension. It was all the same an important break with the past, as the receipt of the pension was not accompanied by any of the moral stigma and legal disadvantages which in those days were always associated with the receipt of poor-law relief. The cost of the pension was borne by the local authorities, who were reimbursed for half their expenditure by the state. In the early part of the twentieth century about a quarter of pensioners received only payments in kind.

Friis's Four Principles.   Friis suggests that four principles have characterised social security measures in Denmark.[3] The first of these was universal coverage irrespective of employment status. In this respect Denmark had much in common with New Zealand and Australia but differed from Germany and the U.K. (except for non-contributory old-age and blind pensions), where benefits in general (up to 1948 in the U.K.) were restricted to employees. The second principle was the exclusion of persons with higher incomes. This was by no means a unique principle, but the normal practice in all countries up to the 1940s. The third was the financing of pensions and benefits mainly out of public revenue and only to a very limited extent from employers' and insured persons' contributions. (In 1968 employers' contributions amounted to only 4 per cent. of total social security expenditure and insured persons' contributions to only 15 per cent.) Here again there was much similarity with New Zealand and Australia and very little with Germany, the U.K. (excluding health services) and, at a later stage, the U.S.A. The last of Friis's principles was administrative decentralisation. In this respect Denmark was similar to most countries in Continental Europe but differed from the Anglo-Saxon countries, where administration was normally central. Pensions in Denmark were administered by the welfare boards of municipalities and village councils, as opposed to the German and Austrian practice of self-governing, autonomous bodies.

Special Features.   Several features of Danish old-age pensions are of special interest. Pensions were adjusted automatically according to the cost of living from the 1930s onwards. The minimum age for pensions was increased twice after the end of the Second World War : in 1947 from the original 60 years to 65 years (60 for single women and the wives of disability and old-age pensioners) and again in 1957, over a transitional period of four years, to 67 (62 for single women and under-age wives). Prior to 1963 the pension rates in country areas were lower than in town areas (the biggest difference being, in 1956, about a quarter).

The Pension Formula. Until 1956 the non-contributory old-age pension was confined to old people with small incomes or no income at all, through the operation of a means test. After that date everybody (except public servants) who satisfied the residence and nationality tests could receive a minimum pension at the age of 67, irrespective of their income. This pension for a married couple was equal to about 9 per cent. of the average wage of an industrial worker. The basic full pension remained subject to an income test as previously. The minimum pension was meant to be the first step towards proper flat-rate subsistence pensions as demogrants. The arguments advanced in favour of national superannuation were similar to those put forward in other countries : the complicated procedure of the means test, the alleged discouragement of saving for old age, the indignity of having to divulge one's personal affairs to the pension authorities and the contrast between the favourable superannuation terms of public servants and the stringent terms for the meagre provisions given to ordinary citizens.

Index-Related Savings. The attempt to provide citizens with some of the advantages of civil service pensions led to the introduction of the Index-Related Insurance and Savings for Old Age Act, 1956. This made it possible for persons between the ages of 18 and 57 (52 for single women) to make 'index contracts' with banks and insurance companies for annuities from the age of 67. The maximum annual payment (premiums) under such contracts was limited to Kr2,000 a year. The premiums as well as the sums insured were subject to cost-of-living adjustments. Thus if prices had increased by 40 per cent. between the date of insurance and the payment of the annuity, Kr140 was due for each Kr100 of annuity which had been purchased. Similarly, contractual annual payments were adjusted whenever prices increased. The premiums paid could be deducted from gross income to arrive at taxable income, while the annuities were taxable like any other income. The deficit under these contracts resulting from price inflation was borne by the exchequer. The measure proved popular with salaried and self-employed persons and in recent years has become increasingly expensive.

Changes in the 1960s. In 1964 a law was passed which provided for the progressive relaxation of the earnings rule for persons who had attained the age of 67 and gave entitlement as from 1970 to basic old-age pensions for all who had reached that age irrespective of their income. In special circumstances, such as ill-health, old-age pensions could be paid to men and women at 60. For all pensioners below 67, however, the income test was retained.

Special Allowances. The basic pension could be increased by a number of allowances : pensioners who had no other (or virtually no other) income had their health insurance contributions paid by the local welfare boards and received a small supplement (which in 1968–9 was Kr1,320 and was received by more than half of all pensioners); an old-age allowance of $5\frac{1}{2}$ per cent. of the basic pension was awarded to persons aged 80 or more; a marriage supplement (Kr924 in 1968–9) was paid in respect of pensioners' wives if they were not entitled to a pension; for persons who postponed claiming a pension for three or five years beyond the age of 67 the pension rate was increased by 10 per cent. or 15 per cent. respectively.

Pension Levels and Expenditure. In 1960 the pension for a single person with no other income was equivalent to 31 per cent. of the average net earnings of a male industrial worker; by early 1969 this proportion had increased to 40 per cent. When both spouses were eligible for a pension they normally received a sum equal to one and a half times the pension paid to a single person. If only one of them was entitled to a pension he or she received a marriage supplement, which increased the total pension by only 11 per cent.

Old-age pensions were the major issue in Danish social security policy throughout the 1950s and 1960s. In writing about policies for old age during this period, Friis says 'major changes in principles and legislation have been introduced nearly every year'. The effect of all these changes was to make pensions available to more old people and to increase the standard of living compared with that of wage-earners, of those pensioners who had little other income.

The combination of the increase in pensions relative to wages, the increase in the proportion of old people becoming entitled to pensions and the rising proportion of old people in the population resulted in an increasingly large share of national income being devoted to old-age pensions. The proportion was 2·6 per cent. in 1954, 3·7 per cent. in 1960 and 4·5 per cent. in 1968. Up to 1956 all expenditure on old-age pensions was met out of government or local authority revenue; after that date the minimum old-age pension was partly financed through a special income-tax. This was levied in 1969 on taxable income at the rate of 3 per cent. and amounted to about a third of the expenditure on all old-age pensions. The flat-rate pension was thus partly financed by a uniform proportionate tax.

Labour-Market Pensions. The Labour Market Supplementary Pension Act, 1964, provided for all employees industrial ('labour-market') pensions in addition to national old-age pensions. These pensions were financed by flat-rate contributions from employers and employees. The annual contribution was Kr260, of which two-thirds was paid by the employer. The maximum pension after a transitional period of 27 years will be Kr2,400 in 1991. Up to 1969 the expenditure on pensions under this scheme was quite small and so were the pensions paid, but the contributions collected resulted in the accumulation of quite substantial funds. The pensions were fixed sums and there were no provisions, as there were under the national old-age pension scheme, for an annual adjustment in line with changes in the earnings index.

Disability Pensions. Disability pensions were first introduced in 1922, under a social insurance scheme, but have been a non-contributory benefit since 1960. After a major amendment in 1965 the scheme covered all Danish citizens between 15 and 67 and was financed mainly out of general tax revenue. Pensions were granted in the case of permanent incapacity for work and consisted of three components which were combined to provide the scale rates. The basic component was the same amount as the basic old-age pension; it was subject to a means test and if income exceeded certain prescribed limits there was no entitlement to the basic component. The other two components – disability and unemployability – were both paid at half the basic component rate and neither was subject to an income test. Persons who were totally and permanently incapacitated qualified for a maximum pension which consisted of all three components (basic, disability and unemployability) and thus equalled twice the basic old-age pension. Persons whose earning capacity was permanently reduced by at least two-thirds qualified for a medium pension, consisting of the basic and the disability components, and thus received a pension which was one and a half times the basic old-age pension. Those whose earning capacity was permanently reduced by at least half were eligible for the minimum pension, which was made up of half of both the basic and the disability components and which thus equalled three-quarters of the basic old-age pension.

A disability pension was payable to all persons whose earning capacity was permanently reduced by at least half, irrespective of their employment status or income. If a man with a substantial income became totally incapacitated, he was entitled to the disability and unemployability components, and if his earning capacity was reduced by half he qualified for half the disability component. Pensions were paid not only to disabled employees and self-employed persons but also to housewives who were incapable of, or severely handicapped in, undertaking normal housework.

Disability pensioners in receipt of maximum or medium pensions also qualified for certain supplementary allowances : a pension supplement (Kr1,320 in 1968–9), a marriage allowance (Kr924 in 1968–9) and children's allowances (about Kr2,000 in 1968–9). The pension supplement was intended for pensioners who had no other, or virtually no other, income and it was therefore subject to a very stringent income test. Pensioners who were incapable of caring for themselves could claim a constant attendance allowance. This was paid irrespective of the pensioner's income at one of two rates – 50 per cent. or 100 per cent. of the basic component – depending on the amount of attendance required.

In the 1960s disability pensions improved even more than old-age pensions relative to earnings. In 1960 the pension for a totally and permanently disabled man or woman who had no income other than the pension was equivalent to 35 per cent. of the average net earnings of a male industrial worker. By early 1969 this proportion had increased to 73 per cent. The corresponding proportions for a married man with two dependent children were 55 per cent. in 1960 and 82 per cent. in 1969. Over the decade the number of disability pensioners increased from 72,000 to 107,000, mainly on account of the amendment to the law in 1965 which considerably extended the classes of persons who qualified for a pension. As a result of the larger number of pensioners and the increase in pension rates, expenditure on disability pensions increased from 0·6 per cent. of national income in 1954 to 1·0 per cent. in 1960 and 1·9 per cent. in 1968.

The large numbers of invalidity pensioners – 23 per 1,000 compared with New Zealand's 3 per 1,000 – can be partly explained by three factors. Because the incidence of invalidity increases rapidly with age, two important factors were : first, the replacement of invalidity pensions with old-age pensions at the age of 67 in Denmark, as opposed to 60 in New Zealand; and second, the less favourable age composition of the population in Denmark (more people above middle age). A third factor was that pensions in Denmark were paid to all irrespective of other income, if their earning capacity was reduced by one-half or more, while in New Zealand they were available only to those who were totally and permanently incapacitated and even then only subject to an income test[4].

Denmark and the Netherlands were the only two among the ten countries in which the invalidity pension for the severely disabled was substantially greater than the old-age pension. This resulted in a reduction of income when disability pensioners reached retirement age. The number of pensioners in Denmark who were in this position was reduced by a rule which provided that after the age of 60 disability pensions could not normally be awarded or changed to a higher or lower scale. It was, all the same, possible to award a claimant over 60 a medium pension if he or she was absolutely incapable of earning any income.

Any change in the nature of the disability of a pensioner meant that his pension was reassessed and it could result in a transfer from one scale to another. However, if a pensioner's disability remained more or less unchanged but his earnings increased, the pension was not normally affected as long as his earnings did not exceed twice the basic component of the pension. The pension's stability was an important inducement to rehabilitation.

History of Dutch Pensions. Statutory provision for old people commenced in the Netherlands in 1913, rather later than in most other countries of Western Europe. The first pension was non-contributory and was paid at the rate of Fl2 a week to people over 70 who had worked as employees for three years after the age of 60; it was increased by half for a married man. In 1919 a contributory pension scheme began. The Disability Act, which became fully operative in that year, imposed on employers the obligation to buy weekly insurance stamps for their employees, which entitled them to modest old-age, invalidity, widows' and orphans' pensions. Neither the 1913 Act nor the Disability Act made any provisions for self-employed persons, who at that time were a substantial proportion of the working population.

A general old-age pension scheme, such as had operated since before the First World War in the U.K., Ireland, Germany, New Zealand and Australia, started in the Netherlands only after the Second World War. This was a non-contributory pension scheme which was introduced as a temporary measure in 1947. It provided all Dutch citizens with pensions at the age of 65, irrespective of their economic status.

The General Old Age Pension Act, 1957, put the provision of old-age pensions on a permanent basis. As from that year, social insurance pensions were financed on the assessment principle. Contributions were levied on all recipients of income aged between 15 and 65 and were collected by the income-tax authorities. In 1969 the contribution for old-age pensions was 9·1 per cent. of taxable income (plus 1·5 per cent. for widows' and orphans' pensions) up to a statutory ceiling of Fl17,450 a year. The contributions from employees were deducted from their wages, but they paid the whole of the contributions without any share being borne by the employers.

Financing of Pensions.   The scheme was subsidised out of general taxation by Fl202 million a year, about 5 per cent. of the total expenditure. This subsidy and the statutory ceiling for contributions were adjusted annually according to changes in the general wage index. The contribution proportion was reassessed every few years in order to make certain that the income of the Old Age Pension Fund approximated to its expenditure. The fund was controlled by the Social Insurance Bank, which administered the scheme. A third of the directors of the bank were appointed by the Minister of Social Affairs and Public Health, a third by employers' organisations and a third by employees' organisations.

Pension Levels.   Flat-rate pensions were paid to all citizens at 65 without any retirement condition. In 1969 the pension was Fl3,744 a year for a single person and Fl5,358 for a married couple, 30 per cent. and 43 per cent. respectively of the standard wage. The pensions were adjusted automatically when the wage index varied by more than 3 per cent. in six months. When the scheme began the full pension was paid to all Dutch citizens who had lived in the Netherlands for six years after their 59th birthday. There was a reduction of 2 per cent. in the pension for each year after 1957 for which no contributions had been paid. On the death of a married person the full pension at the married rate was paid to the surviving spouse for five months; thereafter he or she received the pension at the single person's rate.

Income Redistribution. The Netherlands' provisions for old age – flat-rate pensions financed by proportionate contributions on incomes up to a relatively high ceiling – brought about a vertical redistribution of incomes up to the level of the statutory ceiling. The degree of redistribution was of about the same order as that in Denmark and New Zealand, where pensions were financed out of general taxation. The expenditure on national old-age pensions was about 4·9 per cent. of the national income.

Other Pension Schemes. As in the other countries covered in this survey, public servants in the Netherlands received pensions on very favourable terms. After 40 years' service the pension was normally 70 per cent. of the salary immediately preceding retirement. Public service pensions, which incorporated the general old-age pension, were adjusted annually for changes in the earnings index.

Since 1949 the Minister of Social Affairs and Public Health has been empowered to make membership of an industry-wide scheme compulsory for all employees working in that industry. This power was exercised to compel a minority of employers and employees to participate in the scheme set up by the collective labour agreement to which they were not parties. In two-thirds of all industries the minister had made membership of industry-wide insurance compulsory for all employees. The conduct of these schemes was subject to government regulations and supervision, but they were not subsidised, nor were the payments guaranteed by the state. The contributions paid by employers and employees, as well as the amount and the assessment of the pension, varied between industries.

Disability Pensions. In 1967 the provisions for long-term disability in the Netherlands were completely reorganised and greatly improved. The new insurance scheme covered all employees, except public servants and the staff of the railway company, who had similar schemes of their own. Contributions were levied on all wages and salaries up to Fl89 a day at the rate of 5·1 per cent. in 1969. One-quarter of the contributions were paid by employees and the remainder by the employers.

The long-term disability scheme, like the sickness benefit scheme, was administered by the occupational associations. Benefit was paid after a waiting period of 52 weeks (during which insured persons were entitled to claim sickness benefit) in compensation for total or partial inability to earn as much as could be earned by an able-bodied person of the same age, sex and skills. The amount of disability benefit was related to the degree of a claimant's incapacity and to his previous earnings; it was adjusted for movements in the wage index. No benefit was paid for an incapacity assessed at less than 15 per cent. There were seven benefit grades corresponding to different degrees of disability. Benefit of 40 per cent. of previous earnings (up to a ceiling of Fl89 a day) was paid for a disability assessed at 45-55 per cent., while for a disability of 80 per cent. or more the benefit was 80 per cent. Benefit was increased to 100 per cent. if the beneficiary was totally disabled and required regular attendance and nursing. All beneficiaries were paid a holiday allowance equal to 6 per cent. of the benefit received in the previous year. The award of benefit was independent of other income. It ceased at the age of 65, when beneficiaries became entitled to the old-age pension.

Comparison of Disability Schemes.   In the Netherlands, as in Denmark, disability benefit for severely disabled persons was substantially greater than the old-age pension. Thus in 1969, while the maximum normal disability benefit was Fl19,600[5] a year and the standard wage-earner's disability benefit Fl10,600, the old-age pension was only Fl3,744 for a single person.

While in Denmark some components of the disability pension were demogrants and others means-tested, in the Netherlands compensation for inability to earn was an insurance benefit restricted to employees; it was not available to the self-employed, those incapacitated from birth or housewives. At the same time the minimum degree of disability which gave entitlement to benefit – 16 per cent. – was exceptionally low; it was 50 per cent. in Denmark, Germany and Austria, 85 per cent. in Australia and 100 per cent. in New Zealand.

NEW ZEALAND AND AUSTRALIA

History of New Zealand Pensions.   New Zealand in 1898 was the second country in the world (preceded only by Denmark) to introduce non-contributory old-age pensions. The scheme provided a pension of $36 a year on the basis of a means test for men and women aged 65 years and over who had lived in the colony for at least 25 years. In 1969 the scheme still retained its original purpose – the relief of need among the old – and its main features were unchanged. There had, however, been several important alterations, most of which related to specific provisions. The pension had been renamed *age benefit,* the minimum age reduced to 60, the residence qualification lowered to 20 years and the means test replaced by an income test. Under-age wives, moreover, could now claim benefit and single persons were granted higher benefit rates than married persons.

Deterioration of Pension Levels.   In 1969 the benefit was $13.25 a week for a single person and $24 for a married couple, the latter being equivalent to 41 per cent. of the standard wage. The level of benefit deteriorated in relation to earnings between 1946 and 1970 : the rate of benefit trebled while average earnings quadrupled. In the five-year period 1946-50 the age benefit for a married couple averaged 61 per cent. of average earnings, but in the following three five-year periods this proportion declined progressively, first by 5, then 1, then 4 per cent. Between 1966 and 1970 it was only 49 per cent. During these twenty-five years the Consumer Price Index increased by 170 per cent., with the result that the purchasing power of benefit rose by a mere 11 per cent. The deterioration in the benefit level can also be illustrated by using a different set of figures : it so happened that the number of age beneficiaries was 103,000 in both 1944 and 1971, but between these years the expenditure on age benefit as a proportion of national income declined from 2·16 per cent. to 1·40 per cent.

Invalidity Pensions.   Means-tested invalidity pensions were introduced in 1936 for persons above the age of 16 who were totally blind or permanently incapacitated for work because of accident, illness or congenital defect. The conditions for the award of these pensions (also renamed benefits) have always been similar to those for the award of age benefit. Thus both since 1945 have had the same level of benefit, the same residence qualification and the same income test. The number of beneficiaries has always been relatively small and since 1953 has never exceeded 9,000 persons – 0·6 per cent. of the population aged 16 to 59 years.

The Royal Commission on Social Security recommended a liberalisation of the conditions of award of invalidity benefit :

> We recommend that : . . . The Act be amended to make it clear that invalidity benefits may be granted when there is a severe disablement but the incapacity for work is less than total.[6]

The Commission recognised that social security benefits cannot serve equally the conflicting aims of replacing the income of people who are unemployed and encouraging them to earn money by working. They considered that for the severely disabled the aim of rehabilitation should take precedence over the general principle of relieving need; they therefore recommended that :

> The Department [of Social Security] be given authority in cases where a person is assessed as being severely and permanently incapacitated to determine a special individual level up to which the beneficiary's earnings will be disregarded in the assessment of 'other income' so that the beneficiary will have a positive incentive to rehabilitation.[7]

Both these recommendations would benefit a small group of severely handicapped people at little additional expense.

Superannuation Benefit. The Parliamentary Select Committee which was set up in 1938 to examine the proposed establishment of a national health and superannuation scheme had recommended that the government should consider a gradual liberalisation of the means test for old-age pension with the ultimate object of having superannuation pensions as a demogrant. This recommendation was not accepted by the government; instead universal superannuation benefits were introduced in 1940. These were paid to all persons above the age of 65, without a means or an income test, but subject to the same residence qualifications as age benefit. At its inception the rate of superannuation benefit was only $20 per annum and it was intended that this should be progressively increased by $5 a year until the level was the same as that of age benefit; parity was to be attained by 1968, but it was actually achieved in 1960.

The Labour government in 1938 had expected that it would be possible at some future date to replace the selective age benefit at 60 with universal superannuation at the same age. In support of this they argued that, first, at a certain age people were entitled to benefit by virtue of their past contributions to tax revenue and production, irrespective of their means, and second, strong opposition to the traditional means test encouraged the belief that need could be assumed from the fact of age.

Age Benefit. The position in 1969 was that unmarried women over 55 unable to undertake regular work and all people over 60 were entitled to age benefit if they satisfied the residence qualification and the income test; all persons over 65 were entitled to superannuation benefit on satisfying the residence qualification only. Age benefit thus did not cease at the age of 65; on the contrary, three-quarters of age beneficiaries were above that age and as many as 31 per cent. of all persons over 65 preferred age to superannuation benefit. Age benefit had three advantages over superannuation benefit : first, it was not taxable; second, on the death of the beneficiary there was a payment to the surviving spouse (of three months' benefit); and third, there was an allowance for an under-age wife.

The income test for age benefit was by no means stringent. The Royal Commission found '. . . little evidence to suggest that income-tested benefits . . . significantly discourage working or saving, or undermine individual initiative'.[8] Referring to 1971, they stated :

> . . . it is possible for potential beneficiaries to build up large assets without affecting the amount of benefit payable to them . . . an age beneficiary, for example, may have a debt-free house *plus* one or more cars *plus* unlimited personal effects *plus* approximately $10,000 worth of investments earning $6\frac{1}{2}$ per cent. a year, without either his eligibility for the benefit or the amount of the benefit being affected.[9]

The Royal Commission considered that an allowable income equal to the rate of benefit was excessive and remarked :

> One simply cannot have an equitable selective social security system based on the elimination of need unless all three relevant income support factors – the benefit, the allowable income level, and the rate of benefit abatement – are considered together, and unless one carefully examines the relationship between the total attainable incomes of beneficiaries and those of working non-beneficiaries . . .[10]

This reasoning led the Commission to recommend an increase in benefit rates, a reduction in allowable income levels and a reduction in benefit abatement. For reasons to which reference has already been made, the Commission was opposed to earnings-related benefits and favoured rates which would enable beneficiaries to maintain standards of living not markedly different from those of the rest of the community. With this object in view they also recommended that benefits be related to both the ruling rate of wages paid to building and engineering labourers and the lower quartile level of adult male earnings. The benefit for married persons was to be set close to 80 per cent. of these earnings after payment of income tax. The benefit for unmarried persons was to be 60 per cent. of the married rate. The Commission considered that benefit rates should be reviewed at least once a year, but did not favour a formula of automatic adjustment. They did not think that the review of benefits should be removed from the political arena.

Supplementary Assistance.   Since 1951 supplementary assistance has been available to social security beneficiaries and others. The object of this assistance was to compensate beneficiaries for certain extra living costs (such as high rent, but not those due to family size and composition, which were already taken into account in determining the benefit rate). A minimum tolerable standard of living for all was aimed at, based on the 'belonging' and 'participating' principles; those who, because of special costs, could not reach this standard with the basic benefit rate were to be helped to do so with supplementary assistance.

The award of assistance was subject to a means test, which covered property and capital as well as income. Assets beyond a prescribed amount which were readily convertible into cash without an undue reduction in living standards were taken into consideration in determining both eligibility for and the rate of assistance. Other capital and property was valued and assumed to yield an income at a prescribed rate, which could be higher than that which the assets were actually earning. A formula was applied in determining the 'assessed living cost' (calculated to cover all daily living expenses except the cost of accommodation). However, the amount of assets disregarded, the rate at which capital and property were assumed to yield interest and the formula used to determine living costs were all unpublished and unknown even to the claimant.

In reviewing the operation of supplementary assistance the Royal Commission noted the widespread criticism of the secrecy in which the scheme was administered but, without any discussion or elucidation, accepted the view of the Department of Social Security that there were many arguments against revealing the administration procedures. This reflects an attitude which is quite common among administrators of poor law and public assistance, but quite incompatible with enlightened social policy in the 1970s.

In March 1969 some 13,000 continuing grants of supplementary assistance were in force. The maximum paid was normally $3·50 a week for single persons and $5 for married couples. More than three-quarters of all grants were paid to invalids and old persons. 10 per cent. of all invalidity benefit, 8 per cent. of all age benefits and less than 1 per cent. of all superannuation benefits were increased with supplementary grants.

History of Australian Pensions. New South Wales introduced in 1900 a non-contributory old-age pension scheme which followed closely the precedent set by New Zealand two years earlier. Both schemes had the same minimum pensionable age and the same residential qualification. Their pensions were moreover both paid at standard rates under clearly defined rules and did not depend on the exercise of discretion by officials or committees. Claimants who did not qualify for the maximum pension received a lower rate which was assessed according to statutory rules. The attempt to distinguish between deserving and undeserving persons under both schemes led to the exclusion of three groups of persons, described in almost identical terms : those who had not led a sober and reputable life during the five years before applying for a pension, those who had deserted their spouse or children for six months or more at any time, and those who had been imprisoned for specific periods. Further similarities between the two schemes were evident in their respective means tests, which had many common features.

The two schemes did, however, differ in three respects. First, the standard pension rate in New South Wales was $52 a year, nearly 45 per cent. higher than that in New Zealand. Second, in New Zealand the pension of a couple both of whom were pensioners was twice that of a single person, whereas in New South Wales it was only one and a half times as much. This made the pension of such a couple only 11 per cent. higher in New South Wales than it was in New Zealand. Third, an old-age pension was granted in New South Wales to a man or woman aged between 60 and 65 who was otherwise qualified for the pension and 'unable from physical unfitness to earn his own living', whereas in New Zealand there was no such provision.

A non-contributory invalidity pension scheme was introduced in New South Wales in 1907 – earlier than anywhere else. This provided pensions to invalids over the age of 16 years at the same rates and virtually on the same conditions as old-age pensions. The definition of invalidity was very restrictive. A claimant had to show that he was 'permanently incapacitated for work'. He also had to have resided in New South Wales for five years before he was eligible for a pension. He was not, however, required to prove that he was of good moral character. While old-age pensions were awarded on the basis of a means test, which covered the income and property of the claimant and his spouse, the claimant of invalidity pension had also to show that his close relatives did not adequately maintain him. This was not a family means test proper as the claimant only had to show that they 'did not' maintain him, not that they were unable to do so.

New Zealand and Australia in their old-age and invalidity legislation pioneered a new type of social security provision. They did not subsidise the funds of the trade unions or friendly societies, as did Denmark and the Netherlands, or set up social insurance schemes, as did Germany and Austria, but introduced provisions which gave entitlement to pensions financed out of general revenue to persons who satisfied prescribed statutory conditions. This policy was not adopted without much controversy and dissension. In fact, New South Wales in 1908 passed the Subventions for Friendly Societies Act, which was based on premises quite different from those of the Invalidity and Accident Pension Act of the previous year. The main provision of the 1908 Act was the subsidising of friendly societies from tax revenue to reimburse them in part for the benefits they paid to members who had been sick for more than a year. The subsidy was assessed to equal the cost of all benefit paid to men over 65 and women over 60, plus half the benefit paid to younger members.

The purpose of these provisions was to encourage self-help and prudence, but the effect, like that of all schemes of this type, was to assist men in regular work at relatively high wages; those whose needs were greatest – labourers, casual workers, persons with congenital disabilities – were helped least. Grants of this nature, however, remained an isolated occurrence. There was no other state or Federal legislation passed after the New South Wales Act, subsidising cash benefits paid by non-statutory bodies.

Victoria and Queensland had also introduced old-age pensions before 1908 when the Commonwealth Invalidity and Old Age

Pension Act replaced all state legislation in that field. This Act followed closely the New South Wales legislation and also incorporated some amendments in means-tested provisions which had been made in the New Zealand Old Age Pension Act, 1905. It is of interest to note that the Commonwealth Act, unlike the New South Wales scheme, provided the same rate of pension for single and married persons. It contained moreover a provision, which came into force in 1910, to lower the minimum pensionable age of women to 60. Both these measures were of great benefit to older couples. Between 1908 and 1910 the pension received by couples resident in New South Wales had doubled for some and increased for all by at least one-third, while the pension for single men (including widowers) remained unaltered.

The main characteristics of Australian age and invalidity pension schemes, like those of New Zealand, changed only little in their first sixty years, although the details were changed frequently. Contributory pensions and universal superannuation pensions were much discussed and at times widely canvassed, but did not find their way on to the statute book.

Entitlement, Pension Levels and Supplementary Assistance. In 1969 age pensions were payable to men of 65 and over and to women of 60 and over who had lived in Australia for at least ten years. Invalidity pensions were payable to persons aged 16 and over who were permanently incapacitated for work to the extent of at least 85 per cent. or permanently blind. For incapacity or blindness which occurred outside Australia the residence qualification was the same as for the age pension; otherwise it was five years. The maximum standard rate of both pensions was $15 a week for a single person and $26·50 a week for a married couple (when both were receiving a pension), the latter being equal to 32 per cent. of the standard wage. Pensions were increased by an allowance of $7 a week for the dependent wife of an invalidity pensioner, but the age pensioner received this allowance only if his wife was not in receipt of a pension and either had the care of a dependent child or was permanently incapacitated.

All pensions except those paid to blind persons were subject to a means test. This was not unduly severe : assets disregarded in the assessment included the pensioner's house, car, furniture and personal effects, as well as any income from property or gifts from relatives.

The means assessed were his annual income plus $2 for each complete $20 of his net property above $400. The rate of pension was reduced by half of the amount by which the means assessed exceeded $520.[11] A single (widowed or divorced) pensioner who had no other income could thus have savings of $5,600 and still receive the maximum standard rate of pension; if his savings were £20,000 he could still be entitled to a small pension of $60 a year. Single (widowed or divorced) pensioners who paid rent or had to pay for board and lodging could also claim a supplementary allowance of up to $2 a week subject to a means test. This was awarded at the maximum rate to pensioners whose assessed means did not exceed $1 a week and it was not available to pensioners whose means exceeded $3 a week.

About 60 per cent. of all persons of pensionable age received an age pension in the financial year 1969–70 and some four-fifths of these (48 per cent. of all persons of pensionable age) received the maximum pension at the single or married rate. Approximately 1·8 per cent. of all persons above the age of 16 but below the minimum pensionable age received an invalidity pension. Nearly a third of all single age and invalidity pensioners lived on their own and had so little extra income that they received supplementary assistance.

Between 1946 and 1970 the age pension of a couple both of whom were pensioners more than quadrupled while the Consumer Price Index trebled. Thus the purchasing power of pensions rose by about 35 per cent. over that period. All the same, pensions did not keep up with average earnings which increased four and a half times over the same period.

The Melbourne Poverty Survey. In Melbourne, according to the findings of Henderson and his associates, 14 per cent. of households headed by men of pensionable age and 26 per cent. of those headed by women of pensionable age had incomes below the poverty level. At that time the maximum age pension for a single person was below the poverty line, while that for a couple both of whom were pensioners was above it. A large proportion of old people were not considered to be in need (although according to their income they were in poverty) because of their low housing costs, their ownership of assets and the help they received from their families.

The authors of the Melbourne survey recommended a number of changes in age and invalidity pensions : first, an increase in the wife's allowance to such a level that the total amount paid to a pensioner and his non-pensioner wife would be the same as that paid to a couple both of whom were pensioners – this has been the case in New Zealand since 1945; second, an increase in supplementary assistance up to a maximum of $4 a week and the extension of assistance to married couples – supplementary assistance in New Zealand up to a maximum of $5 a week could be paid to any pensioner; third, a rise in the maximum pension for single persons to at least 60 per cent. of that for a couple – this accords with the recommendation of the Royal Commission on Social Security in New Zealand; fourth, a rise in the basic pension rate each year in step with rises in the average earnings index – the New Zealand Royal Commission was not in favour of automatic pension adjustments.[12]

Downing's National Superannuation Proposals. R. I. Downing, a well-known expert on social problems and public finance in Australia and joint editor of the *Economic Record,* published in 1968 a paper advocating the setting-up of a rather ingenious national superannuation plan.[13] The details of this are, by the nature of the subject, complex and cannot easily be summarised in a couple of paragraphs, but some of the suggestions are original and their adoption might well be considered by other countries. Downing noted the decline of pensions in relation to wages in the previous twenty-five years and the inability of most people of working age to provide adequately for their retirement in an economy which was characterised by continually rising prices and wages. He proposed a scheme based on assessment (benefits to be financed by current contributions) and compulsory for all recipients of earned incomes up to $90 a week (approximately 130 per cent. of the average earnings of employed male units). The Federal government was to subsidise the plan by the same amount as was previously spent on age and invalidity pensions. The remainder of the cost was to be borne by insured persons and in the case of employees was to be shared between them and their employers in the ratio of 1 :2. Pensions were to vary inversely with revalued average lifetime earnings, within specified limits. For low-paid workers there was to be 100 per cent. earnings replacement; for those having average earnings of $90 a week the replacement was to be 67 per cent.; for those with higher incomes it was to be limited to $60 a week. The contributions were to be a greater percentage of the earnings of the higher-paid workers than of the low paid. The progressive scale of the contributions was made possible by concentrating the Federal subsidy on pensions for the lower paid. It was not proposed, however, to bring about any vertical redistribution of incomes between different income groups beyond that which already occurred in Australia in the late 1960s.

Downing suggested a radical solution to the vexed problem of people covered by private superannuation schemes :

> Earners already in superannuation schemes would switch to the national scheme when it came into operation, in respect of their earnings up to the ceiling of $90 a week. Their accrued entitlements to that date should be held until their retirement. . . .[14]

He also showed that the effect of his proposals on the accumulation of capital funds would be quite marginal.

Downing's arguments in favour of a national superannuation scheme are persuasive and his proposals contain several interesting features, but the time may not yet be ripe for such a radical break with Australian traditions.

U.K. AND IRELAND

History of U.K. Pensions.   Old-age pensions were much discussed in the latter part of the nineteenth century. Between 1885 and 1900 they were the subject of two Select Committees, one unofficial parliamentary committee, one Royal Commission, one committee of experts and one departmental committee.[15] The Old Age Pensions Act, 1908, was the first real departure from the Poor Law, but was little influenced by the deliberations which preceded it. The scheme set up by the Act provided non-contributory ('gratuitous') pensions of 25p a week to all men and women when they reached the age of 70; the award of a pension was subject to a means test, a character test, and residence and nationality qualifications. The full pension was paid to persons whose yearly means did not exceed £21; the pension of those whose yearly means exceeded this sum was reduced by 5p in four equal stages, ceasing when their means exceeded £31·50.

The U.K. scheme was similar to that in New Zealand, but there were three important differences : the U.K. pension was half the rate which had been paid in New Zealand since 1905, the amount of income exempt from assessment was a third of the corresponding amount in New Zealand and the minimum pensionable age was five years higher. The 1908 Act was criticised for providing 'a pension which was too low at an age which was too high after a means test which was too severe'. The validity of this criticism may be judged by the following figures : in 1914 the old-age pension of a single person was 22 per cent. of a labourer's wage; in the same year about two-thirds of all persons over the age of 70 received pensions in England and Wales; some 94 per cent. of all pensions were paid at the maximum rate.

In 1919 the pension was raised to 50p a week, but on account of the rise in prices which had taken place during the war this was barely sufficient to restore the purchasing power of pensions to their 1914 level.

The Blind Persons Act, 1920, provided that persons who were blind and who had attained the age of 50 (40 after 1938) should receive a pension exactly the same as the old-age pension they would have received when they were 70. The blind both in the U.K. and in most other countries received better treatment than other totally and permanently disabled persons.

A major change in the character of pension provisions took place in 1925. The Widows', Orphans' and Old Age Contributory Pensions Act of that year granted a contributory pension to all those covered by health insurance, when they reached 65. The wife of a contributory pensioner received a pension on her husband's insurance, also at 65. When contributory pensioners reached 70 they became entitled to a non-contributory pension without a means test.

In 1928, after the provisions of the 1925 Act had come into force, all employees, except some public servants and non-manual workers earning more than £260 per annum, were entitled to a pension of 50p a week at the age of 65. The cost of this contributory pension scheme was shared equally between employers and employees. The non-contributory pension of 50p at the age of 70 remained available, subject to the four statutory tests, to all who were not covered by insurance. By the end of the 1930s more than two-thirds of all persons over 65 and about four-fifths of all persons over 70 received state pensions. The pension rate was still 50p a week, but its purchasing power was some 40 per cent. greater than when the rate had first been fixed in 1919, owing to the fall in prices. The minimum pensionable age for insured women and wives of contributory pensioners was reduced to 60 in 1940.

The comprehensive national insurance scheme which started in

1948 introduced a number of major changes in income provisions for the old, but the minimum pensionable ages and the flat-rate pensions and contributions remained unaltered. The old-age pension was replaced with a retirement pension which, up to the age of 70, could only be claimed on retirement and which was abated in respect of part-time earnings above a quite modest sum. The pension rate was supposed to be adequate for subsistence. Beveridge had stated :

> Pensions adequate for subsistence without other means should be given only to people who, after reaching a minimum age for retirement, have in fact retired from work. To give a full subsistence income to every citizen on his or her reaching the age of 65 or 60 would impose an unjustifiable and harmful burden on all citizens below that age.[16]

The rate of pension on retirement was increased for those who postponed retirement beyond the minimum pensionable age.

National insurance, which gave entitlement to retirement pensions, was extended to all employees (except married women and most widows, for whom it was optional) as well as to the self-employed and the non-employed. Married women qualifying on their husbands' insurance received a pension of about 62 per cent. of the standard rate, while married women qualifying on their own insurance received the standard rate. A retired married man whose dependent wife was under 60 was awarded an increase for her, equivalent to the pension of a wife qualifying on her husband's insurance.

Pension Levels and Supplementary Benefit.   At the end of 1969 the retirement pension for a single person was £5 and for a married couple £8·10, the latter being equivalent to 30 per cent. of the standard wage. Between 1948 and 1969 the pension of a married couple increased by 300 per cent., earnings of adult male manual workers by 260 per cent. and prices by 120 per cent. Thus the purchasing power of pensions had increased by more than 81 per cent. and that of earnings by 63 per cent.[17]

More than one in four pensioners received a supplementary benefit pension in addition to the retirement pension. The rate of this supplementary pension was the amount by which a pensioner's requirements exceeded his resources. The requirements were laid down in statutory rules and included scale rates slightly higher than retirement pensions, plus a rent allowance which in all but exceptional circumstances equalled the actual rent paid. The resources to be taken into account (which included the retirement pension) and to be disregarded were also laid down in statutory rules. Most retirement pensioners who had no regular income in addition to their pension qualified for supplementary benefit. The average benefit that retirement pensioners received was £1·88 a week.

Growth of Pensions. Between 1948 and 1969 the number of persons above the minimum retirement age increased by just over a quarter (2·1 million) while the number receiving a pension increased by three-quarters (3 million). The disproportionate increase in pensioners was due partly to there being more persons who on retirement satisfied the contribution conditions for the receipt of a pension and partly to there being fewer men and women postponing retirement beyond the minimum pensionable age.

Long-Term Disability Benefit. Disablement benefit for insured employees was provided under the National Insurance Act, 1911, by Approved Societies. The benefit was payable after sickness benefit had been paid for 26 weeks if the incapacity continued. Between 1912, when payments started, and 1942 the rate of disablement benefit for men was half that of sickness benefit. It was originally fixed at 25p a week, level with the non-contributory old-age pension, but was only three-quarters of the pension rate throughout the 1920s and 1930s. During this period disablement benefit, like sickness benefit but unlike unemployment benefit, was not supplemented by dependants' allowances. The rate in 1939 was equivalent to less than 11 per cent. of the average earnings of a male manual worker. Neither the old-age pension nor disablement benefit was meant to be sufficient for even a subsistence standard of living; they were merely to supplement other resources such as savings, charity, benefits from friendly societies or trade unions and help from members of the family.

When the new comprehensive system of national insurance was introduced in 1948, disablement benefit was replaced with sickness benefit which became payable for an unlimited period, provided the claimant had been insured as an employee or a self-employed person for at least three years and that he was incapable of work because of some specific disease or bodily or mental disablement. The rate of benefit from then on was independent of the duration of the incapacity and was the same as that of all other social security benefits and pensions. Those receiving sickness benefit could apply for national assistance (supplementary benefit after 1966) on the same terms as retirement pensioners.

The White Paper 'Provision for Old Age'.   Since the late 1950s income provisions for the old have been the subject of intense party-political controversy. The Labour Party favoured a national super-annuation scheme with earnings-related contributions and pensions involving some vertical redistribution of incomes, while the Conservative Party advocated the encouragement of private pensions.

The first major change in national insurance provisions took place in 1961 under a Conservative government, when a graduated pension scheme commenced. The objectives of this scheme, as stated in the White Paper *Provision for Old Age,* were :

(1) To place the National Insurance scheme on a sound financial basis.
(2) To institute provision for employed persons who cannot be covered by an appropriate occupational scheme to obtain some measure of pension related to their earnings.
(3) To preserve and encourage the best development of occupational pension schemes.[18]

The first objective was achieved by imposing a contribution of 8½ per cent. on employees' earnings between £9 and £15 a week (£18 after 1963). This was in addition to the flat-rate contribution, and both contributions were shared equally between employers and employees. The receipt of the graduated contributions relieved the Exchequer of the need to increase subsidies to the flat-rate scheme. Every £7·50 paid by a man and every £9 paid by a woman in graduated contributions gave entitlement to an increment to the flat-rate pension of £1·30 a year. Employers who had private pension schemes providing pensions as favourable as the maximum pension obtainable from the state scheme could contract their employees out of the state scheme. These employees and their employers had to pay higher flat-rate contributions but no graduated contributions.

The government's second objective – some measure of pensions related to earnings – was achieved only to a limited degree, as the pensions were fixed amounts which could not be varied in line with changes in prices and earnings. Any variation in rates would have required retrospective adjustments in the value of benefits which had been secured by past contributions. The nature of the contracting-out provision made any adjustment in state-scheme benefits impossible without putting contracted-out employees at a grave disadvantage.[19]

The third objective was achieved in ample measure; the number of employees covered by occupational pension schemes increased greatly in the 1960s.

The Labour Government's National Superannuation Proposals. The Labour Government in 1969, after having been in office for five years, proposed what they termed 'the most fundamental changes in social security since the present national insurance scheme was introduced soon after the Second World War'.[20] The details of these proposals were, by the nature of the subject, quite complicated, but the main points can be summarised fairly easily. The flat-rate contributions and benefits were to be replaced by earnings-related contributions and benefits; employees' pension contributions were to be 4¾ per cent. of earnings up to a maximum of one and a half times the average earnings of adult male manual workers, while employers' contributions were to be 4½ per cent. of their total payroll, with no earnings ceilings. The Exchequer was to contribute as hitherto 18 per cent. of the combined contributions of insured persons and their employers.

Pensions were to be 60 per cent. of earnings up to half the average earnings of manual workers and 25 per cent. of the remainder up to the scheme's ceiling. The pension for men with average earnings was thus 42½ per cent. and those for men with three-quarters of and one and a half times average earnings were 49 per cent. and 37 per cent. respectively. Pensions were based on the average lifetime earnings revalued in line with changes in national average earnings. The scheme was thus designed to provide a dynamic pension. Full rights to the new pensions were to build up gradually over twenty years. Pensions for those retiring during these twenty years were to be at intermediate rates calculated by combining pensions earned under the old flat-rate scheme with the new pensions.

It was proposed not to alter the minimum retirement age of 65 for men and 60 for women, but the scheme was to be compulsory for all employees, including married women. Pensions for men up to the age of 70 and for women up to the age of 65 were to be paid as hitherto only to people who had retired from regular employment.

Self-employed persons were to continue paying contributions at a flat rate and were to receive a pension based on earnings of half the national average. Their exclusion from the earnings-related scheme was due to 'practical difficulties' of administration. Invalidity pensions were to be paid to all who were still incapacitated after having drawn sickness benefit for 28 weeks and were not to be restricted to people who were permanently invalided. The rate of invalidity pension was to be the same as that of retirement pensions, allowing credits at half the national average earnings for the years remaining up to the pension age. Invalidity pensioners were to receive in addition flat-rate increases for dependent wives and children. The effect of these provisions was not only to relate pensions to earnings but also to give a higher pension to people falling sick late rather than early in life.

The most controversial part of the proposals related to the place of occupational pensions within the national superannuation scheme. The proposals had provided scope for occupational pensions by excluding the self-employed from the earnings-related scheme and by limiting contributions to one and a half times the average wage. They had also rejected the practice prevalent in most countries of leaving occupational schemes to 'live on top' of the state scheme. Instead they proposed that all employees in occupational pension schemes be contracted out of part of the new superannuation scheme. The terms on which such partial contracting-out (abatement) was to be permitted could not be agreed with the Life Offices Association or the National Association of Pension Funds, and this led to the determined opposition of these bodies to the Labour government's proposals.[21] On the defeat of the government in June 1970 these proposals lapsed.

The White Paper 'Strategy for Pensions'. The incoming Conservative government in a White Paper published in 1971 proposed very different but equally fundamental changes.[22] These included the financing of basic flat-rate benefits with earnings-related instead of flat-rate contributions, the introduction of a State Reserve scheme to provide earnings-related pensions on commercial lines without any state subsidy for employees not covered by occupational pension schemes, and the complete exemption from the State Reserve scheme of members of recognised occupational pension schemes. In order to get recognition an occupational pension scheme would have to provide personal pensions for men at an annual rate of not less than 1 per cent. of whole-life earnings (up to a prescribed annual maximum and without revaluation) and a widow's pension at half the husband's rate. Some protection of the value of the pension was also required.

The government's intentions were stated quite unequivocally :

> The standards for recognition [of occupational pension schemes] are designed to ensure that recognised schemes will be providing benefits which, taken as a whole, compare favourably with those in the reserve scheme.[23]

The details of the Conservative government's scheme, which was to operate from April 1975, had not been published at the time of writing (June 1972). It seems certain, however, that the disagreement between the Labour and Conservative parties about the objectives of pension schemes and the means of achieving them are so profound that any scheme put forward by one government will be fundamentally modified if not repealed whenever the party in opposition takes office. In none of the other nine countries has there been such deep-rooted divergence on a major issue of social policy.

History of Irish Pensions.   When the Irish Free State (Irish Republic) was founded in 1922 it inherited from the British administration not only the old Poor Law but also the old-age and blind pension schemes and the monetary health insurance provisions (sickness and disablement benefit). These pensions and benefits were paid at the same rate and on the same conditions in Ireland as they were in Great Britain. As Ireland was a much poorer country, however, the cash payments must have appeared less meagre there than in Britain.

Neither pension nor benefit schemes were modified in any fundamental respect during the state's first thirty years. The Social Welfare Act, 1952, replaced the separate schemes providing unemployment and national health benefits and widows' and orphans' pensions with one simple, co-ordinated and compulsory social insurance scheme to which all employees (excluding public servants and non-manual workers earning more than a prescribed amount) and their employers made weekly flat-rate contributions and which paid benefits also at uniform flat rates.

Disability benefit was substituted for sickness and disablement benefit, and was paid for as long as the incapacity lasted. The continuous payment of disability benefit depended on having been in insured employment for at least three years and being 'incapable of work by reason of some specific disease or bodily or mental disablement'. The new benefit was increased in respect of adult and child dependants. The 1952 Act had many features in common with the British National Insurance Act, 1946; it differed from this Act in excluding the self-employed and the higher-paid salaried workers.[24] The rate of disability benefit in 1969 was £3·25 for a single person and £7·37 for a married couple with two children, the latter being equivalent to 38 per cent. of the standard wage.

The Health Act, 1953, provided for the payment of maintenance allowances by Local Health Authorities to chronically disabled persons over 16 who did not qualify for disability benefit without time limit (because they had not paid 156 contributions or because they were self-employed), if they could neither maintain themselves nor be maintained by their close relatives. The maximum rate of allowance, which was £3 a week in 1969, was determined by the Minister of Health. Allowances were paid only to persons whose disability had lasted or was expected to last for at least one year and who were substantially handicapped in undertaking work of a kind which but for their disablement would be suited to their age, experience and qualifications. In spite of these stringent conditions these allowances were paid to 23,000 people in 1969.

Until 1961 the non-contributory pension at the age of 70 was the only provision for old age in the Republic. In that year a contributory old-age pension scheme was set up for men and women who had reached 70. The terms of award of this pension were quite liberal : all employees who had been covered by social insurance were entitled to it. There was no means test or retirement condition for the pension, which was supplemented by an allowance in respect of a wife regardless of her age. The contributory old-age pension was awarded at an age which was higher than in other Western European countries, but it was estimated that in the late 1960s more than half of all insured men and women aged between 65 and 69 received either disability benefit or unemployment benefit.[25] While five-sixths of all men and women over 70 received some public maintenance, less than a third received a contributory pension; the remainder drew the non-contributory pension which was awarded subject to a means test. The maximum rate of this pension was some 10 per cent. less than that of the contributory pension. It was awarded without an increase for a dependent wife, which meant that many couples, where the man was over 70 and older than his wife, had to manage on one pension.

Improvement in Pension Levels. Between 1953 and 1969 retail prices increased by 72 per cent., while the non-contributory pension increased by 250 per cent. (from £1·08 to £3·75 a week) and average weekly earnings of industrial workers increased by 175 per cent. In this sixteen year period the purchasing power of non-contributory pensions thus increased by more than 100 per cent. and that of industrial earnings by 60 per cent. The very old participated in the general increase in standards of living, particularly in the 1960s, to a greater degree than the population of working age. In 1969 the non-contributory old-age pension for a single person over 70 was 19 per cent. of the standard wage and the contributory pension was on average about one-tenth greater. The gap between cash benefits in the Republic and in Northern Ireland narrowed quite markedly in the 1960s.[26]

Retirement Pensions. In 1970 a retirement pension scheme commenced for insured persons aged between 65 and 69. These pensions were paid at the same rate as disability and unemployment benefit and were increased in respect of adult and child dependants by the same amounts. When retirement pensioners reached 70 they transferred to the contributory old-age pension which had no retirement condition and was paid at a rate some 10 per cent. above the retirement pension.

CANADA

History of Canadian Pensions. Canada had in 1969 three forms of income maintenance for old people : universal, flat rate pensions (under the Old Age Security Act, 1951), income-tested supplements (under the Guaranteed Income Supplement Amendment of 1966) and contributory, earnings-related pensions (under the Canada Pension Plan of 1965 and its Quebec counterpart).

The first Federal legislation which was concerned with financial assistance to old persons was a Federal–Provincial programme, introduced in 1927, under which the Federal government made grants to the provinces to cover part of their expenditure on old-age assistance. However, the terms on which assistance was granted, the rate of assistance and the administration of the programmes remained the sole concern of the provincial governments. The various provincial schemes did not establish rights to pensions under prescribed conditions but left wide discretionary powers to the authorities administering the schemes.

Old-Age Security Pensions.   A proper national system of pensions was only set up in 1951 under the Old Age Security Act. Under this Act pensions were paid to all citizens over the age of 70 who satisfied a ten-year residence qualification, but they were not subject to an income test or retirement. The wife of a married pensioner received the pension only when she reached 70. In spite of the high pension age there was no increase for under-age wives. The rate of pension was at first $40 a month but by 1963 it was $75, having been increased in several stages. Pensions were financed by a 4 per cent. levy on the incomes of individuals up to a ceiling of $3,000 a year ($6,000 in 1969), a 3 per cent. tax on corporate incomes and a 3 per cent. tax on the sales of manufacturers.

In 1965 the old-age security pension scheme was modified in two respects : between 1966 and 1970 the pensionable age was to be progressively lowered from 70 to 65 years and the rate of pension as from 1968 was to be adjusted annually in accordance with movements in the Pension Index, which itself varied with changes in the Consumer Price Index. The annual adjustment was limited to a maximum of 2 per cent. This escalation clause had increased the pension rate to $79·58 a month by 1970.

The Guaranteed Income Supplement.   In the meantime, in 1966, a further amendment to the Old Age Security Act introduced a guaranteed income supplement for pensioners who had little or no income other than their pensions. The original rate of the supplement was $30 a month, but after 1967 it was fixed at 40 per cent. of the old-age security pension.

The combined pension and supplement of an old person who had no other income amounted to $1,310 in 1969 and to twice that amount for a couple both of whom were over 66, the minimum pensionable age in that year. These rates should be compared with the low-income cut-offs suggested by the Dominion Bureau of Statistics for 1967 – $1,740 for unattached individuals and $2,900 for a family of two. In 1969 the average earnings of all male employees in Canada was $7,298. (This happened to be almost identical with the standard wage.) For a couple the combined rate was thus 36 per cent. of average male earnings, but on account of differences in earning levels this proportion varied widely between the provinces. It was highest, at

57 per cent., for the very small population of Prince Edward Island, where earnings were lower than anywhere else, but was only 32 per cent. for the large population of Ontario, where earnings were highest.

Pensioners received the guaranteed income supplement at a reduced rate if they had some income in addition to their pension. The supplement was reduced by $1 a month for every $2 a month of taxable income in the previous year over and above the pension and any supplement that was received; no supplement was paid, therefore, when other income in the previous year had exceeded $768. Among the over-65s some 23 per cent. of the men and 35 per cent. of the women received the supplement at the full rate, while a further 17 per cent. of the men and 16 per cent. of the women received it at a reduced rate. As was to be expected, the proportion of pensioners claiming the supplement increased with age and varied widely between the provinces – less than half in Ontario but as large as 84 per cent. in Newfoundland.

The Canada Pension Plan. The Canada Pension Plan, which was enacted in 1965, provided an earnings-related retirement pension (as well as disability and survivors' pensions as supplementary benefits) for almost all members of the labour force. The plan covered all employees who earned more than $600 a year and all self-employed persons who earned $800 or more, provided they were between 18 and 70 years old. It was financed by contributions from employees, employers and self-employed persons. The first $600 of each contributor's annual earnings were exempt from contributions; the employee paid 1·8 per cent. on earnings above that amount up to a ceiling of $5,000 and his employer made a matching contribution. The self-employed had to contribute 3·6 per cent. of their income between $600 and $5,000 a year, as long as they earned at least $800. The contribution ceilings between 1968 and 1976 were to be adjusted annually in line with changes in the Consumer Price Index, but the maximum adjustment in any year was restricted to 2 per cent., as it was for old-age security pensions.

The retirement pension was to be 25 per cent. of average adjusted lifetime pensionable earnings. All earnings, including the $600 a year on which no contributions were payable, up to the contribution ceiling were pensionable. Earnings of past years were adjusted so that they bore the same relationship to the contribution ceiling in force when the pension commenced as they had borne to the ceiling prevailing in the year in which they were earned. The effect of these provisions can be illustrated with an example. Earnings of $4,000 in 1966, when the contribution limit was $5,000, were adjusted to $4,240 if retirement took place in 1970, when the ceiling was $5,300. If the annual adjustment in the contribution ceiling had not been restricted to a maximum of 2 per cent., the retirement pensions calculated in this way would have been inflation-proof, but as prices rose by appreciably more than 2 per cent and earnings rose even faster, the statutory adjustment of past earnings was quite inadequate.

The retirement pension was based on total adjusted pensionable earnings averaged over the period from the commencement of the scheme on 1 January 1966, or from the age of 18, whichever was the later, to the date on which the pension was claimed, but in no case over less than 120 months. The consequence of the last provision was that only partial retirement pensions were payable during the first ten years of the programme, up to 1976. There was, however, no qualifying period for retirement pensions. A man who had earned $3,600 in 1966 and retired at the end of the year was entitled to a retirement pension of $7.50[27] a month ($90 a year) in 1967. A contributor was thus able to qualify for a pension equal to 2·5 per cent. of his average adjusted earnings in 1967, 5 per cent. in 1968 and so on up to 25 per cent. of earnings in 1976. The maximum retirement pension which could be earned in January 1969, three years after the commencement of the programme, was $31·45 a month. After pensions had been awarded they were adjusted annually in line with changes in the Pension Index, subject to the 2 per cent. ceiling. After 1975 they were to be adjusted in line with changes in an Earnings Index, without any ceiling. The scheme provided that after 1975 certain periods of low earnings could be disregarded in determining the average earnings on which retirement pensions were based.

Contributors of any age received the retirement pension irrespective of any unearned income (including investments, annuities and private pension plans) and those above the age of 70 received it also irrespective of any earned income. For those aged 65-69 entitlement to a pension was subject to retirement, but annual employment earnings under $900 were not taken into consideration; if earnings were between $900 and $1,500 the pension was reduced by half of the excess over $900, and if earnings were above $1,500 the pension was reduced by $300 plus the excess of earnings over $1,500. However, irrespective of the amount earned over the year, the pension was paid in full for any month in which earnings did not exceed $75. All these limits were annually adjusted as from 1968 in line with changes in the Pension Index, subject to the 2 per cent. ceiling. There were no increases in retirement pensions for dependants, but a married woman could receive a retirement pension in her own right and was entitled to the old-age security pension on reaching the age of 65.

The White Paper Income Security for Canadians. In 1970 the income-maintenance provisions for pensioners were reviewed in the White Paper *Income Security for Canadians.* This resulted in several major changes in policy, some of which were implemented in 1971 while others were planned to come into operation in 1973. The purpose of these changes was mainly to reallocate resources so as to render more assistance to those in greatest need, but also partly to adjust the programme to changes in prices and earnings, which had been greater than anticipated in the mid-1960s.

The following changes were implemented in 1971 : the rate of the old-age security pension was fixed at $80 a month (a minimal increase over the rate for 1970); the automatic adjustment of this pension for changes in prices was abolished; the link between this pension and the guaranteed income supplement was discontinued; the maximum supplement was raised to $55 for single pensioners and $95 for a couple both of whom were pensioners; pensioners qualifying for the supplement had the combined amount of the old-age security pension and the supplement adjusted upwards for changes in the Pension Index, subject to an annual ceiling of 2 per cent. All these changes increased the selectivity of pension provisions. The purchasing power of the universal old-age security pension was allowed to depreciate further while pension increases were concentrated on those who had little or no other income. The greater increase in the supplement for single pensioners than in that for married couples was also designed to help those who were worst off.

Serious considerations had been given to the replacement of the universal old-age security pension with a more selective pension scheme, but the government decided against such a drastic measure for four reasons.[28] First, a large proportion of old people had such low incomes that they would qualify in any case for a more selective pension. In 1971 half of all single old people were estimated to have annual incomes of less than $200 and 70 per cent. annual incomes of less than $1,300. Second, the pensions were subject to income tax and thus already selective to a limited extent. Third, many people had made provisions for their retirement expecting to receive these pensions and companies had established superannuation plans to top them up. These people regarded the pension as a right; a failure to provide it would have been considered a breach of trust. Fourth, the commitment to paying universal pensions was all the firmer as the old-age security pensions had been financed in part for almost twenty years by a surcharge on personal income tax; people felt, therefore, not only that they were entitled to the pension but also that they had paid for it.

When the plan had commenced in 1966 the maximum contribution limit had been set at $5,000 a year which was the average wage for that year. By 1970 the average wage had increased to $6,400, while the contribution ceiling had increased to only $5,300. It was anticipated that average earnings would be $7,800 by 1975 but that the contribution ceiling would have increased to only $5,800. There was consequently a strong probability that an increasing proportion of contributors would have earnings at or above the contribution limit; thus a scheme which had been designed to provide pensions related to previous earnings would soon be providing flat-rate pensions for the majority of contributors. The relatively low contribution ceiling also meant that the adjustment of pensions was insufficient to bring them into line with earnings prevailing at the time of retirement.

The Federal government could not change any aspect of the Canada Pension Plan until 1973. This was because the Canada Pension Plan Act, 1965, required that

> . . . provincial approval be obtained by each of at least two-thirds of the provinces having not less than two-thirds of the population of all provinces before any substantial changes are made in the Plan. Three years' notice must be given to the provinces before changes in the level of benefits or contribution rates can be effective.[29]

Thus, although the Federal government wanted to introduce an increase in the contribution ceiling, this could not be done until 1973.

The government proposed a three-stage increase in the contribution ceiling so that it would correspond by 1975 with the expected average earnings level. After that year the plan provided for the ceiling to be adjusted in accordance with an Earnings Index based upon an eight-year moving average of all wages and salaries in

Canada. The government also proposed that pensions in payment should be adjusted in line with the proposed amendments.

Criticisms of the Canada Pension Plan. The earnings-related retirement pension scheme has been criticised as follows :

> Setting aside the quite misleading insurance terminology, the Canada Pension Plan is . . . at the present time, primarily a means of financing provincial investment expenditures through a regressive payroll tax . . . The historical reasons why the C.P.P. was set up in this deceptive format are well known. Pressure from provincial governments led to its being made into an enforced savings plan – which hits the low-income earner hardest – for the use of provincial governments.[30]

This strongly worded denunciation appears to be essentially correct. The plan was based on charging contributions which were vastly greater than would have been required to meet the cost of the benefits proposed for many years to come. Not only were pensions limited to persons retiring after 1966, but the pension formula was designed so as to pay only partial pensions for the first ten years. As a result, expenditure on benefits in 1970 (after the plan had been in operation for four years) was only $89 million, while revenue was $1,020 million and accumulated balances were $3,843 million.[31] The Chief Actuary of the Federal government estimated that if the proposals contained in the White Paper were implemented, assuming a moderate level of inflation,[32] the balance in the Pension Fund would increase until 1995, when it would have reached the gigantic sum of $23,200 million, while benefits in that year would be only $7,600 million.[33] The accumulation of such balances is, of course, not necessary when a pension plan is set up, but a deliberate policy decision.[34] The Canada Pension Plan was required to lend the large surpluses that it was expected to build up in its first twenty years to the provinces on a basis proportionate to the sums paid by contributors in each province. Any sums not taken up by the provinces were to be lent to the Federal government.

The contributions paid by employees and the self-employed are rightly described as regressive. While the exemption of the first $600 of annual earnings from the levy introduced a slightly progressive element, this was more than offset by the relatively low contribution ceiling. The employer's contributions, however, were not regressive, but their effect was very similar to a general sales tax. The contributions were also correctly described as forced savings in that they financed collective investment for the benefit of future generations by means of a compulsory levy.

Disability Pensions. In Canada, as in six of the other countries of this survey, benefits for prolonged disability were closely linked with those for the old. Federal aid to the provinces on the lines of the 1927 scheme of old-age assistance was provided for blind persons from 1937 and for permanently and totally disabled persons from 1955. Under the Canada Pension Plan, contributors who suffered from a severe and prolonged physical or mental disability were provided with pensions as supplementary benefits. Entitlement to these pensions was subject to stringent conditions. A disability was regarded as 'severe' if it rendered the contributor incapable of pursuing regularly any substantially gainful occupation and as 'prolonged' if it was expected to be of long and indefinite duration or to result in death. Furthermore, contributors qualified for a pension only if they had been members of the plan for five out of the ten years preceding the onset of the disability; thus the first pensions only became payable in 1970.

The pension, which was paid after a waiting period of three months, was made up of two components : a flat rate of $25 a month (adjusted according to movements in the Pension Index) and an earnings-related amount of $18\frac{3}{4}$ per cent. of adjusted average earnings (the 120 months average rule applying only to retirement pensions). This formula gave a contributor whose earnings were equal to the contribution ceiling an income-compensation ratio of 24 per cent. in 1970, but for the majority of male contributors, whose earnings were higher, the compensation ratio was lower.

The disability pensioner was worse off than the old-age pensioner in some respects. The 24 per cent. compensation ratio was about a fifth less than the combined old-age security and retirement pensions received by old persons who had incomes equal to the contribution ceiling. When the retirement pension is paid at the full rate in 1976, if the disability pension were unchanged, the gap between the two pensions would be even greater. Disability pensioners were also at a disadvantage in that they were not entitled to the guaranteed income supplement.

Neither a disability pensioner nor an old-age pensioner received an allowance for a dependent wife under the Canada Pension Plan, but disability pensioners could claim an allowance of $25 a month for up to four dependent children (only $12·50 for fifth and subsequent children).

The amendments to the Canada Pension Plan which are intended to be put into force in 1973 will improve the disability pension scheme in several respects.[35] The two components of the pension will both be increased. The flat-rate component will be identical with the level of the old-age security pension and the earnings-related component will be increased from 18¾ per cent. to 25 per cent. so as to equal the retirement pension. Moreover, an allowance at the level of the flat-rate component will be paid in respect of the wives of disability pensioners who are under 65 and who have the care of dependent children. These changes will raise the income support given to the disabled to the level of that given to the old. However, even the modified scheme will not have any constant attendance allowance for the severely disabled nor an allowance in respect of a wife (unless she has dependent children).

The disability pension scheme will continue to apply only to persons who have been disabled after 1970 and who have paid contributions for at least five years before the onset of the disability. All those disabled in previous years as well as all disabled persons who have never been in remunerative employment will have to rely in the future, as they have done in the past, on the provincial social assistance schemes.

The Canada and Quebec Pension Plans. The Canada Pension Plan was administered by the Department of National Health and Welfare and the contributions were collected by the Department of National Revenue. There was a separate Quebec Pension Plan which was closely co-ordinated with the Canada Pension Plan. The two operated virtually as a single unit. Benefit credits accrued under either of the plans were portable throughout Canada.

U.S.A.

Reasons for Late Development. In the U.S.A. the development of social security provisions for all groups of people in need, including the old, lagged behind the development of similar provisions in the other countries of this survey except Canada.[36] Why this happened is not easy to explain, but the attitudes and interests which delayed the introduction of any type of old-age pension for several decades after such pensions had been set up in New Zealand, Australia and the U.K. were presumably not very different from those which have so far successfully opposed the setting-up of a national health service or a national health insurance scheme.

One of these attitudes was unbounded confidence in the efficacy of individual effort in all spheres of activity. There was a firm belief, unshaken by any evidence to the contrary, that such effort could adequately protect prudent and deserving citizens against all the contingencies of life; the corollary of this view – that the undeserving should only receive public support after a searching inquiry into their means, under conditions which do not encourage unnecessary applications – was held equally firmly. Another deep-rooted attitude was the fear among the well-off sections of society that 'welfare ethics' would ruin the sturdy independence of the American character, to which the nation owed its greatness. The interests opposed to the development of social security provisions in the U.S.A. were not so very different from those in other countries, but they were more influential. The commercial insurance industry, for instance, which was in all countries opposed to the spread of income-maintenance provisions, had more political influence in the U.S.A. than elsewhere. The organised labour movement was, for a variety of reasons, even less in favour of social insurance in the U.S.A. than it had been in the U.K.

The federal system of government has sometimes been blamed for the difficulties met in establishing social security provisions in America. This theory is difficult to substantiate. Germany had a federal constitution in the period when the pioneer social legislation was passed. The federal constitution of Australia did not prevent the setting-up of an old-age pension scheme soon after the federation was founded. The political will, backed by public support, is not easily restrained by constitutional machinery or the judgement of any court. Such devices may delay legislation for relatively short periods but not for decades. (This is well illustrated by the delay of the National Insurance Act, 1911, by the House of Lords in the U.K.).

The causes of the absence of social security provisions in the U.S.A., therefore, must not be sought in constitutional law but in people's attitudes and beliefs, the power of economic interests and the economic conditions of the first three decades of this century. A. H. Birch, in a well-documented study of federalism and social legislation, formed the view that

> It would be quite wrong to think that this situation was the result of constitutional difficulties. The plain fact is that the social outlook of the nineteenth century continued to prevail in the United States until the continuing depression of the early 30s forced a change. In the boom atmosphere of the 1920s only a small minority urged insurance against a slump which most people were confident would not arrive, and while there was plenty of room, and need, for welfare services for the old and young, the atmosphere was not favourable to measures which could be held to weaken individual responsibility.[37]

Development of Old-Age Pensions. A Federal scheme of old-age pensions for employees in industry and commerce was first set up by the Social Security Act, 1935. One argument advanced in favour of this legislation was that 'the depression had wiped out much of the life time savings of the aged'.[38] Although this pension scheme was enacted in 1935, no pensions had in fact been paid by 1939, when it was extensively amended. The 1935 Act, before amendment, had several features characteristic of private insurance plans. Pensions were based on cumulative lifetime earnings after 1936, there were no allowances for dependants and contributions financed pensions without any aid from public funds. One of the results of these provisions would have been very low pension levels for many years. Other features of the scheme were more characteristic of social insurance. Contributions were compulsory and were shared between employees and their employers; the funds which accumulated had to be invested in government securities; the scheme was administered by an agency of the Federal government; pensions for contributors under the age of 72 were subject to retirement. Two other provisions of the Act were common to both private and social insurance, but not characteristic of any other form of public assistance for the old : contributors' rights to pensions were clearly defined in law and pensions were paid irrespective of means and unearned income.

When the 1935 Act was amended in 1939, it became less like a private pension scheme. The basis for computing pensions was changed to average monthly earnings in insured employment. This made it possible to pay reasonably adequate pensions to many contributors who were already in the second half of their working life. At the same time, allowances were introduced for adult and child dependants and for the widows and orphans of contributors.

After 1939 the scope of the Social Security Act broadened. The proportion of the working population that was covered was greatly increased, especially in the 1950s. In 1940 only 58 per cent. of all persons in remunerative employment had been covered by social security, but by 1969 this proportion had increased to 90 per cent. In that year virtually all employees (with the exception of most Federal employees and some state and local government employees) and all self-employed persons were covered. Still excluded from the private sector were casual, domestic and farm workers, low-income self-employed persons and some employees of non-profit-making organisations. Coverage was more comprehensive than that of either workmen's compensation or unemployment insurance. Employees were covered irrespective of the number working for any one employer.

Disability Pensions. Two types of disability benefit were introduced in 1956 : one for severely disabled workers aged 50-64 (any age up to 64 after 1960) whose disability was expected to be of long or indefinite duration (expected to last at least 12 months after 1965), and the other for the adult disabled children of deceased and retired workers, if they had become disabled before 18. The provision for adult disabled children was an innovation in social insurance legislation; it gave to these invalids a status somewhat similar to that of a dependent spouse or a widow. Dependants' allowances for disability pensioners were introduced in 1958.

Entitlement to Pensions. The minimum qualifying contribution period for the reward of a retirement pension was reduced several times. The 1939 amendment had fixed it at half the period between 1936 and the contributor's 65th birthday. By 1961 this had become a quarter of the period between 1950 and the 65th birthday. In the mid-1960s a modified eligibility requirement for persons over 72 before 1968 was introduced with the result that after 1966 virtually all these old people qualified for a special (lower) pension, unless they were receiving Federal-aided public assistance or a government pension. These special pensions were paid for out of general revenue.

The result of the extension of coverage and the easing of the eligibility requirements was a substantial increase in the number of pensioners. In 1950 a retirement pension was received by 170 people out of every 1,000 over the age of 65; by 1960 this proportion had increased to 623 per 1,000 and in 1969 it was 874. The proportion entitled to a pension at 65 was always greater than that actually receiving a pension because some contributors deferred retirement beyond the minimum pensionable age.

Pension Levels. The rate of pensions in payment was increased six times between 1950 and 1970. For most of these years pension rates increased somewhat faster than prices, but markedly slower than net earnings. Thus the purchasing power of the pensions of contributors who had retired in 1950 had increased by 15 per cent. between their retirement and 1968 (March) but had declined by 14 per cent. during the same period in relation to net earnings. The corresponding proportions for the pensions of contributors who had retired in 1959 were 4 per cent. and 8 per cent.[39] The increase in the purchasing power of the average pension in payment was much greater : 41 per cent. between 1950 and 1968 and 16 per cent. between 1959 and 1968. The large increase in average pension levels was partly a reflection of the fact that pensions were related to earnings, which had increased faster than prices.

Age of Retirement. The minimum age for retirement on full pension has not been altered since it was first fixed at 65 in the 1930s; since 1956 women have had the option of retiring on a reduced pension at any age above 62 and this option was extended to men in 1961. The pensions of contributors who retired before 65 were actuarially reduced and remained reduced for as long as they were drawn. The reduction was 5/9th of 1 per cent. of the full pension for each month below the age of 65 for which the pension was claimed. The number of contributors retiring on a reduced pension was remarkably high. In 1969 nearly half of all men and two-thirds of all women who started to draw cash benefit were below 65.

Contribution Ceilings and Levels. The contribution ceiling of $3,000, fixed in the original Social Security Act, covered in 1937 the full earnings of 97 per cent. of the contributors and 92 per cent. of the earnings of all people in insured employment. Between 1937 and 1968 the ceiling was raised on five occasions to compensate for the rising level of earnings, but none of the increases was sufficient to restore the ceiling to the relative position it had occupied in 1937. Since 1951 contributions have had to be paid on only about 80 per cent. of all earnings in the years in which higher ceilings were introduced, while in the intervening years this proportion was even smaller. The ceiling of $7,800 which was introduced in 1968 (and still in force in 1969) was estimated to cover in its first year the total earnings of only 60 per cent. of all male contributors in full-time employment. If it had been intended to restore coverage to the 1937 level (92 per cent. of the earnings of all persons in insured employment), the ceiling would have had to be raised to about $15,000.

Contributions from the beginning were shared equally between employees and their employers; for self-employed persons they were one and a half times the employees' rate. The combined contribution rate that employers and employees had to pay for entitlement to cash benefits (excluding health insurance) was gradually increased from 3 per cent. in 1950 to 8·4 per cent. in 1969; it will be 10 per cent. in 1973. These increases were made because the scope of the programme was broadened and because the ratio of over 65s to the working population was rising.

The Pension Formula.   The formula for determining a contributor's retirement pension had to be adjusted whenever the contribution ceiling was increased, but it was always weighted in favour of the lower paid. In calculating the average monthly earnings on which the pension was based in 1970, all income earned before 1950 was disregarded together with any income earned thereafter which was above the contribution ceiling; income in the five years (not necessarily consecutive) between 1950 and the 65th birthday (62nd birthday for women) in which earnings were least was also disregarded. Years with high earnings after the age of 65 for men and 62 for women could be substituted for earlier years of lower earnings. The pension in 1970 was approximately 82 per cent. of the first $110 of the average monthly wage, plus about 30 per cent. of the next $540, with a minimum pension of $64.[40] The basic retirement pension was increased by about 50 per cent. for a wife who either cared for a dependent or disabled child or was above the age of 65. (This increase could be awarded at an actuarially reduced rate for a wife aged 62.) There was also an increase of 50 per cent. for each dependent child.

The average retirement pension for a man, without reduction for early retirement, was $116[41] in 1969 – about 17 per cent. of the standard wage; for a couple both of whom were over 65 the average pension was about 25 per cent. of the standard wage. For men who had opted for retirement before the age of 65 the average pension was some $15 less. These rates were well below the poverty level as defined by the Social Security Administration – $145 a month for a single man over 65.[42]

The social security provisions in the U.S.A. provided a 'floor of protection' rather than a minimum subsistence level. They were adjusted on an *ad hoc* basis after lengthy debates and bargaining in Congress. The contribution rates for employees and the self-employed were regressive because the contribution ceiling was less than the monthly earnings of the majority of male contributors.

Ideology and the Adequacy of Pensions. An inquiry carried out by the Social Security Administration in 1968, 'Income of People aged 65 and Older,'[43] commented on the adequacy of retirement pensions :

> . . . it is evident that social security benefits were not themselves enough to assure a reasonable level of living during retirement . . . Beneficiaries managed fairly well if they had some employment or if they had a second pension. Since few people can count on working throughout their retirement, the combination of benefit income and earnings does not represent a level of income on which retirees . . . can rely for life. Those entitled to a second pension have more assurance, but only about 2 in 10 of the regular beneficiaries are so fortunate . . .
>
> With roughly half the regular beneficiary units having neither current work experience nor a second pension . . . it is not surprising that so many had little except benefits.[44]

Opposition to raising the pension levels is not primarily based on the cost of such measures but on the deeply held conviction that private provisions are some-how superior to public ones; the limited scale of private pension schemes is only seen as evidence that they ought to have more encouragement. This attitude is held by Robert J. Myers, and he describes the effect on private insurance of expanding public social insurance :

> The next step of the expansionists [following the raising of the contribution ceiling to around $15,000] would be to double the present benefit level – or, to begin with, to increase it by at least 50 per cent. This step, combined with the previous one, would then make it virtually unnecessary to have private pension plans, private insurance, and other forms of long-term private savings for the vast majority of the population. The benefit payments would, under the expansionist approach, be automatically adjusted for changes in general *earnings* (not merely for changes

in *prices*) in order to maintain the so-called adequacy of the benefits. In this manner, virtually no individual and group supplementation would ever be needed.[45]

The diminution of private insurance suggests to Myers the prospect of governmental control not only of insurance but also of industry (through cutting back private investment funds). Thus, quite apart from being contrary to the ethics of the 'American way of life', a rise in social security pension levels is seen as part of a direct threat to the national economy.

Expenditure on Pensions.   The total expenditure on social security pensions in 1955 had been about 1·3 per cent. of the G.N.P.; by 1960 this proportion had become about 2·2 per cent. and in 1969 it was about 2·9 per cent. (Approximately 70 per cent. of the 1969 total was spent on retirement pensions, 20 per cent. on survivors' pensions and 10 per cent. on disability pensions.) The increases in the proportion of G.N.P. spent on pensions in 1960 and 1969 correspond with massive increases in the number of beneficiaries in these years : from 8 million in 1955 to 15 million in 1960 and to 25 million in 1969. The average rate of the retirement pension increased between 1955 and 1969 by 62 per cent., while the G.N.P. per head increased by 91 per cent. This confirms what was found by comparing changes in pension rates with changes in net earnings : pensioners did not participate fully in the rising national prosperity. However, the proportion of pensioners among the over-65s increased over these fourteen years from 401 to 847 per 1,000.

Public Service Pensions.   As in all other countries, the pension provisions for civil servants were much more generous than the public provisions for other retired persons. Civil service pensions in the U.S.A., however, were not quite as generous as those in the Continental countries, especially those for short-service officers. The minimum pensionable age varied with the length of service – from 55 after 30 years' service to 62 after five years' service. The pension was based on the 'average salary', which was the highest average annual basic salary of any three consecutive years. The pension was 1·5 per cent. of the average salary times five for the first five years, plus 1·75 per cent. of the average salary times five for the next five years, plus 2·0 per cent. of the average salary times the number of years' service in excess of ten years. Thus for ten years' service the pension was

16·25 per cent. of the average salary; the maximum pension of 80 per cent. of the average salary was reached after 42 years' service. After the pensions were awarded they were adjusted automatically for changes in retail prices. The scheme was financed by contributions of 7 per cent. of salary from both the officers and the employing agency, without any contribution ceiling. It was remodelled in 1969 so that it became self-financing and would not require any grants from public funds.[46]

REVIEW

In all ten countries some provision of a social security character was made for certain groups of old and disabled people, but the nature of these provisions varied widely. They varied to such an extent and operated within such heterogeneous statutory frameworks that international comparisons of some aspects of these provisions (such as expenditure, or the number of old-age pensioners per 1,000 population of a particular age) are of dubious validity and could be very misleading. Instead, therefore, specific features of the schemes in each of the ten countries will be briefly summarised and contrasted.

The Minimum Pensionable Age. The provisions for the old were designated *old-age pensions, age pensions, retirement pensions, age benefit* and *superannuation benefit.* The minimum pensionable age varied from 55 (for unmarried women in New Zealand who 'for health reasons were unable to engage in regular employment') to 70 (for both contributory and non-contributory old-age pensioners in Ireland). The most common minimum pensionable age for men was 65; this was the case in Austria, Germany, the U.K., the Netherlands, Canada (as from 1970), the U.S.A., New Zealand (superannuation benefit) and Australia. Men in Germany and Austria could claim a pension at any age over 60 if they had been unemployed for the previous 12 months, and in the U.S.A. men could claim an actuarially reduced pension from the age of 62. For women in four of the above eight countries (Austria, Germany, the U.K. and Australia) the minimum pensionable age was 60 and in the remaining four (the Netherlands, New Zealand – superannuation benefit – Canada and the U.S.A.) it was the same age as that for men. The minimum age for the retirement pension instituted in Ireland in 1971 was 65 for both men and women. In Denmark the minimum age was 67 for men and married women and 62 for single women, but in special circumstances, such as ill-health, the minimum age was reduced to 60. Age benefit in New Zealand could be claimed by both men and women at the age of 60.

The position of women under these retirement and old-age schemes also varied greatly between countries in other respects. Married men could receive an increase in their pensions for under-age wives of any age in Ireland (contributory old-age pensions), the U.K. and New Zealand (age benefit) and for wives aged 62 in Denmark and the U.S.A. (at actuarially reduced rates). There were various practices when a recipient of widow's pension reached the age for a retirement or old-age pension. In most of the ten countries – Denmark, the Netherlands, the U.K., Canada (old-age security pension), New Zealand and Australia – the majority of women above the minimum pensionable age received an old-age or retirement pension irrespective of whether they were single, married or widowed, while in others – Austria, Germany, Canada (retirement pension) and the U.S.A. – a widow, whatever her age, could not claim a retirement pension on her husband's insurance but could receive a widow's pension under prescribed conditions, plus a retirement pension in respect of her own contributions. In these countries a widow could thus receive two pensions; in fact, in Austria and Germany she could receive even more than two. The rules were often quite complex; in the U.K., for instance, all women who received a widow's pension transferred at 65 to the retirement pension, but between 60 and 64 they could opt for either a widow's or a retirement pension. In Ireland widows whose husbands had been covered by social insurance received a contributory widow's pension irrespective of their age, while other widows received, or transferred to, a non-contributory old-age pension from the age of 70.

Similar situations arose in the case of invalidity pensioners, disability pensioners and recipients of long-term sickness benefit. When they reached the appropriate age they normally transferred to retirement or old-age pensions in Ireland and the six countries where widows did this – Denmark, the Netherlands, the U.K., Canada (old-age security pensions), New Zealand and Australia. In Austria, Germany and the U.S.A., on the other hand, invalidity pensions were paid without an age limit.

The Criteria for Disability. The wide differences between the various countries' statutory definitions of invalidity (or disability or long-term sickness) make a valid comparison of the number of invalidity pensioners per 1,000 population in these countries very difficult. In the Netherlands benefit was paid for any incapacity in excess of 15 per cent., in Denmark the degree of incapacity had to be at least half and in Austria and Germany it had to be more than half. In Canada and the U.S.A. inability 'to pursue any substantially gainful occupation' was required (in Canada for an indefinite period, in the U.S.A. for at least 12 months). Invalidity pensions in Australia were paid to persons who were 'permanently incapacitated for work to the extent of at least 85 per cent.', while in New Zealand invalids' benefit was paid to persons who were 'permanently incapacitated for work'. In Ireland and the U.K. insured persons who satisfied the contribution requirements received sickness benefit for an unlimited period if they were incapable of work 'by reason of some specific disease or bodily or mental disablement'. However, even a comparison of the various 'percentages' of incapacity used by several countries for determining eligibility for (or the rate of) benefit is of dubious validity, as they were assessed according not only to different medical criteria but also to different legal and economic criteria.

Level of Disability Pensions.   In some countries the rate of the invalidity or disability pension was the same as the retirement or old-age pension (the U.K., the U.S.A., New Zealand and Australia), in some the rate of disability pension for severely disabled persons was higher (Denmark and the Netherlands) and in some it was lower (Austria, Germany, Ireland and Canada). In Canada the rate of disability pensions after 1973 will be the same as the pensions paid to retired persons. In Ireland the disability pension was the same as the retirement pension but lower than the contributory old-age pension, while in Austria and Germany the difference between the invalidity and retirement pensions, which partly depended on the age at which the disability occurred, was often quite substantial.

In the Netherlands the work-incapacity benefit was paid at seven different rates depending on the degree of incapacity; in Denmark there were three rates of disability pension and in Germany two. In some countries pensions were paid at the onset of the disability (Ireland, the U.K., New Zealand and Australia), in others after a waiting period in which sickness benefit was paid (Austria, Germany, Denmark and the Netherlands), while in Canada and the U.S.A. disability pensions were only paid after three and seven months respectively, with no entitlement (except in four states in the U.S.A.) to temporary disability benefit during the waiting period.

The Netherlands was the only country where those suffering a severe disability could receive only one pension; in all the other countries persons receiving employment injury pensions or workmen's compensation could also, in certain circumstances, receive other social security benefits or pensions.

Limitations in Cover of Disability Pensions.　Only in Denmark, New Zealand and Australia were invalidity pensions paid to all citizens irrespective of their employment status; in the other seven countries they were only paid to persons who satisfied prescribed social insurance conditions. Disabled persons in these seven countries who did not receive disability pensions had to rely on social assistance, which was awarded on widely varying terms in the different countries and in the U.S.A. and Canada on terms which varied widely between the different jurisdictions within the country. Denmark was the only country where a pension was paid to a severely disabled married woman who was not entitled to social insurance benefit in her own right.

Link between Disability and Old-Age Pensions.　In five of the ten countries the disability pension scheme was closely linked with, or part of, the old-age pension scheme. This was the case in Austria, Germany, Denmark, Canada and the U.S.A., while in the Netherlands, the U.K. and Ireland long-term sickness benefit was linked with, or part of, the temporary disability provisions. In New Zealand and Australia invalidity pensions (benefits) were part of the respective unified social security systems.

Entitlement to Old-Age Pensions.　Entitlement to old-age or retirement pensions was based on insurance contributions in seven countries – Austria, Germany, Ireland (contributory old-age pension), the U.K., the Netherlands, Canada (retirement pension) and the U.S.A. Pensions paid to the over-67s in Denmark and the over-65s in New Zealand (superannuation benefit) were demogrants, as were old-age security pensions in Canada. Old-age pensions in Australia, Ireland (non-contributory) and Denmark (below the age of 67) and age benefit in New Zealand were awarded on the basis of a means or income test. In New Zealand and Australia supplementary benefits were paid in addition to the ordinary pension rates after a more stringent means test. The insurance pensions of a large proportion of pensioners were augmented on the basis of an income test in Austria (equalisation payments), the U.K. (supplementary benefit pensions) and Canada (guaranteed income supplements). In the other four countries insurance pensions were augmented by means-tested assistance only in comparatively rare circumstances.

In the Netherlands, Canada and the U.S.A. the pension provisions for the self-employed were virtually the same as those for employees. The means-tested pensions in Australia and the income-tested pensions and the demogrants in New Zealand were paid to all citizens irrespective of their employment status. Austria and Germany had separate schemes for various groups of self-employed persons. These schemes were not universal and many of them, for instance the farmers' pension schemes, paid lower rates of benefit. The Irish social insurance scheme did not cover the self-employed, who could, however, apply for the means-tested, non-contributory old-age pensions. In Denmark and the U.K. the basic retirement pension was paid to the self-employed and employees on equal terms, but the graduated pension in the U.K. and the labour-market pension in Denmark were only available to employees.

Flat-Rate and Earnings-Related Pensions. The demogrants in Denmark (old-age pension), Canada (old-age security pension) and New Zealand (superannuation benefit) were paid at one standard rate. The social assistance type of pension in New Zealand (age benefit) and Australia (age pension) was paid at a standard rate which was abated if other income exceeded prescribed limits. Social insurance pensions in Ireland, the U.K. (retirement pensions) and the Netherlands were paid at standard flat rates which were reduced if the minimum contribution requirements were not satisfied. Insurance pensions in Austria and Germany were related to both past earnings and the length of insured employment; this was also the case in Canada and the U.S.A., but the basis of assessment was rather different. Past earnings in Germany and Austria were revalued in line with changes in earnings and in Canada (up to 1976) in line with changes in prices. Age and disability pensions in the Netherlands were automatically adjusted according to movements in an earnings index and in Denmark according to movements in a price index. In Austria and Germany pensions in payment were not automatically adjusted but, after 1958, were adjusted according to a statutory formula based on changes in the earnings of some years previously. The implementation of these adjustments was at the government's discretion. In Ireland, the U.K., the U.S.A., New Zealand and Australia pensions in payment were adjusted at regular index or formula.

Income Ceilings. In Ireland non-manual employees earning more than £1,600 were not covered by social insurance and thus not entitled to either retirement pensions (after 1971) or contributory old-age pensions. In none of the other countries having social insurance pensions were employees or the self-employed excluded from participation in social insurance schemes on account of their earnings exceeding prescribed amounts. However, in the four countries which had earnings-related pensions – Austria, Germany, Canada and the U.S.A. – contributions were limited to a statutory ceiling and the maximum pension rates were limited by these ceilings. As a proportion of the standard wage these ceilings in 1969 were : Austria, 157 per cent. (including an allowance for special bonuses); Germany, 135 per cent.; Canada, 71 per cent.; and the U.S.A., 93 per cent. The low percentages in the two North American countries reflect the relatively low proportions of total earnings covered.

Compensation Ratios. It is very difficult to compute with any degree of certainty the compensation ratio of retirement or old-age pensions. In Germany the average pension received by men under the manual workers' scheme in 1969 was only DM3,972 – about 34 per cent. of the average earnings of all men and women in manual and non-manual employment (equivalent to 26 per cent. of the standard wage). The corresponding proportion for men under the non-manual workers' scheme was 56 per cent. (equivalent to 44 per cent. of the standard wage).[47] This was the case in spite of the provision of a pension that was 67·5 per cent. of the basis of assessment after 45 years in insured employment.

Pension levels in the U.S.A. were much lower. The maximum pension possible for a man retiring in 1968 was $156 – about 24 per cent. of the maximum contribution ceiling, which itself was well below average male earnings in that year. The average pension paid to men who had retired at the age of 65 was $115·50 in 1969, some 18 per cent. of the contribution ceiling (equivalent to 17 per cent. of the standard wage). For the large proportion of men who retired between

62 and 65 the compensation ratios were even lower. These pensions levels certainly allowed ample scope for the expansion of occupational pension schemes.

In the U.K. in 1969 the retirement pension of £5 was about 19 per cent. of the standard wage. This could be increased by supplementary benefit pensions in case of need, entitlement to small graduated pensions and postponement of retirement beyond the age of 65.

When comparing the compensation ratios of retirement pensions it should be remembered that there was great variation in allowances for wives. In Germany there was no allowance. In the U.S.A. there was an allowance of 50 per cent. of the husband's pension for a wife who was over 65 when her husband retired and of 40 per cent. for a wife who was 62 when her husband retired; for younger wives there was no allowance. All wives in the U.K. under 60 received an allowance of 62 per cent. of the husband's basic pension and wives above that age received a pension on their husband's insurance.

A Tentative Prognosis. Some of the basic policy considerations behind retirement pensions and possible future trends in this field have been discussed in Chapter 2. In Austria and Germany there was a trend towards income-related retirement pensions with the ultimate object of replacing some two-thirds of income for up to 85 or even 90 per cent. of the working population. In the Netherlands, where both long-term disability pensions (work-incapacity benefit) and short-term sickness benefit were related to earnings, there appears to be some possibility of the old-age pension scheme developing in the same direction. The Danish labour-market pensions may possibly at some stage be modified to become dynamic and related to income. Within the framework of the E.E.C. and following the spirit of Article 118 of the Treaty of Rome, the retirement pension schemes of Germany, the Netherlands and Denmark may well be less dissimilar in the years to come than they were in 1969. If this is so, it seems probable that the pattern and ideology of the German scheme will prevail.

In the U.K. the retirement pension proposals put forward by the Conservative government which came into office in 1970 are somewhat similar to the system operating in the Netherlands – compulsory, earnings-related contributions with a reasonably high contribution ceiling financing flat-rate pensions which are supplemented by industry-wide, compulsory occupational pension schemes. However, this similarity is deceptive. The British Conservative government is committed to the principle of selectivity in the social services, the discouragement of public provisions, the encouragement of private enterprise and the reduction of taxes on personal and corporate income to a greater extent than is advocated in the other countries of Western Europe. Its approach to social security provisions, in spirit though not in the methods used, has more in common with that of the North American countries. However, as has been remarked earlier, a change in government in the U.K. would probably lead to major changes in the pension scheme proposed in 1971.

Ireland faces the particular problem that a larger proportion of the population than in the other countries of this study is self-employed and was, in 1969, not covered by any contributory pension scheme. Many of these self-employed persons had very low incomes and this was one of the factors which made it difficult to set up a pension scheme for them. The insurance industry in Ireland is well established, an important source of private savings and not without political influence.[48] The government has always supported the extension of private insurance provisions for retirement, and it seems likely that it will continue to do so. This makes it probable that pension policy in Ireland will not deviate much from that in the U.K., as long as there is a Conservative government in London.

In Canada, the U.S.A. and Australia, social security pension provisions were well below the subsistence level; they were meant to provide a floor on which other provisions could be built. In New Zealand pension policy appears to have been settled for some time ahead as the result of the government's acceptance in 1972 of the recommendations of the Royal Commission on Social Security. Pensions will be adequate to give old people the feeling that they belong to their community and to enable them to participate in its normal pursuits; the pension of a couple will be equal to approximately 80 per cent. of the lower quartile of male workers' earnings.

Possible Reasons for Changes in Pension Levels.   In considering the rates of old-age pensions and the changes in these rates in the 1950s and 1960s, the ten countries fall into two groups – European and non-European. In the European countries rising proportions of old people tended to go together with increases in pension rates relative to earnings, while in the non-European countries relatively stable proportions of old people (owing to large-scale immigration of under-65s in spite of rising numbers of old people) accompanied pension rates which did not rise relative to earnings (except in Canada, where pensions were very low in the 1950s).

This apparent pattern may be explicable in terms of the political power wielded by old people, which will increase as the proportion of the voting population that they form increases. (In fact if old people formed a low proportion of the electorate they could constitute a positive political deterrent to pension increases.) It might have been expected that a high proportion of old people would be a factor discouraging pension increases, as the financial burden incurred by large-scale increases would have to be borne by the working population. If this was a factor, it was not such a powerful one as that of the political weight carried by the electorate over 65. In 1969 old people formed as much as 20 per cent. of the electorate in Austria and as little as 12 per cent. in Australia, while in the other countries the proportions ranged between these two, and (except in the U.S.A. and the Netherlands) these proportions were consistently higher in the European countries than in the non-European ones. In the same year old-age pensions relative to earnings were higher in the European countries than in the other four.

Although the conclusions reached here appear to be supported by the data and developments in the 1950s and 1960s, they should only be accepted with considerable reservation. It may well be that political, economic and ideological factors quite unconnected with the number and proportion of old people in a country are decisive in determining the level of pension rates.

Pensions in North America. The rate of pension is one important characteristic of an old-age pension scheme; another is the proportion of old people who are covered by the scheme. It was in the latter respect that changes in the U.S.A. were most important. In Canada the dividing line between the poor-law type of social assistance and old-age pensions proper dates only from the early 1950s. In spite of the many and glaring shortcomings of the three old-age pension schemes prevalent in Canada at the end of the 1960s, they do show a considerable level of sophistication.

CHAPTER VII

Unemployment

The Inevitability of Unemployment. The rising standard of living which all the ten countries have enjoyed since the war has been the result of production increasing faster than population. Each worker on average produced more, so that in 1970, for example, only two men produced the goods and services which it took three men to produce in 1960. Rising productivity (output per man-year), however it is brought about, contributes to making men redundant: the man who loses his old job become available to produce something else. This additional output is reflected in the ever higher standard of living for which society strives. Thus redundancy of labour is an inherent feature of economic growth and not the consequence of poor economic planning or incompetent industrial management. Ideally, the man who becomes redundant should be able to find new employment without any difficulty, but in practice this does not always happen.

One of the recognised major objectives of government is the maintenance of a high and stable level of employment.[1] This cannot be achieved solely by counteracting cyclical fluctuations through monetary policy and demand management, but requires also other measures, for example industrial training programmes, regional capital investment and more opportunities and incentives for geographical labour mobility. However, a high and stable level of employment is in certain circumstances incompatible with other objectives of public policy – stable prices or a correction of an imbalance of payments.

It may well be that in retrospect the 1950s and 1960s will appear as a golden age of low unemployment, relatively stable prices, rapid economic growth and few industrial disputes. There is at present little prospect of creating an economic structure in which all men and women can be certain of employment at all times. On the contrary, the sharpening conflict of sectional interests resulting in spiralling prices might well lead to higher levels of unemployment in the future than have been experienced in the last two decades.

The Case for Low Levels of Compensation. Whatever the omens for the future may be, the unemployed, like the poor, have always been with us. In the nineteenth and well into the twentieth century public support for the unemployed was meagre and based on the principle of 'least eligibility'. This was, in this context, the belief that the position of a man out of work should be worse than that of a man in the most humble and low-paid job. There were three distinct justifications for holding this principle : it was believed that, first, the unemployed person had to have an incentive to seek work; second, the worker's fear of dismissal and unemployment was an effective device for maintaining industrial discipline and thereby promoting production; third, a man had to have an inducement to move from a place where there was no work to places where he could find work. The principle of least eligibility also had the advantages of minimising the financial cost of supporting the unemployed and keeping the rates low.

The underlying assumption supporting this general attitude was that unemployment was not a misfortune but a manifestation of personal shortcomings and moral failings. The general view among those who shaped public opinion was that the unemployed were work-shy, 'too fond of the bottle', malingerers and trouble-makers. Herbert Spencer in England and William Graham Sumner in America advanced the view that persons with such undesirable characteristics were neither fit nor deserving to survive. Their comforting doctrine (comforting to the rich) provided a ready-made case for resisting the demands of taxation and any degree of communal responsibility. Sumner, a man of considerable influence about the turn of the century, a professor of political and social science at Yale, a priest of the Protestant Episcopal Church and the president of the American Sociological Society in 1909, wrote in 1885 : 'The law of the survival of the fittest was not made by man. We can only by interfering with it produce the survival of the unfittest.'[2] The same moral indignation as is felt today by the many in the U.S.A. who see the poor as 'living high on welfare handouts' was felt by 'right-thinking and respectable' people everywhere in the past and is still felt by not a few in all ten countries.

The Case for Generous Compensation.   Most of the situations which result in involuntary loss of earnings are, at least in the short run, not capable of being influenced by government policy. The number of sick, disabled, widowed and old is not easily affected, although the number entitled to social security benefit owing to these conditions can be modified without much difficulty by changes in legislation. Unemployment belongs to a different category. It is the only contingency resulting in an involuntary loss of earnings which may be caused or prevented by government action. The fact that a government can within limits influence the level of employment is now as widely accepted as the fact that the unemployed are generally, but not invariably, not to blame for their plight. If it is accepted that some people are unemployed as the result of government measures aimed at slowing down the rate of inflation and others as the result of such rapid technological progress that in a few areas jobs vanish faster than new ones arise, the case for generous compensation for those who lose their employment for these reasons seems very strong.

All statutory support for the unemployed, whether by way of social insurance or social assistance, is based on the recognition that unemployment is more often than not involuntary and that it is more of a misfortune than a fault. There are in particular three arguments in favour of a high level of compensation. First, it accords more with the modern concept of communal responsibility and seems morally superior to the common law dictum that (except in unlawful acts) 'the loss lies where it falls'. This view is generously expressed by R. C. Geary, a former director of the Irish Central Statistical Office and the first director of the Economic and Social Research Institute in Dublin, who wrote in 1970 :

> In the classical words of the unemployment Acts a person qualified for aid when 'able and willing to work but unable to find suitable employment'. That such people, through no fault of their own, should find their earnings reduced by 68 per cent. to a level which must be near subsistence, is an affront to natural justice and a burden on the conscience of citizens in general.
>
> The ideal would be that every employee should have a civil service type contract, whereby his income is reduced, or ceases altogether, only because of grave misdemeanour; it should not be reduced on involuntary unemployment. Apart from cost, there would appear to be no difficulty about administering such a scheme using the existing social security system.[3]

A second argument for generous unemployment compensation is based on the economic reasoning advanced by Lord Keynes in the 1930s. This demonstrated that the level of employment depends on spending for either consumption or investment and that saving in excess of investment reduces employment. A high level of unemployment compensation both nationally and regionally tends to maintain the level of purchasing power and thereby the level of employment, while a low level of unemployment compensation has the opposite effect and thus actually contributes to unemployment.

Lastly, high unemployment compensation is likely to increase productivity in certain circumstances. The willingness of workers to accept new types of machinery and other changes requiring a re-organisation of work schedules is an important factor in determining the rate at which productivity will rise. Reorganisation frequently results in redundancy and workers have an understandable reluctance to co-operate in measures which will make some of them lose their jobs and livelihood. The more favourable the situation of the men who became redundant, the more likely it is that workers will refrain from resisting alterations in methods of production and new manning schedules.

Statutory Disqualification. For the last twenty-five years all ten countries have provided, at least for a limited period, insurance benefit or assistance for the majority of men and women who are able to work but who cannot find any suitable employment. These schemes all incorporated a number of grounds for disqualification which were meant to distinguish between voluntary and involuntary unemployment. The grounds for disqualification were very similar in all countries as they were all based on the original British legislation and included: voluntary leaving without good cause, discharge for misconduct, refusal to accept an offer of suitable work, the loss of employment due to a trade dispute, refusal to undergo training provided and making fraudulent claims. Only the last of these disqualifications refers to a condition which can be established with reasonable ease; the other five as well as the words 'able and willing to work' give considerable scope for stringent or lenient interpretation.

The question of what employment is suitable is often difficult to decide as it relates to a particular person and not to a particular job. The variety of relevant criteria which can be taken into account in determining whether work is suitable is illustrated by a clause contained in many of the U.S. state laws which gives seven such criteria :

> In determining whether or not any work is suitable for an individual, the commission shall consider the degree of risk involved in his health, safety and morals, his physical fitness and prior training and experience, his length of unemployment and prospects for securing local work in his customary occupation, and the distance of the available work from his residence.[4]

Some of the other grounds for disqualification, such as 'industrial misconduct' and 'leaving voluntarily without good cause' are similarly difficult to define.[5] Any scheme of unemployment insurance or assistance is inherently more complex to administer than other income-maintenance programmes. The administrative decisions, possibly reversed or confirmed on appeal, are likely to reflect the social climate prevailing in a society.

Disqualification for industrial misconduct can be a powerful weapon of industrial discipline, and refusal of benefit as the result of strikes or lockouts can be used to influence the conduct of industrial disputes. Income-maintenance provisions for the unemployed are inherently the most controversial of any social security cash benefits.

The Case for Full Employment.   In the field of social security the most remarkable change, comparing the 1920s and 1930s with the twenty-five years following the Second World War, has been the ubiquitous decline in unemployment. The proportion of aggregate expenditure on social security cash payments which is spent on unemployment benefit and relief has declined everywhere. However, the social effect of the reduction in unemployment far outweighs the economic benefit and the reduced financial burden on public funds. All the ten countries attained for at least a few years what Lord Beveridge defined as full employment :

> [A state in which] unemployment is reduced to short intervals of standing by, with the certainty that very soon one will be wanted in one's old job again or will be wanted in a new job that is within one's powers.[6]

This he considered as superior to any other state of employment :

> . . . the labour market should always be a seller's market rather than a buyer's market. A person who has difficulty in buying the labour that he wants suffers inconvenience or reduction of profits. A person who cannot sell his labour is in effect told that he is of no use. The first difficulty causes annoyance or loss. The

other is a personal catastrophe. This difference remains even if an adequate income is provided, by insurance or otherwise, during unemployment; the feeling of not being wanted demoralises.[7]

Nothing increases the dignity of labour and the self-respect of the man who has nothing to sell but his labour, as much as the knowledge that what he has to sell is in keen demand.

History of Unemployment Insurance. In the last quarter of the nineteenth century trade unions of skilled workers already paid unemployment benefit to their members on a substantial scale. Early in the twentieth century the government adopted a number of measures which gave some limited assistance to the unemployed outside the framework of the Poor Law. On the initiative of Winston Churchill a national system of labour exchanges was set up by William Beveridge in 1909 with the object of improving the mechanism of the labour market. Beveridge became the first Director of Labour Exchanges, and he and Churchill were also the architects of the unemployment insurance scheme which formed Part II of the National Insurance Act, 1911. This was the first national compulsory unemployment insurance scheme set up in any country.

It provided for insurance against unemployment in certain industries which had marked fluctuations of employment. When the scheme came into operation in 1912 it covered $2\frac{1}{4}$ million manual workers. The Unemployment Insurance Act, 1920, extended cover to virtually all manual workers in private industry and commerce (a special scheme for agricultural workers was set up in 1936) and also to non-manual workers earning less than £250 a year. Under the original Act benefit was 35p a week limited to 15 weeks (and no more than one week's benefit for five weeks' contributions). Workers and their employers each contributed $2\frac{1}{2}$d (about 1p) a week and the Treasury contributed a sum equal to one-third of the combined contributions of employers and workers.

The scheme developed very differently from what had been envisaged in 1912. During the war years 1914–18 the level of unemployment was low but the steep rise in prices reduced the purchasing power of the benefit. The Act of 1920 increased benefit rates to 75p for men and 60p for women but this did not even bring them back to the values of 1912. In the following year allowances for adult and child dependants were introduced in conditions of great distress caused by unemployment, in an atmosphere of panic and in fear of rising working-class militancy. Between 1920 and 1930 the purchasing power of benefit paid to a married man with two children increased more than three-fold, partly on account of the dependants' allowances which were raised on three occasions, partly owing to an increase in the basic rate but mainly owing to a decline in prices of more than 40 per cent. over the decade. Simultaneously, in the severe depression following the First World War the limitations in the duration of benefit were relaxed and for some years virtually suspended.

The British unemployment scheme was designed to have an insurance character, although not to the extent of covering 'all the responsibilities of the unemployed person in all circumstances, but rather to supplement private effort in mitigating distress due to involuntary unemployment',[8] However, in the exigencies of the prolonged and severe unemployment of the period between the wars, it altered its character several times. The changes in policy and administration are too numerous to be recorded, but the governments of those days considered unemployment insurance not only as a means of mitigating the distress caused by unemployment but also, particularly in the 1920s, as an important device for combating militancy and political upheaval.

The National Insurance Act, 1946, adhered to all the major features of the 1911 Act. Flat-rate contributions were shared equally between employers and employees, giving entitlement to flat-rate benefits limited in duration by the previous employment record. However, the flat rate was now, according to the Beveridge recommendation, 'to be sufficient without further resources to provide the minimum income needed for subsistence in all normal cases'.[9] Unemployment insurance was extended to all employees irrespective of income and became part of a comprehensive national insurance scheme providing against all contingencies of interruption and cessation of earnings. The unemployed who had exhausted their entitlement to insurance benefit could apply for national assistance which was awarded on the basis of an income test. For householders (but not for others) the level of national assistance, which included an allowance for the net rent actually paid, was after 1948 considerably higher than that of insurance benefit. For this reason an appreciable proportion of insurance beneficiaries applied also for national assistance (renamed supplementary benefit in 1966).

Benefit Levels. In November 1969 the standard rate of benefit was £5 a week (£6·75 from October 1972) for a single person and £8·10 (£10·80) for a married couple if the wife did not work. This was increased for each dependant child by £1·55 (£2·10) less the value of any family allowance received by the mother. The benefit was normally payable for 52 weeks, after a waiting period of three days. Persons who had exhausted their benefit could claim supplementary benefit subject to an income test. For a married man with two children whose wife was not working, benefit was approximately 41 per cent. of the standard weekly wage plus family allowances. The supplementary benefit which such a family could claim averaged about 50 per cent. (depending on the rent paid and the age of children) of the standard wage. As neither supplementary benefit nor insurance benefit were earnings-related, they were proportionally higher for the man with a small wage than for the man with a high wage.

The Wage Stop. Supplementary benefit by a provision known as the 'wage stop' was restricted to an amount such that the claimant's income while unemployed was not greater than it would have been if he were working full-time in his normal occupation. This proviso was in accordance with the principle

> that it would be unfair to the man who was working, but earning less than the supplementary benefit level, if his counterpart who was unemployed received a higher income. Thus the wage stop was intended to leave the unemployed claimant neither better nor worse off than he would be when working.[10]

In 1969 approximately 10 to 14 per cent. of all unemployed men receiving supplementary benefit were subject to the wage stop.

Earnings-Related Benefits. In 1965 the flat-rate unemployment benefit was increased by an earnings-related supplement for all who had earned at least £450 in the preceding financial year. This supplement was paid after a waiting period of 12 days at a rate of one-third of the sum by which the average weekly earnings (up to £30) exceeded £9. For the standard wage-earner with an income of £26·60 per week the supplement thus amounted to £5·87 and increased the aggregate benefit of a single man by 117 per cent. but that of a married man with two children by only 52 per cent. The duration of the earnings-related supplement was limited to 26 weeks. It was also restricted so that the total benefit including dependants' and earnings-related supplements did not exceed 85 per cent. of average weekly earnings in the preceding financial year. In November 1969 about 35 per cent. of the men and 19 per cent. of the women who received unemployment benefit also received the earnings-related supplement.[11]

The introduction of the earnings-related supplement was a major break with the Beveridge concept of flat-rate subsistence benefits. At the time this was justified by the inadequacy of flat-rate benefits to meet the needs of a modern consumer society. The scale of commitments which people undertake for rents, mortgages and hire-purchase agreements are related to their normal earnings. They cannot be adjusted quickly when faced with a sudden loss of income due to sickness or unemployment. In order to avoid anxiety and financial difficulties, it was therefore necessary to relate benefits to earnings. A second quite different reason in favour of this change was the desire to diminish the reluctance of workers to accept the large-scale redundancies which were anticipated as a result of industrial re-organisation. The new benefit was to enable the male worker and especially the skilled higher-paid worker to carry on without undue financial pressure while he was looking for a new job.

Minimum Notice and Redundancy Payments.   There was a somewhat similar motivation behind the Contracts of Employment Act, 1963. It gave to all employees entitlement to minimum periods of notice of termination of employment. The length of notice varied with the time an employee had been continuously employed. As from 1972, one week's notice was required after 13 weeks' continuous employment, rising to eight weeks' notice after 15 years' continuous employment. An employee who was not given the opportunity of working normally during the period of notice was to be paid for each week of notice at least at his weekly rate of pay in the 12 weeks before notice was given. This Act improved the employment security of workers who had been in the same job for some time.

The Redundancy Payments Act, 1965, was another measure designed to assist industrial reorganisation. It required employers to make lump-sum compensation payments, related to pay, length of service and age, to employees made redundant. 'Redundancy' was defined as termination of contract on account of the diminution or cessation of an employer's needs for employees to do work of a particular kind. Employees who had at least two years' service became entitled to half a week's pay for each year of employment at age 18 to 22, to one week's pay at age 22 to 41 and to one and a half weeks' pay at age 41 to 65 (60 for women). The maximum service for compensation was 20 years and weekly earnings in excess of £40 were ignored in calculating redundancy payment. Thus the standard wage-earner aged 55 who had worked for one employer for 15 years became entitled to compensation, which was exempt from income-tax, equal to 22 weeks' pay – about £586. Redundancy pay was designed to be more favourable for the older rather than the younger worker, the man who held a job for some time rather than the one who moved around and the man with a good wage rather than the lowest paid.

The compensation was paid by the employer, but in 1969 he could claim from the Redundancy Fund set up under the Act reimbursement of half the sum he had paid out. This fund was financed by employers' contributions of 6·3p a week in respect of employed men and 2·9p in respect of women. The lower contributions for women reflected both their lower average earnings and their shorter average periods of continuous employment.

Half of the redundancy pay was thus, like other social risks, pooled and borne by industry as a whole, while the other half was an imposition on the employer who had made workers redundant. (This arrangement was somewhat similar to merit rating and self-insurance). It thus imposed the same burden on industries and firms where redundancies were caused by declining trade as on firms where they were the result of reorganisation leading to greater productivity.

The three measures introduced in the 1960s to make redundancy more acceptable to workers and thereby assist industrial reorganisation and technical innovation undoubtedly had some degree of success. They were supplemented by more liberal redundancy compensation schemes in some industries in the public sector – coal-mining, railways, docks and steelmaking. However, the increasing level of unemployment, which reached more than 1 million by the end of 1971, brought about a wave of strikes protesting against redundancies. In the Britain of the early 1970s the fear of losing one's job had become greater than it had been for the previous thirty years. Between 1960 and 1969 unemployment averaged about 1·8 per cent., but in the last three months of 1971 it exceeded 4 per cent. In these circumstances, notice of termination of employment, short-term earnings-related benefits and redundancy payments continued to be social security measures of intrinsic worth, but had become of little use in promoting industrial reorganisation.

Persons Receiving Benefit.   The registered unemployed are, at any time, only a proportion of those 'able and willing to work but unable to find suitable employment'. Some men and women past the minimum retirement age would prefer to continue working but retire when they fail to keep their jobs. Young boys and girls who had intended to start work at 15 or 16 continue in school for another year or two. Married women who like to go out to work do not register for employment when they know that there are no suitable employment opportunities in their area. In times of full employment when there are more vacancies than jobs some people, when they lose a job or leave it voluntarily, remain unemployed for a short time while they look around but do not register at an employment exchange. For all these reasons the number actually unemployed is normally greater than that registered as unemployed. Conversely, among those registered are some who, for various reasons which may be judged good or bad, are not willing to work; others are physically or mentally unfit to perform any type of work which is likely to be available.

In November 1969 just over a fifth of the men and just over a third of the women who were registered as unemployed received no benefit of any kind. Married women who had opted not to pay national insurance contributions had no claim to unemployment benefit and did not receive supplementary benefit if they lived with their husbands. Men did not receive any benefit in three circumstances: lack of entitlement to unemployment benefit owing to the statutory disqualifications to which reference was made in the previous section; lack of entitlement to supplementary benefit owing to the existence of other income, for example employer's pension, wife's earnings or capital in excess of about £2,500; failure to apply for supplementary benefit. The proportion of registered unemployed not receiving benefit varied with changes in economic conditions and with the number of registered unemployed.

Reorganisation of Employment and Training Services.   At the end of 1971 the Department of Employment announced a major programme of reorganising the employment services. One of the consequences of this was that as from 1974 unemployment benefit would be paid by post instead of, as at present, in cash at the employment exchanges. The details of the new payment scheme have not yet been published, but it was made clear that

> The Employment Service will continue to retain its responsibilities for protecting the National Insurance Fund against abuse by reporting prima-facie cases of refusal of, or failure to apply for suitable employment and of any restrictions on availability for work of people drawing benefit. Registration for employment with the Employment Service will still be a condition for the receipt of unemployment benefit. . . .[12]

Early in 1972 the Department of Employment published a plan for a massive expansion in vocational training.[13] This was based on an increasing realisation that changes in the pattern of skills would be needed to secure full employment and that organised training was the most efficient way to prepare people for new employment. Already in July 1971 the allowance paid to trainees at vocational training centres had been increased so that on average they were some £5 a week above the comparable rate of unemployment benefit. The official intention for the future was to keep these allowances sufficiently high to act as an inducement to the unemployed to undertake training. However, the allowance paid to a single man at the time when it was increased in July 1971 was equal to only about a third of the average wage of a man working in industry and about half the earnings of a low-paid worker, hardly sufficient to be a genuine inducement but a step in the right direction.

IRELAND

History of Unemployment Support. When the state was founded in 1921, unemployment insurance under the U.K. National Insurance Act, 1911, had already been in operation for nine years. The exclusion of agricultural workers from insurance cover under the U.K. legislation had, however, prevented the largest group of employees in Ireland from benefiting by the scheme. All the essentials of the U.K. provisions as they operated in 1921 after the introduction of dependants' allowances remained unaltered in Ireland up to 1969. Indeed, the 1921 personal rates of benefit remained unaltered for the next 26 years.[14]

The unemployed not in receipt of insurance benefit had to rely until 1933 on poor-law relief from the local authorities. In that year an unemployment assistance programme was introduced which utilised the administrative arrangements of the unemployment insurance scheme and transferred the major share of the cost of supporting the unemployed to the Exchequer. The rate of unemployment assistance varied with the applicant's family circumstances, means and place of residence. Assistance was unlimited in duration but subject to statutory disqualifications similar to those of unemployment insurance. The inherent difficulty of unemployment assistance peculiar to Ireland was the large number of smallholders and their relatives who worked more or less part-time on their farms but also sought wage-earning employment.

The major change in the structure of social security provisions occurred when the Social Welfare Act, 1952, amalgamated unemployment and other types of social insurance with the various assistance programmes to form one unified scheme. At the same time unemployment insurance was extended to agricultural workers. Non-manual employees earning more than a prescribed income (£1,200 in 1969 and £1,600 as from 1971), however, were still excluded from all social insurance coverage.

The endemic nature of unemployment in Ireland was emphasised by Geary and Hughes in the opening sentences of their research paper on this subject:

> In Ireland less attention is paid to the chronically high Irish unemployment rate than the gravity of the problem merits. Indeed, the reason it is more or less tacitly tolerated may be its permanent character.[15]

In Ireland as in all developed countries there were fewer unemployed in the 1950s and 1960s than there had been in the 1920s and 1930s, but Ireland had in the 1960s the highest unemployment rate of any of the countries of this study. In that decade the unemployment rate, excluding agriculture, fishing and domestic service, averaged 6·1 per cent.[16] In November 1969 as many as 57,000 men and women were registered as unemployed, including 21,000 not engaged in commerce or industry.[17]

Levels of Unemployment Support.   In January 1970 the standard rate of unemployment benefit was £3.75 for an adult, increased by

£3·12½ for an adult dependant and 77½p for each of the first two dependent children. The average compensation rate for the standard wage-earner with two children in 1969–70 was about 43 per cent. The duration of unemployment benefit was limited to 52 weeks except for persons aged 65 years and over who, if they fulfilled the statutory conditions, received unemployment benefit without time limit until they qualified for a contributory old-age pension at the age of 70 years.

The maximum rate of unemployment assistance for an adult in January 1970 was £3·07½, with increases of £2·80 for an adult dependant and 62½p for each of the first two dependent children. This for a family of four was about 15 per cent. less than unemployment insurance benefit. In non-urban areas unemployment assistance for adults was paid at slightly lower rates – 40p per week less for a married couple. The maximum non-urban rate of unemployment assistance for a family of four was in 1969–70 equal to about 54 per cent. of the average minimum weekly wage for a male agricultural worker, which was at the time £12·55 per week.

No information is available about the number of people who unsuccessfully applied for unemployment assistance. In a society where a substantial minority of self-employed farmers as well as most agricultural workers had very low incomes, it is inherently difficult to provide unemployment assistance at adequate subsistence rates.

The Redundancy Payments Act. Some interesting and novel provisions were contained in the Redundancy Payments Act, 1967, which had objectives in some respects similar to three British schemes : the Contracts of Employment Act, 1963, the Redundancy Payments Act, 1965, and the earnings-related short-term supplement to unemployment benefit introduced in 1966. The Irish Act, which was amended in 1971, provided a lump-sum compensation and a weekly redundancy payment. The lump sum equalled half a week's pay for each year of continuous employment between the ages of 16 and 41 and one week's pay for each year of continuous employment over the age of 41 years, plus one additional week's pay. The standard wage-earner who became redundant at the age of 50 years after 15 years' continuous employment thus became entitled to 13 weeks' pay – £252 at 1969 wage rates. The lump sum was not restricted after 1971 to any specific amount or number of weeks. Employees qualified for compensation after two years' continuous employment. The scheme only covered employees for whom social insurance was compulsory, but non-manual workers continued to be covered by the scheme for four years after they had exceeded the income limit for compulsory insurance.

In addition to the lump-sum payment, a redundant worker was entitled, if unemployed, to half his normal pay as from the fourth day of unemployment. This entitlement was for a minimum period of four weeks and a maximum of one week for each year (years after the age of 41 counting as two) of continuous employment. These weekly payments were in addition to unemployment or disability benefits, but the aggregate payments could not exceed 90 per cent. of what had been the normal pay. The weekly payments ceased when work was recommenced. They were, however, revived by subsequent periods of unemployment and disability.

The lump-sum compensation was paid by the employer who could claim a rebate of 50 per cent. from the special Redundancy Fund which had been set up under the 1965 Act. This rebate could only be claimed if the employer had given the employee at least two weeks' notice of termination of contract. For each additional weeks' notice he could claim a further $2\frac{1}{2}$ per cent. rebate subject to a maximum rebate of 65 per cent. The purpose of these higher rebates was to provide a strong incentive to employers to give the longest possible notice of redundancy to their staff. The weekly payments were made by the Department of Labour and were a direct charge against the Redundancy Fund, which was financed by weekly flat-rate contributions of employers and employees shared in the ratio of 2 : 1.

The appeals machinery set up by the Act broke with previous Irish practice. Disputes about claims to unemployment insurance benefit or unemployment assistance were determined by Appeals Officers appointed by the Minister of Social Welfare. These officers held statutory appointments and were independent in the sense that they were not subject to direction in deciding any issue. The Appeals Tribunal under the Redundancy Payments Act was more like the British local appeals tribunals under the National Insurance scheme. The Irish tribunal consisted of a legally qualified chairman and one member nominated by trade unions and one by bodies representing employers.

The Promotion of Employment Act. The Federal Placement and Unemployment Act, 1927, instituted the first German contributory system of unemployment insurance some forty years after the other branches of social insurance had been set up. The main tenets of the original law were followed in all subsequent legislation. The emphasis on the different facets of the employment service, however, has varied over the years. The present law, the Promotion of Employment Act, 1969, as its title implies, enlarged the scope of the service and also improved the conditions on which benefit was awarded. The primary object of the new law was the prevention of unemployment by means of a positive employment policy; the support of the unemployed had become a secondary objective. The wide realisation of the need to adapt the skills and vocational qualifications of workers to changes in production and technology had been an important influence in the making of the law.

The Federal Labour Office (Bundesanstalt für Arbeit) which administered the Act was empowered to encourage all branches of vocational education : vocational training (the acquisition of the knowledge and skills required to practise a trade or occupation), vocational further education (the supplementation, improvement and expansion of existing knowledge and expertise), vocational retraining (the acquisition of the knowledge and expertise required to change to a different occupation) and vocational rehabilitation (measures to enable people who were mentally or physically handicapped or psychologically disturbed to remain or become self-supporting).

The Federal Labour Office assisted vocational training to a limited extent by grants and loans to young people as well as adults. Such assistance, however, was only given to people who lacked (or whose parents lacked) the necessary means of financing their own training. Persons who undertook vocational further education, vocational retraining or vocational rehabilitation received maintenance allowances according to statutory scales. These allowances were related to the income which had been earned before training began. In 1970 the standard allowance for the first six months of training was 130 per cent. and thereafter 140 per cent. of the appropriate earnings-related unemployment benefit. This was equal to 81 and 88 per cent. respectively of net earnings for a single person. A married man received in addition DM14·40 for each member of his family, subject to his total allowance not exceeding 95 per cent. of what had been his net income. Furthermore, the standard allowance was increased by 4 per cent. every six months after the first year of attending a course. The Federal Labour Office also financed the three types of vocational education and assisted with all expenses incidental to attending the courses.

Since 1969, in order to encourage expenditure by individuals on vocational education, a sum of up to DM900 spent on training for an occupation in which a taxpayer was not engaged could be deducted as an expense for the purposes of income-tax. Expenditure without limit, incurred on education or training related to the occupation in which the taxpayer was engaged, was another permissible tax deduction.[18] (In the U.K. expenditure on vocational education was not in any circumstances a permissible tax deduction.).

Measures to Stabilise Employment.   The Federal Labour Office also administered a variety of measures designed to stabilise employment and to create new employment opportunities. One such measure was the compensation, subject to prescribed conditions, of workers on short time for the full amount of their lost earnings. This benefited on average as many as 143,000 in the unfavourable employment conditions of 1967, but a mere 1,300 in the more favourable conditions of 1969. The number benefiting at some time during these years was of course much greater. Another measure granted benefits varying between 63 and 80 per cent. of normal net earnings to workers in the building industry who, on account of bad weather conditions, were prevented from working in the winter months. In 1968–9 such benefits were paid in respect of the loss of nearly 35 million working days at a cost of DM823 million. The purpose of this measure was twofold : to maintain the income of these workers and to enable builders to offer continuous employment to their regular work-force. The Federal Labour Office also subsidised builders on prescribed scales for any work they undertook in January or February; the object of this was to indemnify them for the cost of protective devices needed to enable work to continue at that time of year.

There were also a number of grants and loans to induce employers to provide work for the older unemployed who had been out of a job for some time. The Federal Labour Office was moreover empowered to make reintegration allowances on a quite generous scale to people seeking work. These covered expenses related to travelling, moving house, maintaining two households and purchasing tools and equipment. Such allowances were restricted to people who could not be expected to bear these expenses themselves.

Unemployment Insurance. As from 1968 virtually all employees except civil servants and part-time workers were compulsorily insured against unemployment, including non-manual workers with incomes above a specified amount who until then had been exempt. Employees had to contribute to the funds of the Federal Labour Office a maximum of 1 per cent. of their wages or salaries up to DM1,800 per month. This was matched by identical contributions from their employers. The combined contribution actually levied as from 1964 was 1·3 per cent. The contribution ceiling as from 1969 was the same as that for pension insurance. It was reassessed annually so as to equal twice the average earnings of all manual and non-manual workers (covered by pension insurance) in the first three years of the last four years.

Unemployment benefit was awarded subject to the usual statutory disqualifications. The duration of benefit was determined by the number of weeks worked in the last three years and was limited to a maximum of 52 weeks. Benefit as from 1970 was paid from the day following the termination of employment. The previous rule requiring three waiting days was rescinded as it was considered incompatible with sound social policy to leave a man without an income, even for a short period. An applicant was entitled to unemployment benefit even if he worked part-time for up to 20 hours a week and even if, on account of a disability, he was not able to work for the number of hours customary in his occupation. A man who did not receive a pension in respect of incapacity for work was entitled to benefit, as long as he was able to work for a minimum of 20 hours a week. The period for which benefit was withheld on account of a statutory disqualification was reduced by the 1969 Act to between two and four weeks, depending upon circumstances; it had previously been between two and eight weeks.

The standard rate of benefit depended on the normal earnings in the 20 days preceding unemployment, up to the contribution ceiling of DM1,800 per month in 1970. It was 62·5 per cent. of the relevant net earnings of a single man and corresponded to between 42 and 60 per cent. of gross earnings. On account of variations in tax liability, the proportion was lower the higher the income. For the standard wage-earner the level of compensation in 1969 was about 45 per cent. The standard rate of benefit was supplemented by an allowance of DM12 a week for each dependant, with the proviso that the total benefit did not exceed 80 per cent. of the net earnings of a married man with two dependent children.

An unemployed person could have a net income of DM15 a week without losing any entitlement to benefit, but his benefit was reduced by half the amount by which his net income exceeded this sum. Thus the standard wage-earner, when he became unemployed, could earn in a part-time job DM100 a week and still be entitled to about DM86 unemployment benefit, as long as he did not work for more than 20 hours a week.

The unemployed who had either exhausted their benefit or not qualified for it could claim unemployment assistance subject to an income test. This test was applied not only to the applicant and his spouse but also to his parents and any of his children living at home. Assistance was not limited in duration and was awarded according to rules which, allowing for the necessary adaptations to the nature of the scheme, were similar to those for the award of unemployment benefit. For recipients who had exhausted their claim to benefit, assistance was based on pre-unemployment earnings; for all others it was based on an estimate of future earnings. For the family with many children the maximum assistance rate was the same as the maximum benefit rate, while for the single standard wage-earner assistance was less by some 16 per cent. Dependants' allowances were the same under both schemes.

Throughout the 1960s the unemployment rate averaged a mere 1 per cent., but in 1967, the worst year of the decade. it exceeded 2 per cent.

All the funds of the Federal Labour Office were derived from the contributions of employers and employees. In 1969 about 30 per cent. of the total contribution income (about 0·4 per cent. of all wages liable to contributions) was spent on 'bad weather' benefits and 'all the year round employment' grants to workers and employers in the building industry. (This ought to be considered as a subsidy of quite a substantial amount to that industry). Another 17 per cent. went on vocational education and reintegration allowances, while only a quarter was needed for the financial support of the unemployed. This quarter included the expenditure not only on unemployment benefit but also on assistance payments to those who had exhausted their benefit.[19] The Federal Exchequer financed the unemployment assistance of those who had not previously received benefit.

Comparison between the German and the U.K. Provisions for the Unemployed. It is interesting to note that in Germany unemployment benefit was awarded on terms distinctly more generous than those in the U.K. In Germany the 1969 Act abolished waiting days and liberalised the rules relating to benefit for men involved in trade disputes. The opposite happened in the U.K. in 1971 when waiting-day rules were made more onerous and payments to men involved in a dispute were further restricted.[20] In the U.K. most spare-time or part-time earnings and in any case all earnings in excess of 33p a day (£1·98 a week) led to the forfeit of benefit, while in Germany the unemployed were able to have quite substantial part-time earnings and work up to 20 hours a week and yet still draw benefit (although at a reduced rate). In general, benefits for single men and married men whose wives were working were higher (in relation to earnings) in Germany than in the U.K.; for other married men the position was more complex and varied according to income and the duration of unemployment. Periods of statutory notice terminating unemployment were generally longer in Germany than in the U.K. However, Germany had statutory redundancy payment schemes only in the mining and the iron and steel industries, while the U.K. had a universal scheme from 1965.

Austria. The Austrian and German employment services had much in common; they were based on the same principles and shared many characteristics. In Austria, however, the rates of benefit in relation to earnings were lower and the conditions attached to the award of benefits were more restrictive. The average rate of unemployment in Austria in the 1960s was 2·7 per cent., almost three times that in Germany.

With the exception of public servants and casual workers all employees in Austria were compulsorily insured against unemployment. The qualifying period for entitlement to benefit was more stringent than it was in Germany and the duration was limited to a maximum of 30 weeks. Benefit commenced on the eighth day of unemployment. The standard rate of benefit varied with earnings of up to Sch4,050 a month (Sch90 to Sch324 a week in 1969 when the standard weekly wage was Sch1,225) and was an inverse proportion of earnings (60 to 33 per cent.). It was supplemented by an allowance of Sch30 a week for the first and Sch24 for each additional dependant, plus very small rent and cost-of-living allowances. The standard benefit was reduced by any income in excess of Sch1,200 a month and for lesser incomes by one-half of any pension or benefit from public funds. These deductions, however, could not exceed half the standard benefit.

After exhausting benefit the unemployed could claim unemployment relief subject to an income test. The rate of relief and the conditions on which it was granted were similar to those for the award of benefit.

In Austria, as in Germany, there were schemes for granting benefit to workers on short time and to workers in the building industry who were prevented from working in the winter months owing to bad weather conditions. Subsidies and loans were granted to provide additional employment of a type which was 'economically useful and in the public interest'. Such assistance could not exceed the savings in unemployment benefit and relief resulting directly from the consequent reduction in unemployment.

Employees contributed 1 per cent. of their wages up to Sch4,050 a month (about 75 per cent. of the standard wage) to unemployment insurance and related employment services. Employees in the building industry and their employers each contributed an additional 0·5 per cent. of wages for the financing of the 'bad weather' benefits; any additional expenditure on these schemes was borne by the Exchequer.

DENMARK AND THE NETHERLANDS

The Danish Voluntary Unemployment Insurance Scheme. Denmark was the only European country of this study in which unemployment insurance was voluntary. Among employees outside the public service only half were insured against unemployment. Also, in contrast to the other countries the insurance scheme was not administered by a government department as in the U.K., Ireland and Austria, nor by self-governing occupational associations of employers and employees as in Germany and the Netherlands, but by trade unions. They administered special unemployment funds which had been recognised, supervised and subsidised by the government since 1907.

Unemployment insurance was voluntary in the sense that the law did not make it compulsory for any group of employees, but not in the sense that the decision whether to insure or not was left to the individual. The rules of the trade unions obliged their members to join and contribute to the union's unemployment fund, and as membership of a trade union was in many economic activities more or less a condition of employment, the individual generally had little choice in practice. It was also possible to join the unemployment fund of a union without being a member, but this was comparatively rare. Entitlement to unemployment benefit was subject to the same statutory disqualifications as it was in other countries. The unemployment funds were separate legal entities and were not permitted to pay benefit to their members if they were unemployed owing to an industrial dispute.

In the mid-1960s there were some 65 separate funds ranging in membership from 100 to 250,000 and comprising a total of 800,000. The benefits were largely financed by members' contributions which varied widely between different funds, and which were particularly high for unskilled workers. Local social service committees were empowered to pay up to half the unemployment insurance contribution of some of these low-paid workers. Benefit was paid after six waiting days had passed. The rate of daily benefit varied according to the length of membership of the fund and was higher for householders than for others. There were also a number of special allowances for rent and fuel as well as children's supplements. Benefit for the single man was about a quarter and for the married man with two children about half the average wage.[21]

The scheme was improved and revised in several respects in 1967. Waiting days were abolished and benefit was paid as from the first day of unemployment. Benefits were simplified and increased and the various allowances were rescinded. The level of benefit was increased to about three-fifths of average earnings for the single man as well as the married man with two children, but continued to be limited to 80 per cent. of pre-unemployment earnings. As from 1967, benefit was adjusted annually according to the movement of the wage index of industry. In 1968–9 the daily cash benefit paid for six days a week and liable to income-tax was at the most Kr61·50 and averaged Kr55. The unemployment funds were empowered to assist those seeking employment by the payment of travel and removal grants and by granting lodging allowances.

The result of the various improvements was an increase in the average level of benefit between 1962 and 1968 of about 140 per cent., while wages during this period increased by only 65 per cent. The financing of the scheme was also drastically changed. In 1962 employees' contributions financed more than half the benefits paid and were related to the risk of unemployment to which the members of a fund were exposed. By 1968 the position had altered considerably : contributions from the insured were the same irrespective of the fund to which they belonged, were on average 44 per cent. lower than they had been six years previously and were financing only 11 per cent. of the benefits paid. In 1962 the average annual contributions had been almost equal to two and a half days' wages, while in 1968 they were equal to less than one day's wage. Employers' contributions to the financing of unemployment insurance had always been at a relatively low level, but in 1968 the combined contribution of the state and the local authorities amounted to 82 per cent. of the total expenditure. This proportion was somewhat exceptional, however, as it was related to a level of unemployment which happened to be higher in that year than in any other during the 1960s.[22]

Aspects of Voluntary Insurance. The limitation of unemployment insurance to half the employee population might be undesirable from two quite different points of view. First, by restricting insurance to those who are most likely to be unemployed, it offends against the principle that social insurance should distribute risks over the whole of society and not cover only those who are most exposed to a particular risk. This would have been a justified criticism of Danish unemployment insurance up to 1967, but could hardly be applied thereafter when more than four-fifths of the cost of benefit was borne by the public purse. The term 'insurance' applied to the post-1967 income-maintenance programme for the unemployed might be considered a misnomer. The second reason why the limitation of unemployment insurance to only half the population might be regarded as undesirable is that it leaves substantial sections of employees without any certain support if they lose their employment. This was a justified criticism of Danish unemployment insurance in 1969 and will be remedied by the proposals of the Social Reform

Commission to which reference has already been made.

In Denmark the government was responsible for the employment services, including local and regional employment exchanges and vocational training and rehabilitation, and their administration was quite separate from that of the cash payments to the unemployed.

Level of Unemployment. The level of unemployment in Denmark in the 1960s averaged 3·1 per cent. according to the published statistics. This was a higher rate than in the other European countries except Ireland. A comparison of these unemployment rates is, however, misleading and likely to exaggerate unemployment in Denmark. The rate for Austria, Germany, the U.K. and the Netherlands expressed the number of unemployed registered at employment exchanges as a proportion of all employees, while that for Denmark referred to the beneficiaries as a proportion of the members of the trade union unemployment funds.

Unemployment Insurance in the Netherlands. In the Netherlands, as in Denmark, the government started to subsidise the trade union unemployment funds early in this century.[23] During the inter-war period there was considerable discussion and controversy about the introduction of an unemployment insurance scheme. The role of the trade unions and the share of the cost to be borne by the employers were two of the major political disagreements. Legislation was proposed in the late 1930s but delayed by the war and the first Unemployment Insurance Act was only passed in 1949 and came into force in 1952.

In 1969 all employees were covered by unemployment insurance and also some self-employed persons whose status was similar to that of employees. Any insured person who had been working for at least 130 days in the same branch of industry or trade during the 12 months preceding unemployment was entitled to receive interim unemployment benefit from the occupational association of that industry for up to eight weeks. If he continued to be unemployed beyond this period he was entitled to unemployment benefit for a further 18 weeks under a national scheme. Any employee who did not qualify for interim benefit became entitled right away to unemployment benefit under the general scheme if he had been an employee for a minimum prescribed period.

Benefit Levels and Special Features. The rates of unemployment and interim unemployment benefit were the same : 80 per cent. of 100/106 of the daily wage up to a maximum of F189. This was supplemented by a 6 per cent. holiday allowance payable in a lump sum. The relevant daily wage was that earned on average during the three months preceding unemployment. The benefit was adjusted according to the movements of the general wage index. Two features relating to the rate of benefit are of special interest. First, benefit was paid at a reduced rate during periods of partial unemployment, as it was in Germany. Second, a person who accepted employment at a lower wage than he received before he became unemployed, or who accepted lower wages in order to avoid unemployment, was guaranteed unemployment benefit based on his previous higher earnings in the case of his becoming unemployed again within a period of two and a half years.

Financing. Interim unemployment benefit was financed by contributions shared equally between employers and employees. These averaged 0·6 per cent. of wages up to a maximum of F189 a day, but varied between the occupational associations. In those associations in which the level of unemployment was above average, contributions were also above average and vice versa. This arrangement thus incorporated a limited degree of risk rating in unemployment insurance. Unemployment benefit proper was financed by contributions which were identical for all types of employment and fixed at 0·8 per cent. for 1969. Half of this was borne by the government and one-quarter each by employers and employees.

Unemployment Relief. After exhausting unemployment benefit there was an entitlement to unemployment relief from the local authorities subject to an income test. Relief was limited in duration to two years and was granted (subject to the general disqualifications which applied to benefit and relief alike) on much the same terms and conditions as benefit. The rate of relief was 75 per cent. of what had been the pre-unemployment daily wage, adjusted according to movements in the wage index. The whole of the cost was borne by the government who reimbursed the local authorities for all their expenditure on relief.

The unemployment rate in the Netherlands averaged about 1 per cent. in the 1960s and was about the same as that in Germany.

NEW ZEALAND AND AUSTRALIA

History of the Provisions for the Unemployed in New Zealand. New Zealand had no unemployment insurance, but it was the first English-speaking country to support the unemployed by a system financed by compulsory earnings-related contributions. Prior to the setting-up of the Unemployment Board in 1930 the relief of the unemployed had been shared between the government and local bodies. The Board was instituted to establish labour exchanges, to encourage training and the promotion of employment in industry and to provide sustenance for the unemployed. It was financed as from 1931 by a registration fee of $2 to be paid by all males over 20 years and an emergency unemployment charge of $1\frac{1}{4}$ per cent. on all wages, salaries and other incomes. This charge was later increased and was levied at $3\frac{1}{3}$ per cent. between 1935 and 1939.[24] The comprehensive social security plan which was introduced in 1939 was financed in the same way as the Unemployment Board had been; the charge was renamed social security tax and raised to 5 per cent.

The unemployment charge of 1931 differed from a social insurance contribution in that it gave no entitlement to the award of benefit. It was in the nature of a specially designated tax. The Unemployment Board adopted the policy that work should be performed in return for relief, and from 1930 to 1933, during some of the worst years of unemployment, that policy was implemented.[25] Sustenance without work for men over 50 years or unfit for manual work, who could not be placed on approved relief schemes, commenced in 1934. It was only two years later that uniform sustenance payments throughout New Zealand were established. They were paid in 1938 at a basic rate of 40 cents a week compared with what were then the basic old-age and invalidity pensions of $2.25 and $2 respectively.[26] Thus more than twenty years after the payment of unemployment benefits without a means test had commenced in the U.K., the relief of the unemployed in New Zealand was still subject to a 'work test', and when sustenance without work finally prevailed it was granted at most inadequate rates.

At the start of the comprehensive social security plan the basic rate of unemployment benefit, which was subject to a means test, was fixed at $2 a week. This was a substantial increase but was still only two-thirds of the old-age pension. The basic unemployment benefit was raised to the level of other means-tested benefits and pensions only in 1945.

Levels of Benefit and Unemployment.   Unemployment benefit in 1969 was paid at a maximum rate of $13.25 for a single man or woman and $24 for a married couple when the wife was not working. This was reduced by any personal earned income of the beneficiary and also by any other income, including the earned income of his wife, in excess of $11 a week. Benefit was payable after seven waiting days, subject to the usual disqualifications, for an unlimited duration. The benefit for a single man was equal to about 23 per cent. of the standard wage.

The level of registered unemployment in the 1960s was very low by any standards; it averaged 2,000 (out of a labour force of 1 million) and in five of the ten years was less than 1,000. The number receiving unemployment benefit in 1971 was about two-thirds of those registered as unemployed.[27]

Recommendations of the Royal Commission.   The Royal Commission on Social Security examined the desirability of changes in the unemployment benefit scheme, which had remained basically unaltered for more than thirty years.[28] They rejected the proposals for an earnings-related benefit on three counts : it could not be applied to those seeking to enter the work-force as they had no earnings record on which benefit could be based; an earnings-related benefit might exceed the wage which a man was able to earn in the future; earnings-related benefits could not be financed by earnings-related contributions on account of 'the hazards of unemployment, which can reach disaster proportions'. The Commission did not rule out the possibility that at some unspecified future date it might be considered worth while to introduce an insurance scheme, but in the meantime 'The flat-rate system with benefits adjusted to family responsibilities is . . . the surest and best basis for [the maintenance of an adequate standard of living for all].'[29] These arguments seem remarkably weak to be put forward in 1972. They fail to take account of the unemployment insurance schemes of the Netherlands and Germany, of the short-term earnings-related benefits in the U.K. and of the Canadian White Paper, *Unemployment Insurance,* published in 1970.

The Commission also rejected the proposal which was strongly urged on it that benefit should be paid irrespective of whether the husband or wife of the unemployed person was earning : '. . . to exclude the earnings of the husband or wife from the assessment of eligibility, would be to pay the benefit where the need did not exist'.[30] The Commission did, however, favour some liberalisation of the income test and recommended that the first $10 a week of personal earned income should be treated as 'other income'. This meant that the man whose wife was not working and who had no other income could earn that much without a reduction of his benefit.

A suggestion to abolish or shorten the seven-day waiting period was also unfavourably received. The Commission acknowledged that a week without any income might be a hardship and felt that the Social Security Commission might have been too rigid in applying the waiting days rule, but considered that nothing more was required than an examination of the possibility of exercising more freely the discretion which the law permitted.[31]

The exceptionally low level of unemployment in the decade prior to the deliberation of the Royal Commission must have been an important factor influencing their attitude towards unemployment benefit. In this economic climate the political pressure favouring drastic changes in an established system which affected only a handful of people must have been minimal. In the Royal Commission's Report, which contained 480 pages (excluding appendices), the chapter on unemployment benefit was a mere 13 pages. This probably reflected accurately the importance public opinion attached to this subject.

History of the Provisions for the Unemployed in Australia.   Australia was the only other among the ten countries which had no unemployment insurance scheme. Proposals for the introduction of such a scheme had already been discussed prior to the First World War and came up again in a different form in the 1920s and 1950s, but none of them gained sufficient support to be implemented.[32]

Even a national unemployment assistance scheme with benefit subject to an income test commenced only in 1945, decidedly later than in any of the other countries in this survey. Prior to that date relief was granted by the states and local bodies almost exclusively in kind, except in Queensland which had an unemployment insurance scheme in the 1920s.

The scheme initiated in 1945 was in several respects similar to the New Zealand Social Security Act. While in Australia applicants for invalidity, age and widows' pensions were subjected to a means test, the award of unemployment and sickness benefit was (as in New Zealand) based on an income test; this meant that only the income derived from capital, but not the possession of capital, was taken into consideration in determining eligibility and the rate of benefit. Australia and New Zealand had similar statutory disqualifications from benefit, counted the earnings of the wife as income of the applicant and had a seven-day waiting period. The Australian unemployment benefit scheme has not altered in any of its major characteristics since its inception.

Level of Benefit.   In 1969 the maximum rate of benefit for an adult was $10 a week plus $7 for a dependent spouse. Any income in excess of $6 was deducted from the benefit. The income not deducted could include personal earned income and in this respect appeared to be slightly more liberal than the New Zealand rules. However, the maximum rate of benefit was equal to only 12 per cent. of the standard wage, and even including the amount not deducted came to only 19 per cent., well below the corresponding proportion in New Zealand. The maximum rate of unemployment and sickness benefit was only two-thirds of the rate of age and invalidity pensions. This had also been the case in New Zealand prior to 1945, but in that country since then the rates of all income-tested benefits have been identical. (In New Zealand the term 'pension' was not used and only supplementary benefits were subject to a means test.)

Poverty and the Level of Unemployment.   At the time of the Melbourne Poverty Survey unemployment benefit for a married couple was some 28 per cent. below the poverty level adopted in that study. However, Henderson and his associates found little evidence of poverty caused by long-term unemployment.[33] This was mainly due to the very small number of unemployed in Melbourne at that time.

The level of unemployment in the late 1960s was very low. In 1969 it averaged 75,000, about 1·4 per cent. of the labour force. In contrast to most other countries the unemployment rate for both married and single women was higher than that for men – twice as high in every year between 1966 and 1970. The absolute number of male and female unemployed was about the same, but twice as many men as women received unemployment benefit.

History of Unemployment Insurance. Unemployment insurance was a joint Federal–state responsibility, unlike workmen's compensation which had always been solely a state responsibility and O.A.S.D.H.I. which was solely a Federal programme. Wisconsin in 1932 was the first state to pass an unemployment insurance law. The Social Security Act, 1935, provided an inducement, in the form of a tax-offset, for states to introduce unemployment insurance schemes. This was achieved by imposing a Federal wage tax on all employers in commerce and industry who had eight or more employees and allowing those employers who paid contributions to an approved state unemployment insurance scheme to credit these contributions up to 90 per cent. against the Federal tax. As a result of this provision all states had enacted unemployment insurance laws by 1937.

For a state insurance scheme to be approved, adherence to certain standards was required. Benefits had to be paid through public employment offices and the schemes could not .deny benefit to a worker on the grounds that he had refused to accept work at substandard wages or to join or resign from a trade union. There were also requirements relating to prompt and accurate payment of benefits. All other major issues, including duration and levels of benefit, conditions of eligibility and methods of financing the schemes, were left for the states to decide.

Criticism of the State Schemes. The 50 state programmes operating in 1969 differed in many important particulars, but can in general be criticised on a number of counts. The cover was too restricted, the level of benefit too meagre, the waiting period too long, the duration of benefit too short, the taxable base too low and the financing was accompanied by undesirable side-effects.

About 20 per cent. of all employees were not covered by unemployment insurance. The exclusions varied between different jurisdictions. Domestic workers (except in New York) and agricultural workers (including those in processing) were usually excluded. Half the states excluded employees working for employers of fewer than four workers, although as from 1972 after a change in Federal law all employees in commerce and industry were covered. In most states public employees, except those in the Federal service, were not covered compulsorily, although in some states certain public authorities could elect to have their employees included.

The level of benefit was usually a nominal 50 per cent. of previous earnings, frequently expressed as a fraction of the earnings in the calendar quarter with the highest earnings in the base period (often the first four of the last five calendar quarters). All the state laws, however, set a maximum on the amount of weekly benefit a worker could receive; these ranged in 1970 from $40 to $86 a week. In only ten states was the benefit increased by allowances for dependants and in these the maximum plus allowances ranged from $52 to $123. The effect of these dollar maximums was to limit the average weekly benefit (including allowances) for total unemployment to $50, equal to 37 per cent. of previous weekly earnings. This proportion ranged in the different states from 26 to 45 per cent. and was less than 30 per cent. in four of them.[34]

When unemployment schemes commenced in the 1930s, a waiting period of two or three weeks was the norm. By 1969 three states had abolished the waiting period and in the remainder it had been reduced to one week. It has been suggested that the time needed to process the initial claim for benefit was one of the reasons for the one-week waiting period and that the length of the waiting period was no longer an issue in these programmes.[35] It seems strange that American ingenuity in organisation could not equal that of the Germans who paid earnings-related unemployment benefit without any waiting days. In any case, if the time for processing is the justification for the waiting days, some retroactive payment in the case of prolonged unemployment would be appropriate.

In all states the duration of benefit was limited to a maximum number of weeks; in all but one this was not less than 26 weeks and in a few it was 36 weeks. Benefit extended up to 39 weeks was payable during periods of high unemployment to workers who had exhausted their benefit, under a Federal–state programme.[36] In 1970 about 1¼ million beneficiaries, equal in number to a quarter of all who had received benefit at some time during the year, were still unemployed when they had exhausted their claim to benefit. The unemployed in this position were not covered by any national follow-up programme. Unemployment was not one of the four categories of monetary public assistance for which the states received Federal aid. Some states and a large number of local authorities denied public assistance to unemployed but employable workers.[37] The economic position of the long-term unemployed in the U.S.A. was in general much worse than that in any other country of this study.

The grounds for statutory disqualification from benefit were similar to those in other countries, but the penalties attached to disqualification were frequently more severe. An official publication of the Department of Health, Education and Welfare summarised them :

> In all jurisdictions, disqualification serves at least to delay a worker's receipt of benefits. The disqualification may be for a specific period . . . or for the entire period of unemployment following the disqualifying act. Some States not only postpone the payment of benefits but also reduce the amount due to the claimant. A few States may cancel all benefit rights of a disqualified worker; then he can receive no benefits under the system until he returns to work and has earned enough wage credits to qualify again.[38]

The Federal wage tax in 1935 was levied on wages up to $3,000 a year which was at that time also the earnings base for the O.A.S.I. programme. Thereafter the earnings ceiling for the Federal social insurance programme was raised several times and stood at $7,800 in 1969, but the base for the wage tax had remained unaltered. (It was raised to $4,200 in 1972.) The financing pattern of the state unemployment insurance programmes was influenced by the wage-tax ceiling because, as mentioned above, employers could credit the contributions that they paid under the approved state laws up to 90 per cent. against the 3·2 per cent. wage tax. When the Federal tax ceiling was raised in 1972 the states had either to increase their contribution base correspondingly or to find that employers were liable to pay to the Federal government the whole of the tax on the amount by which the ceiling was raised, without an offset. In 1969 the tax ceiling was still $3,000 and this was also the base for unemployment insurance contributions in most states, although in two-fifths it had been increased somewhat, most frequently to $3,600 per annum. The combined result of the ceilings in contribution assessment and the rapid rise in wages was that unemployment contributions were levied on only half the wages of covered employees. This in turn tended to restrict increases in the maximum duration and amount of weekly benefits. It even resulted in contributions lagging behind benefits paid out in years of relatively high unemployment like 1970. (The ratio of benefits to contributions in 1970 was 1·54.)

Experience Rating. Another reason for the low contribution receipts was the universal practice of experience rating – varying an employer's contribution with his 'experience with unemployment'. This was encouraged by the Social Security Act, 1935, which allowed full tax credit for reductions in an employer's contributions on the basis of his employment record. The original idea had been that the carrot of lower contributions would be an incentive for employers to stabilise employment in much the same way as merit rating in workmen's compensation was to be an incentive to provide safe working conditions. Another object of experience rating was the allocation of the cost of unemployment benefits to industries so that it would be properly reflected in the price of goods. Consumers who bought goods from firms which made workers unemployed, it was argued, ought to bear the cost of this unemployment. A third argument in favour of experience rating was that employers would be encouraged to participate in the programmes by helping to police the system against unjustified claims and by influencing legislation. The extent to which the first two objectives were rational, capable of achievement or have been achieved in practice is debatable, but the third objective was undoubtedly achieved in ample measure – employers were encouraged to oppose increases in benefits and to advocate more stringent disqualification rules. Every employer had a financial incentive to contest the claims to benefit of his former employees.

The practice of experience rating was of major importance in all states in the financing of unemployment insurance. In 1970 it resulted in a reduction of the standard contribution of 2·7 per cent. to a national average of 1·3 per cent., with state averages ranging from 0·4 to 3·5 per cent.[39]

Supplementary Unemployment Benefit.   Supplementary unemployment benefit plans operating in the U.S.A. have had a great deal of publicity. They were first negotiated in the automobile industry in 1955 and in the following year in the steel industry. Such schemes also operated in some sections of the electrical engineering and the clothing industries. The unemployment compensation negotiated under these schemes was appreciably more generous than that under the state schemes, and all but one of the states did not consider such payment as a disqualification from unemployment compensation.

It should, however, be stressed that the proportion of all employees covered by the supplemental unemployment schemes was a mere 3·9 per cent. of all employees in private industry in 1969 and had hardly increased since 1961, when it was 3·6 per cent. The total cost of these schemes was a derisory $3 per $10,000 wages in every year between 1967 and 1970.

Level of Unemployment.   In the 1960s unemployment in the U.S.A. was relatively high; the average rate among those insured against unemployment was 3·5 per cent. This varied from 5·6 per cent. in 1961 to 2·1 per cent. in 1969.[40] There were also marked variations between the states : in 1970 six had an average rate of less than 2 per cent. while eleven had a rate above 4 per cent.

Absence of Federal Responsibility.   The U.S.A. was the only one among the ten countries in which the financing and administration of unemployment benefit was not a central government responsibility. Central governments through fiscal and monetary policy can influence the level of economic activity and thereby the level of employment, but it was not within the power of the states to do this. It seems therefore somewhat peculiar that state policies have predominated in unemployment insurance for so long. William Lloyd Mitchell, when he had retired as Commissioner of the Social Security Administration, wrote in 1964 :

> American unemployment insurance was set up, and still operates, on a Federal–State basis. Whether this plan is a wise one is debatable. It cannot be denied that there are certain intangible values in using the Federal–State partnership to bring the operation of social programs as close as possible to the people they serve . . . But, on the other hand, unemployment does not normally respect State boundaries, nor can it be dealt with effectively on a State-by-State basis . . . Fifty separate State governments cannot be expected to be as promptly and faithfully responsive to national policy and direction as would be the case in a straight Federal operation.[41]

The shortcomings of the U.S. unemployment income-support system were manifold and blatant. Experience rating in particular was a divisive practice which resulted in a conflict of interests between employers and the unemployed. It is difficult to defend the system as a social policy measure, although some may think that as an economic policy it made more sense.

Unemployment Insurance.   A national compulsory and contributory unemployment insurance scheme was introduced in 1941. The Federal Parliament had already in 1935 passed a law to set up such a scheme, but this had been declared unconstitutional by the Privy Council.

Approximately 80 per cent of employees were protected by unemployment insurance in 1969. Most public servants and non-manual employees earning more than $7,800 were excluded, but agricultural workers were covered. Benefits varied with previous earnings, employment history and family status. The maximum earnings taken into account for contribution and benefit purposes were $100 a week. Up to that amount the basic benefit was a slightly inverse proportion of earnings. It was increased in respect of one dependant, but not more than one, by $4 a week in the lowest and $11 in the highest wage class. Benefits, including increases for dependants, equalled 43 per cent. of earnings, but were only paid after seven waiting days. Benefit rates were based on average weekly contributions for the last 30 weeks in the two years preceding the claim and were limited in duration to one week for every two weeks' contributions, subject to a maximum of 52 weeks.

Contributions to the scheme were shared equally between employers and employees; the rates applying to each of the wage classes were slightly progressive, varying from 0·7 to 1·4 per cent. of earnings. The Federal government contributed one-fifth of the combined employer–employee contributions and bore the cost of administration. Seasonal benefits on less strict contribution conditions were awarded to claimants during the five and a half months' period commencing in the first week of December. The maximum earnings limit of $100 for assessment of benefit meant that the unemployment compensation ratio for the single standard wage-earner (with an income of $140) was only 30 per cent. and that for the married man with children only 38 per cent.

Unemployment Relief.   As from 1956 the Federal government had contributed half the cost of public relief of the unemployed and their dependants; the other half was shared between the provinces and the local authorities. In 1966 this unemployment relief programme was incorporated in the Canada Assistance plan, a comprehensive public assistance measure to complement other income-security programmes. This plan, however, involved the Federal government neither in administrative responsibilities nor in the determination of the conditions and level of assistance. These remained within the discretion of the provinces and local authorities and therefore differed widely. The operation of the plan was severely criticised in the White Paper *Income Security for Canadians* :

> A fundamental weakness in the administration of social assistance in Canada is the failure to recognise that persons unable to support themselves have a right to assistance . . .
>
> People are often denied assistance, even when the alternative options of employment, training or rehabilitation are not really available . . .
>
> Rates of assistance often remain too low to provide for a reasonably adequate level of support . . .
>
> It is common practice for the unemployed, whose need is assumed to be of relatively short duration, to be provided with only emergency issues for food on a week-by-week basis . . .
>
> The practices followed in the administration of assistance have often reflected the belief of some administrators, and a significant segment of the public, that there are large numbers of persons who would rather receive assistance than work. The evidence available suggests that belief to be wrong. Punitive practices followed in assistance administration are neither appropriate nor useful.[42]

These few sentences illustrate the quite detailed account of the shortcomings of social assistance contained in that White Paper. The prescriptions of the White Paper have been the object of considerable controversy, but few would want to disagree with its diagnosis. A society which in its official publications criticises so vigorously its own policies and institutions would appear to be fundamentally sound and decent.

The Unemployment Insurance Act, 1971. In June 1970 the government had issued a White Paper, *Unemployment Insurance,* the major proposals of which were incorporated in the Unemployment Insurance Act, 1971. This extended compulsory insurance to all employees under 70 years with a very few exceptions; these included casual workers, persons earning less than $25 a week, employees of provincial government (who could opt for coverage) and persons receiving pensions under the Canada and Quebec Pension Plans. The exclusion of employees who earned more than a prescribed amount from compulsory insurance was abolished. The White Paper had estimated that unemployment insurance would cover more than 96 per cent of all employees.

The scheme was financed by employees' contributions of 0·8 per cent. of earnings up to $7,800 a year. This limit applied to 1972 and thereafter was adjusted annually in accordance with changes in the wage index. The employers' contribution for small enterprises (and for large enterprises up to 1975) was 140 per cent. of that of their employees. Large enterprises (with a wages bill in excess of $78,000 in 1972) will as from 1975 pay a contribution based on the enterprise's average redundancy rate over a three-year period. The contribution based on experience rating was to be at least equal to that of their employees and at most twice as much. The aggregate contributions of employees and employers were to finance all benefits as long as the national average level of unemployment did not exceed 4 per cent. The Federal government was to subsidise the scheme when unemployment exceeded that level and also when unemployment in any region exceeded 5 per cent.

The eligibility requirements for benefit were liberalised and 20 weeks in insurable employment in the previous 52 weeks was sufficient for the receipt of full benefit. This could be paid for a period of up to 51 weeks, depending on the applicant's employment record and on national and regional unemployment rates. Benefit was two-thirds of the average earnings in the qualifying period. This could be increased by up to 75 per cent. by dependants' allowances, but was in 1972 subject to a maximum of $100 a week (two-thirds of the contribution ceiling of $150 a week). Benefit was paid after a waiting period of two weeks (previously one week) and was subject to income tax (previously tax-exempt). The maximum period of disqualification from receiving benefit (owing to voluntary withdrawal from work, dismissal for misconduct or refusing a suitable employment offer) was reduced from six weeks to three weeks.

The new unemployment scheme is in many respects – increased coverage, lower qualifying periods, higher benefit rates tied to a wage index, reduced periods of disqualification – a marked improvement and puts provisions for the unemployed in Canada well ahead of those in any of the states in the U.S.A. The introduction of experience rating and the extension of the waiting period from one to two weeks were more controversial measures. The new benefit rates were designed to give a benefit of two-thirds of average earnings to people whose wages were at or below the national average. As men's wages were on average higher than women's, this meant that the benefit was less than the statutory proportion for most men and was unlikely to exceed half pay for most skilled workers. The inclusion of non-manual workers whose earnings exceeded the previous ceiling for compulsory insurance was a recognition of the fact that this group also faced the hazard of unemployment, but the benefit they could expect was well below the statutory proportion.

Level of Unemployment. The Canadian unemployment rate in the 1960s averaged 5·1 per cent., ranging from a low of 3·6 per cent. in 1966 to a high of 7·0 per cent. in 1960. The rates of the five employment regions also showed wide variations in 1969; when the national average was 4·7 per cent., the rate for Ontario was 3·1 per cent. and that for Quebec 6·9 per cent. An unemployment rate ranging from 4·0 to 5·1 per cent. was considered as compatible with full employment.

REVIEW

Distinctions between Categories of Social Beneficiaries. The six main categories of persons who suffer from interruptions or cessation of income can be divided into two groups : those which were larger and those which were smaller in the post-Second World War era than in the inter-war years. In all the ten countries the proportion of the old (over 65) has increased and so has that of the sick and of invalids to a smaller and less well-defined extent. The proportion of the unemployed and of widows (under 65) has declined sharply everywhere and that of the work-injured has diminished to a less marked degree.

The persons belonging to some of these categories can be counted more easily than those belonging to others. Widows and the old can be precisely defined; they are enumerated at regular population censuses, their numbers do not vary greatly from year to year and are not directly affected by any social security benefits to which there may be entitlement.[43] Invalids, the sick and the work-injured are more difficult to define; their numbers are partly determined by medical assessment which may vary both over time and between countries; changes in economic and technological circumstances may increase or diminish the incidence of these contingencies, and the existence and the level of social security provisions may influence their number claiming benefit.

Unemployment Statistics. Some reference to the difficulty of enumerating the unemployed – those able and willing to work but unable to find suitable employment – has already been made in the beginning of this chapter and in the section referring to the U.K. Unemployment is without doubt frequently a less precise condition than old age or widowhood, but normally more capable of external assessment than sickness. The criteria for defining unemployment (like those for defining sickness) vary over time and between countries. The legal regulations for administering unemployment benefit use terms such as "suitable', 'available', 'able', and 'willing' to which very different meanings can be attached.

The ten countries used four different methods of compiling unemployment statistics. Canada, the U.S.A. and Australia conducted household sample surveys for the collection of data on demographic and labour-force characteristics. In these surveys

> *Unemployed persons* comprise all those who, during survey week, did no work at all, and who either,
>
> (a) did not have a job or business and were actively looking for work (including those who stated that they would have looked for work if they had not been temporarily ill or believed no work was available, or had not already made definite arrangements to start work in a new job after survey week), or
>
> (b) were laid off from their jobs without pay for the whole week.
>
> A person who either lost his job or was laid off *during* survey week, but did some work at his job during that week, is classified as employed.[44]

The validity of the findings of such surveys depended on the truthfulness of the respondents in their replies to questions which referred both to facts (did he have a job?) and surmise (did he believe that no work was available?). In these three countries the unemployment rate was the number of unemployed as a proportion of all employed and unemployed persons, including among the employed both employees and selfemployed.

The second method of compilation, based on compulsory unemployment insurance statistics, was used in Ireland. The percentage unemployed, excluding those normally working in agriculture, fishing and private domestic service, was obtained by relating the number of currently insured persons on the 'live register' (for employment at the local employment offices) to the estimated currently insured population. This method tended to give the unemployment rate an upward bias as it excluded three groups of employed persons among whom unemployment was low or non-existent : persons in public employment, salaried employees whose earnings exceeded £1,200 a year and self-employed persons in trade and industry. As the minimum retirement age in 1969 was 70 years, the live register contained a number of persons aged between 65 and 69 who in most other countries would not be included in the labour force. The percentage unemployed excluded all those seeking employment who had no previous attachment to the labour force, especially small farmers and their relations assisting them, as well as married women.

The Danish unemployment percentage expressed unemployment among insured members of trade unions funds. As membership of the funds accounted for only half of all employees (excluding those in the public service), it is not possible to establish how far this percentage was representative of the general state of unemployment. For reasons referred to above, it is, however, more than probable that the rate of unemployment among that half of the population who were not members of the funds was always lower.

Austria, Germany, the U.K. and the Netherlands published an unemployment rate which expressed the registered unemployed as a percentage of all insured against unemployment. For various reasons, however, the unemployment rates of even these four countries were not strictly comparable. First, in the U.K. the insured population included all employees as well as the self-employed, while in the other three countries only employees (excluding public servants) were insured. Second, the number registering for employment was affected by several factors which varied between countries, one of the most important of these being the relative advantage to be derived from registration.

New Zealand recorded the number of persons registering for employment at the employment exchanges but did not compile an unemployment rate.

All four methods of compiling unemployment rates are useful and reasonably reliable indicators of changes in the level of unemployment within a country, but they are only of limited validity in comparing the levels of unemployment of different countries. Changes in the level of unemployment do not only direct attention to social needs but are also indicators of the success or failure of a government's economic policy. Unemployment is the only one among the six major social contingencies which could and did change quite rapidly within a short period of time.

Levels of Benefit.   Benefit for unemployment lasting a few weeks or months was awarded without an income test to the great majority of the short-term unemployed in all countries except New Zealand and Australia. In six countries the maximum (normal) rate of unemployment benefit was the same as that of sickness benefit. In three of these – Ireland, New Zealand and Australia – it was the same flat rate. In the U.K. the basic flat rate and the earnings-related supplement were identical for both contingencies. The Netherlands and Canada (after 1971) had rates for both benefits proportionate to earnings subject to the same maximums. In Austria and Germany the unemployed fared decidedly worse than the temporarily disabled, while in Denmark and the U.S.A. the opposite was the case. The relatively favourable position of the short-term unemployed in the U.S.A. as compared with the position of those suffering a temporary disability was due to the latter's not being entitled to any statutory benefit in all but four states.

As long ago as 1952 the I.L.O. Social Security (Minimum Standards) Convention had fixed 45 per cent as the minimum compensation ratio for an unemployed man with two children. In 1969 benefits for the standard wage-earner in Austria, Canada, the U.S.A. and Australia were still well below this level. Benefits in Germany, the U.K. (third to 28th week), Denmark and the Netherlands were above it, while Ireland, the U.K. (up to the second and after the 28th week) and New Zealand had compensation ratios at about that level. In the last three countries compensation for the majority of the unemployed, whose wages were below the standard wage, was up to the ratio laid down in the Convention.

Means Tests for the Long-Term Unemployed.   New Zealand and Australia were the only countries in which the level of income maintenance and the conditions attached to its award were the same irrespective of the duration of unemployment. In the other countries the condition of the long-term was worse than that of the short-term unemployed. This was most decidedly the case in Canada and the U.S.A. which had no national support programmes for the long-term unemployed. In these two countries unemployment relief was the responsibility of the states or provinces and the local authorities. Relief was generally awarded without rules and absolute refusal of support was by no means uncommon. When relief was granted it was usually discretionary and often depended on the availability of funds in the budgets of local authorities.

All six European countries had in 1969 some structured assistance schemes for the long-term unemployed. This had not, however, been the case in Ireland up to 1966, nor was it again as from 1971 when occupiers of smallholdings were disqualified from unemployment assistance, to which they would otherwise have been entitled, between March and November by an Unemployment Period Order. All men resident in rural areas who had no dependants were disqualified between certain dates in June and November by a second Unemployment Period Order. The avowed purpose of the first Order was to give 'encouragement' to occupiers during the summer months to cultivate their land, that of the second to make men accept work as labourers which was said to be available at that time of year to anyone who wanted employment.

In the European countries assistance to persons who had been unemployed for more than 52 weeks and often also to those unemployed for shorter periods was subject to a means test. In this it differed from invalidity, old-age and widows' pensions and employment injury compensation, all four of which were awarded 'as of right' to all insured persons without a time limit. Sickness benefit, except in the U.K. and Ireland, was limited in time, but the great majority of the long-term incapacitated in Austria, Germany and Denmark became entitled to invalidity pensions, while in the Netherlands the transfer to long-term incapacity benefit after expiry of sickness benefit was virtually automatic.

Beveridge's Recommendations. The means-test rule in the European countries thus distinguished unemployment quite markedly from other social contingencies. It is interesting to recall the views expressed by Beveridge on this subject some thirty years earlier. He recommended 'making . . . unemployment benefit at full rate indefinite in duration, subject to requirement of attendance at a work or training centre after a limited period of unemployment'. He argued that in the case of a lengthy interruption of earnings the need for wage replacement tended to increase rather than decrease and that measures to prevent a deterioration in morale became more urgent. This led him to state :

> To reduce the income of an unemployed . . . person, either directly or by application of a means test, because the unemployment . . . has lasted for a certain period, is wrong in principle.

Beveridge therefore advocated payment of benefit without time limit, subject to two provisos :

(1) Men and women in receipt of unemployment benefit cannot be allowed to hold out indefinitely for work of the type to which they are used or in their present places of residence, if there is work which they could do available at the standard wage for that work.

(2) Men and women who have been unemployed for a certain period should be required as a condition of continued benefit to attend a work or training centre, such attendance being designed both as a means of preventing habituation to idleness and as a means of improving capacity for earning.[45]

Beveridge's arguments (which are given here only in bare outline) and recommendations seem more reasonable and fair than the practice of any of the ten countries. It is indeed remarkable that even in the countries which had long periods of high employment (for example the Netherlands and Germany), the duration of unemployment benefit without a means test was still limited. In Austria and the U.K. assistance subject to a means test for a married man was no less than insurance benefit; in the other countries it was less, but in the Netherlands only by a relatively small amount.

The low levels of unemployment in the 1960s may not have been an appropriate environment for the development of the training centres which Beveridge advocated. All the six European countries, however, have made some limited progress in this field and all envisage more development in the future. In 1969 the various vocational education schemes in Germany were the most advanced. The implementation of such schemes, however, is expensive and beset with many practical difficulties. One of the greatest of these is to make the training of undoubted benefit to the unemployed and thereby maintain or raise their morale. Moreover, any training scheme has to avoid two dangers : that of appearing to the unemployed as a work test of a punitive nature and that of appearing to men at work so favourable that they are tempted to become unemployed in order to receive training. All countries succeeded in avoiding the second danger; the terms on which training was provided anywhere were rarely sufficiently attractive to make it popular. The first danger was also overcome by the simple device of having only a very limited amount of training.

The Incidence of Unemployment. No age group and few occupations or professions are immune from unemployment, although it follows a general pattern with distinct and ubiquitous characteristics. Unemployment tends to be highest among the very young, especially those who have never had a job, and the 'old' (comprising any age over 40). While it is difficult to anticipate with any degree of certainty which employments will expand and which will contract, because political, economic and technological changes are so unpredictable, certain jobs are more prone to unemployment than others : it is least among public servants, comparatively low among administrative, technical and professional salaried staff and highest among unskilled and semi-skilled manual workers. Moreover, in most countries and in all where there is more than a marginal level of unemployment, proportionately more men than women are unemployed.

In the decade of the 1960s the level of employment was fairly high and stable in most countries, with the marked exception of Ireland which faced problems of particular difficulty, and to a lesser degree Canada and the U.S.A. There was some relation, although not a very marked one, between the level of unemployment benefit and the level of unemployment. The Netherlands and Germany had comparatively high levels of support and low levels of unemployment, while the U.S.A. and Canada had low levels of support (very low for the long-term unemployed) and a comparatively high level of unemployment. Australia had, conversely, the lowest level of support combined with a very low level of unemployment.

The lack of public concern about the welfare of the unemployed and the consequent lack of political pressure for improving their conditions can easily be understood in the high-employment economy of Australia. There were too few people to make a fuss and there was the widespread and not unreasonable view that 'there are plenty of jobs for all who are able and willing to work'. However, not all those registered for employment may have been able to undertake the jobs which were available. The Australian labour-force statistics show that in the boom conditions of 1970, when only 0·9 per cent. of all men were unemployed, as many as 2·4 per cent. of all youths between 15 and 19 were looking for work.[46]

New Zealand had as high a level of employment as Australia, but had consistently a markedly higher standard of income maintenance.

Poverty and Unemployment.   In theory the income support of people able and willing to work but unable to find suitable employment is quite distinct from two other issues : first, the condition of a man with a family, especially a large family, in full-time employment but with an income insufficient to keep him out of poverty; and second, the voluntary unemployment of people who are able but unwilling to work.

Any earnings-related benefit for the unemployed will fail to keep everyone above an officially designated poverty line unless either a minimum benefit is awarded which varies with family circumstances or some alternative arrangements are made for the support of the family. A programme which incorporates such a minimum benefit will have to pay some men with very low wages (about the lowest decile) and large families (more than two children) benefit at rates which exceed their wages when in full-time employment. This would be a financial incentive to unemployment and be quite unacceptable as a public policy in any country. The magnitude of the low wage-earner problem depends on the dispersal of earnings and the difference between the median wage and the poverty base of the single man. If the lowest decile wage-earner has an income of 90 per cent of the median wage there is not likely to be much of a problem, but if his income is 60 per cent. of the median wage the problem will be much greater. If the poverty base is merely sufficient to keep body and soul together, the number affected will be much less than if poverty is expressed as a fairly high proportion of the median wage (viewing poverty as a relative state of deprivation). The problem is further aggravated by two other factors : the correlation between low incomes and large families and the relatively high proness of unskilled workers to become redundant.

The only way of overcoming the problem of paying some men when they are unemployed more than when they are at work is to adopt a universal family allowance programme. This is the subject of the next chapter. The alternative is to keep the support level of the unemployed low wage-earners with large families below the poverty base;

this is the practice in Ireland, the U.K., Canada, the U.S.A. and Australia (and possibly also in some of the other five countries). Positive and free family-planning services can make some contribution to reducing poverty among the low paid, but as policies in this field have been generally negative and restrictive in the past, little is known about the extent to which such programmes can be effective. Changing social attitudes to abortion and sterilisation may make some impact in the future.

Anybody who claims to be involuntarily unemployed should be considered as such until he implicitly or explicitly refuses offers of suitable employment. If he does he is not involuntarily unemployed and he should be supported, if at all, by a programme different from that of the unemployed. Such a policy might make the issue of what is 'refusal of suitable employment' even more important than it is at present; it would also make it essential to have a proper machinery for appeals against decisions taken by civil servants in the first instance. It is suggested that in all the countries of this survey the adoption of such a policy would greatly facilitate a rational and reasonably generous support programme for the unemployed.

The moral case for supporting a man who is able and willing to work but unable to find suitable employment at or approaching the level of his normal earnings, or at least at the New Zealand 'belonging' standard, is undoubtedly strong. An examination of the practice in the ten countries shows, however, that the case has not been persuasive. The three countries with the highest compensation ratios for the single standard wage-earner were the Netherlands with 80 per cent., Denmark with 50 per cent. and Germany with 45 per cent.

The Cost of Improving Benefits. At the levels of unemployment prevailing in the 1960s the fiscal burden of unemployment compensation at levels approximating to normal earnings would not have been particularly heavy in any country. In some, for example Germany, it would have been quite a minor imposition, requiring at most an increase in the combined contributions of employers and employees from 1·3 to 1·6 per cent. of earnings up to the maximum contribution level. The Canadian unemployment insurance scheme, which was based on a combined contribution of employers and employees of just under 2 per cent. of earnings, financed a compensation ratio of two-thirds without any state subsidy as long as unemployment did not exceed a monthly average of 4 per cent. An increase in contributions from 2 to 3 per cent. would thus have been sufficient to give full wage replacement to all the unemployed whose earnings were at or below the national average. If the U.S.A. had levied contributions on wages up to $7,800 a year (the ceiling fixed in the Canadian Act), average benefits could have been increased from about one-third to about two-thirds of average earnings. The same result could have been achieved by leaving the contribution ceiling unaltered but doing away with experience rating, which would have meant employers contributing 2·7 per cent. instead of the 1·4 per cent. they paid in 1969.

The low levels of compensation were thus not due to the fiscal burden which higher levels would have imposed on the economy. They must have been due to arguments more persuasive to policy-makers than (what above was called) the moral case.

American Attitudes to Unemployment.   The low-compensation lobby can point out that the U.S.A., in the thirty-five years following the setting-up of their unemployment scheme and in the absence of any proper system of unemployment assistance, has experienced an unprecedented economic expansion (in absolute if not in relative terms) which has increased enormously the standard of living of most of its citizens. It can be argued, and indeed is argued by the Nixon administration, that what in this chapter has been referred to as the shortcomings of the unemployment support programme and the very absence of a welfare state have been part of the package which made this progress possible. This view is shared by many influential people in the U.S.A. and many millions who endorse it with their votes at elections. This attitude, however, is not supported by developments in those countries of this study – the Netherlands, Denmark and Germany – which have experienced during the last two decades a rapid rate of economic growth combined with reasonably generous unemployment support programmes and levels of unemployment well below those prevailing in the U.S.A.

It does not of course follow that had the U.S.A. taken over the Netherlands' unemployment insurance scheme it would have experienced the Netherlands' rate of economic growth. Unfortunately the side-effects of any social policy in a particular economic and political environment and within a certain institutional framework cannot be predicted with any degree of certainty. The issues are too complex and the vagaries of human nature too great. It can be asserted with confidence that 'being tough with the unemployed' is not the only road to economic progress; it is more difficult to contradict the belief that at some times, in some conditions, it is one of several possible roads. Recent history lends support to the view that it is a road which many like to tread.

CHAPTER VIII

Family Endowment

Varieties of State Assistance.   State assistance to parents in the cost of rearing their children is the normal practice in all ten countries. The assistance rendered in kind by way of free or subsidised services – health, education, school meals, welfare food – is always more costly than the provisions which increase the parent's disposable income – family allowances, income tax, children's exemptions and increments to social insurance and social assistance payments.

In every country, with the possible exception of the U.S.A., the cost of state assistance for many children attending school exceeds the amounts parents spend on their children. The cost of free primary and secondary education for that age group accounts for well over half of all state assistance their parents receive.[1]

Education.   Free education of children is not merely the most expensive service rendered to parents but is also the least controversial. Certain aspects of education – church schools, comprehensive secondary education, racial integration, the minimum school-leaving age – have been the objects of intense controversy, but the principle of the cost of education being a communal rather than a parental responsibility is universally accepted. Socialised medicine is a disparaging term, but nobody talks of socialised education.

The minimum of nine or ten years' free, universal and compulsory education, which is the norm in the ten countries, benefits (or at least is meant to benefit) children as individuals and in this sense provides assistance to their parents. However, the compulsory nature of education makes it simultaneously a financial burden on the least well-off parents by postponing the age at which their children can start to earn a wage, and it is the children of these parents who normally leave school at the earliest age possible. An increase in the minimum school-leaving age from 15 to 16 years deprives both the children themselves and their parents of the wages the children could have earned in their 16th year. (The extension of compulsory school attendance is, of course, of no consequence to the parents whose children would in any case have stayed on at school.). Thus, compulsory education, though providing assistance to parents, may legitimately give rise to pressure for additional assistance to some parents in the form of disposable income. The importance of this issue can possibly be best appreciated if it is realised that the aggregate family allowances, from birth up to the children's 16th birthday, received by parents having two children was, at 1971 rates, in Germany, Ireland, the U.K., Canada and Australia about the same as or less than the two children could have earned in their 16th year.

Free and subsidised education has two other characteristics which are relevant to family endowment: the length of education children receive is generally directly related to their parents' income and the cost of education varies broadly with the age of the child; for example, a year at primary school involves less cost than a year at university. From this it follows that public expenditure on education tends to be greater for the children of the higher than of the lower income groups. This too is a matter of some magnitude. At a conservative estimate the cost to public funds of educating an average university graduate is at least three times greater than that of a child leaving school at 15 years.

It would, however, be erroneous to consider free education as nothing but a family endowment. The expenditure of £5,000 on a bright boy to enable him to qualify as a chartered electrical engineer will not only benefit him but increase the country's productive capacity and thereby the standard of living of many people on whose education much less has been spent. Education is thus partly a capital investment which yields diffuse benefits. This goes some way in explaining why education is so widely financed out of the public purse. At various times in different places the free education of children has been advocated in order to make them better Christians, better workers or better citizens. Education is considered so essential that a prescribed minimum is made compulsory and thereby completely removed from the discretion of the parents and the operation of market forces. More than the minimum is considered so desirable that it is offered to parents free of charge or at a subsidised rate. Both compulsion and subsidies increase the quantity and quality of education which many children receive to well beyond what their parents would be willing or able to pay for, if they had to bear the full cost.

Objectives and Means. State assistance to parents, other than through education, has been advocated as a means of achieving a variety of objectives; some of these are inconsistent with each other and some are vague and ill-defined. The objectives most widely discussed have included an increase in the number of births, the encouragement of prudent parents to have more children, the reduction of poverty, greater equality of opportunity for children irrespective of their parents' income, an increase in national wealth by investment in human beings and a diminution of differences in standards of living of people with similar incomes but different family circumstances.

The means of achieving these objectives clearly differ. The most efficient way of reducing poverty is to concentrate all available resources on those who are poorest. A similar policy might be appropriate for increasing the degree of equality of opportunity. Restricting allowances to men who have incomes above the national average and otherwise varying them directly with income might be most effective if the objective is to encourage 'prudent' parents to have more children. To achieve greater equality in standards of living of people who have similar incomes but different family circumstances might require allowances proportionate to income. A policy setting out to bring about a growth in G.N.P. may aim at allocating allowances partly on the basis of attainment in intelligence tests and partly inversely related to the parents' income. The efficacy of a family endowment scheme can only be assessed in relation to the objectives it sets out to achieve.

Family allowances, income-tax relief and supplements in respect of children to other social security cash benefits were the three major methods employed in the ten countries to augment parents' disposable incomes in certain circumstances. Denmark gave no tax relief and the U.S.A. awarded no family allowances. The other eight countries employed all three methods. The family allowance scheme in operation in 1971 had a number of common characteristics. They were paid to virtually all families who had at least three or more children at a flat rate which was neither related to income nor dependent on an income or a needs test. The family allowance scheme of the ten countries of this study will now be looked at individually and a general review will follow.

History of Family Allowances. New Zealand in 1926 was the first country to introduce a family allowance scheme. 'This embodied the principle of the state bearing to some extent the responsibility for the well-being of the families of those who were in poorer circumstances'.[2] The scheme was non-contributory and granted a small allowance to low-income families in respect of third and subsequent children below the age of 15 years. In the spirit of that time, illegitimate, alien and Asiatic children were excluded but the allowance for invalid children could be continued beyond the age limit. This scheme remained unaltered for the next twelve years, after which time the age limit was raised to 16 and the allowance increased and renamed *family benefit*. In 1940 the benefit was extended to the second and in 1941 to the first child in a family. The means test was abolished in 1946 and benefit was paid from then on for all children under 16 living in families. By 1947, after the removal of the means test and the extension of benefit to all children, the objective of the scheme had altered substantially. Originally it was designed to help parents with large families who were in the lowest income bracket, but twenty years later it had become a universal family endowment. In essence it was now a device for paying 3 per cent. of the national income raised by taxation proportionate to income to families proportionate to the number of children in the family.[3]

In 1969 a family benefit of $1·50 per week was paid for each child under the age of 16 whose parents were normally resident in New Zealand. The benefit was extended until the end of the year in which the child had his 18th birthday, if he continued in full-time education or was totally incapacitated from earning his living. The benefit was exempt from tax and was normally paid to the mother.

In New Zealand, as in most of the other countries under review, family allowances were changed less frequently than other social benefits. The basic rate of social security benefits has been changed twenty-one times since the present scheme commenced in 1939, but during these thirty years family benefit has only been increased three times – in 1942, in 1944 and in 1958.

Special Features of Family Allowances. Two features of family benefits in New Zealand are of special interest. First, at the discretion

of the Social Security Commission, benefits for up to 52 weeks may
be paid in advance in a lump sum on the birth of a first child of a
marriage and when any child commences the first year of secondary-
school education. Second, parents were able to purchase or to improve
a house by capitalising benefits in respect of one or more children
from the age of one year up to the age of 16 years, subject to the
sum advanced to any family being not less than $400 and not more
than $2,000 :

> Eligibility to capitalise benefits is determined by the [Social
> Security] Department, which in doing so is required to have
> regard to the income and assets of the applicants to be satisfied
> that there is need for capitalisation to finance a housing pro-
> position, that is, that the applicants could not reasonably be
> expected to arrange finance from any other source. On the
> other hand the Department is required to consider whether
> the loss of family benefit by regular cash instalments would
> cause hardship to the applicant.[4]

In 1969–70, 8,000 applications for capitalisation were granted.
The encouragement of parents to become owner-occupiers may be
desirable from several points of view, but there is the possibility of
this scheme having the undesirable side-effect of tempting parents
to have more children.

Supplements to Social Security Benefits.   Between 1939 and 1968
there was no supplementation of social security benefits in respect
of dependent children. In the latter year, family maintenance
allowances (F.M.A.s) were introduced as a discretionary supplement
to age, invalidity, sickness and unemployment benefits. Sole parents
received the same benefit as widowed mothers, and the poorest
married couples were compensated at least partially for the gradual
erosion of the universal family benefit. In 1949 family benefit for
couples who had two and four children was equal to 20 per cent.
and 40 per cent. respectively of the basic rate of social security
benefit. By 1969 these proportions had declined to 12½ per cent. and
25 per cent and even with the F.M.A. were only 15 per cent. and
36½ per cent. F.M.A.s were paid on average to some 4,000 persons
in respect of 12,000 children – less than 3 per cent. of the children
receiving family benefits.

Tax Exemptions.   Special income-tax exemptions for dependent

children restricted to parents who had low incomes were first introduced in 1913. They have been modified since that date on many
occasions. In 1969 all parents of dependent children under 16 (under
18 years if still at school) received an exemption of $135 for the first
four children and $140 for subsequent children. As married couples
were liable to tax on all income in excess of $515 per annum, the
children's tax exemptions benefited virtually all parents who had
an income. As tax rates were progressive and not, as in Germany
and the U.K., proportionate over a long income range, the value of
the exemption increased with income, ranging from $11 per annum
to $91. For a man of average income the value of tax relief was
about $35 per child, less than half the $78 he received in family
benefit.

Recommendations of the Royal Commission. The Report of the
Royal Commission on Social Security in New Zealand published in
1972 contains a comprehensive discussion of assistance to families.[5]
The Commission considered universal family benefit as an important
investment in people as well as a means of alleviating poverty or
meeting needs. The Commission set out to ensure that the cost of
rearing children at all levels of income was equitably spread throughout the community. A transfer of income from non-parents to parents,
irrespective of income, appeared to them justified on account of the
unequal distribution of dependent children among households.

The Commission, while recognising that the cost of maintaining
a child increases with age, considered that from the point of view
of family income and living standards this is offset by a number of
countervailing factors : children of 15 years and over are, in a full-
employment economy, able to earn some money in their spare time;
the arrival of the first child frequently reduces family income by the
mother's ceasing to work, while it simultaneously increases expenditure; the father's earnings are usually higher when the children are
older; the probability of the mother resuming work increases with
the age of the children. The Commission recommended, because of
these factors, that family benefit should not vary according to age
or the number of children in the family. The fact that special income-
tax exemptions were less for parents with low than with high
incomes – $28 in 1971 at an income of $2,000 per year for the first
child but $68 at an income of $14,000 – was viewed by the Commission as running 'counter to the emphasis which social security

must place on greater help for those in greatest need'.[6] It therefore recommended the abolition of tax concessions to parents and their replacement by a higher rate of family benefit of $3 per week. This would increase the aggregate assistance received by all parents but would be of much greater benefit to the badly off than the well off. A rate of $3 per week represented 60 per cent. of what the Commission estimated to be the family food expenditure per head in 1970.

The existing F.M.A. would be replaced by a standard scale of benefits for 'family groups', augmented according to the number of dependent children. After family benefit was taken into account, the same aggregate benefits would be received by family groups of the same size, for instance a married couple with no children and a sole parent with one child, or a married couple with three children and a sole parent with four.

In view of the recommended higher rate of family benefit and the economies of scale which should accrue in large families, it was recommended that the standard benefit should not be increased in respect of the fourth and subsequent children of a couple or the fifth and subsequent children of a sole parent.

The Commission arrived at its decision and recommendations by examining and evaluating the evidence submitted; it noted that research into family problems in New Zealand was deficient, but did not sponsor any research of its own.

All the recommendations of the Royal Commission relating to family benefit were accepted by the government in June 1972.[7] As from July 1972 family benefit was increased to $3 per week, the special child tax exemptions were terminated and the F.M.A. replaced by increased standard benefits for beneficiaries with dependent children.

AUSTRALIA

History of Family Allowances. In Australia child endowment was widely debated in the inter-war period. In 1920 the Commonwealth government introduced a scheme for its civil service, and in 1927 a universal family endowment scheme commenced in New South Wales, covering all children under 14 years in low-income families. Two years later the latter scheme was amended so as to exclude the first child in the family. For the first six years the scheme was financed by a payroll tax, but thereafter it was paid out of general revenue.

In 1928 the Royal Commission on Child Endowment recommended in a majority report that the Commonwealth government should not introduce child endowment. Their arguments were similar to those made in many other parts of the world : the country could not afford it; wages were adequate, if spent wisely, to support even a fairly large family; state support would weaken parental responsibility and reduce the incentive to provide for oneself; there were other more pressing needs in social services. The government accepted the report and justified this with, *inter alia,* two further reasons : a reluctance to adopt a policy which would in effect lead to a reduction in the minimum wage of men who had no dependent children and the undesirability of legislating for child endowment without having the power to control basic wages. The latter was at that time the prerogative of the state governments.

A universal system of family endowment commenced in Australia in 1941. In the phraseology of the government of the day, it was 'a means of providing that no matter how much the war pinches our incomes the basic needs of the family will be satisfied.[8] It enabled an increase in the statutory basic wages and the resultant inflationary pressure to be postponed by limiting increases of income to those whose needs were greatest. As the endowment scheme was considered as 'a logical adjunct to the wages system', it was financed, to the extent to which it made payments to employees, by a payroll tax of $2\frac{1}{2}$ per cent. Much of the remainder of the cost was intended to be covered by the removal of child income-tax exemptions for all but the first child in the family. These, however, were partially restored in 1942.

In 1964 the rate of endowment for children under 16 years was 50 cents a week for the first, $1 for the second, $1·50 for the third and subsequent children and $1·50 for full-time students aged 16-21. In 1967 there were cumulative increases of 25 cents a week for fourth and successive children. These allowances were not assessed as income for tax purposes. Between 1948 and 1969 the Consumer Price Index increased by 150 per cent. but throughout this period the rate of endowment for the second child remained unaltered so that its purchasing power declined by 60 per cent. The rate for the first child has never been raised and its purchasing power by 1969 had declined by 50 per cent. since it was introduced in 1950.

Supplements to Social Security Benefits. Additional benefits of
$2·50 per week for the first child and $3·50 for other dependent
children under 16 were paid to age and invalidity pensioners and
to persons in receipt of unemployment and sickness benefit. In 1969
these additional benefits were equal to 35 per cent. and 76 per cent.
of the basic rate of sickness and unemployment benefit of couples
who had two and four children respectively. Family endowment
increased these proportions to 44 per cent. and 104 per cent. This
apparently generous support of dependent children is, however,
deceptive, as the basic allowance for a married couple without
children was a mere 21 per cent. of the standard wage and the
aggregate benefit for a couple with four children was only 42 per
cent. In New Zealand the corresponding proportion was 56 per cent.

Tax Exemptions. Parents received tax relief for dependent children;[9] they were allowed to deduct from their taxable incomes $208
for the first dependent child and students aged 16 to 21 and $156
for other dependent children. The value of these exemptions to the
standard wage-earner was about $65 for the former and about $46
for the latter. For three children under 16 the child endowment was
$156, virtually the same as the tax relief received by the standard
wage-earner. For persons with higher incomes tax relief exceeded
child endowment, and for those with lower incomes fell short of it.
The larger the number of children, the greater was the value of
family endowment compared with tax relief.

Recommendations of the Melbourne Poverty Survey.[10]   The Melbourne Poverty Survey found that in 1966 about 43 per cent. of
families without fathers and 22 per cent. of families with four or
more dependent children had incomes below or only marginally (20
per cent.) above the poverty line. Henderson and his associates
considered an increase in child endowment rates as the obvious
remedy for poverty among these families. They recommended an
increase to $3·50 per week in the rate for the third child and to
$4·50 for fourth and subsequent children. These increases, according
to their calculation, would in 1969 have cost $108 million and would
have been sufficient to raise out of poverty all large families in which
the father was employed. One way of meeting this expenditure, they
suggested, was to withdraw children's tax exemptions and thereby
increase revenue by $160 million. To offset the hardship this would

have caused to low-income families with one or two children, they further suggested an increase of 50 cents per week in child endowment rates for first and second children, at a cost of $71 million in partial compensation for the withdrawal of tax exemptions. The net cost of these three suggestions would have been $19 million.

CANADA

History of Family Allowances. Family allowances date back to 1944 when they were introduced by the Federal government with the approval of all the political parties. The allowances were paid to all parents irrespective of income and were related to the age of the child. The rates of allowance, which covered all children in the family, were originally fixed at $5 per month for children under 6, $6 between the ages of 6 and 9, $7 between 9 and 12 and $8 between 13 and 16. The rates for the second and fourth age range were still the same twenty-five years later, while those for the other two had been increased by $1 in 1957. Youth allowances at the rate of $10 per month for children aged 16 and 17 who attended school or were disabled commenced in nine provinces in 1964 and in Quebec three years earlier. The cost of both type of allowance was paid out of general Federal revenue. For the first two years of their operation family allowances were subject to income-tax, but they have since been exempted.[11]

The purpose of family allowances was summarised in a recent White Paper :

> These allowances are intended to provide for the additional needs of families with children to ensure better opportunities for children. They are also intended to compensate families for the inability of wage rates to take into account the number of dependants a worker has; workers with low wages and several children have insufficient income to raise and educate them. Since unemployment insurance only affords protection for one dependant, family allowances help families, particularly low-income families, when the worker is unemployed. Also, in the case of social assistance, adequate maintenance for a family with a number of children may mean a higher income on assistance than can be obtained through employment. Family allowances are paid whether a person is employed or unemployed and therefore make it possible to provide more adequate income support to these families without reducing the incentive for the bread-winner to return to work. The program was initially intended

also to bolster income and employment in the post-war period by providing a steady flow of income security payments into the consumer spending stream. Youth allowances were designed to encourage students to remain in school until 18 at least, and to provide some income security for handicapped children unable to attend school and not yet eligible for disabled persons' allowances.[12]

The purchasing power of family allowances had by 1969 declined by more than half since the end of the war and their efficacy in achieving the objectives quoted was therefore much less than it had been in the 1940s. The provinces of Newfoundland and Quebec supplemented the Federal family allowance provisions with schemes of their own.

Supplements to Social Security Benefits.   Supplements to social insurance benefits for dependent children were received by comparatively few parents. Old-age and work-injury pensioners did not receive such supplements. As there was no sickness benefit scheme, there was no provision for the children whose father was ill. Unemployment benefit was supplemented by $4 to $11 per week, varying according to wage class, but this was in respect of one dependant only. This could be a child dependant in a singe-parent family or in a family where the wife was working and thus not qualifying as a dependant. Child supplements of $25 per month for the first four children and $22·50 for other children were paid to invalidity pensioners and marginally higher supplements to widowed mothers. All these supplements were well below a tolerable subsistence level. The 'low-income' level for a child in a two-parent family was assessed at $580 per annum by the Dominion Bureau of Statistics in 1967. In the same year the Quebec paper *Guidelines for a New Quebec Family Allowance Policy* estimated the minimum cost of caring for a child to be between $25 and $30 per month, varying with the size of the family.

Tax Exemptions.   In 1969 taxpayers received an exemption of $300 for each dependent child under 16 and $550 for older children. This represented for a standard wage-earner, whose marginal tax rate was 28 per cent. (including provincial income-tax), tax reliefs of $84 and $154 respectively. A man with twice this income would be relieved of almost twice that amount of tax on account of the progressive nature of the tax schedules. The loss of revenue due to these exemptions was $450 million in respect of children under 16 years, while the cost of family allowances was $560 million.

Criticisms of the Family Support Programme. The family support programmes as they operated in 1969 were widely criticised in many quarters. The Royal Commission on the Status of Women in Canada in the chapter of their report entitled 'Taxation and Child Care Allowances' commented :

> We believe that the State should give adequate compensation for the cost of true dependants, whether that cost is measured in cash outlays or in time devoted to care and supervision, or both. This compensation should be given to all families that support such dependants, whether the mother stays at home or works outside.

> We considered recommending a substantial increase in the present exemptions (amount deducted from the taxable income) for dependants, which would further reduce a family's taxable income, but rejected the idea because exemptions by their very nature provide a larger benefit to families in higher income groups than to those in lower income groups.

> Tax credits (amounts deducted from the tax payable) are preferable to exemptions. Tax credits are independent of the size of income and do not benefit the rich, at least in dollars, more than the poor . . . but tax credits also have shortcomings : they benefit only those whose income is high enough to be taxed. They do not provide adequate relief for families who have no taxable income or whose tax liabilities are so small that they could not use the full credit. . . .

> Consequently, the solution we recommend is to provide substantial cash allowances for dependent children. . . . We suggest an allowance in the order of $500 a year for each dependent child (under 16 years). . . . This allowance should be taxed to avoid subsidising wealthy families and to enable the government to recoup part of the money distributed. It would replace the present system of Family Allowances and the income-tax exemption for a dependent child under 16 years of age.[13]

The report neither gave nor discussed the cost of these recommendations, but on the basis of published figures it appears that the net cost, taking into account the reduction in the married persons' allowance also recommended by the Commission, would have been about $1,000 million,[14] equivalent in 1969 to 1·3 per cent. of G.N.P.

at market prices. The recommendations would have redistributed income vertically from the well off to the less well off, as well as from persons having no or only one dependent child to those responsible for larger families.[15]

The White Paper *Income Security for Canadians* referred to family allowances as a 'high-cost technique' and an 'inefficient anti-poverty tool', criticised the allowances for being both too low and in aggregate too costly and suggested that they would be more effective if rearranged in such a way as to be selective.[16] It therefore proposed the replacement of family allowances by a Family Income Security Plan. The main features of this plan were : a benefit for each child of $16 per month to be given to families with incomes of less than $4,500 per annum; benefits gradually reducing to $5 per child to be given to families with incomes up to $10,000; no benefit to be given to families with incomes above that amount; all benefits to be subject to income-tax.

It was estimated that under this plan 20 per cent. of all families would receive the maximum benefit and be better off by some 135 per cent., about 60 per cent. of all families would be better off to varying degrees than under the previous scheme and some 30 per cent. would lose their entitlement to benefit. The net cost of the plan was estimated to be the same as the 1970 expenditure on family allowances. The higher benefit rates to the majority of families would be financed by $270 million worth of benefit withdrawn from higher-income families and $100 million in tax recovered from beneficiaries.[17] The core of the plan thus was to provide some limited amelioration of poverty among the poorest families and somewhat higher net benefits for families of below-average incomes, at the expense of families who have above-average incomes. The rate of benefit was to vary with income but not with the size of the family or the age of the children. The standard wage-earner with an income of $7,000 in 1969 would receive $10 for each child irrespective of whether he had one child or six children.

These proposals were criticised by the Canadian Council on Social Development.[18] The Council wished to adhere to a scheme in which family allowances were universal and deplored the White Paper proposals as dividing families into 'haves' and 'have-nots'. Within a universal scheme it desired to give special emphasis to the needs of the lower-income families. The Council concurred with the view expressed in the White Paper that 'there are three basic criteria for determining the need for variations in [family allowance] benefits : family size, age of children and family income',[19] but criticised the proposed plan for not taking into account the age of children and the family size. In particular, it considered it inequitable to pay identical benefit rates to families with the same income but different numbers of children. The absence of a built-in escalation clause to meet rises in consumer prices was also censured.

The Council made a number of recommendations for a reformed family allowance programme. These include a universal flat-rate benefit for all dependent children under 18, taking into account the age of the children; a family allowance tax with rates directly related to income – a zero tax at low incomes and a 100 per cent. retrieval of the allowance at very high incomes; elimination of tax exemption for dependent children under 18; lower family allowance tax rates for larger families; an escalation clause to allow for price changes in consumer goods and services.

These recommendations would provide greater benefits for families with low incomes and a reduction in benefits for some families with high incomes. They would, however, at reasonably adequate levels of benefit, be more expensive to implement than the Family Income Security Plan. The Council suggested that the cost of increased assistance to low-income families should not be borne only by families with dependent children but also by other taxpayers and especially those with high incomes.

In June 1971 the Minister of National Health and Welfare announced that the proposed Family Income Security Plan would be modified in several respects before legislation for its implementation was introduced.[20]

History of Family Allowances. A universal scheme of children's allowances commenced in Ireland in 1944. This provided an allowance of 12½p per week for third and subsequent children under the age of 16 to all parents irrespective of their income or occupation. Monthly allowances were substituted for weekly ones and extended to second children in 1952 and to first children in 1963. The scheme was financed out of general revenue. When it was first introduced, income-tax relief for third and subsequent children was reduced so as to increase parents' tax liability by the same amount that they received in children's allowances.[21] This 'claw-back' was discontinued after a short time but was reintroduced in 1969 to cover the increases in allowances given in that year.

The rates of allowance, which were exempt from income-tax, were then 50p per month for the first child, £1·50 for the second and £2 (increased to £2·25 in 1970) for the third and subsequent children. In the first twenty-five years of the scheme, children's allowances for a family with three children increased more than eightfold. In 1969 some 330,000 families received allowances in respect of 970,000 children. There were then on average nearly three children in every family receiving allowances.

Supplements to Social Security Benefits and Civil Service Pay. Social insurance beneficiaries received increases of 77½p (£1·35 in 1972) per week for the first two children and 52½p (£1 in 1972) for subsequent children. For recipients of social assistance subject to an income test, the increases were 62½p (£1·15 in 1972) for the first two children and 37½p (75p in 1972) for subsequent children. These increases were in addition to the universal children's allowances.

Some state employees received supplements in respect of children as part of their salary; these were subject to income-tax and were in addition to the universal allowances. All schoolteachers and most civil servants received £35 per annum in respect of each child.

Tax Exemptions.   Parents have received tax relief for dependent children since the foundation of the state. In 1969 this was given by way of a tax exemption of £150 for children over 11 years and £135 for younger children.[22] The exemptions were reduced by £15 for all but one child under 16 years in respect of which universal children's allowances had been paid. The value of this relief, at the standard rate of tax of 35 per cent. up to incomes of some £5,000 per annum, was £53 or £47. This was about twice as much as the universal allowances payable in respect of children under 16, and for younger children, even after the claw-back, was £42 compared with the top rate of the universal allowance of £24 per year. The value of tax relief was also substantially greater than the increases in respect of children given to social insurance and social assistance beneficiaries. Parents with incomes of £565 or less were exempt from income-tax and therefore could not benefit from tax relief for children. Even families with three children under 11 could only fully benefit from this relief if their income exceeded £1,075 per annum.

Policy Objectives. The introduction of children's allowances towards the end of the Second World War was influenced by the recommendations of the Beveridge Report in Great Britain. The avowed purpose of the children's allowances was to effect a redistribution of income in favour of families. In a society where a large proportion of men and women do not marry and, among those who do, many marry at a relatively late age and have large families, inequalities in standards of living of people who have the same income but different family circumstances are comparatively great.

The extension of children's allowances to first children and the increase in allowances for third and subsequent children in 1963 was intended to compensate families for the increase in prices of food and clothing resulting from the imposition in that year of a turnover tax on almost all goods and services.

In his 1972 budget speech the Minister of Finance announced that the universal children's allowances scheme was being reviewed.[23] As no committee had been appointed to undertake such a review, it must be assumed that the minister was referring to a study at official level.

UNITED KINGDOM

History and Policy Objectives of Family Allowances. Family allowances for second and subsequent children were paid to all parents irrespective of their income and occupational status. They were paid out of general government revenue and, contrary to the practice of other countries, were liable to tax as earned income.

This scheme, which commenced in 1946, implemented a recommendation of the Beveridge Report, *Social Insurance and Allied Services*.[24] Lord Beveridge had referred to the 30 per cent. increase in real wages in the first thirty years of this century and the evidence (of several surveys of the inter-war years) showing that this had by no means eliminated poverty among large families. His recommendations were based on two propositions :

First, it is unreasonable to seek to guarantee an income sufficient for subsistence, while earnings are interrupted by unemployment . . . without ensuring sufficient income during earning. Social insurance should be part of a policy of a national minimum. But a national minimum for families of every size cannot in practice be secured by a wage system, which must be based on the product of a man's labour and not on the size of his family. . . .

Second, it is dangerous to allow benefit during unemployment . . . to equal or exceed earnings during work. But, without allowances for children, during earning and non-earning alike, this danger cannot be avoided. . . . To secure [greater fluidity of labour] the gap between income during earning and interruption of earning should be as large as possible for every man. It cannot be kept large for men with large families, except either by making their benefit in unemployment . . . inadequate, or by giving allowances for children in time of earning and non-earning alike.[25]

Lord Beveridge advocated a policy of sharing the cost of children between the community and parents and referred to allowances relieving parents of the whole cost of their children as 'an unnecessary and undesirable inroad on the responsibilities of parents'.[26] He suggested that this policy should be implemented by paying for every child in a family, except the first, an allowance sufficient to cover maintenance at the minimum acceptable subsistence standard. For the first child no allowance was to be paid while the parents were earning, as 'few men's wages are insufficient to cover at least two adults and one child.[26] The maintenance of the first child was to be the minimum share in the cost of rearing a family which had to be borne by the parents.

The family allowance scheme proposed by Lord Beveridge was incorporated in the Family Allowance Act, 1945, but the allowance was fixed at such a low figure that in effect the policy underlying his proposals was rejected. He had recommended an allowance of 40p per week, equal to one-fifth of the benefit to be paid to a married couple when their earnings were interrupted, while the allowance provided by the 1945 Act was only 25p, that is, a mere 62 per cent. of what was considered necessary to cover the minimum needs of a child. Since then family allowances have remained the Cinderella of the social services.

They were increased to 40p in 1952 and for second children remained at that level for 16 years, while for third and subsequent children there was an increase to 50p in 1956 but no further increase for the next 12 years. By 1968 the purchasing power of the allowance for second children had declined by 39 per cent. and that for third and subsequent children by 31 per cent. since they had last been adjusted. In 1968 the allowances for all children were increased in two stages by 50p and in 1969 were 90p and £1 respectively. The extent to which family allowances fell short of the Beveridge concept can be seen by expressing the allowance paid for three children as a percentage of the standard rate of national insurance benefit received by a married couple. Beveridge had proposed 40 per cent.; in 1948, when the National Insurance Act came into operation, it was 24 per cent.; by 1967 it had declined to 12 per cent., but by 1969 it was back to 24 per cent. On the basis of the Beveridge recommendation the rate of allowance should have been £1·62 in 1969 – one-fifth of a married couple's insurance benefit of £8·10 – and have risen to £2·18 in 1972, when it was still about 93p on average.

The allowance was normally paid to the mother at a post office. Initially it covered children up to the time when they started work or the July following their 16th birthday, whichever was the earlier date. The upper limit was raised to the 18th birthday in 1956 and to the 19th in 1964.

One suggestion made by Beveridge, 'in practice, the allowances should not be uniform but graded by age, since the needs of children increase rapidly with age',[27] has not been implemented.

Supplements to Social Security Benefits. When the national insurance scheme commenced in 1946, increases for child dependants of beneficiaries were confined to the first child as other children were covered by family allowances. Beveridge had recommended that the increase in benefit in respect of the first child should be at the same rate as that of family allowances and that both should be sufficient for maintenance at the minimum tolerable standard of living. As, however, family allowances had been fixed at 25p per week, about two-thirds of that minimum, it was necessary to provide for first children an increase of 37½p, and it would have been reasonable to give increases of 12½p for second and subsequent children. This was done in 1951, but it was only from 1952 onwards, after family allowances had been increased to 40p, that the increase in respect of a first child of a beneficiary was the same as family allowances plus the increases for second and subsequent children. The rule of providing the same aggregate income including family allowances for the first two children of a beneficiary has been followed since; for third and subsequent children, for no very evident reason, the aggregate income was marginally higher between 1956 and 1968.

Beveridge had recommended an increased benefit for a child equal to 20 per cent. of the national insurance benefit for a married couple. The proportion adopted in 1946 was 18 per cent. and since then has varied between these two percentages. This has meant that the increase for a child has been about half that for an adult dependant.

Initially the increase for the child dependants of a widow had been the same as that for other beneficiaries, but since 1956 they have been at a higher rate. This may be explained by three factors : first, the number of widows with dependent children is small in relation to other types of beneficiaries and therefore liberality to widows is comparatively inexpensive; second, it is virtually certain that high benefit rates for widows will neither increase their number nor that of their child dependants; third, widows enjoy public sympathy even among those who suspect every unemployed to be work-shy and every disabled to be a malingerer. The 1969 increases for child dependants of widows were £2·45 for the first child, £1·55 for the second and £1·45 for third and subsequent children; the corresponding benefits for other beneficiaries were less by 90p per week.

Tax Exemptions.   Tax exemptions for dependent children were first introduced in 1920. They varied with the age of the child but not with family rank. In 1969 the exemptions were £115 per annum for children under 11 years, £140 for children between 11 and 16 years and £165 for older children. These exemptions were reduced by £42 per child for whom a full year's family allowance had been received. The purpose of this reduction, colloquially known as the 'claw-back', was to reduce income-tax relief by an amount equivalent to that by which family allowances had been increased in 1968. The procedure had been suggested in the Beveridge Report :

> Insofar as it appears that . . . allowances to all families irrespective of their means would mean giving money to prosperous people without need, this can be corrected by an adjustment of the rebates of income-tax now allowed for children. This does not mean that . . . allowances should replace tax rebates. The problems of taxation and of allowance are distinct and involve different considerations.[28]

An appropriate reduction in tax exemptions to offset an increase in family allowances leaves the income of families paying tax at the standard rate unaffected and concentrates the net expenditure and the corresponding benefit of increasing family allowances on those families whose income is too low to pay tax at the standard rate. The claw-back had, however, the incidental effect of increasing the money the mother drew at the post office while reducing the money the father received in his wage packet. This redistribution of income within the family was one of the reasons why politicians hesitated to use the claw-back device. There was also apprehension that the men affected might agitate for higher wages and salaries, to compensate them for their increased tax liability. As men with two or more children receiving allowances accounted for only one-fifth of all men working, there was the danger that the resulting pay increase would greatly exceed the amount by which taxes had increased. The inflationary conditions in the post-devaluation Britain of the late 1960s made it difficult to verify the validity of these apprehensions.

As family allowances were subject to income-tax, any increase in allowances, quite irrespective of the claw-back, increased the income the mother drew at the post office while simultaneously reducing the father's pay-packet by about 32 per cent. of the cash increase enjoyed by the mother. Only fathers with very low incomes or very large families were exempt from this increased tax liability. The claw-back thus merely accentuated the selectivity within universality and the degree of income redistribution within the family.

The value of tax exemptions in 1969 for parents who paid tax at the standard rate was £47 for children under 11 years for whom no family allowance was received and £30 for second and subsequent children in a family that was covered by these allowances. For children over 16 years the corresponding amounts were £68 and £51 respectively. The net benefit of family allowance to parents paying income-tax at the standard rate was £32 for second and £35 for third and subsequent children.

The Family Income Supplement. In 1971 a new means-tested family support scheme for the working poor was introduced. This enabled any man, widow, divorcee, deserted wife or unmarried mother with at least one dependent child under 16 or still attending school to claim a Family Income Supplement if he or she was in full-time employment. This supplement, subject to a maximum limit, was one-half of the difference between a family's normal gross income and a prescribed amount. This was originally fixed at £15 for a family with one child plus £2 for each additional child, but was raised to £18 before the scheme was commenced and to £20 in April 1972. The maximum limit, which was fixed in 1970 at £3, was raised to £4 in 1971 and to £5 in the following year. Thus a deserted wife with two children earning £12·50 per week and receiving 90p in family allowance would be entitled in 1972 to half the difference between £22 and £13·40, that is, to £4·30; if her income increased to £13·50 her supplement would decline to £3·80.

The scheme was designed to assist between one-half and one-third of working families whose gross income was below the means-tested supplementary benefit scales for the disabled. It does not, however, provide a guaranteed minimum family income. As women's wages are usually lower than men's, and as the prescribed amount is the same for a married couple with one child as for a single parent with one child, the supplementation scheme benefits fatherless families more than standard families. In 1972 the prescribed amounts were so low that a family with two dependent children where the father earned 70 per cent. of the average earnings of a male adult manual worker was not entitled to a supplement. The number of awards made by the end of 1971 was 93,000. As with other means-tested schemes, a substantial proportion of those entitled to benefit failed to apply for a variety of reasons.

The level and structure of family support in Britain has been criticised widely. Since 1965 the Child Poverty Action Group has become the channel through which much of this criticism has been voiced. The Group advocates substantial family allowances both to reduce poverty and to create equity in standards of living between families with children and households without dependent children. It proposed a carefully costed plan[29] in 1970 which contained three elements : family allowances of 175p per week for each child in the family including the first (compared with existing allowances of 90p for the second and 100p for the third and subsequent children), the termination of child tax exemptions, and family allowances, except for the first 100p per week of each family's allowance, to be taxable (compared with the whole allowance being subject to tax). The net cost of this proposal was estimated to be £250 million per year and an alternative proposal giving an allowance of 125p instead of 175p for the first or only child in the family was estimated to cost £80 million per year. The Family Income Supplement scheme which was announced in 1970 a few weeks after the C.P.A.G.'s proposals had been submitted was estimated to cost £8 million.

The Group censured the Family Income Supplement on several counts : families needed to plead poverty, which on past experience always leads to a failure to claim by many people entitled to benefit;[30] the scheme was restricted to one-half or less of all poor families in which the breadwinner was in full-time employment; the scheme acted as a disincentive for a man to work overtime or for his wife to go out to work, because of the reduction in supplement whenever family income increased; the administrative cost of the scheme was relatively high; many families whose incomes were marginally above the limit set by the scheme would fail to benefit.

The C.P.A.G. proposals were similar to those of the Royal Commission on Social Security in New Zealand, which were implemented in 1972, to those of the Royal Commission on the Status of Women in Canada, to those of the Henderson recommendations in the Melbourne survey and to those of the Sozialenquête-Kommission in Germany. They are, however, diametrically opposed to the ideology of the British 1970 Conservative government which, like the Canadian 1968 Liberal government, was strongly committed to 'selectivity' in social security provisions.

DENMARK

History and Policy Objectives of Family Allowances. Children's allowances for children up to 16 were first introduced in 1950 to compensate parents in part for the termination of certain food and clothing subsidies. They were increased in 1953 and 1955, again to relieve parents of the effect of both withdrawal of subsidies and increased sales taxes.[31] These allowances were scaled according to the parents' income and residence. The income limit beyond which parents lost their eligibility to children's allowances was, however, sufficiently high to enable some 90 per cent. of all children under 16 years to qualify. The allowances were paid at the same rate to all children in the same family, irrespective of their ages and the number of children in the family. The maximum rate in Copenhagen was about a third higher than the maximum rate in the rural areas.

Prior to 1961 parents were also entitled to child tax exemptions for children under 16 years; these also varied according to place of residence, but increased with the number of children in the family. Exemptions were claimed in respect of virtually all children, but on account of the progressive nature of income tax they were of greatest benefit to those taxpayers with the highest income. This was the major reason why these tax remissions were discontinued in 1961 and replaced by restructured and increased children's allowances. Since that date children's allowances have been uniform all over the country, are no longer dependent on parental income and are paid up to a child's 18th birthday. The rate of allowance was increased on five occasions between 1961 and 1970. In 1969 it was Kr.855 per annum for the first four children and Kr.905 for subsequent children (increased to Kr.1,100 for all children in 1970). Until 1970 the family allowance had been paid by tax offices and normally been offset against taxes due. From that date onwards the allowances were paid by the social security offices.[32]

Other Provisions for Children.   Child pensions were paid to orphans, to children of widows and widowers and to children of invalidity and old-age pensioners. The standard pension of Kr.3,684 in 1970 was paid for orphans only, other children receiving three-fifths of the standard pension. These pensions were adjusted annually, according to changes in the cost-of-living index. Prior to 1969 they were subject to an income test, but as from that date they were paid to all persons entitled to them, irrespective of income. There were no supplements in respect of children in sickness, unemployment or industrial injury insurance.

Maintenance payments imposed on a parent by a court could be paid in advance by a local authority to the other parent or any other person having the custody of the child or children. The maximum which could be paid, if the father was liable, was three-fifths of the standard child pension; the maximum if the mother was liable was two-fifths of that pension. Nearly 100,000 children were covered by such advance payments in 1968–9. The local authorities recovered 58 per cent. of the sums advanced, but even so the net cost of this scheme was Kr.74 million.

There were a number of other services and subsidies provided for families with children. The most important and expensive of these was a sophisticated rent allowance which provided a subsidy which varied directly with the number of children and the level of rent and inversely with the family income.

History of Family Allowances. Family allowances for third and subsequent children of employees were first introduced in 1939 and subsequently were extended to all children in the family as well as to certain social security beneficiaries and some categories of the self-employed. In 1963 a general family allowance scheme covering the whole population was introduced and simultaneously two special schemes, one for employees and one for the self-employed, came into force.[33]

All three schemes provided quarterly allowances varying with a child's rank in the family but not with his age or his parents' income. Under the general scheme no allowance was payable for the first two children; the rates in 1969 were Fl137 for the third child and Fl184 for fourth and fifth children. The special scheme for employees provided allowances for the first two children at rates of Fl121 and Fl137 per quarter respectively. The self-employed received allowances for the first two children if their income was less than Fl7,450 per annum and for the second child only if their income was between Fl7,450 and Fl7,950. The rate of allowance for the self-employed was the same as that for employees.

Employers contributed a payroll tax of 2 per cent. of earnings up to Fl17,450 to the general scheme and of 3·3 per cent. of earnings to the employees' scheme, neither of which could be recovered from their employees. The self-employed paid a levy of 2 per cent. of their incomes up to the same amount to the tax authorities as their contributions to the general scheme. The entire cost of the special scheme for the low-income self-employed was paid out of general revenue.

Special Features of Family Allowances. The Netherlands' family allowance schemes had two features of special interest. All allowances were dynamic; the statutes provided for automatic adjustment in the rate of allowances in accordance with changes in the wages index. This meant that they not merely maintained their purchasing power when prices increased but that their real value increased in line with the rising purchasing power of wages. The other feature was that some parents were entitled to two or even three allowances in respect of one child. This double and treble counting was meant to relate allowances to special needs.

Parents were entitled to family allowances for the following dependent children :

(1) each child under 16 – counts as two children if largely (to the extent of more than half) dependent on the parent and away from home because of education or permanent illness;

(2) each child between 16 and 27 largely dependent on the parent and receiving full-time education counts as two, or if away from home and almost entirely (90 per cent. or more) dependent on the parent, counts as three;

(3) each child between 16 and 27 largely dependent on the parent and permanently ill, counts as two;

(4) one child between 16 and 27 mainly employed in keeping house or, if there are at least three other children under 27 in the household, helping in looking after the household, counts as two.

Tax Exemptions.   Child tax exemptions were granted in two ways.[34] First, there was an exemption of Fl420 for each child; the same four criteria that applied in child allowances applied here – thus the exemption could be claimed two or three times over in respect of one child. Second, further relief for those entitled to child allowances was given. This varied according to both income level and number of children; again one child could count as several by the same four criteria. The standard-wage family with one child would save about Fl250, and with three children about Fl730. Relief increased with income and with the number of children (within certain limits). Tax concessions for the standard wage-earner were thus much lower than the family allowances received in cash under the special employees' scheme – Fl484 for one-child and Fll,580 for three-child families. For higher incomes the tax remission was at the maximum Fl623 for each dependent child.

GERMANY

History of Family Allowances.   During the inter-war years a few family endowment schemes were operated by private firms. The first universal scheme was introduced by Hitler in 1935 in order to encourage an increase in the number of births. This provided allowances for fifth and subsequent children in a family and later was extended to third and fourth children. It was discontinued at the collapse of Germany in 1945.

A new scheme commenced in 1955.[35] This gave an allowance of DM25 per month for third and subsequent children to all parents in remunerative employment irrespective of income and means. A year later this was widened to include all parents resident in the country excluding only social insurance pensioners and persons employed in the public service. The second child in the family was included as from 1961, subject to the parents' income not exceeding DM7,200 per annum. Until 1964 allowances for third and subsequent children were financed by a 1 per cent. payroll tax and a corresponding tax on the self-employed, while the allowance for second children, which was designed to compensate parents for not benefiting from income-tax relief for children, was paid out of general revenue. After that date, under a remodelled scheme, all children's allowances were paid out of general revenue.

In 1969 allowances were awarded in respect of second and subsequent children, but allowances to parents who had two childen only were restricted to those who had an income of less than DM7,800 per annum (DM13,200 as from 1970). The rate of allowance, which was exempt from income-tax, was DM25 per month for the second child, DM50 for the third (increased to DM60 in 1970), DM60 for the fourth and DM70 for fifth and subsequent children. Allowances were due until the children attained the age of 18, or 25 if they continued in full-time education. These allowances were paid to 1·8 million families irrespective of their income and means, for 4·7 million children and to 300,000 families who had two children only. Expenditure on the universal children's allowances, including the cost of administration, was DM2,700 million – approximately DM540 per child per year.

Supplements to Social Security Benefits and Civil Service Pay. Social insurance pensioners' children's supplements differed according to the nature of the pension received. Old-age and invalidity pensioners were paid a flat rate of DM82 per month for every child. This was determined so as to equal 10 per cent. of the average earnings of all insured pensioners in the first three years of the last four years prior to the date when the supplements were paid. Accident insurance pensioners received a supplement of 10 per cent. of their pension for each child, subject to a maximum of DM200 per month and a minimum equal to the universal children's allowances. The unemployed received DM12 per week per child (DM52 per month).

These supplements were exempt from tax and were more liberal than the universal scheme for families of all sizes. The cost of these family supplements to social insurance pensioners was DM980 million in 1969.[36]

Public servants benefited from three family allowance schemes. All received a children's allowance of DM50 per month for all children in the family. In addition, officers received local supplements and manual workers social supplements for all children at the uniform rate of DM40 for the first child, DM47 for the second to fifth children and DM58 for all other children. These three allowances were liable to income-tax and to social insurance contributions where appropriate. The gross cost of public service family allowances was DM3,100 million in respect of 3·2 million children in 1969 – approximately DM1,000 per child per year. These allowances were not only substantially higher than those under the universal scheme but they were paid in respect of all first and second children.

Tax Exemptions.   Parents since 1920 have been entitled to relief from income-tax in respect of their dependent children. In 1969 this was given by way of tax exemptions of DM1,200 for the first child, DM1,680 for the second and DM1,800 for third and subsequent children. The value of the tax exemption for the standard weekly wage-earner was DM19 per month for the first child, DM27 for the second and DM29 for the third and subsequent children. For couples paying tax at the progressive rate in respect of earnings above DM16,000, the maximum value of the exemption for the third child was DM80 per month.

A three-child family earning less than DM16,000 received the same amount in universal children's allowances as in tax relief in respect of children – DM75 from each. When the family was larger the children's allowances exceeded tax exemptions, when smaller the tax exemptions exceeded the children's allowances. When earnings exceeded DM16,000 the value of tax exemptions increased, and when earnings were low the value of tax exemptions declined. The revenue loss on account of tax exemptions for children was estimated to be DM4,200 million.

Policy Objectives.   There was much opposition to the reintroduction of children's allowances in 1954.[37] They were considered as encouraging large families and a resurrection of the tarnished population policy of Hitler's Germany. The alleged interference with the privacy of the family by the state was opposed fiercely. It was argued that married couples should decide how many children they wished to have and that they alone ought to be responsible for all the consequences of their decisions. To have and to rear children, it was suggested, was one of the greatest pleasures and satisfactions in life which was not offset by the acceptance of greater economic burdens. The view was canvassed that the state was only entitled to assist families if, without such assistance, the family would sink below a tolerable minimum standard of living and thereby endanger the proper physical and mental development of the children. For this purpose a social assistance scheme rather than universal children's allowances was the appropriate device. A third strand of the opposition was the condemnation of the waste involved in paying allowances to many who were not in need of support and the corresponding excessive administrative cost. The policy of giving something to everybody was seen as typical of a welfare-state mentality designed to make all citizens amenable to the wishes of the authorities. The higher allowances for fourth and subsequent children, which were introduced in the middle 1960s, were condemned as favouring parents with low incomes and large families. This was considered as objectionable in its effect on population structure, eugenics and G.N.P.

The advocates of children's allowances had as their primary objective an increase in the disposable income of families. The allowances were to reduce the economic burden of rearing a family and to raise the standard of living of parents compared with that of single persons and couples without dependent children.

Family allowances for public servants were originally confined to established civil service officers (*Beamte*). These officers were paid remuneration appropriate to the level of their responsibilities and sufficient to make them devote all their energies to honest public service without the need to augment their income in any other way. Family allowances were paid in recognition of the fact that officers who had families would otherwise be reduced to a standard of living incompatible with the responsibility of their position. The avowed objective of family allowances was to raise the standard of living of officers with dependent children to that of officers who did not have to support a family. The extension of this historic and slightly archaic concept to some 3 million public servants, including nearly a million manual workers, as part of the process of assimilating conditions of service, robbed it of the validity it may have possessed in the past. In any case a flat-rate allowance varying marginally with the rank of the child is not the most appropriate method of equalising the standards of living of people who have the same income but different family responsibilities; this is more effectively done by allowances related or possibly even proportionate to income.

The diversity of social security provisions, the administrative autonomy of the various agencies and the cherished concept of self-government are the only possible explanations of the multiplicity of supplements for dependent children. It is not easy to justify the wide differences in supplements paid to the unemployed, the accident insurance pensioners and the invalidity insurance pensioners. Among the social security supplements paid in respect of dependent children, the scheme of the social assistance agencies is logically the most satisfactory. This grants allowances related to the age of the child and has a more realistic appreciation of the cost of rearing children than schemes relating allowances solely to the rank of the child in the family.

Tax exemptions for children were considered as a recognition of the citizen's dual responsibility : to support his family and to support the collective expenditure of the society of which he was a member. At any level of income, the greater the number of his dependants the less was his ability to contribute to collective expenditure. The purpose of children's tax exemptions was to equalise the taxable capacity of people who have the same income but differ in their family responsibilities. The justification for tax exemptions increasing with rank of the child, especially for third and subsequent children prior to 1965, was that levels of remuneration were normally geared to the support of one or two children and that parents who had more children would therefore suffer a correspondingly greater reduction in taxable capacity. As the cost of maintaining a child is partly related to its age, the logical application of the equalising principle would require exemptions to vary with age as well as with rank. However, as the cost of rearing a child is also much influenced by the father's income, tax relief should, on the basis of the equalising principle, be related to income. This is actually the case on account of the progressive nature of the German income-tax system which, even with exemptions unrelated to income, causes tax relief resulting from these exemptions to increase with income.

In Germany the family is also supported by several other measures, especially in the field of housing and education maintenance grants. The multiplicity of family support measures, however, are quite uncoordinated and strive simultaneously to achieve objectives which are often incompatible with each other.

Recommendations of the Sozialenquête-Kommission. The Sozial-enquête-Kommission, the nearest German equivalent of a Royal Commission, recommended in the late 1960s that (1) the universal children's allowances and children's tax exemptions should be combined; (2) this unified allowance should be graded by the child's rank in the family but not by parental income; and (3) it should normally be offset against liability to income-tax, but when the allowance exceeds tax liability it should be paid to employees with their wages.[38]

AUSTRIA

History of Family Allowances. An official publication of the National Federation of Austrian Social Insurance Institutions[39] states that family allowances are granted 'in order to further marriage and the maintenance of the family'. This reads somewhat strangely, but presumably represents a motivation which prevailed at one time.

A system of family allowances for employees was introduced in 1948 and extended to the self-employed in 1954. In 1969 all employed and self-employed persons as well as social insurance beneficiaries were entitled to family allowances in respect of all children under the age of 18 dependant on them. The allowances varied with the family rank of the child but not with the parents' income or the child's age.[40] The rate of the monthly allowance, which was paid for 14 months a year, was Sch200 for the first child, Sch220 for the second, Sch260 for the third, Sch290 for the fourth and Sch 320 for fifth and subsequent children, plus a supplement of Sch175 to families of three or more children.

These allowances were normally paid in conjunction with wages by employers, with benefit by the sickness funds or with pensions by the pension institutes. Employers offset the sums paid out in allowances against income-tax, while the social security agencies reclaimed them from the revenue authorities. Allowances to the self-employed were either offset against their income-tax liabilities or paid out by the local tax offices.

The employees' allowances were financed by a 6 per cent payroll tax and those of the self-employed were financed partly by a surcharge on their income-tax or, in the case of farmers, their land tax, and partly by contributions from the provincial governments.

Supplements to Social Security Benefits.   Sickness benefit was increased by 5 per cent. basic entitlement for each dependent child subject to total benefit not exceeding 75 per cent. of pre-sickness earnings. Pensions in respect of old age and invalidity were increased by the same percentage, but by at least Sch76 per month for each child. Unemployment benefit was increased by a weekly flat rate of Sch24 per child, subject to a maximum of 80 per cent. of pre-unemployment earnings.

Tax Exemptions.   Since 1967 parents have received child tax exemption of Sch7,000 per annum for the first and second child and Sch8,000 for third and subsequent children. Prior to that date the exemption was given by way of a percentage reduction on a regressive scale of the rate of tax chargeable.[41] For the standard wage-earner in 1969, the value of this exemption was Sch2,380 for each of the first two children and Sch2,720 for subsequent children. This compares with family allowances of Sch2,800 for the first and Sch3,080 for the second child. The tax threshold was so low that the child tax exemption benefited virtually all parents, but as income-tax was progressive it was of greater benefit to parents with high incomes than it was to those with low incomes.

U.S.A.

Child Poverty.   The U.S.A. is the only one among the ten countries of this study and moreover the only one among all the developed countries which has no universal family support programme. Standards of living in the U.S.A. are by any criteria much higher than anywhere else. All the same, a substantial proportion of the population (about one-eighth) live below what is officially designated as the poverty level. As in other countries, the proportion of children in poverty (in the U.S.A., one-seventh) is somewhat greater than that of all persons in poverty. Moreover, the proportion in poverty of certain groups of children is very much higher; for example, in minority racial groups nearly two-fifths and in fatherless families more than half are in poverty. The Bureau of the Census[42] estimated that the income deficit of poor families with children under 18, that is, the amount required to lift them above the poverty level, was $4,900 million in 1969, about one-half of 1 per cent. of the country's G.N.P. The absence of universal family endowment is thus not due to lack of ascertained need.

Tax Exemptions. Parents were assisted by three different programmes in 1969. They received a tax exemption of $600 per year for each child.[43] This reduced the tax liability of the standard wage-earner by about $150 and that of a man earning more than $200,000 by $420. There was of course no tax saving for those with no taxable income. The revenue loss due to these tax exemptions was estimated to be $7,500 million[44] in 1967 and will have been somewhat greater in 1969. In any case it was substantially more than the income deficit of poor families.

Supplements to Social Security Benefits. The Federal old-age, survivors', disability and health insurance (O.A.S.D.H.I.) was the second programme providing support for children. Retired and disabled workers received a payment of 50 per cent. of their primary insurance amount (basic pension) in respect of every dependent child under 18 or up to 21 if at school. A payment of 75 per cent. of the primary insurance amount was made to the children of deceased workers.[45] The average monthly benefit paid to children of retired, disabled and deceased workers at the end of 1969 was $39, $35 and $71 respectively. About $3\frac{1}{4}$ million children under 18 – about one in 20 of all children of that age – benefited from these provisions. A fairly small number of children benefited under a variety of other social insurance schemes : unemployment insurance (ten states granted child supplements), workmen's compensation (17 states granted child supplements) and railroad and veterans' compensations.

Aid to Families with Dependent Children. Within provisions set forth in Federal law, all states granted financial aid to certain categories of needy families with dependent children (A.F.D.C.). Each state established the conditions under which needy families might receive assistance and determined how much they should receive. Prior to the 1960s, aid was restricted by Federal law to families where the need was caused by the incapacity or death of a parent or a parent's continued absence from home. Later this was extended to cover need caused by the parent's unemployment. However, by 1969 the great majority of states had not incorporated this liberalisation of Federal law into their own state legislation. The A.F.D.C. schemes, with eligibility requirements largely determined by the states, have been widely considered to be socially disruptive. In 1968 Wilbur J. Cohen, the then Secretary of Health, Education and Welfare, criticised state laws and explained the reasons for the reluctance to liberalise them :

> . . . the Federal Government assists States to make payments to families with the father unemployed. In the 29 which do not take advantage of this Federal offer and continue to provide aid only if the father is disabled or absent from home, the assistance program is correctly criticised on the grounds that it sets up an incentive for the unemployed worker to leave home.
>
> Support for an assistance program that applies to all in need and that pays adequate amounts has been faced with hard going because of the incredible longevity of myths about those whom the program are supposed to aid : that the poor live high on welfare handouts and that the poor are lazy and don't want to work.
>
> The myths persist despite the fact that more than 80 per cent. of the households that do receive aid are still poor afterwards, despite the fact that most of the welfare recipients are not employable, and despite the fact that 80 per cent. of the working-age men who are poor have jobs, and about 75 per cent. of them are in full-time jobs.[46]

The number of children covered by the A.F.D.C. programmes in 1969 was about $5\frac{1}{2}$ million and had increased to 7 million – about one-tenth of all children under 18 – by 1970. The average monthly payment to families covered by these programmes was $176 in 1969 ($187 in 1970) and for a family of a mother and three children averaged about $180, or $2,160 per year.[47] At that time the poverty level for a non-farm family of this composition, as defined by the Social Security Administration, was $3,725 per year.[48]

The average payment per recipient (including the child's or children's parents) varied widely between the states : in 1969 it was as low as $12 in Mississippi and as much as $69 in Massachusetts, while national average was $45.[49].

For a better understanding of the position of children in poverty two important developments should be emphasised. In the ten years leading up to 1969 the proportion of children in families below the poverty level declined for a variety of reasons from 27 to 14 per cent. and the real purchasing power of the A.F.D.C. benefit per recipient increased by about 40 per cent. However unsatisfactory the position of many children may have been at the end of the 1960s, it was vastly better than it had been at the start of the decade.[50]

The Family Assistance System. In August 1969 the President (Richard Nixon), shortly after taking office, sent to Congress a number of welfare reform proposals. The most important of these, which received great publicity at the time, was a negative income-tax scheme which was to be called the Family Assistance System (F.A.S.). This was meant to replace the A.F.D.C. programmes and to provide a guaranteed minimum income to all families with at least one dependent child. The minimum was to be $500 for each of the first two family members and $300 for each subsequent member. For a family of four who had no other income the minimum was thus $1,600, at a time when the official poverty level for a non-farm family of this size with a male head was $3,745.[48]

The scheme provided that for earnings up to $720 the minimum should not be reduced, but that for earnings beyond this amount the allowance would be reduced by 50 cents for each dollar earned. A family of four was thus to be eligible for assistance up to an annual income of $3,920.

This scheme had not been accepted by Congress by 1972. It was by any standards a very moderate proposal which would have given families with no other income a standard of living not even half-way up to the official subsistence (poverty) level. It was at the time argued by some that, however inadequate, the scheme should be viewed as 'the thin end of the wedge' and was capable of improvement in the course of time. This view, however, is quite erroneous for the reasons given by Cohen (to which reference has been made on p. 45 above, a year before Nixon's message to Congress.

Three of the reasons for the institution of universal child endowment schemes by other countries – an investment in the future, a move towards social cohesion by avoiding a personal means test and income redistribution in favour of families with dependent children – have as yet found little public support in the U.S.A. Several academic writers have produced a variety of schemes of great ingenuity endeavouring to counter all the objections raised against such policies, but to no avail.[51] It appears that the American electorate adheres firmly to the beliefs that it is the responsibility of each family to take care of itself, that the state's intervention is to be limited to cases where the need is well established, and even then it is to be minimal rather than adequate. The New Zealand principle of giving to all families at a level of income which enables them to *belong* to society is not a popular doctrine in the U.S.A. at present.

REVIEW

Family Support Programmes in Kind.   Family or children's allowances, tax remissions and child supplements to social security beneficiaries are easy to quantify but are only part of the aggregate family support. Some countries have in addition less costly social security benefits of a similar nature. Maturity grants of varying but modest amounts were paid in 1969 in all countries except Canada, the U.S.A. and New Zealand. Maternity allowances at rates equivalent to full wages were paid for several weeks before and after confinement to women working as employees in Austria, Germany and the Netherlands, and at the same rate as sickness benefit in Ireland, the U.K. and Denmark; the other four countries had no such schemes.

Free and subsidised services, including education, to which reference has already been made, housing and school meals and milk, are other forms of family support but are not social security provisions according to the definition used in this study. Health services are part of the social security system and by their nature are of considerable benefit to parents of dependent children. In 1969 most children received health care without charge or at only nominal charges in Austria, Germany, the U.K., Denmark and the Netherlands, but parents had normally to pay for at least part of health care in the other five countries. A given sum of money, however, spent on free health services for all children would do more both to relieve poverty and give direct assistance where it is most needed, than if it were spent on universal children's allowances.

The Value of Family Allowances.   Family cash allowances were relatively modest in all nine countries. In none were they equivalent for the two-child family to even 10 per cent. of the income of the standard wage-earner (see Table 8 :1). In Austria and the Netherlands the rates of allowances for larger families were comparatively generous. They were equivalent for a three-child family in Austria to 19 per cent. and in the Netherlands to 13 per cent. of the income of the standard wage-earner. In the other seven countries the corresponding proportion was 8 per cent. or less.

TABLE 8:1 *Children's Allowances and Tax Remissions as a Proportion of the Standard Weekly Wage, 1969.*

	Children's allowances for families with			Tax remission for families with
Children:	One	Two	Three	Three
	%	%	%	%
Austria	4	9	19	12
Germany	–	–	6	6
Ireland	1	2	5	13
U.K.	–	3	7	8
Denmark	2	5	7	–
Netherlands	4	8	13	6
Canada	1	3	4	3
U.S.A.	–	–	–	5
New Zealand	3	5	8	4
Australia	1	2	4	4

As family allowances were paid at a flat rate they were an inverse proportion of income. For a man earning three-quarters of the standard wage the proportion of children's allowances to income was one-third higher than that shown in the table; for example, for a three child family in Germany children's allowances were equivalent to 6 per cent. of the income of the standard wage-earner, but to 8 per cent. of that of the man earning three-quarters of the standard wage. Conversely, on account of the progressive nature of income-tax schemes, child tax relief was directly related to income. For the man with a very low income tax relief tended to zero, while it was greatest for the very rich.

For the standard wage-earner with three dependent children the value of children's allowances was about the same as that of tax relief in Germany, Canada ·and Australia, it was greater in Austria, the Netherlands and New Zealand and less in Ireland and the U.K. For the same family, the combined support of children's allowances and child tax relief was greatest in Austria, the Netherlands and Ireland and least in the U.S.A. (where there are no children's allowances), Denmark (where there is no longer any tax relief), Australia and Canada.

A marked characteristic of children's allowances was their tendency to depreciate in purchasing power more than other social security benefits. In six of the countries, Germany, Ireland, the U.K., Canada, New Zealand and Australia, the rates have remained unaltered for considerable periods. This and the generally low level of children's allowances suggests that the political pressure for raising these allowances was less than that for increases in other social security benefits. This might have been due to the fact that in all these countries only a minority of households contained dependent children. This was because most men work for 45 to 50 years but have dependent children under 16 normally for only 20 years or less. As some men and women do not marry and about 8 per cent. of married couples have no children, it follows that those caring for children are always in a minority, even among those below retirement age. Another possible explanation for the low political pressure in favour of children's allowances is that children, in contrast to other social security beneficiaries, have no votes.

Entitlement to Family Allowances.   The maximum ages of children giving entitlement to children's allowances in specified circumstances differed widely : Austria, 27; Germany, 25 (but no limit if invalid); Ireland, 16; the U.K., 19; Denmark, 18; and Australia, 21. These maximum limits in all countries except Ireland referred to children who were either invalids or in full-time education. They were thus in some respects similar to invalidity benefits and education grants. On balance it seems desirable to give adult invalids a benefit in their own right as happened in the U.K. and New Zealand, rather than providing a benefit payable to their parents. Education grants to students are more in the spirit of the time than family allowances to their parents; they also have the advantage of being able to take account of a student's attainment and the requirements of manpower policy. Family allowances for children in their late teens and twenties tend to mitigate poverty very little and to benefit mainly the relatively better-off parents whose children are those most likely to continue at school and college up to these ages.

Children's or family allowances were independent of parental income except in Germany in the case of the second child in a two-child family and in Britain where the allowances were subject to tax and the 'claw-back' and thus of greater net benefit to the least well off.

Allowances Graded by Rank and Age. In 1972 New Zealand and Denmark had flat-rate family allowances which were independent of the family rank and age of the child; these two countries were also the only ones which did not grant any tax remissions in respect of children. The other five European countries and Australia had family allowances which increased with the rank of the child, but the degree of increase differed widely. Thus in 1969 the allowance for a four-child family exceeded that for a two-child family by 149 per cent. in Austria, by 440 per cent. in Germany, by 225 per cent. in Ireland, by 210 per cent. in the U.K., by 124 per cent. in the Netherlands (employees' scheme) and by 214 per cent. in Australia. The higher this ratio, the greater was the concentration of benefit on the larger family. This was achieved by paying no allowance for the first child in Germany and the U.K., and only a very low one in Ireland and Australia. Austria, Germany and the Netherlands also favoured the larger family in their tax remissions for children, while Australia had a higher tax exemption for the first child in the family than for other children under 16. Ireland, Canada and the U.K. graded child tax exemptions by age and not by family rank. In 1972 no country except Canada graded family allowances by the age of the child, though the double-counting method in the Netherlands did bring this about to some extent.

The limited evidence available as regards the cost of maintaining children of different ages indicate that cost rises with age.[52] The reasons why a child's age was not taken into account in determining family allowance rates were presumably the countervailing factors advanced by the New Zealand Royal Commission. An increase in allowances with the rank of the child is justified by the fact that at any income the economic burden of a fourth child is greater than that of a second child, in the sense that in the ten countries of this study except Ireland the two-child family is considered as the norm and any additional child presents a somewhat abnormal cost.

Methods of Paying Allowances. The administration and method of paying family allowances may be of considerable social importance. In Austria and the Netherlands, where these allowances were mainly financed by a payroll tax, adjustments of rates with changes in prices or wages were more frequent than in most of the other countries, with the possible exception of Denmark, where the allowances were financed out of general revenue. If the allowance is paid direct to the mother, the impact on family finance may be different from that in countries like Austria where the allowance was paid as an integral part of the main source of income. The frequency of payment may be a matter of importance, especially for poor families. Only in the U.K. was the allowance paid weekly, while in the Netherlands it was paid quarterly and in the other countries at a monthly or four-weekly rate. The higher the allowance and the more it is considered as a supplement to other social security benefits, the greater is the argument for enabling the parent to draw the benefit at a weekly rate. The maximum satisfaction of parents in different income circumstances and the minimisation of administrative costs may be achieved by offering parents a choice of the interval at which they receive their allowance.

Population Explosion. As regards the level of financial support given to the family, the concluding paragraph of the chapter on 'Assistance to the Family' in the Report of the New Zealand Royal Commission deserves to be quoted in full :

> It may seem strange to some that at a time when the 'population explosion' is regarded as a threat to mankind's very survival, and when we are being told that New Zealand's birthrate is too high, we have yet chosen to lay even greater emphasis on social security provision for children and for those who care for them. We have not done this in ignorance of or in despite of the need for world population control. But the responsibility of social security, as we see it, is to care for those who are in the community. This must not be subordinated to other aims. However desirable these may be they must be pursued by other means.[53]

Allowances for Public Servants. Some countries had special children's allowance schemes for public servants. In Germany all public servants received more generous children's allowances than those paid under the universal scheme from which they were excluded.

Ireland paid most public servants children's allowances as part of their remuneration as well as the allowances which were paid to all residents under the universal scheme. The Netherlands provided special children's allowances for first and second children to teachers and other public servants. Australia, prior to the introduction of universal children's allowances, had a special scheme for public employees.

One of the possible objectives of a family allowance scheme is a diminution in the differences between standards of living of people who have the same income but different family circumstances. A married man supporting a wife and two young children at any income is decidedly worse off than an unmarried man, or an older man whose children are no longer dependent on him and whose wife possibly goes out to work. Children's allowances can contribute to closing this gap. As the general trend in favour of equal pay for men and women was more pronounced in the public services than in many other types of employment, the arguments in favour of special public service children's allowances appear reasonable. This is all the more so as universal children's allowances for one and two-child families remained quite low in relation to average earnings and even lower in relation to the somewhat higher salaries of teachers and civil servants.

Income Redistribution over the Life-Span. Children's allowances have another desirable effect to which often insufficient weight is attached : they redistribute income over the life-span. Individuals benefit when they are dependent children and when they care for dependent children, and contribute before they have a family of their own and after their children have ceased to be dependent. Even men and women who never marry and couples who have no children benefit from the 'investment in human beings' aspect of children's allowances. There is also the often forgotten fact that when the childless retire it is not their pension which provides them with transport, heat, food and entertainment but the work currently performed by other people's children.

Supplements to Social Security Benefits. The New Zealand Social Security Act, 1938, and the Beveridge Report intended the level of family allowances to be adequate for the maintenance of children at an acceptable subsistence standard. Their parents were therefore

not thought to require any child supplements when they were unemployed or disabled. The general tendency of family allowances
to lag behind increases in other social security benefits and in prices
meant that even in these two countries, a few years after the restructuring of the social security systems, child supplements for social
security beneficiaries had to be introduced.

In 1969 the Netherlands was the only country which did not
provide increases in respect of children for any type of social security
benefit. This was because benefits at 80 per cent. of previous earnings
plus family allowances were considered adequate maintenance for
families of all sizes. Canada provided a child supplement only to
invalidity pensioners and the unemployed, and both were fixed in
terms of dollars. In the U.S.A. earnings-related old-age and invalidity
pensions were increased by half for a dependent child, but only
one-third of the states incorporated child supplements in their workmen's compensation schemes and even fewer, one-fifth, had child
supplements in unemployment insurance. Austria and Germany had
a variety of child supplements, some 4, 5 or 10 per cent. of an
earnings-related benefit.[54] In Denmark old-age and invalidity pensioners were entitled to a child's special supplement which was a
fixed amount unrelated to the basic benefit but annually adjusted to
take account of changes in prices. There were no increases in respect
of children paid to sickness insurance beneficiaries. The U.K. provided increases in respect of children to all beneficiaries; these were
equivalent, including the family allowance, to about one-fifth of the
standard benefit paid to a married couple. Ireland had much the
same system but the proportion in relation to a couple's standard
benefit was somewhat lower. In Australia the supplement, including
family endowment, paid for the first child of unemployed or sick
parents was some 18 per cent. of the maximum benefit they received;
the corresponding proportion in New Zealand was 6 per cent.

However, these figures are somewhat misleading : in Australia the
basic benefit for a married couple was only 21 per cent. of the
standard wage while in New Zealand it was 41 per cent. This illustrates the important point that the level or even absence of child
supplements is not indicative of the degree of state support received
by the family in unemployment or sickness. The proper indication
of this is the aggregate benefit as a percentage of original earnings
or of the standard wage. The lower the basic rate of benefit, the
stronger is the case for generous child supplements.

Vertical Income Redistribution. Family allowances in all countries tended to redistribute income not only to those with dependent children but also, to some very limited extent, vertically to the least well off. In all countries families with low incomes paid fewer taxes in terms of money than those with higher incomes, and as all families receive the same rate of allowance there must have been some degree of income redistribution. Family allowances represented in 1966 about 3 per cent. of consumption expenditure in Austria and the Netherlands and 1½ per cent. or less in the other seven countries. It is not likely that their relative proportion has changed markedly in the subsequent five years. If it is assumed that the least well-off fifth of the population had a quarter of all the children, then even in Austria and the Netherlands they would have received in family allowances at most the equivalent of 0·75 per cent. of total consumption expenditure. Actually their net receipts would have been less, as even the least well off in all countries pay taxes on a variety of consumer goods. The element of vertical redistribution through the family allowances was therefore universally so small in aggregate as to border on the insignificant. This, however, does not in any way detract from the importance of the allowance to the least well-off families.

CHAPTER IX

Conclusions

Scope of the Study. This study has concentrated on four approaches to social policy : a brief history of the provisions in each of the ten countries, a comparison of the provisions in force in 1969, the economic and social implications of these provisions and the general direction in which benefit levels have moved. This seemed a reasonable limitation of the scope of study, but left unanswered three questions which students of social policy often ask : What factors explain the differences between the various national schemes? What factors explain the differences in benefit levels between countries? To what extent do existing schemes meet social needs? None of these questions is easy to answer.

The Three Unanswered Questions. It is often very difficult to specify the crucial considerations behind any social policy decision, let alone make international comparisons of these considerations. Most political decisions are not simply the result of logically applying a coherent programme based on ideological commitment, and social policy decisions are no exception to this rule. They are the result of many varied and often opposing influences. The impact of one powerful personality has sometimes been the major force behind the content or form of a particular scheme. At other times decisions have been reached after interested parties have struck bargains, the terms of which may not have been put into writing and occasionally not even into words, although this informality has not made them any less binding on the parties concerned.

Government decisions in all countries are cloaked in secrecy, and the material for a critical examination of why a particular decision was taken is often not available. The avowed reasons are, of course, not necessarily the genuine ones. Financial contributions from insurance companies or trade unions to the funds of political parties may well have had some influence on the provisions of social insurance schemes. The insurance companies and the trade unions wield power in diverse ways, but in quite a few cases it will have been in the interests of all concerned to keep these matters out of the public eye.

Detailed case studies of the origin and history of particular social security schemes, moreover, cannot find a place in a comparative study of five schemes in ten countries. Such studies have to be meticulous and searching; ill-documented, general or superficial explanations would only be misleading.

It is not astonishing but all the same noteworthy that the decisions taken by any one government often appear quite inconsistent. Few governments are, in the words used by Robert Myers, wholly 'moderate' or wholly 'expansionist'. This can be illustrated by some examples. The National Party government of New Zealand in 1972 accepted the recommendations of the Royal Commission on Personal Injury, which were progressive, controversial and presented a major break with established tradition, at the same time as those of the Royal Commission on Social Security, which were conservative and traditional. The major social reforms undertaken in Germany by the Christian Democratic (Conservative) government in the 1950s and early 1960s greatly benefited employees but left many of the self-employed, especially those in agriculture, inadequately or totally unprotected against most social contingencies.

In examining the development of social policy in any country, what has been omitted deserves as much attention as what has been covered. The relative deterioration of social security standards in New Zealand throughout the 1960s, for example, was not the result of action but of inaction, not of winding up particular schemes or of 'undermining the welfare state' but of leaving it alone, i.e., failing to increase benefit rates in line with changes in earnings.

Answering the second question is as difficult as answering the first because the factors which make for differences in benefit levels between countries are somewhat similar to those which make for the differences in provisions between the various schemes – a conglomeration of ideology, history and the sway of pressure groups of various kinds. The insurance companies and medical associations do not merely influence the content of particular schemes but also indirectly the general level of benefits. The changes over the last thirty years in the nature of inequality of both income distribution (which were highlighted by Galbraith in *The Affluent Society*) and the life-styles of different social classes (which were discussed in Chapter 2 above) may well have restrained the political pressure for higher benefit standards in the richer of the ten countries, although in those countries the pressure was never very pronounced.

The third question which has been left unanswered – the extent to which existing schemes meet social needs – poses rather different problems. This question can be answered by cross-national studies[1] or studies covering one country only.[2] They have to be conducted by household surveys and must take into account not only statutory and non-statutory income-maintenance provisions but also savings, earnings and other income as well as certain expenditure items such as rents. Furthermore, social needs can often not be met by cash payments alone but require such services as housing, domiciliary help and health care.

Two Further Limitations.   The historical sketches attempt to outline the historical developments which have led up to the positions of the various schemes in different countries in 1969. It would have been preferable to have related these developments to the political and economic backgrounds against which they took place, but this was well beyond the scope of this study. It would also have been desirable to have related public social security provisions to both fiscal provisions of a social security nature and non-statutory social security provisions, but the material for such studies is not readily available in the case of most countries.

Public social security schemes in the ten countries differed in many respects. In this concluding chapter it is not necessary to recapitulate all the differences which have been discussed in previous chapters, but it is of interest to refer to some of them by way of example without attempting to give a comprehensive account.

Administration.   In all ten countries children's allowances were administered by government departments. The only income-maintenance services normally provided by commercial insurance companies were workmen's compensation in Denmark, most of the states of the U.S.A., New Zealand and Australia and temporary disability insurance in some of the few states in the U.S.A. which had compulsory schemes.

Social security cash benefit in the four non-English-speaking European countries were usually provided by a multiplicity of self-governing autonomous bodies which were composed of representatives of employers and employees. An exception to this was the administration of social pensions in Denmark which was undertaken by committees which were closely linked with the local authorities. These bodies and committees were not merely administrative agencies but exercised varying degrees of discretion in the award of benefits and (particularly in Germany and the Netherlands) had limited discretionary powers in determining contribution rates. This system meant that insured persons might receive different benefits for identical contributions or pay different contributions for identical benefits.

In the English-speaking countries cash benefits were administered by government departments or government agencies. In Ireland, the U.K., New Zealand and Australia unified benefit schemes were administered by one department or agency. The Australian states and Irish local authorities spent only relatively small sums on relief. In Canada the provinces administered all assistance programmes (although most of them were aided by Federal funds) and workmen's compensation schemes. Quebec had its own pension plan, which was virtually identical with the Canada Pension Plan, and its own supplementary family support programme.

The states in the U.S.A. were responsible for workmen's compensation and temporary disability schemes as well as for all assistance schemes (most of which were aided by Federal funds). Unemployment insurance schemes were also a state provision but they were administered subject to minimum standards laid down in Federal law. The major social security schemes of the U.S.A. (the O.A.S.D.H.I.) and of Canada (the Canada Pension Plan) were Federal schemes administered by Federal agencies.

Characteristics of Schemes. Children's allowances were demogrants in all countries (except Germany in the case of second children in two-child families and the Netherlands) and so were national old-age pensions in Denmark, old-age security pensions in Canada, superannuation benefit in New Zealand and one component of the Danish invalidity pension.

Selectivity in the award of cash benefits (in the sense of making the award of a particular benefit – not necessarily all benefits – subject to income or means tests) was a common practice in most of the ten countries. Thus all cash benefits in New Zealand (except workmen's compensation and superannuation benefit) and Australia (except workman's compensation) were subject to an income or a means test. Such tests were also often applied in supplementation of demogrants and insurance benefits, for example the guaranteed income supplement (for old-age security pensions) in Canada, the special pension supplements to national old-age pensions in Denmark, and the supplements to insurance benefits in Austria and the U.K. In Denmark old-age pensions of persons below the age of 67 and some components of the invalidity pension were also subject to an income test. Such tests were relatively unimportant (numerically) in Germany and the Netherlands while social assistance schemes were important (numerically) in the states of the U.S.A., the provinces of Canada and in Ireland.

Employers were under a statutory obligation to provide sick pay in Germany to all employees for up to six weeks' incapacity and in Austria and Denmark to salaried employees for a limited period. The W.C.A.s in Denmark, most of the states of the U.S.A., New Zealand and Australia imposed an obligation on employers to provide compensation for their employees. Certain redundancy payments in Ireland and the U.K. were also statutory obligations imposed on employers.

Financing. Social assistance schemes subject to means tests were normally financed out of general taxation and this was usually, but not invariably, also the case for demogrants. There was, however, a designated wage tax for children's allowances in Austria; old-age pensions in Denmark and Canada were partly financed by special income taxes. In some countries, for example Ireland and Denmark, social insurance schemes were heavily subsidised out of general revenue while in others, for example the U.S.A. and Canada, all benefits were financed out of contributions. In Germany, pension insurance was subsidised out of general revenue but sickness insurance was not. Although the Exchequer paid part of the cost of all social insurance schemes in the U.K., it was a much smaller proportion than in Ireland or Denmark.

Earnings-related insurance contributions of both employers and employees were subject to income ceilings in all countries.

Risk rating was applied to contributions or premiums for employment injury schemes in six countries (not in Austria, the Netherlands, Ireland or the U.K.). In five of these six countries (not in Canada) merit rating was also common. This device was also widely applied in the unemployment insurance schemes in the states of the U.S.A. and will be applied in 1975 in the Canadian unemployment insurance scheme. The proportion of insurance contributions borne by employers and employees respectively varied widely between countries and between schemes.

Number Covered. The proportion of the population covered by the various social security schemes has greatly increased in all countries over the last thirty years. All children in families were covered by children's allowances in Austria, Ireland, Denmark, Canada, New Zealand and Australia. In Germany and the U.K. first children (and in Germany also some second children) were not covered, nor were the first two children of most self-employed persons in the Netherlands.

Social insurance tended to cover all employees but there were many important exceptions : in Ireland non-manual employees earning more than £1,200 (£1,600 after 1971) were excluded; in Denmark only half of all employees were covered by unemployment insurance; in the U.S.A. agricultural workers, domestic servants, casual workers and employees of firms employing less than a specified number of staff were frequently excluded from the schemes operated by the states – workmen's compensation, unemployment insurance and temporary disability insurance; in the U.K. married women and most widows were not compulsorily insured but could opt to be covered by insurance. Civil servants and other public servants in all countries had special schemes under which they enjoyed much more favourable terms than social security beneficiaries.

The social insurance cover extended to the self-employed was more restrictive, but in 1969 much less so than it had been prior to the second World War. The unified social insurance scheme of the U.K., the O.A.S.D.H.I. in the U.S.A., the Canada and Quebec Pension Plans and the Netherlands old-age pension insurance covered virtually all self-employed persons. In Austria and Germany there were a number of old-age pension schemes for various groups of self-employed persons, but the cover was far from complete and the terms were often less favourable than those for employees.

In some countries the number of social security beneficiaries was difficult to ascertain as many of them received two or more benefits simultaneously. In those countries for which reasonably accurate estimates of the number of beneficiaries can be made, the proportion of the population covered by social security payments (excluding children's allowances) varied widely : Ireland, 24 per cent.; the U.K., 23 per cent.; the U.S.A., 19 per cent.; New Zealand, 11 per cent.; and Australia, 9 per cent. The relatively low proportions in New Zealand and Australia are explained partly by the relatively low proportions of their populations which are over 65 and partly by the selective nature of their social security provisions.

Conditions of Award. The circumstances giving entitlement to benefit varied widely. The minimum pensionable age ranged from 55 (single women in New Zealand who were unable to work) to 70 (for contributory and non-contributory pensions in Ireland). In Austria and Germany persons who had been unemployed for a specified period could claim old-age pensions before the normal age. A claimant of invalidity benefit had to have a disability of only 15 per cent. in the Netherlands but of 100 per cent. in New Zealand. Commuting accidents in Austria and Germany were considered as 'arising out of and in the course of employment' but were not normally considered as such in Ireland or the U.K. Benefit for temporary disability (sick pay) was paid without any waiting days in Germany but subject to a waiting period of one week in Denmark, the U.S.A., New Zealand and Australia. (As from 1971 the waiting period in Canada was two weeks.)

In Denmark and the Netherlands medical certification of incapacity was not normally required for the award of temporary disability insurance benefit, but in the other eight countries (in Canada, from 1971) the award of benefit was conditional on certification.

Temporary disability benefit was paid only after a substantial qualifying period in Ireland and the U.K., but in Austria and Germany it was paid to all insured persons irrespective of the length of time for which they had been insured. Old-age pensions were paid subject to retirement conditions in Austria, the U.K., Canada (retirement pensions) and the U.S.A. but not subject to such a condition in Germany, Ireland (contributory old-age pensions), Denmark, the Netherlands, Canada (old-age security pensions) and New Zealand (superannuation benefit). Almost any part-time employment disqualified the unemployed from receipt of unemployment benefit in Ireland and the U.K. but quite substantial earnings were not a disqualification from benefit in Austria and Germany. The severity of the statutory disqualification from unemployment benefit also varied widely. It was most severe in some of the states of the U.S.A. but comparatively liberal in Germany.

Assessment of Benefit. The assessment of temporary disability insurance benefit and old-age insurance pensions should give some indication of the variation in benefit assessment. Temporary disability benefit was paid at flat rates irrespective of earnings in Ireland and Denmark as well as in the U.K. for the first two weeks of incapacity and from the 29th week. In the other four countries which had insurance schemes – Austria, Germany, the Netherlands and the U.S.A. (four states) – and in the U.K. from the third to the 28th week, benefits were related to previous earnings. The period of earnings taken into account in assessing benefits ranged from four weeks preceding the onset of incapacity in Germany to one year, which might include earnings of as much as two years prior to the onset, in the U.K.

There was a great variety of factors involved in assessing old-age pensions. They were paid at flat rates in Ireland and the Netherlands; they had a small earnings-related component in the U.K.; they were proportionate to earnings in Austria, Germany and Canada (retirement pensions) and were assessed by a formula which had a bias towards the lower paid in the U.S.A. In all these five countries the earnings taken into account in assessing pensions were restricted by income ceilings. These were appreciably above the average earnings of male manual workers in Austria and Germany but below such earnings in Canada and the U.S.A. Past earnings were revalued according to sophisticated and complex formulae in Austria and Germany, according to a simple formula in Canada and on an *ad hoc* basis in the U.S.A. The peculiar characteristics of the graduated pension scheme in the U.K. made it impossible to revalue past earnings.

The age of the pensioner's wife could be relevant : there was no supplementation in respect of a dependent wife in Austria or Germany and there was supplementation only for a wife aged 62 or above (unless she cared for dependent children) in the U.S.A., whereas there was supplementation for a wife of any age in Ireland, the U.K. and the Netherlands. Another factor was the age of retirement : pensions were reduced by 20 per cent. of the basic amount in the U.S.A. for men and women who retired at 62 instead of the normal age of 65; in the U.K. there were no provisions for men who retired below the age of 65, while the minimum pensionable age for women was 60 years. There were sometimes increments for deferred retirement : for married men in the U.K. there was an increment of 42 per cent. of the basic pension for five years' deferment, but there were no such increments in the U.S.A. For a man retiring at the age of 65 in 1969 the minimum period of insured employment giving entitlement to a pension was 15 years in Austria and Germany, just under five years in the U.S.A. and just over five years in the U.K.

The amount of the pension also depended on the total length of insurance cover : it was proportionate to the period of insurance in Germany, increased disproportionately with the length of insurance in Austria and was reduced by 2 per cent. for each year of unexcused contributions in the Netherlands. The relationship of earnings-related pensions to pre-retirement earnings usually depended on a complicated formula in which the revaluation of past earnings and the most recent earnings taken into account were important components.

The above paragraphs should have demonstrated that even among countries which have as much in common as the ten of this study, differences in social security provisions are not marginal but substantial.

Three Difficulties in Comparing Benefit Levels.   An attempt to compare the levels of benefit of a particular scheme, for example temporary disability benefits or pensions for the old, presents quite a number of difficulties.

First, benefit levels are assessed according to so many different criteria that an overall comparison of levels is impossible. The most reasonable way out of this difficulty is to compare the benefits received by persons who are equivalent in all relevant respects : age, sex, marital status (common law wives were not entitled to depen-dants' allowances in Ireland and the U.S.A. but were covered in the U.K. if caring for the dependent children of the beneficiary), health, employment status, occupation, dependants (number, ages, disabili-ties and whether in full-time education), length of residence and period of insurance, earnings over a specified period before the onset of benefit or pension entitlement and the amount of earned and unearned income of the beneficiary, his wife and other dependants.

Variation in any of these factors could quite possibly result in major changes in benefit and might even result in a complete cessation of benefit. Whether the benefit level of a particular country compares well or badly with that of another will thus be much influenced by the relevant characteristics of the persons whose benefits are compared. This is a problem similar to that of index numbers where the choice of the base influences the measured change.

A second difficulty is the period selected for comparison. In the case of interruptions of earnings, entitlement to benefit was often delayed by waiting days. For some benefits in a few countries there were retroactive payments for waiting days after a specified period of incapacity or unemployment. In a few countries the nature and levels of statutory income replacements changed after comparatively short periods of incapacity. Because of these three factors a comparison of temporary disability benefit received by persons who are identical in all respects in different countries will give quite different results according to whether the comparison refers to the first week, the seventh week, or the first seven weeks of incapacity. Thus here too, whether the benefit level of a particular country compares well or badly with that of another will be much influenced by an arbitrary decision – in this case the period selected for comparison.

The third difficulty in comparing levels of benefit is to find a common unit in which the benefit of different countries can be expressed. The conversion of local currencies into U.S. dollars gives results which, as has been shown in Chapter 3, are quite misleading. Any meaningful comparison must be of ratios of benefits to some income level, either that of the past earnings of the particular beneficiaries or some national standard. In the case of past earnings these ratios are to some extent influenced by the definition of income (should piecework and overtime earnings, commission, bonuses and holiday pay be included?) and the period over which income is measured. The latter is a point of some substance as the earnings of manual workers, especially when they near retirement, are often quite irregular.

Methods of Comparison. A comparison of compensation ratios relating to the past earnings of beneficiaries, at a time when rising prices are the norm, is only valid for short-term benefits. For long-term pensions such a method only makes sense if it refers to the time when the pension was first awarded. In flat-rate benefit schemes such ratios are inversely related to previous income.

The alternative to such ratios, the comparison of benefits as proportions of some national standard, is often more meaningful and practical. The most appropriate standard for this purpose would be the median earnings of adult male manual workers. These figures are not available for a recent year for all countries, and even the corresponding average earnings are not regularly published. For this reason benefits in this study are compared with the standard wage (see Appendix II) – an approximation to the average wage.

Benefits received by the standard wage-earner expressed as a proportion of the standard wage give some indication of how the average man fares, but do not show the relative position of the man who earns 50 per cent. more or 25 per cent. less. Here again, whether the benefit level of one country compares well or badly with that of another will be much influenced by an arbitrary decision – the relative pre-contingency income levels of the persons whose incomes are compared.

The results of comparing the benefit levels of a particular scheme are thus much influenced by the relevant characteristics (more than a dozen) of the persons who are compared, by the period selected for comparison and by the relative pre-contingency income levels of the beneficiaries. For these reasons any tables setting out to compare benefits received in different countries are likely to over-simplify the position. Social Security provisions are designed to cover a variety of needs and to serve certain social ends (for example to encourage the willingness to work and save, discourage malingering and militancy, keep down the level of taxation and promote private enterprise). Thus these objectives, which were often incompatible with each other, led in different countries to a great variety of provisions resulting in many different benefit levels in broadly similar circumstances. Any straightforward, accurate and comprehensive comparison of the benefit levels of a particular scheme is thus, by the nature of the subject, impossible, and any attempt to make such a comparison may well prove more misleading than enlightening.

The League Table.   The restricted validity of comparisons of social security expenditure as a proportion of G.N.P. has been discussed in Chapter 3. However, in spite of all the problems which arise in making detailed comparisons some general conclusions can be drawn from this study. No single country provided the best standards in all

TABLE 9:1 *League Table of the Standards of Seven Social Security Schemes in 1969*

	Employment Injury	Temporary Disability	Invalidity	Old Age	Unemployment	Family Endowment	Health Service	Scores T	Scores B
Austria						T		1	—
Germany	T	T		T	T			4	—
Ireland				B			B	—	2
U.K.							T	1	—
Denmark			T	T			T	3	—
Netherlands	T	T	T		T	T		5	—
Canada		B	B					—	2
U.S.A.	B	B	B		B	B	B	—	6
New Zealand								—	—
Australia	B			B	B	B		—	4

Notes: T=top; B=bottom

five schemes (six, if invalidity is counted separately from old age) which have been discussed. There appeared to be some factors, which are far from clear, which made countries develop some schemes more than others. A league table of a very general nature can be drawn up for all the schemes (see Table 9.1). However, it was quite possible and even likely that a beneficiary in certain circumstances did receive a relatively greater benefit in a country at the bottom end of the table than he would in one at the top end.

This league table is based on personal judgement and not on slide-rule calculation, as a number of particulars have to be taken into account which, like apples and pears, cannot be added up. Any attempt to produce indices by attaching weights to the different particulars would have to be so arbitrary that the results would be much less meaningful than those based on judgement.

In assessing benefit standards for employment injury schemes at least seven particulars have to be taken into account : waiting days, compensation ratios[3] for temporary and permanent total disability, income ceilings which restrict compensation payments, time limits on payments, adjustment of benefits after award in line with price or earnings changes and the proportion of employees not protected by the scheme. In the countries which have a federal system of government there is the further complication of differences between the various state or provincial benefit standards. The Netherlands scored high in all particulars. In several particulars Canada scored higher than Germany but was not placed in the top two because in most provinces the income ceiling was relatively low, compensation was not adjusted in line with rising prices and a substantial number of the most vulnerable employees were not protected. On these three particulars Germany scored higher and this was judged to be more important than the fact that the permanent total disability compensation ratio was 75 per cent. in the Canadian provinces but only two-thirds in Germany. The U.S.A. and Australia were placed at the bottom of the table partly on account of their low effective compensation ratios for temporary disability and partly because the schemes of most states in both countries limited the time for which compensation could be paid. The only other country which had a time limit on compensation was New Zealand, but it had higher compensation ratios.

Benefit standards for temporary disability schemes were assessed on the basis of five particulars : waiting days, compensation ratios, income ceilings, maximum duration of benefit and the proportion of the working population covered. Canada had no scheme at all and thus was clearly at the bottom; it was joined there by the U.S.A. where three-quarters of employees in private industry were neither protected by any compulsory insurance scheme nor entitled to benefit under an assistance scheme. Australia, where the compensation ratio was very low and which also had a one-week waiting period, was considered for placing at the bottom. However, the availability of even a very low level of selective benefit to all the working population was judged to be superior to the U.S. provisions. Germany was placed at the top of the table in spite of its relatively low income ceiling on account of its scheme of wage-payment continuation for the first six weeks of incapacity, its relatively high compensation ratio and the absence of waiting days. The Netherlands was also placed at the top because it had the highest compensation ratio and effectively no waiting days but, like Germany, it provided no protection for most of the self-employed.

Particulars taken into account in placing the invalidity schemes included waiting periods, compensation ratios, liberality of supplementary allowances, adjustment of pensions in line with changing earnings or prices, definitions of invalidity and the proportion of the working population covered. Denmark and the Netherlands were without doubt the countries with the highest standards. Both had high compensation ratios for total disability and paid reduced pensions for partial disability. Pensions were automatically adjusted in Denmark for movements in the price index and in the Netherlands for movements in the earnings index. These two countries also had reasonable supplementary allowances for the most severely disabled and were the only ones among the ten in which pensions for the totally disabled were markedly higher than old-age pensions. At the bottom of the table Canada paid no disability pensions at all in 1969. In the following year, when the Canada Pension Plan provisions for the disabled had come into operation, the pension was awarded on such restrictive conditions, was so meagre in amount and had so long a waiting period that the country's position at the bottom of the table would have been unaltered. The other country at the bottom of the table was the U.S.A. where the waiting period was seven months, the compensation ratio and the income ceiling both low and the conditions for award onerous. Australia also had a low compensation ratio but the conditions for award were somewhat less severe and there was no long waiting period.

The scores of old-age pension schemes were based on compensation ratios, supplementation for wives, age of retirement, whether a pension was conditional on retirement, the adjustment of pensions in line with changing prices and earnings and the proportion of the population covered. Denmark and Germany were placed at the top of the table because they adjusted pensions regularly for changes in prices and had the highest compensation ratios for both single persons and for couples.

Pensions in Germany and as from 1970 also in Denmark were not subject to a retirement condition. The Danish old-age pension was normally only paid at the age of 67 but it was paid to virtually all people above this age. In Germany pension cover for the self-employed was not comprehensive and their pensions were often at lower levels than those of employees. Ireland was placed at the bottom of the table because the minimum age for the receipt of a pension was 70 for both men and women. (As from 1970 the retirement age for insured employees was 65.) About half of all men over 70 received non-contributory pensions which were not supplemented in respect of under-age wives. Australia, the other country at the bottom of the table, had a means-tested pension at 65 for men and women which also did not normally provide any supplementation for under-age wives. The Australian compensation ratio was the lowest among the ten countries.

The ranking of unemployment benefit schemes took into account waiting days, compensation ratios, the amount of part-time earnings disregarded, income ceilings, the application of merit rating and the proportion of the population covered. The Netherlands was undoubtedly at the top of the league with a relatively high income ceiling, an exceptionally high compensation ratio (80 per cent.) and the absence of waiting days. The other country at the top was Germany which also had no waiting days but had an appreciably lower compensation ratio. In both countries all employees were covered and comparatively generous amounts of part-time earnings were disregarded. Australia was placed at the bottom of the table. It had seven waiting days, an exceptionally low compensation ratio and only very low amounts of part-time earnings were disregarded. The U.S.A. was judged to have the second lowest standard of service on account of the absence of structured (categorical) provisions for persons not, or no longer, entitled to unemployment insurance benefit, the severity of statutory disqualifications (in some states) and the socially disruptive effect of merit rating. The average compensation ratio was somewhat lower in the U.S.A. than in Canada and both countries had a waiting period of one week.

Family endowment was ranked by one criterion only : the level of benefits paid (to one-, two- and three-child families) as a proportion of the standard wage. On this basis Austria was at the top of the league followed by the Netherlands. These two countries had markedly higher levels of family endowment (see Table 8 : 1) than any others. The U.S.A. had no family endowment scheme and thus was once again at the bottom of the table, where it was joined by Australia. In Ireland benefits for three-child families but not for smaller ones were higher than those in Australia, while benefits in Canada for two-child families but not for others were also higher than in Australia. In Germany there were no allowances for one-child families and those for the second child in two-child families were selective, but three-child families received a higher allowance than in the other three countries mentioned.

The organisation of health care has not been discussed in this study; the health service provisions have merely been outlined in Appendix I. There is, however, little difficulty in placing the ten countries in the table. The U.S.A. was clearly at the bottom as it provided, with few exceptions, no publicly financed or subsidised individual health services for persons below the age of 65. The other country at the bottom was Ireland where the great majority of the urban working class had to pay for all general practitioner and pharmaceutical services. The free general medical services for the least well off (designated up to 1971 as 'the lower income group') were a good example of the maxim that 'a service for the poor is a poor service'. (The quality of the health services was improved by the Health Act, 1970.) At the top of the table was the United Kingdom which provided a comprehensive National Health Service for all the population which was, with only very minor exceptions, free at the point of consumption. The other country which was placed at the top of the league was Denmark. In contrast to Austria, Germany and the Netherlands, it provided a service for all the population rather than one which basically served only employees and some groups of the self-employed. If the placing had referred not to 1969 but to 1972, Canada would have had a strong claim for moving to the top of the table.

The method of scoring adopted gives 14 top and 14 bottom positions for the seven social security schemes covered. Five of the European countries occupy the 14 top positions while 12 of the bottom positions are occupied by three of the countries outside Europe. None of the five countries which scored top positions in any service scored bottom positions in another, and none of the four which scored bottom positions in any service scored top position in any other. New Zealand was the only country for which no scores were recorded. The Netherlands, Germany and Denmark (in that order) were at the top of the league; the U.S.A. was at the bottom preceded by Australia.

These scores are no more than reasonable approximations. Another method of scoring (for example placing six rather than four countries for each scheme, even on the same personal basis of assessment) might have led to somewhat different results.

The Four Pairs. The social security services of the four pairs of countries (Austria and Germany, Ireland and the U.K., Canada and the U.S.A., New Zealand and Australia) can be compared under four headings: expenditure, standards of benefit, organisation and characteristics of provisions.

Expenditure on social security as a proportion of G.N.P. in 1966 was given in Table 3:1 and Fig. 3:1. The four pairs showed some similarity: Austria and Germany were the two countries with the highest proportions while Canada and the U.S.A. were among the three which had the lowest. Ireland and the U.K. had proportions which were, in relation to those of all the ten, neither high nor low. New Zealand's expenditure proportion was markedly higher than that of Australia, but the proportions for this pair of countries were much closer in 1966 than they had been in 1961 or in 1952.

It is of interest to note that among three of these four pairs it was the richer and more populous country which had the lower expenditure proportion. The opposite might have been expected, but it was only in the U.K. that the proportion was higher than in Ireland. These expenditure proportions are widely quoted and relatively easy to compute but, as was suggested in Chapter 3, their meaning should be interpreted with great care. The differences in the proportions between the countries of a pair shown in Table 3:1 are smaller than the wide variations within countries in the expenditure on public social security provisions as a proportion of the aggregate personal incomes of regions, states or provinces. In most national social security schemes provinces or states which have either low levels of income per head or relatively high needs (e.g., more unemployed, children or old) – the two often go together – tend to have high expenditure proportions relative to those in other parts of the country. This was the case for Northern Ireland in the U.K., Connaught in Ireland, Newfoundland in Canada and Alabama in the U.S.A.

The assessment of standards of particular social security schemes (Table 9 : 1) shows only two instances where a pair were either both at the top or the bottom of the league table. Canada and the U.S.A. were bottom for both the temporary disability and invalidity schemes. The aggregate score for the seven social security schemes shows Austria and Germany scoring no bottom positions while Canada and the U.S.A., as well as New Zealand and Australia, scored no top positions. The only pair which scored both top and bottom positions was Ireland and the U.K. The league table, like the expenditure proportions, shows some similarities between the pairs, but in neither of these respects did the pairs have marked common characteristics.

The similarity between the pairs in the organisation of social security services was more marked. For the administration of social insurance schemes Austria and Germany had three different types of self-governing, autonomous agencies, composed of elected representatives of employers and employees : sickness funds, pension institutes and accident insurance institutes. In both countries the sickness funds provided health services and paid sickness benefit. These agencies exercised some discretion in fixing contribution rates and awarding certain non-statutory benefits. They also collected the contributions levied by the pension and accident insurance institutes. In these two countries the organisation of children's allowances and unemployment insurance was more dissimilar than that for other social security schemes.

In Ireland and the U.K. as well as in New Zealand and Australia one government department was responsible for the administration of virtually all cash benefits – demogrants, social assistance and insurance benefits. The administration of cash benefits in Canada and the U.S.A. was more complex. Social assistance in both countries was primarily a provincial (state) or local responsibility. Demogrants in Canada and social insurance for old age, disability and survivors were administered by the Federal governments. Unemployment insurance schemes in the U.S.A. were the responsibility of the states, subject to minimum standards laid down by the Federal government, while in Canada a Federal scheme was administered by an Unemployment Insurance Commission which had tripartite membership. In Canada each province had its own workmen's compensation scheme but all schemes were of a public social security type, while in the U.S.A. the diversity among the workmen's compensation schemes provided by the states was very great.

The similarity in the characteristics of the social security schemes of the pairs was even greater. Attention has been drawn to the similarities in previous chapters and a brief recapitulation of some of the main points will suffice. The Austrian and German social security services were mainly of a social insurance character. They provided earnings-related benefits which were financed by earnings-related contributions up to statutory income ceilings. In sickness insurance, health services were rendered independent of income but were financed by earnings-related contributions; this led to some vertical income redistribution. Otherwise the German schemes brought about only a minimum of such redistribution. The Austrian pension formula, which was markedly different from the German, had some bias towards the lower paid and also incorporated an income guarantee (equalisation allowance). The schemes of the two countries differed in many particulars, e.g., German accident (employment injury) insurance contributions were risk-rated as well as experience-rated while the Austrian were uniform percentages which differed only between manual and non-manual workers; in Austria children's allowances were paid in respect of all children while in Germany no allowance was paid for the first child in the family; in Germany wage payment continuation covered all employees while in Austria it applied only to salaried staff.

The Irish and U.K. social insurance systems had many common characteristics. They both provided basically flat-rate benefits for flat-rate contributions. Ireland has tended to follow U.K. legislation after a time-lag of a few years.[4] One of the most long-lasting differences in the scheme of the two countries was removed in 1967 when the Irish W.C.A. was repealed and replaced by provisions which were very similar to the employment injury legislation operating in the U.K. since 1948. The Irish social insurance system covered only manual workers, and salaried staff earning less than £1,200 per year, while in the U.K. all the population was covered by social insurance. For this reason many more people in Ireland than in the U.K. had to rely on social assistance as their sole means of support. The minimum pensionable age in Ireland in 1969 was 70 years while in the U.K. is was 60 for women and 65 for men. The health service in Ireland was less comprehensive than that in the U.K. and Home Assistance,[5] the Irish 'provider of last resort', was more discretionary and less structured than the supplementary benefit scheme in the U.K.

The New Zealand and Australian social security schemes were selective and imposed needs tests for the award of all benefits except children's allowances and, in New Zealand, superannuation benefit at the age of 65. Benefits were paid to categories of persons according to prescribed rules which left considerable discretion to the authorities making the award. There was a marked tendency for Australian legislation to follow that of New Zealand. Age pensions in Australia were paid to men and women at the age of 65 without any supplementation for under-age wives, while in New Zealand there was such supplementation and age benefit could be claimed at 60.

An examination of the social security systems of these three pairs of countries confirms the supposition that the two countries of each pair have many more common than divergent characteristics. There can be no doubt at all that the systems of each pair had more in common with each other than either had with the system of any other country. The prevalence of common characteristics is nothing like as pronounced between the fourth pair, Canada and the U.S.A.

Canada paid children's allowances and old-age security pensions as demogrants and had a national guaranteed income supplement, subject to an income test, to old-age security pensions. Schemes of this nature did not exist in the U.S.A. The Canadian Federal Unemployment insurance scheme involved quite substantial regional income redistribution, while unemployment insurance in the U.S.A. was a fragmented service. Individual health care as a publicly financed service was quite well developed in Canada, especially for hospital in-patient treatment, but was virtually non-existent in the U.S.A. for persons below the age of 65. Canada had no temporary disability scheme and had not yet started to pay long-term disability allowances; temporary disability insurance in the U.S.A. covered only a quarter of all employees and there was a long waiting period for disability benefit. The O.A.S.D.H.I. of the U.S.A. and the Canada and Quebec Pension Plans had a number of common features of which not the least important was that both schemes had relatively low income ceilings for earnings-related contributions. Both countries also adhered to social assistance schemes in which –

> The stigma of poor relief and the dole still lingers and is often reinforced by humiliating procedures and policies, the insufficiency of the assistance available and the fear of arbitrary denial of benefits, as well as community attitudes.[6]

The severity and illiberality of social assistance provisions were possibly the most marked common characteristics of the social security systems of the two countries. Assistance payments subject to income or means tests are by their nature not popular with the recipients of assistance anywhere, but in other countries the administration of needs tests was not as harsh as in North America.

Downing, commenting on Australia, wrote :

> Other countries are said to regard the means test as an abhorrent affront to social justice. It does not seem to be so regarded in Australia.
>
> There is certainly some opposition to the means test – but this opposition is possibly strongest among those who are excluded by it from benefits rather than among those who submit themselves to it and thereby qualify for the benefits.[7]

The Canadian and U.S. social security systems may have had more in common with each other than either had with the system of any other country, but to the extent to which this was the case it was due to common negative, not to common positive, characteristics. The various social security schemes of both countries formed even less coherent systems than those of the other eight countries, and if they were to be described as systems they were both *sui generis.*

The two North American countries had a number of common political and economic characteristics which made them more alike to each other than either was to any other country : a federal system of government, close economic links, a similar economic structure and state of development, a common language and a common frontier for several thousand miles. It would be interesting but beyond the scope of this study to speculate why, in spite of all these similarities, the social security schemes of the two countries had developed at such different rates and in 1969 differed in so many respects.

Prognosis.   The development of social security in each of the ten countries will be influenced by some factors which are temporary and local. On balance, but not invariably, left-of-centre governments are 'expansionist' while right-of-centre governments are 'moderate'. The extent to which the results of an election influence the long-term trend of social security provisions is uncertain. However, as the measures introduced by the government of any party are rarely reversed when the other party assumes office, it seems probable that the outcome of elections is of some importance.

The irreversibility of measures which have been implemented favour the expansionists because 'omissions' by a moderate government can be easier rectified than schemes set up by an expansionist government can be repealed. The Nixon administration is as unlikely to extend medicare as it is to abolish it.

At the end of 1972 the governments of the U.K. and the U.S.A. believed in work ethics rather than in welfare ethics, while those of the other eight countries had a more or less pronounced propensity to be expansionist. In the middle 1970s some expansion of social security provisions in those countries should therefore be expected.

Three factors may well be the determining influences in long-term developments : inflation, 'the revolution of rising expectations' and the slowing down and eventual cessation of economic growth. The economic depression of the 1930s which had wiped out the lifetime savings of many old persons in the U.S.A. was thought to have been one of the reasons for the introduction of the social security pension scheme. In the three years leading up to the 1972 price increases in some of the ten countries have been so great that the real value of the savings of many old people has declined sharply. Some investors in property and shares have benefited from inflation, but others who had invested in government bonds, building society shares or without-profit insurance policies lost part of their savings, often as yet without being aware of it. Many occupational pensioners and annuitants have already experienced a decline in their standards of living. If inflation continues at the rate experienced in 1972 for any length of time, the decline in the real purchasing power of old people's savings will be so great that this may be a powerful influence making for the expansion of public social security provisions.

The so-called revolution of rising expectations may well be an influence in the opposite direction. The continuous increase in the standard of living of the great majority of the population in each of the ten countries has encouraged the expectation of cumulatively higher annual increases in real earnings. This desire for higher earnings is further accentuated by a consumer society in which 'keeping up with the Joneses' and competitive striving are held up as social virtues and in which advertisers show great skill in creating progressively more needs. When expectations rise faster than real incomes people may become increasingly frustrated in spite of the annual increases in their standard of living. Such feelings and social values contribute to a 'the devil take the hindmost' mentality, the antithesis of the acceptance of communal responsibilities which is the basis on which social security provisions are built.

When this frustration and appeal to the individual's self-interest occur in societies in which there is great inequality in the distribution of income, where taxation policies and inflation increase the income of the rich while the savings of the less well off erode and the tax burden of the average wage-earner increases, a rise in industrial militancy must be expected. Whether such militancy favours improvement and reform of social security provisions is doubtful, but some moderate pessimism seems justified.

All economic predictions are hazardous, but the prediction that the rate of economic growth over the next few decades will be less in the majority of the ten countries of this study than it has been in the period since the Second World War seems less hazardous than most. The reasons for this were briefly discussed in Chapter 2. In the past, expansion of social security provisions and the resulting redistribution of income between contingency groups, income groups, regions and over the life-span have taken place against a background of rising G.N.P. per head. This was especially pronounced over the last twenty-five years, when the expansion of social security services in all the ten countries was most rapid.

Economic growth for the generations alive today is an accepted phenomenon. It is difficult for us to visualise the strains and tribulations of societies where growth has ceased, but here again some moderate pessimism about the development of social security seems justified.

The Organisation of Medical Care

ACCORDING to the I.L.O. terminology, curative and preventive medical care is a social security provision. A description of the health services of the ten countries in any detail and a discussion of the problems to which they give rise would require another book.[1] The purpose of this appendix, therefore, is merely to sketch in bare outline the provisions made in each of the countries.

One of the most important variables of cash benefits is their amount, and one can, to some extent, compare the cash benefits of different countries as proportions of the standard wage; health services, however, have beyond such quantitative aspects variables of quality : how it feels to be treated in a public ward in Australia cannot easily be compared with how it feels in a 'Class 4' ward in the Netherlands. The quality of the face-to-face relationships in health care varies as much as individual doctors and the atmosphere in different institutions. Moreover, whereas a man who loses his job and cannot get another one has a clear need for income replacement of some sort and will receive it according to the statutory rules, the question of *need* in health care is not always so clear-cut; care may be given to save life or relieve pain or may be more in the nature of an amenity (for instance, plastic surgery, visits to spas, good hospital food). The type of medical care which is possible and considered reasonable changes with advances in medical knowledge, surgery and drug therapy, although measures which are thought to be technically desirable may be socially disadvantageous, for example, district hospitals in the U.K.

The organisation and structure of health services affect not only the nature of the services rendered but also the income, working conditions and morale of the large number of persons who work in these services as employees or independent contractors.

The conflict between the interests of patient and practitioner (and supporting staff) is in some respects similar to that between the interests of customer and retailer or worker and management. Health services are usually more geared to the practitioners' interests, for the professional associations of doctors, dentists and pharmacists, and the insurance agencies which normally support them, exert a crucial influence on the type of health service which is set up. The high social status of practitioners, the nature of their calling, the length of their training, the level of their expertise and their professional solidarity give them the political weight to delay and modify any changes in the scope, structure or administration of health services of which they do not approve. However, in spite of the opposition of practitioners, there has been in all ten countries over the last thirty years a marked increase in the number and proportion of the population who receive either free or subsidised medical care. During the same period there has been a ubiquitous increase in the combined public and private expenditure on health care.

In all countries there was an increased acceptance of the state's responsibility to provide health care for its citizens. The I.L.O. Medical Care and Sickness Benefit Convention, 1969, states in Articles 8 and 9 :

> Each Member shall secure to the persons protected, subject to prescribed conditions, the provision of medical care of a curative or preventive nature . . . with a view to maintaining, restoring or improving the health of the person protected and his ability to work and to attend to his personal needs.[2]

'Persons protected' refers to all employees and their dependants as well as to certain other classes of the economically active population.

In 1969 the nature of the provisions of medical care varied widely. At one extreme, services in the U.S.A. were restricted to the over-65s and minimal care for those in dire need; at the other, services in the U.K. were available to all residents as part of the comprehensive National Health Service, under which treatment was unrelated to income or insurance status.

AUSTRIA[3]

Some 92 per cent. of the population were covered by the statutory, compulsory sickness insurance schemes for employees, public servants, self-employed persons and farmers. The general scheme for employees, which also included social insurance beneficiaries, was the largest and accounted for three-quarters of all who were covered. This scheme granted a comprehensive range of free health services of unlimited duration to insured persons and their dependants. Services were rendered in three different forms : first and most commonly, by doctors, dentists, opticians and pharmacists, who provided services as independent contractors with the insurance institutes; second, in health centres maintained by the institutes and staffed by practitioners employed by them; third and most rarely, by practitioners not under contract. If an insured person opted to consult a practitioner not under contract, he himself had to pay the fees charged, but was reimbursed by the institutes the amount which would have been paid to a practitioner under contract for the same service.

In-patient and out-patient hospital treatment for insured persons was also provided without charge. They had, however, to pay a fee of Sch4 for each prescription (not restricted to an approved list), part of the cost of dentures and 10 per cent. of the first four weeks' hospital charges for a dependant. Practitioners under contract, health centres and hospitals, with the above exceptions, were not allowed to ask insured patients for any payment. The hospital charges made to the insurance institutes were low in relation to cost; the hospitals were financed mainly by the provinces and the local councils.

The three smaller statutory sickness insurance schemes provided equally comprehensive services. The compulsory statutory scheme for self-employed persons covered only certain groups, while for others insurance was voluntary. The benefits of this scheme covered dependants only if the insured person opted to pay an extra contribution for this cover. The public servants' and the farmers' schemes were compulsory without exclusion and covered all dependants. In these schemes certain proportions of practitioners' fees had to be paid by the insured persons and services from practitioners not under contract with the insurance institutions were more common.

GERMANY[4]

Compulsory, statutory sickness insurance covered all manual workers, all non-manual workers whose earnings were less than DM11,860 (DM17,100 in 1971[5]) and almost all social security beneficiaries. After 1971 those employees who were not compulsorily insured could join the statutory scheme voluntarily, as could many self-employed persons whose income did not exceed the compulsory insurance limit for non-manual employees. Public servants had their own sickness insurance scheme, but insurance was not compulsory for farmers[6] or any substantial group of self-employed persons. Prior to 1971 the option of joining the scheme was restricted to a few small groups of self-employed persons and certain social security beneficiaries.

The insurance benefits covered a comprehensive range of health services all of which were rendered by doctors, dentists, opticians, pharmacists and hospitals under contract with the insurance institutes. There was no scheme for the reimbursement of fees paid, nor did the institutes provide any services themselves. Insured persons as well as their dependants were entitled to benefits. These included not only curative but also preventive treatment, health checks and various screening tests.

All services, with a few exceptions, were rendered free of charge. Insured persons had to pay one-fifth of the cost up to DM2.50 of spectacles and each prescription. Children and social security beneficiaries were exempt from this charge. Most dental treatment was free but insured persons had to pay about a third of the cost of dentures. Insured persons who had not claimed any sickness insurance medical benefit for three months received a 'no-claim bonus' of DM10, but not more than three times a year.

The statutory sickness insurance scheme was administered by nearly 2,000 autonomous institutes (sickness funds) and financed by members' contributions. In 1971 about 85 per cent. of the benefits received by members were health services; sickness benefit accounted for the remainder. Contributions were proportionate to earnings. The scheme redistributed income in favour of the lower income groups and families with children.

IRELAND[7]

For entitlement to free individual health care the population after 1970 was divided into three groups : those with full eligibility, those with limited eligibility and the remainder.

The full-eligibility group was defined as 'adult persons unable without undue hardship to arrange general practitioner, medical and surgical services for themselves and their dependants' and the dependants of such persons. The full-eligibility status was determined by officers of the Health Boards by criteria which varied throughout the state. About 30 per cent. of the total population were in this group, but the proportion ranged from 12 per cent. in Dublin to more than 50 per cent. in the area covered by the Western Health Board.

The limited-eligibility group included all employees covered by social insurance, adults whose yearly means were less than £1,200 (£1,600 since 1971) and farmers whose rateable valuation was less than £60 and the dependants of such persons. This group accounted for about 60 per cent. of the population and included the majority of the urban working class.

Some services, such as medicines for certain long-term ailments, immunisation against and hospital treatment of infectious diseases, hospital care of long-term defects in children and various screening tests, were provided for all three groups. Persons with limited eligibility received in addition in-patient and out-patient hospital treatment for all illnesses, maternity and infant care and a refund of expenditure on drugs above a specified sum per month. All services, including those of general practitioners and the provision of drugs, were free to persons with full eligibility.

Until 1972 general practitioner services were provided in dispensaries for persons with full eligibility by part-time salaried doctors, each of whom was responsible for a particular district. Under the Health Act, 1970, persons with full eligibility could choose their doctor from the practitioners participating in the service. These practitioners were under contract with the Health Boards and were paid on a fee-for-service basis.

Even after the major reform and restructuring of health services between 1970 and 1972, Ireland remained the only country in Western Europe where the majority of the population had to pay all general practitioners' fees and normally also the full cost of the drugs they prescribed.

In 1969–70, before the reorganisation had come into force, public expenditure on health services was 3·4 per cent. of the G.N.P.

U.K.[8]

All people, irrespective of their length of residence, income, means or national insurance status, were entitled to comprehensive health services. These, in Beveridge's phraseology, included whatever medical treatment was required in whatever form it was required :

> domiciliary or institutional, general, specialist or consultant, and . . . also the provision of dental, ophthalmic and surgical appliances, nursing and midwifery and rehabilitation after accidents.[9]

When the National Health Service (N.H.S.) commenced in 1948 all services were free. After that date some relatively minor charges were made at various times for medicines, spectacles and dental treatment. Children were exempt from these charges and so were certain other groups, for example persons over the age of 65, who did not have to pay the prescription fee of 20p charged in 1972.

All types of health care could be obtained privately, but it was estimated that at least 95 per cent. of the population availed themselves of the N.H.S. general medical practitioners', consultants' and hospital services. The proportion of the population relying on the N.H.S. for dental services and the supply of spectacles was rather smaller.

Consultants were salaried or, if working part-time, paid on a sessional basis. When the service began general medical practitioners were paid solely by a capitation fee for each person who had registered with them, but this was gradually modified so that by 1971 only about half their remuneration was directly related to the number of patients in their care. Dentists were paid a fee for each service rendered.

The current and capital expenditure on the N.H.S. in 1969 was marginally less than 4 per cent. of the G.N.P. About 3 per cent. of the expenditure was met by payments from persons using the service, 9 per cent. was met by the N.H.S. flat-rate weekly contributions paid by employees and the self-employed, and the remainder came from central and local government taxes.

DENMARK

The national health insurance scheme was administered by autonomous, self-governing sickness funds, most of which covered a local authority area. All persons over the age of 16 were entitled to join a fund, either in Division 'A' or in Division 'B'. The level of income (not capital) determined the division which a person had to join. About five-sixths of all members were in Division 'A', which catered for the lower and middle income groups. More than 95 per cent. of all adults were members of the funds; children under 16 were covered by their parents' membership.

The benefits that 'A' members received included : free medical attention from general practitioners and specialists, free hospital in-patient treatment and care, three-quarters of the cost of medicines which were on the list approved by the Minister of Social Affairs, at least half the cost of spectacles and conservative dental treatment, free home nursing and free maternity benefit. General practitioners in Copenhagen were paid a capitation fee; in the rest of the country they received a lower capitation fee but also charged the funds for each service they rendered. Specialists were also paid separately for each service; they treated 'A' members only if they were referred to them by their general practitioner. 'B' members received treatment from general practitioners, specialists, dentists and opticians as private patients and had to pay whatever fees they were charged. The funds reimbursed them the amount that the practitioners would have received for rendering the same service to an 'A' member. 'B' members received in-patient hospital treatment in a public ward, pharmaceutical services, maternity benefit and home nursing on the same terms as 'A' members.

About 95 per cent. of the cost of hospital treatment was paid by the central government and local authorities; the remainder was financed by the funds. Some three-quarters of the expenditure of the sickness funds was met by the flat-rate contributions from their members, which were about 10 per cent. higher for 'B' than for 'A' members.

The aggregate public expenditure on health services by the sickness funds, the central government and the local authorities was about $5\frac{1}{2}$ per cent. of the G.N.P.

NETHERLANDS

Compulsory health insurance covered all employees (except public servants) with earnings of less than Fl14,850 in 1969 (about 120 per cent. of the standard wage) and all social insurance and social assistance beneficiaries except old-age pensioners. Other persons of working age with incomes of less than the statutory limit for employees could voluntarily insure themselves with the social health insurance funds. This option was also open to persons over 65 who had incomes of less than about 70 per cent. of the statutory limit for employees. The dependants of these three groups were entitled to health insurance benefits free of charge.

Employees contributed 3·75 per cent. of their income and this was matched by similar contributions from their employers. The contributions of old people and the voluntarily insured were related to earnings and subsidised out of general revenue. The three groups covered compulsorily or voluntarily by social health insurance accounted for about 70 per cent. of the population. The remainder had to make their own arrangements. Most of them joined private health insurance schemes.

The social health insurance benefits were free and reasonably comprehensive. General medical practitioners received an annual fee for each person registered with them and were not permitted to charge any fees to insured patients. Dentists were paid specific fees for each service; patients who attended for regular inspections received all services, apart from the provision of dentures, free of charge. Insured persons registered with a pharmacist and received prescribed medicine without charge, but proprietary medicines were only supplied free when no substitutes of the same quality were available.

The first year of hospital in-patient treatment was given free, as an insurance benefit, in the lowest of three or four hospital classes. In addition to social health insurance, everybody who resided in the Netherlands (not only employees) was covered by the long-term hospital insurance plan, which financed hospital care after the first 12 months of in-patient treatment.

CANADA[10]

Health services were financed jointly by the Federal and provincial governments. Levels of service and charges were not uniform throughout the country. Provincial hospital insurance schemes were estimated to cover 99 per cent. of the population. In-patient services had to include, by Federal law, accommodation, meals, nursing, diagnostic procedures, drugs and the use of operating rooms. In addition, some out-patient services were provided, which were usually fairly comprehensive. In most provinces hospital care was free, but in some, for example Alberta and British Columbia, moderate charges charges were made.

By 1971 virtually the whole population was covered by medical insurance schemes – known as *medicare* – which were administered by the provincial governments but eligible, from 1968, for Federal grants of 50 per cent. of expenditure. In order to qualify for these grants four criteria had to be satisfied : first, comprehensive coverage for all medically necessary services rendered by a physician or surgeon; second, universal availability of services to eligible residents and coverage of at least 95 per cent. of the eligible provincial population; third, portability of benefits between provinces; fourth, administration by a public authority on a non-profit-making basis.[11] Charges could be made if they did not render necessary medical care inaccessible to persons with low incomes.

In all provinces but Quebec the public insurance body paid medical practitioners 90 per cent. of the negotiated current fee schedule; in Quebec participating doctors were paid by the insurance body and were not allowed to make additional charges to their patients. In the other provinces such charges were legal. In all provinces patients had to pay for prescribed medicines.

The term 'insurance' applied to either the hospital scheme or medicare is a misnomer. In some provinces individuals made no direct contribution to either scheme.

Individual private and public health-care expenditure in 1970 amounted to 5·2 per cent. of the G.N.P.[12]

U.S.A.[13]

The U.S.A. had no national health service and for persons under 65 it had neither a national health insurance scheme nor any plan for subsidising private health insurance. A health insurance system for virtually all persons over 65 was introduced in 1966. It provided for up to 90 days of in-patient hospital treatment for any spell of sickness, subject to the payment of the first $40 and a further $10 a day for any stay exceeding 60 days. A further 60 days of hospital care was provided, once only, subject to the patient's paying $20 a day. (Beneficiaries' payments were increased by 30 per cent. in 1970.) The scheme was financed by a 1·2 per cent. payroll tax on employees (shared equally between employers and employees) and a similar tax on the self-employed.

About 95 per cent. of all people over 65 were also enrolled in the Supplementary Medical Insurance system, a voluntary scheme subsidised by the government, which also commenced in 1966. The monthly contribution was $5·30 and the main benefits were partial reimbursement of the cost of medical care at home, in the surgery and in hospital. Patients had to pay the first $50 a year and 20 per cent. of the cost in excess of that amount.[14]

The expenditure on individual health care was financed to the extent of 39 per cent. by direct payments from consumers, 25 per cent. by private insurance benefits, 23 per cent. by the Federal government and 12 per cent. by the state and local authorities. In 1949–50, twenty years earlier, direct payments had accounted for 68 per cent., private insurance benefits for 9 per cent. and public expenditure for 20 per cent.[15]

Among the population under 65 about 84 per cent. were insured for hospital care, 48 per cent. for medical care apart from that received as hospital in-patients, 53 per cent. for prescribed drugs and 6 per cent. for dental treatment.[16] The operating expenses of all private insurance agencies averaged 14 per cent. of the premiums paid and those of insurance companies 20 per cent.[17] Most private insurance covered only a proportion of the expenditure incurred.

Between 1965 and 1971 aggregate private and public expenditure on health care increased from 5·9 per cent. to 7·4 per cent. of the G.N.P.[18] During the same period the Consumer Price Index increased by 28 per cent., the medical-care component of this index by 43 per cent. and hospital daily service charges by 84 per cent.[19]

NEW ZEALAND[20]

The state provided all accommodation and treatment in public hospitals and subsidised it in private ones. One-sixth of all occupied beds (excluding psychiatric ones) were in private hospitals. The state also paid specified sums towards the cost of each medical service rendered by general medical practitioners and certain specialists. These payments were not increased between 1941, when they commenced, and 1972, except that as from 1969 higher payments were made for services rendered to pensioners and social security beneficiaries. Patients were charged a 'fee-for-service', which in 1970 averaged about three times the sum paid by the state. The full cost of medicines and drugs supplied by pharmacists on medical prescriptions was normally paid by the state. Free dental services were available to children up to the age of 16.

The government's expenditure on health services was financed out of general tax revenue. All health service benefits were universal, irrespective of means and income, with the exception to which reference has been made above.

The New Zealand government encouraged the expansion of the private hospital system in the 1950s and 1960s by making loans on favourable terms for the building of new hospitals and alterations to existing hospitals.[21] The role of private hospitals within the health service is a controversial issue. Dr. W. B. Sutch[22] alleges that

> . . . the taxpayers' funds are being diverted to help pay for the medical attention of those with higher incomes, at a time when those on low incomes cannot, in many cases, get the medical attention they require just as much as (or more than) the better off. In fact, surgery in some cases in private hospitals may be and probably is a misplacing of medical priorities . . .[23]

His contention that 'Since 1950 the provision of medical and hospital attention in New Zealand has become more restricted in coverage, less free and less universal'[24] seems to be one of substance.

AUSTRALIA[25]

The major purpose of the Commonwealth health service subsidies was to encourage and reward self-help through voluntary insurance. The Commonwealth medical benefit scheme subsidised voluntary insurance with registered agencies to meet part of the cost of medical practitioners' and specialists' services. About three-quarters of the population were covered by such insurance. The government subsidy met some 45 per cent. of the benefit paid. For a general practitioner consultation this was set in such a way that contributors had to pay 80 cents of the 'most common fee' charged.

Patients who were protected by private hospital insurance received a Commonwealth hospital benefit of $2 for each day of in-patient care. This was paid through the contributor's hospital benefit organisation. As from 1970 the same benefit was paid to hospitals for uninsured persons who were treated and accommodated free of charge.

The pharmaceutical benefit and the nursing-home benefit were not limited to voluntarily insured persons. All persons who received medical treatment were, on prescription, supplied with medicines from a comprehensive range. The patient paid only the first 50 cents of the cost of each prescription and the Federal government paid the remainder. Nursing homes received subsidies of $2 or $5 per in-patient day according to the nature of the treatment or care provided.

As from 1970 low-income families and persons receiving unemployment, sickness and special benefits were eligible for free medical insurance and free hospital insurance up to the public ward charges. Families whose incomes were slightly above the eligibility limits for free insurance (which did not vary with family size) could buy insurance at reduced rates. The persons covered by these provisions received free hospital care but had to pay that part of the medical fee which was not included in the insurance benefit. Poor persons, however, were frequently treated by hospital doctors free of charge.

The Pensioners Medical Service, which covered nearly 10 per cent. of the population, provided in 1970 free general practitioner services, a wide range of free medicine and free in-patient hospital care to age, invalid and widow pensioners who were able to satisfy the means test in force immediately before October 1969. General practitioners participating in this scheme were paid on a fee-for-service basis.

APPENDIX II

The Standard Wage

AN international comparison of the levels of social security benefits expressed in national currencies presents considerable difficulties, one of which is, of course, that the purchasing power of benefits is affected by differences in standards of living. The most meaningful comparison, however, might be in terms of the relation to the wage levels of unskilled and skilled male workers in specific industries. Such figures are not available on a uniform basis for all ten countries. The nearest approximation is the wages (earnings per week) in manufacturing industries which are published annually in the *I.L.O. Yearbook of Labour Statistics*. These data give for most countries only one figure, which refers to the weekly earnings of both men and women, while for some countries they give the weekly earnings of men and women separately (U.K. and Australia) and for a third group they give only the hourly earnings of men and women combined. By reference to the *I.L.O. Yearbook* tables giving the hours worked per week and the number of each sex employed, it is possible to obtain for all countries the average weekly earnings in manufacturing industries of men and women combined (see Table AII). These figures, however, are too low to be representative of male earnings. It was therefore considered appropriate in this study to increase them by 25 per cent. This proportion is the same as that in the Employment Injury Benefits Convention, 1964, Article 19, paragraph 6 :

> For the purpose of this Article, a skilled manual male employee shall be –
> . . .
> (*d*) a person whose earnings are equal to 125 per cent. of the average earnings of all the persons protected.[1]

In this study the combined male and female average earnings in manufacturing industries, plus 25 per cent., are referred to as the *standard wage* and the man who earnes this wage as the *standard*

325

TABLE A II   *Standard Wage*, 1969

I	II	III	IV	V	VI	VII	VIII
Country	Period	Sex	Earnings per period	Weekly Hours	Number Employed	Earnings per week	Standard[b] Wage
Austria	Month	M & F	Sch4,263			Sch4,263[a]	Sch5,329
Germany ...	Week	M & F	DM232			DM261	DM290
Ireland	Week	M & F	£15·46			£15·5	£19·4
U.K.	Week	M F	£25·55 £12·10		5·9 m 2·7 m	£21·3	£26·6
Denmark ...	Hour	M & F	Kr14·1	37·4		Kr527	Kr659
Netherlands ...	Week	M & F	Fl192·8			Fl192·8	Fl241
Canada ...	Week	M & F	$111·7			$111·7	$139·6
U.S.A. ...	Week	M & F	$129·5			$129·5	$161·9
New Zealand ...	Hour	M & F	$1·14	40·5		$46·2	$57·8
Australia ...	Week	M F	$73·3 $41·2		0·99 m 0·32 m	$65·3	$81·6

Source: I.L.O. *Yearbook of Labour Statistics*, 1971.

Column IV: Table 19A.   Column V: Table 13.   Column VI: Table 2.

[a] Per month, which is also the period to which benefits relate.   [b] Column VII plus 25 per cent.

wage-earner.

The comparability of the standard wages of different countries is by no means perfect for a number of reasons, among which two are particularly important. First, the definition of 'weekly earnings' is not uniform; thus the German figures include family allowances paid directly by employers, the Austrian figures include mining and quarrying, the figures for different countries do not always refer to the same period and 'wages' are variously defined, in some countries including supervisory and clerical staff. Second, the average earnings of women are everywhere lower than those of men, but form a different proportion of men's earnings in each country. Moreover, women account for differing proportions of the labour forces in the manufacturing industries of different countries. One further important limitation in standard wage comparisons is that the number employed in manufacturing industries is in all countries only a minority of all those employed.

The standard wage, with all these limitations, is all the same the best available yardstick against which to measure social security benefits. It is, however, far from perfect and should only be used critically and with caution.

Currency Conversion Table, 1969

TABLE A III *Currency Conversion Table, 1969*

	Australia & New Zealand	Austria	Canada	Denmark	Germany	Ireland & U.K.	Nether-lands	U.S.A.
	$	Sch100	$1	Kr10	DM10	£1	Fl10	$1
Australia & New Zealand .... $	1·00	3·39	0·81	1·20	2·23	2·14	2·46	0·893
Austria .... Sch	29·5	100	23·9	35·5	65·8	63·2	72·6	26·3
Canada .... $	1·23	4·18	1·00	1·48	2·75	2·64	3·04	1·10
Denmark .... Kr	8·30	28·2	6·73	10·0	18·5	17·8	20·4	7·41
Germany .... DM	4·48	15·2	3·64	5·40	10·0	9·59	11·0	4·00
Ireland & U.K. ...... £	0·47	1·58	0·376	0·562	1·04	1·00	1·15	0·417
Netherlands .... Fl	4·06	13·8	3·29	4·89	9·06	8·70	10·0	3·63
U.S.A. .... $	1·12	3·80	0·909	1·35	2·50	2·40	2·76	1·00

Source for bottom line: Social Security Programs throughout the World, 1969 (U.S. Department of Health, Education and Welfare) country schedules; remainder: author's calculations.

NOTE: The vertical columns give the value of the national currency in terms of the foreign currency, e.g. Canada $1 equals DM3·64 and Denmark Kr10 equals £0·562 or 56·2p.

Notes and References

CHAPTER I: INTRODUCTION

1. International Labour Office (1972) p. 2.

CHAPTER II: FACTORS INFLUENCING THE LEVEL AND NATURE OF
SOCIAL SECURITY

1. This assumption is only valid if four conditions are satisfied: prices are compared at factor cost; only prices of goods and services entering international trade are considered; the balance of payment of each country is in equilibrium; dollars are converted into national currencies at the same rates as used for the conversion of G.N.P. into dollars. In practice these conditions are rarely met.

2. *United Nations Yearbook of National Accounts Statistics,* 1969, Table 1C.

3. Williamson (1968).

4. Australia has 6, New Zealand 10, Canada 11, the U.S.A. and Germany 9, the Netherlands 11, Ireland 26, the U.K. 15 and Austria 9 regions. Income in Australia, New Zealand, Canada and the U.S.A. refers to personal income, in the U.K. to total net assessed income, in Germany and the Netherlands to net product at factor cost, in Ireland to earned income and in Austria to national income. The data cover one or several years in the 1950s.

5. Lydall (1968).

6. This section draws on some paragraphs in my chapter 'Financ-ing of Social Services' in Townsend and Bosanquet (1972).

7. Beveridge (1942) para. 307.

8. Ibid., para. 9.

9. U.K.: Ministry of Pension and National Insurance (1958) para. 32.

10. U.K.: Department of Health and Social Security (1971a) para. 9.

11. U.S.: Department of Health, Education and Welfare (1968) p. 15.

12. New Zealand: Royal Commission of Inquiry: Social Security in New Zealand (1972) p. 62.

13. Ibid., p. 195.

14. Ibid., p. 230.

15. Canada: Department of National Health and Welfare (1970) pp. 5-6.

16. New Zealand: Royal Commission of Inquiry: Social Security in New Zealand (1972) p. 171.

17. Canada: Department of National Health and Welfare (1970) p. 16.

18. Myers (1970) p. 22.

19. International Labour Office (1972) p. 2.

20. Zöllner (1970) pp. 226-8.

21. New Zealand: Royal Commission of Inquiry: Social Security in New Zealand (1972) p.170.

22. Canada: Department of

National Health and Welfare (1970).

23. U.K.: Department of Health and Social Security (1971a).

24. See Kaim-Caudle (1969a) and Townsend (1968).

25. Lees (1967).

26. Cohen (1968).

27. This is well illustrated by a remark made in Germany to the author in the late 1950s by an unsophisticated opposition member of parliament: 'Our government is dishonest. They have stolen most of our party's social policy.' He was perfectly right, but felt no satisfaction in the government's having not only taken over his party's programme but actually implemented it. He only felt regret about his party's having lost the election.

28. Marmor (1970).

29. New Zealand: Royal Commission of Inquiry: Social Security in New Zealand (1972) p.11.

CHAPTER III: LEVELS AND TRENDS OF SOCIAL SECURITY

1. International Labour Office (1972).

2. Nordic Countries (1971).

3. European Economic Community (1970). Data of 1962-70 were published in European Economic Community (1971b).

4. U.S. Department of Health, Education and Welfare (1970).

5. International Labour Office (1972) p. 2.

6. See Orshansky (1966) and Cohen (1968).

7. Canada (1970).

8. See Canada: Department of National Health and Welfare (1970) p. 6.

9. Downing, in Henderson, Harcourt and Harper (1970) p. 4.

10. Bixeby (1970).

11. For a discussion of the reasons for the increased expenditure on social services in the U.K. between 1963 and 1969, see Kaim-Caudle, in Townsend and Bosanquet (1972).

12. Germany (1970) p. 31.

13. Irish Congress of Trade Unions (1971).

14. U.K.: Department of Health and Social Security (1970a). Tables 92, 112 and 145.

15. New Zealand: Social Security Department (1970). Tables 4, 13 and 23.

16. Australia (1971) pp. 389-97.

17. U.S.A. (1970b). Tables M3, M24, Q4, Q7 and Q8.

CHAPTER IV: EMPLOYMENT INJURY

1. Space does not permit any reference to the issues specific to industrial diseases, permanent partial disability or survivors' pensions.

2. International Labour Office (1964) p. 2.

3. Ibid., pp. 2-3.

4. For a detailed discussion of the U.S. schemes, see Skolnik and Price (1970).

5. U.S. Department of Health, Education and Welfare (1970) p. 228.

6. U.K. Department of Health and Social Security (1972) Tables 45 and 70.

7. Victoria (1970).

8. Ireland: Commission on

Workmen's Compensation (1962) para. 13.

9. New Zealand: Royal Commission of Inquiry: Compensation for Personal Injury in New Zealand (1967) para 86.

10. Beveridge (1942) para. 87.

11. International Labour Office (1964) Article 7, Sections 1 and 2.

12. New Zealand: Royal Commission of Inquiry: Compensation for Personal Injury in New Zealand (1967) para. 171.

13. Beveridge (1942) paras. 78-9.

14. Ibid., para. 80.

15. U.S. Department of Health, Education and Welfare (1968) p 72.

16. New Zealand: Royal Commission of Inquiry: Compensation for Personal Injury in New Zealand (1967) para. 198.

17. Kewley (1965) p. 377.

18. International Labour Office (1964) p. 4.

19. Skolnik and Price (1970) p. 11.

20. Except in Queensland and Western Australia. See Australia: Department of Labour and National Service (1970) Table F.

21. Canada (1971) p. 852.

22. New Zealand: Royal Commission of Inquiry: Compensation for Personal Injury in New Zealand (1967).

23. New Zealand: Select Committee on Compensation for Personal Injury in New Zealand (1970)

24. *Forefront of New Zealand Affairs* (Feb. 1972) p. 1.

25. New Zealand (1971) p. (i).

26. New Zealand: Select Committee on Compensation for Personal Injury in New Zealand (1970) paras. 36-52.

27. New Zealand: Royal Commission of Inquiry: Compensation for Personal Injury in New Zealand (1967) para. 491.

28. New Zealand (1971) Section 24(1)(g).

29. New Zealand: Royal Commission of Inquiry: Compensation for Personal Injury in New Zealand (1967) para. 267.

30. Ibid., Appendix 7, p. 225

31. New Zealand: Select Committee on Compensation for Personal Injury in New Zealand (1970) para. 79.

32. New Zealand: Royal Commission of Inquiry: Compensation for Personal Injury in New Zealand (1967) para. 17.

33. Skolnik and Price (1970) p. 24.

34. Canada: Department of National Health and Welfare (1970) p. 37.

CHAPTER V: TEMPORARY DISABILITY

1. Germany (1966) para. 613, translated by the author.

2. Ibid., para. 614, translated by the author.

3. Rodler and Urbanetz (1971) p. 15.

4. U.K.: Department of Health and Social Security (1972) Tables 25 and 26.

5. Germany (1970) p. 135.

6. The Austrian statistics refer to both men and women and mainly to manual workers; the British exclude most married women and non-industrial civil servants, but include not only salaried employees but also the self-employed; the German cover both men and women but are restricted to manual workers. The statistics in these three

countries refer moreover to different terminal ages and different age distributions.

7. Article 18 (1).

8. Article 26 (1 and 3).

9. *International Social Security Review* (1970) no. 1, p. 13.

10. Beveridge (1942) para 323.

11. Ibid., paras. 124-6.

12. Sir Keith Joseph, *Hansard,* vol. 816, col. 62.

13. These were the net effects; the mechanism of tax collection disguised the advantages of not returning to work.

14. Mr Brian O'Malley, *Hansard,* vol. 820, col. 1562.

15. Andersen (1970).

16. New Zealand: Royal Commission of Inquiry: Social Security in New Zealand (1972) chap. 24, para. 36.

17. Ibid. (1970) Paper 10, p. 13.

18. Germany (1970) p. 184.

19. Only a quarter exercised this option. U.K.: Department of Health and Social Security (1970a) p. 290.

20. Ibid. (1969a) para. 10.

21. Ibid. (1969b) para. 56.

22. Kaim-Caudle (1964) pp. 35-36.

23. The term *disability* in the U.S.A. is synonymous with *invalidity* in other countries.

24. In Denmark the flat rate was raised by 35 per cent. in October, 1969, thereby raising the compensation ratio to approximately the Convention's standard.

25. Denmark and Austria attained the I.L.O. standard by including family allowances which are not incorporated in Table 5:1.

26. Brooks (1971) p. 428.

27. Demark (1972).

28. New Zealand: Royal Commission of Inquiry: Social security

in New Zealand (1970) Paper 16, p. 21.

29. Ibid. (1972) p. 181.

30. Ibid., p. 180.

31. Ibid., p. 179.

32. Ibid., pp. 180-1.

33. Ibid., p. 183.

34. Ibid., p. 184.

35. Price (1972) Table 4, p. 23.

36. Germany (1970) p. 142.

37. The standard contribution conditions were lower for certain special groups, including school-leavers, students, members of H.M. forces, widows and divorced women. See U.K.: Department of Health and Social Security (1970b).

38. U.K.: Central Statistical Office (1971) Table 41.

39. U.K.: Department of Health and Social Security (1972) Tables 32-34.

40. The survey also covered mining, construction, public utilities, transport, insurance, banking, the civil service and local authorities, in most of which substantially higher proportions of wages were paid for periods of sickness.

41. U.K.: *Department of Employment Gazette* (Jan. 1971) Tables 20 and 23, pp. 8, 10.

42. U.K.: Central Statistical Office (1971) Table 20.

43. U.K.: *Departmnet of Employment Gazette* (Jan. 1971) Table 31, p. 18.

44. Ibid. (June 1972) p. 545.

45. Ibid. (Feb. 1971) Table 95, p. 141.

46. Ibid., Table 110, p. 155; for more detailed information, see ibid. (Aug. 1971) pp. 690-710.

47. Price (1972).

48. U.K.: Department of Health and Social Security (1972) Tables 32-34.

CHAPTER VI: OLD AGE AND INVALIDITY

1. Unemployment, employment injury, temporary disability and maternity benefits and invalidity and survivors' pensions.

2. U.K.: Department of Health and Social Security (1969a) para, 123.

3. Friis (1969).

4. See New Zealand: Royal Commission of Inquiry: Social Security in New Zealand (1972) p. 268.

5. $A + \dfrac{6A}{100}$

$$\left(\text{where } A = 260 \times 89 \times \frac{80}{100}\right)$$

6. New Zealand: Royal Commission of Inquiry: Social Security in New Zealand (1972) p. 275.

7. Ibid., p. 378.

8. Ibid., p. 151.

9. Ibid., p. 150.

10. Ibid., p. 143.

11. The liberality of the means test is fairly recent. Prior to 1969 the pension was reduced by $1 for each $1 of means in excess of the prescribed amount, and up to 1960 the pension had been reduced by $2 for every $20 by which the value of assets exceeded $400.

12. The Australian age-pension scheme has frequently taken over provisions first introduced in New Zealand. Thus Australia raised the pension paid to a single person to more than half that paid to a couple (both pensioners) in 1963, following the example set by New Zealand in 1955. (In this, Australia was in fact reverting to the provisions of the New South Wales Pension Act of 1900. Similarly, as from 1968 in Australia payment of benefit was continued to the widow or widower of a beneficiary for three months

after the latter's death, while a similar provision had been in force in New Zealand since 1960.

13. Downing (1968).

14. Ibid., p. 425.

15. See *Encyclopaedia Britannica,* 11th ed., vol. 20, p. 64.

16. Beveridge (1942) para. 244.

17. These figures are only approximations. The purchasing power of wages is also affected by direct taxes, including social insurance contributions. Estimates of the movement of retail prices over comparatively long periods, during which standards and modes of living have changed greatly, must be made with caution.

18. U.K.: Ministry of Pensions and National Insurance (1958) p. 13.

19. For a critical analysis of the graduated pension scheme, see Lynes (1963).

20. U.K.: Department of Health and Social Security (1969a) p. 5.

21. For an assessment of the White Paper, see Lynes (1969).

22. U.K.: Department of Health and Social Security (1971a).

23. Ibid., para. 60.

24. In 1951 the coalition government had introduced a Bill which would have extended social insurance to all employees irrespective of income and provided contributory old-age pensions at 65 for men and 60 for women. The Bill, which would have brought social insurance in Ireland even more into line with Britain, lapsed on the defeat of the government at the general election of 1951.

25. See Kaim-Caudle (1969b).

26. See Coughlin (1972).

27. $\dfrac{25}{100} \times \dfrac{3,600}{120}$

28. Canada: Department of National Health and Welfare (1970) p. 42.

29. Ibid., p. 48.

30. Canada: National Council of Welfare (1971) pp. 19-20.

31. Canada: Department of National Health and Welfare (Research and Statistics Dictorate) (1972) p. 70.

32. 'The moderate inflation estimates assume that from 1975 on, consumer prices will increase by 3 per cent. a year, average earnings by $5\frac{1}{2}$ per cent. a year and interest rates will be $6\frac{1}{2}$ per cent. (Canada: Department of National Health and Welfare, 1970, p. 51).

33. Ibid.

34. The Actuarate Report prepared in 1964, before the Act was passed, had estimated that the balances in the Pension Fund would increase to $8,000 million in 1985 and decline thereafter. See Gerig and Myers (1965) pp. 16-17.

35. Canada: Department of National Health and Welfare (1970) pp. 49-50.

36. For a discussion of attitudes before 1935, see Lubove (1968) chapter 5.

37. Birch (1955) p. 27.

38. U.S. Department of Health, Education and Welfare (1968) p. 5.

39. Price (1968) p. 29.

40. Myers (1970) p. 10.

41. All pensions were increased by 15 per cent. as from January, 1970 (*Social Security Bulletin*, February, 1970, p. 1).

42. U.S. Department of Commerce (1971) Table 510.

43. Bixeby (1970).

44. Ibid., pp. 22-3.

45. Myers (1970) pp. 20-1.

46. For a description and discussion of the civil service retirement programme, see Hart (1970).

47. Germany (1970) pp. 60, 70.

48. One of the two major insurance companies – the Irish Life Assurance – is partly owned by the state and is considered a state-sponsored body.

CHAPTER VII : UNEMPLOYMENT

1. This was first unequivocally stated in the British White Paper *Employment Policy* (Cmd. 6527) in 1944. This announced that the government accepted 'as one of their primary aims and responsibilities the maintenance of a high and stable level of employment after the war' (Beveridge, 1944, p. 260).

2. Quoted in Galbraith (1958) p. 46.

3. Geary and Hughes (1970) p. 26.

4. Quoted in Haber and Murray (1966) p. 289.

5. For a wide-ranging discussion of disqualification in unemployment insurance, see Ibid., chap. 15.

6. Beveridge (1944) p. 18.

7. Ibid., p. 19.

8. U.K.: Inter-Departmental Committee on Public Assistance Administration (1925) para. 34.

9. Beveridge (1942) para. 307.

10. U.K.: Department of Health and Social Security (1971*b*) para. 69.

11. U.K.: Department of Health and Social Security (1970*a*) Table 90.

12. U.K.: Department of Employment (1971) p. 12.

13. U.K.: Department of Employment (1972).

14. Farley (1964) p. 6.

15. Geary and Hughes (1970) p. 1.

16. International Labour Office (1971).

17. Ireland (1969) pp. 295, 319.

18. Germany (1970).

19. Ibid.

20. Social Security Act, 1971, Section 7.

21. Nordic Countries (1968) p. 83.

22. The state's contributions were different for each fund and varied with the average number of benefit days per member.

23. The following paragraphs are mainly based on *International Social Security Review* (1970) no. 1, pp. 31-4.

24. New Zealand: Social Security Department (1950) p. 41.

25. Ibid., p. 30.

26. New Zealand: Royal Commission of Inquiry: Social Security in New Zealand (1972) p. 291.

27. New Zealand: *Monthly Abstract of Statistics* (January 1972) Tables 14 and 17.

28. New Zealand: Royal Commission of Inquiry: Social Security in New Zealand (1972) chap. 15.

29. Ibid., p. 294.

30. Ibid., p. 294.

31. Ibid., p. 295.

32. A discussion of the various proposals to institute unemployment insurance in Australia is contained in Kewley (1965).

33. Australia (1970) p. 186.

34. U.S. Department of Commerce (1971) p. 286.

35. Haber and Murray (1966) p. 200.

36. In addition to this programme, the Employment Security Amendments of 1970, Congress made temporary provisions in the Emergency Unemployment Compensation Act, 1971, for extending unemployment insurance benefits during the first nine months of 1972. These provisions were limited to states where unemployment exceeded 6·5 per cent. for 13 weeks. Extended benefit up to half the amount of their regular compensation could be paid to workers who had exhausted their benefits, but at most for an additional 13 weeks. (See U.S. Department of Health, Education and Welfare, 1972, p. 31.)

37. Haber and Murray (1966) p. 503.

38. U.S. Department of Health, Education and Welfare (1968) p. 51.

39. U.S. Department of Commerce (1971).

40. The labour-force sample survey unemployment percentages were considerably higher. They averaged 4·8 for the decade and were 6·7 in 1961 and 3·5 in 1969.

41. Mitchell (1964) pp. 35-6.

42. Canada: Department of National Health and Welfare (1970) pp. 53-5.

43. There may be an indirect effect in that without benefits or at very low benefits their life-span may be shortened by malnutrition and neglect.

44. Australia (1970) p. 184; see also Canada (1971) p. 853.

45. Beveridge (1942) paras. 128-132.

46. Australia (1970) p. 190.

CHAPTER VIII: FAMILY ENDOWMENT

1. Kaim-Caudle, in Townsend (1968) p. 20.

2. New Zealand: Social Security Department (1950) p. 29.

3. New Zealand: Royal Commission of Inquiry: Social Security in New Zealand (1972) Appendix 11A.

4. New Zealand: Social Security Department (1970) p. 20.

5. New Zealand: Royal Commission of Inquiry: Social Security in New Zealand (1972) chap. 21.

6. Ibid., para. 27, p. 223.

7. *The Post* (New Zealand), 23 June 1972.

8. Kewley (1965) p. 264.

9. U.K.: Board of Inland Revenue (1971) vol. V.

10. Henderson, Harcourt and Harper (1970) p. 20.

11. Canadian Council on Social Development (1971) p. 16.

12. Canada: Department of National Health and Welfare (1970) p. 44.

13. Canada: Royal Commission on the Status of Women (1970) chap. 5, paras. 45-8.

14. Gross cost for 6·9 million children $3,450 million less (*a*) income-tax on allowances, $750 million; (*b*) cost of family allowances, $560 million; (*c*) increase in revenue due to removal of tax exemptions for children, $450 million; (*d*) reduction of married persons' allowance from $2,800 in the White Paper proposals for tax reform to $2,000, a saving of approximately $700 million; (*e*) savings on child supplements by termination or reduction of child supplements to social insurance and assistance beneficiaries.

15. The detailed effects are shown in Table 1 of the Commission's report.

16. Canada: Department of National Health and Welfare (1970) p. 44.

17. Ibid., p. 46.

18. Canadian Council on Social Development (1971).

19. Ibid., p. 11.

20. Canada: Department of National Health and Welfare (Research and Statistics Directorate) (1972) p. 1.

21. Farley (1964) p. 72.

22. U.K.: Board of Inland Revenue (1971) vol. IV.

23. *Irish Times,* 20 April 1972.

24. Beveridge (1942).

25. Ibid., paras. 411-12.

26. Ibid., para. 417.

27. Ibid., para. 421.

28. Ibid., para. 422.

29. Townsend and Atkinson (1970).

30. Atkinson (1969); U.K.: Ministry of Social Security (1967) chap. 2, para. 22.

31. Friis (1969) p. 146.

32. Nordic Countries (1971) p. 116.

33. *International Social Security Review* (1970) No. 1, pp. 50-2.

34. U.K.: Board of Inland Revenue (1971) Vol. V.

35. Germany (1970).

36. Ibid., p. 162.

37. Germany (1966) p. 309.

38. Ibid., p. 317.

39. Rodler and Urbanetz (1971).

40. Ibid., p. 94.

41. U.K.: Board of Inland Revenue (1971) vol. I, p. 122.

42. U.S. Department of Commerce (1971) Table 517.

43. U.K.: Board of Inland Revenue (1971) vol. VIII, p. 108.

44. Projector (1970) p. 8.

45. U.S. Department of Health, Education and Welfare (1968).

46. Cohen (1968) p. 11.

47. U.S. Department of Commerce (1971) Table 463.

48. Ibid., Table 512.

49. U.S.A. (1970*a*) Table M.26.

50. U.S. Department of Commerce (1971) Tables 463 and 513.

51. See projector (1970).

52. Wynn (1970) chap. 3.

53. New Zealand: Royal Commission of Inquiry: Social Security in New Zealand (1972) p. 240.

54. Except for old-age pensions in Germany which were a percentage of the past average earnings of all persons insured.

CHAPTER IX: CONCLUSIONS

1. Ethel Shanas *et al., Old People in Three Industrial Societies* (Routledge & Kegan Paul, London, 1968).

2. Ministry of Pensions and National Insurance, *Financial and Other Circumstances of Retirement Pensioners* (H.M.S.O., 1966).

3. Compensation ratio here and in the following pages refers to the benefit paid to the man who was a standard wage-earner, relative to his pre-contingency earnings.

4. Children's allowances are an exception to this generalisation; they commenced in Ireland in 1944 but in the U.K. only in 1945.

5. 6 Cinnéide (1970).

6. Canada: Department of Health and Welfare (1970) pp. 23-4.

7. Henderson *et al.* (1970) p. 10.

APPENDIX I: THE ORGANISATION OF MEDICAL CARE

1. See, for example, Roemer (1969), an interesting analytical study of eight countries including Germany, the U.K. and Canada; see also Murray (1971), which briefly discusses health service problems in various countries including Germany, Denmark, the Netherlands and the U.S.A.

2. International Labour Office (1969) p. 4.

3. Brooks (1971).

4. See Germany (1970) pp. 128-34; Germany (1966 pp. 196-260; Kastner (1967).

5. Employees were exempt from compulsory insurance if their earnings exceeded 150 per cent. of the income of all persons covered by pension insurance in the first three of the last four years.

6. A compulsory sickness insurance scheme for farmers and retired farmers was introduced in July 1972. This provided much the same benefits as other statutory schemes, for 1·2 million insured persons and the same number of dependants. See *International Social Security Review*, nos. 1–2 (1972) pp. 86–8.

7. See Hensey (1972) for a comprehensive and authoritative account of health services in Ireland.

8. See International Labour Office, Social Security Branch (1967).

9. Beveridge (1942) para. 427.

10. See Hastings (1967) for a description of Canadian health services.

11. Canada: Department of National Health and Welfare (Research and Statistics Directorate) (1972) pp. 13–14.

12. Ibid., p. 127.

13. See Marmor (1970).

14. Myers (1970) pp. 10–12.

15. Rice and Cooper (1972) p. 13.

16. Mueller (1972) p. 4.

17. Ibid., p. 13.

18. Rice and Cooper (1972) p. 4.

19. U.S.A. (1972) Tables M30 and M31.

20. For a description of health services, see New Zealand: Royal Commission of Inquiry: Social Security in New Zealand (1972) chaps. 43–48.

21. New Zealand: Department of Health (1969).

22. A well-known writer on social affairs in New Zealand and a former chairman of the United Nations Social Commission.

23. Sutch (1971) pp. 96–7.

24. Ibid., p. 94.

25. Australia: *Health Insurance* (1969); see also Scotton and Deeble (1968).

APPENDIX II: THE STANDARD WAGE

1. International Labour Office (1964) p. 8.

Bibliography

S.S.B. = *Social Security Bulletin.*

I.S.S.R. = *International Social Security Review.*

ANDERSEN, BENT ROLD (1970), "Some Major Results of a Study of the Coverage and Functioning of Social Agencies and Legislation in Denmark", *ISSR*, no. 2, pp. 326-32.

ATKINSON, A. B. (1969), *Poverty in Britain and the Reform of Social Security,* Univ. of Cambridge, Dept. of Applied Economics, Occasional Paper: 18, Cambridge Univ. Press.

AUSTRALIA (1970), *Labour Report No. 54, 1968 and 1969* (Commonwealth Bureau of Census and Statistics, Canberra).

AUSTRALIA (1971), *Official Yearbook of the Commonwealth of Australia,* (Commonwealth Bureau of Census and Statistics, Canberra).

AUSTRALIA: DEPARTMENT OF LABOUR AND NATIONAL SERVICE (1970) *Conspectus of Workers' Compensation Legislation in Australia and Papua–New Guinea, 1970.*

AUSTRALIA: *Health Insurance* (1969), *Report of the Commonwealth Committee of Enquiry (Chairman:* Mr Justice Nimmon) (Government Printer, Canberra).

BEVERIDGE, W. H. (1942) *Social Insurance and Allied Services* (Report), Cmd 6404 (H.M.S.O.).

BEVERIDGE, W. H. (1944) *Full Employment in a Free Society* (Allen & Unwin, London).

BIRCH, A. H. (1955) *Federalism, Finance and Social Legislation in Canada, Australia and the United States* (Oxford Univ. Press).

BIXEBY, LENORE E. (1970) 'Income of People Aged 65 and Older: Overview from 1968 Survey of the Aged', *S.S.B.*, vol. XXXIII, no. 4 (Apr. 1970) pp. 3–34 (U.S. Dept. of Health, Education and Welfare).

BROOKS, ROBERT (1971) 'Survey of Austrian Sickness Insurance', *I.S.S.R.* no. 3, pp. 410-30.

CANADA (1970) 'A Review of the Role of the Department of National Health and Welfare in Relation to Poverty', Appendix A of the *Proceedings of the Special Senate Committee on Poverty* (Senate of Canada, 2nd Session, 28th Parliament), no. 23, 24 and 26 Feb. 1970, pp. 63-75, as quoted in *S.S.B.*, vol. XXXIII, no. 7 (July 1970) pp. 13-20 (U.S. Dept. of Health, Education and Welfare).

CANADA (1971) *1970–71 Canada Yearbook* (Dominion Bureau of Statistics, Ottawa).

CANADA: DEPARTMENT OF NATIONAL HEALTH AND WELFARE (1970) *Income Security for Canadians* (Ottawa).

CANADA: DEPARTMENT OF NATIONAL HEALTH AND WELFARE (1971) *Annual Report for the Fiscal Year Ended March 31, 1970* (Ottawa).

CANADA: DEPARTMENT OF NATIONAL HEALTH AND WELFARE (RESEARCH AND STATISTICS DIRECTORATE) (1970) *Social Security in Canada, 1969* (Ottawa).

CANADA: DEPARTMENT OF NATIONAL HEALTH AND WELFARE (RESEARCH AND STATISTICS DIRECTORATE (1972) *Health and Welfare Services in Canada, 1971* (Ottawa).

CANADA: MINISTER OF FINANCE (1969) *Proposals for Tax Reform* (White Paper), Hon. E. J. Benson, Minister of Finance.

CANADA: NATIONAL COUNCIL OF WELFARE (1971) *Statement on Income Security* (Ottawa).

CANADA: *Royal Commission on the Status of Women in Canada* (1970) Report of the Royal Commission (Chairman: Mrs Florence Bird) (Information Canada, Ottawa).

CANADIAN COUNCIL ON SOCIAL DEVELOPMENT (1971) *A Policy Statement: Comments and Recommendations on 'The Family Income Security Plan' Proposed in the Federal Government White Paper 'Income Security for Canadians', 1970.*

COHEN, WILBUR J. (1968) 'Ten-Point Program to Abolish Poverty', *S.S.B.*, vol. XXXI, no. 12 (Dec. 1968) pp. 3-13 (U.S. Dept. of Health, Education and Welfare).

COUGHLIN, ANTHONY (1972) 'Social Services North and South', *Hibernia*, 25 Aug. 1972 (Hibernia National Review Ltd., Dublin).

CUTT, JAMES (1970) 'Income Support Programmes for Families with Children: Alternatives for Canada', *I.S.S.R.*, no. 1, pp. 100-12.

DENMARK (1972) *Danish Report to the U.N. Conference of Ministers Responsible for Social Welfare, 1972* (privately circulated).

DOWNING, R. I. (1968) 'National Superannuation: Means Test and Contributions', *Economic Record*, vol. XLIV, no. 108 (Dec. 1968) pp. 407-37.

EUROPEAN ECONOMIC COMMUNITY (1970) Statistical Office, *Sozialstatistik No. 3, 1970.*

EUROPEAN ECONOMIC COMMUNITY (1971a) *Bericht über die Entwicklung der sozialen Lage in der Gemeinschaft im Jahr 1970* (Brussels–Luxemburg).

EUROPEAN ECONOMIC COMMUNITY (1971b) *Social Accounts of the Member States of the E.E.C.*, Statistical Office, *Sozialstatistik No. 2, 1972.*

FARLEY, DESMOND (1964) *Social Insurance and Social Assistance in Ireland* (Institute of Public Administration, Dublin).

FRIIS, HENNING (1969) 'Issues in Social Security Policies in Denmark', in Shirley Jenkins (ed.), *Social Security in International Perspective* (Columbia Univ. Press, New York).

GALBRAITH, JOHN KENNETH (1958) *The Affluent Society* (Hamish Hamilton, London).

GEARY, R. C., and HUGHES, J. G. (1970) *Certain Aspects of Non-Agricultural Unemployment in Ireland,* Paper No. 52 (Economic and Social Research Institute, Dublin).

GERIG, DANIEL S., and MYERS, ROBERT J. (1965) 'Canada Pension Plan of 1965', *S.S.B.,* vol. xxvii, no. 11 (Nov. 1965) pp. 3-17 (U.S. Dept. of Health, Education and Welfare).

GERMANY (1966) *Soziale Sicherung in der Bundesrepublik Deutschland* Bericht der Sozialenquête–Kommission (Kohlammer, Stuttgart).

GERMANY (1969) *Jahresbericht der Bundesregierung 1969* (Presse– und Informationsamt der Bundesregierung) pp. 327-60 (published annually).

GERMANY (1970) *Ubersicht über die Soziale Sicherung* (Bundesminister für Arbeit und Sozialordnung).

HABER, WILLIAM, and MURRAY, MERRILL G. (1966) *Unemployment Insurance in the American Economy* (Irwin, Homewood, Ill.).

HART, MAURICE C. (1970) 'Civil-Service Retirement Program, October 20, 1969', *S.S.B.,* vol. xxxiii, no. 2 (Feb. 1970) pp. 15-25, 33 (U.S. Dept. of Health, Education and Welfare).

HASTINGS, J. E. F. (1968) *Monograph of the Organisation of Medical Care within the Framework of Social Security: Canada* (International Labour Office, Geneva).

HENDERSON, RONALD F., HARCOURT, ALISON, and HARPER, R. J. A. (1970) *People in Poverty: A Melbourne Survey* (Institute of Applied Economic and Social Research, Univ. of Melbourne).

HENSEY, BRENDAN (1972) *The Health Services of Ireland* (Institute of Public Administration, Dublin).

I.L.O. Yearbook of Labour Statistics 1971 (International Labour Office, Geneva, 1972).

INTERNATIONAL LABOUR OFFICE (1952) *Social Security (Minimum Standards) Convention, 1952,* Convention 102 (International Labour Conference, Geneva).

INTERNATIONAL LABOUR OFFICE (1964) *Employment Injury Benefits Convention, 1964,* Convention 121 (International Labour Conference, Geneva).

INTERNATIONAL LABOUR OFFICE (1969) *Medical Care and Sickness Benefits Convention, 1969,* Convention 130 (International Labour Conference, Geneva).

INTERNATIONAL LABOUR OFFICE (1970) *Introduction to Social Security* (Geneva).

INTERNATIONAL LABOUR OFFICE (1972) *The Cost of Social Security: Seventh International Inquiry, 1964–1966* (Geneva).

INTERNATIONAL LABOUR OFFICE, SOCIAL SECURITY BRANCH (1968) *Monograph on the Organisation of Medical Care within the Framework of Social Security: the United Kingdom* (International Labour Office, Geneva).

INTERNATIONAL SOCIAL SECURITY REVIEW (1970) 'Social Security in the Netherlands', *I.S.S.R.,* no. 1, pp. 3-61.

IRELAND (1969) *Irish Statistical Bulletin,* vol. XLIV, no. 4 (Dec. 1969) (Central Statistics Office, The Stationery Office, Dublin).

IRELAND (1971) *Statistical Abstract of Ireland 1969* (Central Statistics Office, The Stationery Office, Dublin).

IRELAND: *Commission on Workmen's Compensation* (1962), Report of the Commission (Chairman: Mr Justice Shannon) (The Stationery Office, Dublin).

IRELAND: DEPARTMENT OF SOCIAL WELFARE (1949) *White Paper containing Government Proposals for Social Security* (The Stationery Office, Dublin).

IRELAND: DEPARTMENT OF SOCIAL WELFARE (1950) *First Report of the Department of Social Welfare: 1947–49* (The Stationery Office, Dublin).

IRISH CONGRESS OF TRADE UNIONS (1971) *Trade Union Information,* no. 166 (Dec. 1971) (Irish Congress of Trade Unions Research Service, Dublin).

JENKINS, SHIRLEY (ed.) (1969) *Social Security in International Perspective* (Columbia Univ. Press, New York).

JENSEN, ORLA (1961) *Social Welfare in Denmark* (Det Danske Selskab, Copenhagen).

KAIM-CAUDLE, P. R. (1964) *Social Security in Ireland and Western Europe* (Economic Research Institute, Dublin).

KAIM-CAUDLE, P. R. (1967) *Social Policy in the Irish Republic* (Routledge & Kegan Paul, London).

KAIM-CAUDLE, P. R. (1969*a*) 'Selectivity and the Social Services', *Lloyds Bank Review,* ed. J. R. Winton, no. 92 (Apr. 1969).

KAIM-CAUDLE, P. R. (1969*b*) 'The Senior Citizen in Irish Society', *Journal of the Institute of Public Administration of Ireland,* vol. XVII, no. 2 (Summer 1969) pp. 101-12.

KAIM-CAUDLE, P. R. (1972) 'Financing of Social Services', Peter Townsend and Nicholas Bosanquet (eds.), *Labour and Inequality* (Fabian Society, London).

KASTNER, FRITZ (1968) *Monograph on the Organisation of Medical Care within the Framework of Social Security: Federal Republic of Germany* (International Labour Office, Geneva).

KEWLEY, T. H. (1965) *Social Security in Australia* (Sydney Univ. Press).

KEWLEY, T. H. (1969) *Australia's Welfare State* (Macmillan of Australia, Melbourne).

KOLODRUBETZ, WALTER W. (1972) 'Two Decades of Employee-Benefit Plans, 1950–70: A Review', *S.S.B.,* vol. XXXV, no. 4 (Apr. 1972) pp. 10-22 (U.S. Dept. of Health, Education and Welfare).

LEES, DENNIS (1967) 'Poor Families and Fiscal Reforms', *Lloyd's Bank Review,* ed. J. R. Winton, no. 86 (Oct. 1967) pp. 1-15.

LUBOVE, ROY (1968) *The Struggle for Social Security 1900–1935* (Harvard Univ. Press, Cambridge, Mass.).

LYDALL, HAROLD (1968) *The Structure of Earnings* (Oxford Univ. Press).

LYNES, TONY (1963) *Pension Rights and Wrongs: A Critique of the Con-*

servative Scheme, Fabian Tract No. 348 (Fabian Society, London).

LYNES, TONY (1969) *Labour's Pension Plan,* Fabian Tract No. 396 (Fabian Society, London).

MARMOR, THEODORE R. (1970) *The Politics of Medicare* (Routledge & Kegan Paul, London).

MILLER, KENNETH E. (1968) *Government and Politics in Denmark* (Houghton Mifflin, Boston).

MITCHELL, WILLIAM LLOYD (1964) *Social Security in America* (Robert B. Luce, Washington, D.C.).

MUELLER, MARJORIE SMITH (1972) 'Private Health Insurance in 1970: Population Coverage, Enrollment and Financial Experience', *S.S.B.,* vol. xxxv, no. 2 (Feb. 1972) pp. 3–19 (U.S. Dept. of Health, Education and Welfare).

MURRAY, D. STARK (1971) *Medical Care: Who Gets the Best Service?,* Fabian Occasional Paper 6 (Fabian Society, London).

MYERS, ROBERT J. (1970) *Expansionism in Social Insurance,* Paper 32 (Institute of Economic Affairs, London).

NEW ZEALAND (1971) *Accident Compensation Bill* (Wellington).

NEW ZEALAND: DEPARTMENT OF HEALTH (1969) *A Review of Hospital and Related Services in New Zealand* (Wellington).

NEW ZEALAND: MONTHLY ABSTRACT OF STATISTICS (Jan. 1972) (Dept. of Statistics, Wellington).

NEW ZEALAND: *Personal Injury* (1969), *A Commentary on the Report of the Royal Commission of Inquiry into Compensation for Personal Injury in New Zealand* (Wellington).

NEW ZEALAND: ROYAL COMMISSION OF INQUIRY: COMPENSATION FOR PERSONAL INJURY IN NEW ZEALAND (1967) *Report of the Royal Commission* (Chairman: Mr Justice Woodhouse) (Wellington).

NEW ZEALAND: ROYAL COMMISSION OF INQUIRY: SOCIAL SECURITY IN NEW ZEALAND (1970), *Papers 1–22.* Submissions from the Social Security Department.

NEW ZEALAND: ROYAL COMMISSION OF INQUIRY: SOCIAL SECURITY IN NEW ZEALAND (1972) *Report of the Royal Commission* (Chairman. Rt. Hon. Sir Thaddeus Pearcey McCarthy) (Wellington).

NEW ZEALAND: SELECT COMMITTEE ON COMPENSATION FOR PERSONAL INJURY IN NEW ZEALAND (1970) *Report of the Select Committee* (Chairman: Mr G. F. Gair, M.P.) (Wellington).

NEW ZEALAND: SOCIAL SECURITY DEPARTMENT (1960) *The Growth and Development of Social Security in New Zealand* (published by the Social Security Department with the co-operation of the Health Department, Wellington).

NEW ZEALAND: SOCIAL SECURITY DEPARTMENT (1970) *Report for the Year Ended 31st March, 1970* (Wellington).

NORDIC COUNTRIES (1951–71) *Social Security in the Nordic Countries,* Statistical Reports of the Nordic Countries, published in 1957 (for 1954; 54/5); 1960 (for 1956: 56/7); 1964 (for 1960: 60/1); no. 11, 1965 (for

1962: 62/3); no. 13, 1968 (for 1964:64/5); no. 16, 1970 (for 1966:66/7); no. 22, 1971 (for 1968: 68/9).

O'Cinneide, Seamus (1970) *A Law for the Poor* (Institute of Public Administration, Dublin).

Oram, C. A. (1969) *Social Policy and Administration in New Zealand* (New Zealand Univ. Press, Wellington).

Orshansky, Mollie (1966) 'Recounting the Poor', *S.S.B.*, vol. xxix, no. 4 (Apr. 1966), pp. 20–37 (U.S. Dept. of Health, Education and Welfare).

Price, Daniel N. (1968) 'O.A.S.D.H.I. Benefits, Prices and Wages: Effect of 1967 Benefit Increase', *S.S.B.*, vol. xxxi, no. 12 (Dec. 1968) pp. 28–35 (U.S. Dept. of Health, Education and Welfare).

Price, Daniel N. (1972) 'Cash Benefits for Short-Term Sickness, 1948–70,' *S.S.B.*, vol. xxxv, no. 1 (Jan. 1972) pp. 19–35 (U.S. Dept. of Health, Education and Welfare).

Projector, Dorothy S. (1970) 'Children's Allowances and Income-Tested Supplements: Costs and Redistributive Effects', *S.S.B.*, vol. xxxiii, no. 2 (Feb. 1970) pp 3–14 (U.S. Dept. of Health, Education and Welfare).

Querido, A. (1968) *Development of Socio-Medical Care in the Netherlands* (Routledge & Kegan Paul, London).

Rice, Dorothy P., and Cooper, Barbara S. (1972) 'National Health Expenditure 1929–71', *S.S.B.*, vol. xxxv, no. 1 (Jan. 1972) pp. 3–18 (U.S. Dept. of Health, Education and Welfare).

Richardson, J. Henry (1960) *Economic and Financial Aspects of Social Security* (Allen & Unwin, London).

Rodler, Othmar and Urbanetz, Hermann (1971) *Social Security in Austria* (National Federation of Austrian Social Insurance Institutions).

Roemer, Milton I. (1969) *The Organisation of Medical Care under Social Security* (International Labour Office, Geneva).

Scotton, R. B., and Deeble, J. S. (1968) 'Compulsory Health Insurance for Australia, *Australian Economic Review*, 4th quarter.

Sinfield, Adrian (1967) *The Long-Term Unemployed* (O.E.C.D., Paris).

Skolnik, Alfred M., and Price, Daniel N. (1970) 'Another Look at Workmen's Compensation', *S.S.B.*, vol. xxxiii, no. 10 (Oct. 1970) pp. 3–25 (U.S. Dept. of Health, Education and Welfare).

Sutch, W. B. (1971) *The Responsible Society in New Zealand* (Whitcombe & Tombs, Christchurch).

Townsend, Peter (1968) *Social Services for All?* (Fabian Society, London).

Townsend, Peter, and Atkinson, Tony (1970) 'The Advantages of Universal Family Allowances', *Poverty,* no. 16–17, pp. 18–21.

Townsend, Peter, and Bosanquet, Nicholas (1972) *Labour and Inequality* (Fabian Society, London).

U.K.: BOARD OF INLAND REVENUE (1971) *Income Taxes Outside the United Kingdom, 1969,* 8 vols. (H.M.S.O.).

U.K.: CENTRAL STATISTICAL OFFICE (1971) *National Income and Expenditure, 1971* (H.M.S.O.).

U.K.: DEPARTMENT OF EMPLOYMENT (1971) *People and Jobs: A Modern Employment Service.*

U.K.: DEPARTMENT OF EMPLOYMENT (1972) *Training for the Future: A Plan for Discussion.*

U.K.: DEPARTMENT OF EMPLOYMENT GAZETTE (Jan. 1971) 'Labour Costs in Great Britain in 1968 – Part 3', *Department of Employment Gazette,* vol. LXXIX, no. 1 pp. 4–20 (H.M.S.O.).

U.K.: DEPARTMENT OF EMPLOYMENT GAZETTE (Feb. 1971) 'New Earnings Survey, 1970 – Part 4', *Department of Employment Gazette,* vol. LXXIX, no. 2, pp. 132–56 (H.M.S.O.).

U.K.: DEPARTMENT OF EMPLOYMENT GAZETTE (Aug. 1971) 'Occupational Pensions and Sick Pay Schemes', *Department of Employment Gazette,* vol. LXXIX, no. 8, pp. 690–710 (H.M.S.O.).

U.K.: DEPARTMENT OF EMPLOYMENT GAZETTE (June 1972) 'Family Expenditure Survey: Subsidiary Occupations', *Department of Employment Gazette,* vol. LXXX, no. 6, pp. 528–534 (H.M.S.O.).

U.K.: DEPARTMENT OF HEALTH AND SOCIAL SECURITY (1969a) *National Superannuation and Social Insurance: Proposals for Earnings-Related Social Security,* Cmnd 3883 (H.M.S.O.).

U.K.: DEPARTMENT OF HEALTH AND SOCIAL SECURITY (1969b) *Social Insurance: Proposals for Earnings-Related Short-Term and Invalidity Benefits,* Cmnd 4124 (H.M.S.O.).

U.K.: DEPARTMENT OF HEALTH AND SOCIAL SECURITY (1970a) *Annual Report, 1969* (H.M.S.O.).

U.K.: DEPARTMENT OF HEALTH AND SOCIAL SECURITY (1970b) *Sickness Benefit,* National Insurance Leaflet 16, Dec. 1970.

U.K.: DEPARTMENT OF HEALTH AND SOCIAL SECURITY (1971a) *Strategy for Pensions: The Future Development of State and Occupational Provision,* Cmnd 4755 (H.M.S.O.).

U.K.: DEPARTMENT OF HEALTH AND SOCIAL SECURITY (1971b) *Supplementary Benefits Handbook,* Supplementary Benefits Commission (H.M.S.O.).

U.K.: DEPARTMENT OF HEALTH AND SOCIAL SECURITY (1972) *Digest of Statistics Analysing Certificates of Incapacity June 1968–May 1969.*

U.K.: INTER-DEPARTMENTAL COMMITTEE ON PUBLIC ASSISTANCE ADMINIS-TRATION (1925) *Report of the Committee on the Co-ordination of Administrative and Executive Arrangements for the Grant of Assistance from Public Funds on account of Sickness, Destitution and Unemployment* Cmd 2011 (H.M.S.O.).

U.K.: MINISTRY OF PENSIONS AND NATIONAL INSURANCE (1958) *Provision for Old Age: The Future Development of the National Insurance Scheme* Cmnd 538 (H.M.S.O.).

U.K.: MINISTRY OF SOCIAL SECURITY (1967) *Circumstances of Families* (H.M.S.O.).

United Nations Demographic Yearbook 1966 (United Nations, New York, 1967).

United Nations Demographic Yearbook 1969 (United Nations, New York, 1970).

United Nations Demographic Yearbook 1970 (United Nations, New York, 1971).

United Nations Monthly Bulletin of Statistics (United Nations, New York, July 1971 and May 1972).

United Nations Statistical Yearbook 1970 (United Nations, New York, 1971).

United Nations Yearbook of National Accounts Statistics 1969 (United Nations, New York, 1970).

United Nations Yearbook of National Accounts Statistics 1970 (United Nations, New York, 1972).

U.S.A. (1970*a*) 'Current Operating Statistics', *S.S.B.*, vol. xxxiii, no. 4 (April 1970) pp. 48–76 (U.S. Dept. of Health, Education and Welfare).

U.S.A. (1970*b*) 'Current Operating Statistics', *S.S.B.*, vol. xxxiii, no. 6 (June 1970) pp. 21–49 (U.S. Dept. of Health, Education and Welfare).

U.S.A. (1972) 'Current Operating Statistics', *S.S.B.*, vol. xxxv, no. 4 (Apr. 1972) pp. 28–56 (U.S. Dept. of Health, Education and Welfare).

U.S. DEPARTMENT OF COMMERCE (1971) *Statistical Abstract of the United States: 1971* (U.S. Dept. of Commerce, Bureau of the Census, Washington).

U.S. DEPARTMENT OF HEALTH, EDUCATION AND WELFARE (1968) *Social Security Programs in the United States* (Washington).

U.S. DEPARTMENT OF HEALTH, EDUCATION AND WELFARE (1970) *Social Security Programs Throughout the World, 1969* (Washington).

U.S. DEPARTMENT OF HEALTH, EDUCATION AND WELFARE (1972) 'Emergency Unemployment Compensation Act of 1971', *S.S.B.*, vol. xxxv, no. 3 (Mar. 1972) p. 31.

VICTORIA (1970) *Yearbook of the State of Victoria* (Melbourne).

WILLIAMSON, J. G. (1968) 'Regional Inequality and the Process of National Development: A Description of the Patterns', chap. 4 in L. Needleman (ed.), *Regional Analysis* (Penguin Books, Harmondsworth).

WYNN, MARGARET (1970) *Family Policy* (Michael Joseph, London).

ZOLLNER, DETLEV (1970) 'Social Insurance Benefits and Earnings Replacement in a Dynamic Economy', *I.S.S.R.*, no. 2, pp. 224–36.

Index

This index was compiled by Mr. H. P. Jolowicz

The following abbreviations have been used in this index: Inst. = Institute;
Int. = international; nat. = national; no. = number; sec. = security;
soc. = social

347